C. Fred Bergsten
and the World Economy

C. Fred Bergsten
and the World Economy

Michael Mussa, editor

PETERSON INSTITUTE FOR INTERNATIONAL ECONOMICS
Washington, DC
December 2006

Michael Mussa, senior fellow since 2001, served as economic counselor and director of the research department at the International Monetary Fund from 1991 to 2001, where he was responsible for advising the management of the Fund and the Fund's Executive Board on broad issues of economic policy and for providing analysis of ongoing developments in the world economy. By appointment of President Ronald Reagan, he served as a member of the Council of Economic Advisers from August 1986 to September 1988. He was a member of the faculty of the Graduate School of Business of the University of Chicago (1976–91) and was on the faculty of the Department of Economics at the University of Rochester (1971–76). During this period he also served as a visiting faculty member at the Graduate Center of the City University of New York, the London School of Economics, and the Graduate Institute of International Studies in Geneva, Switzerland. He is the author of *Argentina and the Fund: From Triumph to Tragedy* (2002).

**PETER G. PETERSON INSTITUTE
FOR INTERNATIONAL ECONOMICS**
1750 Massachusetts Avenue, NW
Washington, DC 20036-1903
(202) 328-9000   FAX: (202) 659-3225
www.petersoninstitute.org

C. Fred Bergsten, *Director*
Valerie Norville, *Director of Publications
and Web Development*
Edward Tureen, *Director of Marketing*

Typesetting by BMWW
Printing by Kirby Lithographic Company, Inc.

Printed in the United States of America
09 08 07   5 4 3 2 1

Library of Congress Cataloging-in-Publication Data

C. Fred Bergsten and the world economy / Michael Mussa, editor.
   p. cm.
   Includes bibliographical references and index.
   ISBN 0-88132-397-7 (978-0-88132-397-9 : alk. paper)
   1. Bergsten, C. Fred, 1941–
2. International economic relations.   3. International trade.   4. Commercial policy. I. Mussa, Michael.   II. Peterson Institute for International Economics.

HF1359.C25 2006
337—dc22   2006038025

Contents

Tables

Figures

Preface

Fred Bergsten is a phenomenon among economists. As a result of his contributions in books, articles, testimony, op-eds, speeches, and media interviews (many of which are listed in the appendix at the end of this volume), Fred Bergsten has become the world's leading analyst and commentator on the wide range of issues of international economic policy. More than this, thanks to his extraordinary entrepreneurial efforts, shrewd management, and energetic marketing, Fred has substantially magnified his individual contributions. Most importantly, he has accomplished this through his creation and direction of the Peter G. Peterson Institute for International Economics—widely and rightly regarded as the world's preeminent think tank for serious, timely, and highly relevant analysis of key issues of international economic policy.

It is serendipitous, therefore, that 2006 marks both the 65th anniversary of Fred's birth and the 25th anniversary of the founding of the Institute. In celebration of these joint anniversaries, Fred's colleagues at the Institute have prepared this festschrift, surveying broad areas of international economic policy in which the Institute and Fred himself have been and remain highly active.

Following my brief appreciation of Fred Bergsten's endeavors as intellectual entrepreneur, the second chapter by Mac Destler and Marcus Noland provides a broad overview of the main areas of the Institute's substantive work for the past 25 years, emphasizing a number of Fred Bergsten's major innovations. Gary Hufbauer and Jeffrey Schott then present a more detailed review of Institute analyses of key trade policy issues and of Fred's contributions to them. Kimberly Elliott follows with a review of the Institute's work on the use of trade sanctions for both political and economic purposes—issues on which the Institute's work by Hufbauer, Schott, and Elliott dominates the literature. Next, Monty Graham examines policies affecting international flows of direct investment, an area in which Fred Bergsten, as an official of the Nixon and Carter administrations, was a key pioneer and that is once again at the forefront of policy debates. Howard Rosen winds up the section on international trade and investment with a review of US trade adjustment assistance policies, for which Fred was an early advocate and remains a vocal proponent.

The Institute's work and Fred's contributions on international macroeconomic policy questions are the subject of the second half of this volume. Morris Goldstein provides a broad overview, and then John Williamson takes up the key issue of exchange rate regimes, including his and Fred's (somewhat quixotic) pursuit of target zones. Edwin Truman analyzes a question that is logically related to proposals for a target zone for the exchange rate of the US dollar: whether and when wide swings in the dollar's real effective exchange rate over the past three decades have conveyed important signals about the need for adjustments in economic policies. Next, Martin Baily and Robert Lawrence examine the concept of "competitiveness," reevaluating the analysis and recommendations of the Competitiveness Policy Council, which Fred chaired from 1991 to 1997.

Turning to subjects more directly related to the world's developing countries, William Cline reviews and updates the Institute's extensive work on Third World debt, another subject on which Fred Bergsten was an early and important contributor. I then return to the subject with which the Institute began its long list of publications: controversies concerning lending by the International Monetary Fund. Goldstein follows with a call for the IMF to reinvigorate its activities and fulfill its mandate for exchange rate surveillance, with particular reference to China's extraordinary efforts to maintain a massively undervalued currency. In the grand tradition of the Institute's support of vigorous debate on controversial issues, Randall Henning then offers a political science perspective on a subject that has attracted a good deal of Fred Bergsten's interest and energy: building the institutions of international economic relations. In this context, Henning reaches somewhat different conclusions from Goldstein concerning the methods and usefulness of IMF exchange rate surveillance. Finally, J. David Richardson concludes our festschrift with a plea for more effective public communication of the key ideas and results of international economic policy analysis—an endeavor in which C. Fred Bergsten particularly excels.

Even a brief perusal of the Institute's publication catalog reveals that many important subjects are not covered in this volume. Most important among these omissions is the work on foreign economies and on US economic relations with these countries, subjects that have attracted a good deal of Fred Bergsten's attention over the years. Also omitted is a review of the Institute's extensive work on issues relating to particular industries or sectors and to the environment. All of these issues, in addition to those covered in this volume, remain on the Institute and Fred Bergsten's agenda.

Research on issues relating to economic development and problems of world poverty has traditionally played a relatively minor role in the work of the Institute. This deficiency is being remedied by the Institute's sister organization, the Center for Global Development, which was established five years ago at the instigation of Fred Bergsten and with generous support from Edward W. Scott, Jr. Under the direction of Nancy Birdsall, the Center has already established its independent reputation as a leading policy research institute in its field.

The Peter G. Peterson Institute for International Economics is a private, nonprofit institution for the study and discussion of international economic policy. Its purpose is to analyze important issues in that area and to develop and communicate practical new approaches for dealing with them. The Institute is completely nonpartisan.

The Institute is funded by a highly diversified group of philanthropic foundations, private corporations, and interested individuals. Major institutional grants are now being received from the William M. Keck, Jr. Foundation and the Starr Foundation. About 30 percent of the Institute's resources in our latest fiscal year were provided by contributors outside the United States, including about 12 percent from Japan.

The Institute's Board of Directors bears overall responsibilities for the Institute and gives general guidance and approval to its research program, including the identification of topics that are likely to become important over the medium run (one to three years) and that should be addressed by the Institute. The director, working closely with the staff and outside Advisory Committee, is responsible for the development of particular projects and makes the final decision to publish an individual study.

The Institute hopes that its studies and other activities will contribute to building a stronger foundation for international economic policy around the world. We invite readers of these publications to let us know how they think we can best accomplish this objective.

MICHAEL MUSSA
October 2006

C. Fred Bergsten and Richard N. Cooper with Vice President Walter Mondale on Air Force One

With President Jimmy Carter

With President Richard Nixon

With Secretary of State Henry Kissinger

Fred's swearing-in ceremony at the US Treasury with Secretary Henry Blumenthal and family, Mark and Virginia Bergsten

With Federal Reserve Chairman Paul A. Volcker and Chancellor of West Germany Helmut Schmidt

With Karl Otto Pöhl, president of Deutsche Bundesbank

With Japanese Finance Minister Kiichi Miyazawa

With Secretary of the Treasury James A. Baker III

With President George Bush

With US Trade Representative Carla A. Hills

With President Bill Clinton

With Secretary of Commerce Ron Brown

With Indonesian President Haji Mohammed Suharto (right)

With Chinese President Jian Zemin

Pre-Summit Preparatory Conference
April 10-11, 2000
The Tokyo Foundation

At a conference to develop proposals for the G-8 Okinawa Summit, April 2000

Left to right: Nancy Birdsall, president, Center for Global Development; Bono of U2; Fred; and Ed Scott, chairman of the Board, Center for Global Development

With Michael Jordan

With J. Bradford Jensen, deputy director, Peterson Institute

With college basketball uniform

With Institute Board of Directors Chairman Peter G. Peterson and Federal Reserve Chairman Alan Greenspan

With Peter G. Peterson

With Mexican President Vicente Fox

With Anthony M. Solomon, honorary chairman of the Executive Committee, Peterson Institute

With Reynold Levy, chairman of the Executive Committee, Peterson Institute

With US Trade Representative Robert Zoellick

With Mexican President Ernesto Zedillo

With Robert E. Rubin, director and chariman of the Executive Committee, Citigroup

With Rodrigo de Rato, managing director, International Monetary Fund

Peterson Institute 25th Anniversary Gala discussion panel, Andrea Mitchell, Jean-Claude Trichet, Alan Greenspan, Heizo Takenaka, and Robert Rubin

With Institute Board member and Dean Jessica Einhorn, Johns Hopkins University, School of Advanced International Studies

Les Gelb, Council on Foreign Relations and Peter G. Peterson

With Institute Board member and Caterpillar CEO James W. Owens

Peter G. Peterson and Institute Board member and AIG CEO Maurice R. Greenberg

With Institute Board of Directors Vice Chairman and UTC CEO George David and Peter G. Peterson

Peterson Institute staff, 2006

With son Mark and wife Virginia

C. Fred Bergsten:
Intellectual Entrepreneur

MICHAEL MUSSA

C. Fred Bergsten's extensive contributions to the debate on key issues of international economic policy are examined extensively in subsequent chapters of this volume. This introduction reflects briefly on Fred's enormous contributions, beyond what appears on his bibliography (listed in appendix A). Most important is his role as the intellectual entrepreneur who has created, directed, and developed the Institute for International Economics—now renamed the Peter G. Peterson Institute for International Economics—as the world's leading think tank for the analysis of international economic policy.

In extolling Fred Bergsten's performance as an intellectual entrepreneur, I shall not need to appeal to one of Fred's favorite marketing strategies—"responsible excess." The plain fact is that without Fred's very broad knowledge of international economics, his extraordinary energy in fundraising and marketing, his keen insight and foresight in perceiving critical policy issues as (or especially before) they become important, and his skill in selecting a team of key staff and in motivating and directing their activities, there simply would be no Institute for International Economics as we know it today.

Fred's talents are mutually reinforcing. His selection and direction of staff and his capacity to foresee key policy issues clearly depend on his own substantive knowledge of international economics (and politics). But it's also true that his broad and deep substantive knowledge derives in

---

Michael Mussa has been a senior fellow at the Institute since 2001.

part from the fact that Fred personally reads and approves all of the Institute's research proposals, policy briefs, policy analyses, monographs, and books, and this in turn contributes to his outstanding ability to market the Institute's intellectual product. In seminars, public debates, and meetings with government officials or business leaders, Fred can readily cite the Institute publication (sometimes forthcoming) that provides the relevant fact, analysis, or empirical result. As the genial host of the Institute's many public meetings, Fred is always prepared with the pertinent question or comment to get the discussion rolling or restart it if it begins to flag.

Some scholars disdain the grubby business of securing financing to support their intellectual endeavors. Others just don't like writing research proposals or other aspects of fundraising. Fred is not shy about asking for financial support for the Institute. More important, he is very effective at securing it. This success, of course, owes a good deal to the generosity of people like Peter G. Peterson, Anthony M. Solomon, David Rockefeller, the Niarchos Foundation, and others and to the decision of the German Marshall Fund (GMF) to provide the Institute with a very large start-up grant. This support initially came on the basis of Fred Bergsten's original proposal to found an institute focused on international economic policy. It continues to come because of confidence in Fred's ability to lead such an endeavor and to deliver the timely, relevant analyses of key international economic policy issues that are highly valued by those who make or influence policy in and out of government.

Fred's deep involvement in the intellectual work of the Institute is vital to his effectiveness as a fundraiser. People and organizations who contribute substantial sums to a think tank generally want the person in charge to be knowledgeable about the substance and to be able to provide effective leadership on the substance to his or her colleagues. The fact that Fred handles the fundraising activities virtually by himself not only frees colleagues from a task for which Fred has such a strong absolute and comparative advantage but also contributes significantly to the Institute's key strengths as an intellectual endeavor. The funding is already there, and it supports a group of experts who can work quickly and competently, and write clearly and forcefully, on a wide range of international economic policy questions. If Fred has an insight on an issue that the Institute should address, he does not need to apply for funding or search for relevant staff. He can immediately deploy available people (including himself) to prepare the relevant analysis. Similarly, when one of us has an issue for analysis, we can quickly arrange for Fred to review it. With the aid of the Institute's superb publications staff, the whole process from initial idea to public release of a detailed and persuasive study can proceed very rapidly. All this facilitates the Institute's renowned ability to diagnose critical policy issues as they become important and to prepare and disseminate timely, relevant, and highly competent analyses.

As with others who achieve well beyond the norm, Fred's success owes a good deal to his personality. He is quite a character. The following remarks reflect on some key aspects of Fred's personality that have contributed importantly to his success and that of the Institute. They draw heavily on interviews that Howard Rosen conducted with Fred's friends and supporters in preparation for the celebration of the Institute's 25th anniversary.

Evangelist for the Open Economy

Those who have seen Fred Bergsten in operation—at a seminar, in a debate, or as the host of innumerable Institute luncheons to launch new publications—should not be surprised to learn that Fred is the son of a Methodist minister. Like most professionally trained economists, Fred understands the logical analysis establishing that an open international economic system—free of artificial impediments to the mutually beneficial exchange of goods, services, assets, and technology—will serve the economic interests of all nations. More than most, he is aware of the substantial benefits conferred on this country and the rest of the world by the open international economic system that has developed since the Second World War under the leadership of the United States. With Fred, however, these are more than matters of intellectual understanding; they support a moral conviction to go forward and persuade others to pursue the virtues of openness and to forsake the evils of protectionism in all its forms.

Stuart Eizenstat first got to know Fred when he was serving as President Carter's domestic policy adviser in the White House and Fred was the assistant secretary for international affairs in the Treasury. They continued their association in later years, including the period when Eizenstat was a senior official in the State and Treasury Departments during the Clinton administration. Eizenstat speaks eloquently of Fred's evangelism and its effectiveness:

> Well, I think that in many ways the Institute has made me a much more fervent believer in the importance of an open trade and investment climate. I come from a more liberal Democratic background, and I've been really concerned about how my own party has drifted into a more anti-trade, anti-investment attitude. And I would say that Fred himself, through our work together in the Carter administration and since we've left the work he's done at the Institute have really reinforced for me the fact that there is no turning back on globalization, there is no turning back on free trade, that these are positives on a net-net basis, that we have an open foreign exchange and foreign investment climate, that we have to encourage countries to reform. And I would say that when I was ambassador to the European Union that Fred's studies gave me the ammunition to encourage the European Commission and the member states to adapt more open and flexible policies as well.

Others clearly appreciate the evangelical element in Fred's character and its importance to his success. Aside from Fred himself, Peter G. Peterson has played the greatest role in the development of the Institute through his hugely generous financial support, his chairmanship of the Institute's Board of Directors, and his continuing intellectual involvement in the work of the Institute—contributions recognized in the renaming of the Institute. Peterson comments thus on the role of Fred's evangelism in the Institute's success:

> I don't think it's an accident that we've been named the most influential think tank in the country. One reason . . . we are influential dates back to Fred Bergsten's talent, not only in defining issues that are going to be very relevant but in promoting them. . . . He's a great outreach guy, and when the Institute does a project, like we're now doing on China, for example, I've seen hundreds of references to our China project. Part of this is because Fred believes that outreach is a very important part of our mission, and you'll see Fred and his colleagues testifying, and you'll hear press conferences, you'll see visits to the White House. . . . Only then does the policy work that we do . . . maximize its effect.

As president of the GMF, Frank Loy played a critical role in the founding of the Institute. Based on a proposal from Fred Bergsten, the GMF, under Loy's leadership, agreed to provide an initial grant of $4 million—one-quarter of the Fund's entire budget—to get the Institute started. Loy reflects on the qualities that made Fred an attractive candidate to lead the new institute:

> Well, I think we all recognized an intellectual nimbleness, an ability to articulate views that is much better than you find among many others, and we . . . guessed that he had leadership capabilities. We hadn't much to go on at the time, but just looking at him, and talking about him, we came to that conclusion.

Fred Bergsten is a man with a message. The name of the Institute he directs signals the core of that message: the Institute *for* International Economics. Consistent with the logical analysis and empirical research of the economics profession, the Institute and Fred tend to have a positive orientation toward most aspects of globalization. Aside from this well-known orientation, however, neither Fred nor the Institute are politically partisan, nor do they ignore that globalization can have ill effects that should be alleviated, nor do they promote the interest of the United States at the expense of other countries. These qualifications are an essential part of Fred's evangelism and are critical for the success of the Institute.

Leslie Gelb has known Fred since childhood, worked with him closely when they were both assistant secretaries (at State and Treasury) in the Carter administration, and has continued a close association since then. He comments on the importance of nonpartisanship:

> I don't think that the Institute is partisan at all, which is one of its real virtues, one of the key things about the place it occupies . . . in the universe of think tanks.

People don't believe that the Institute has a score to settle or a political game to play; . . . its work really is about solving problems.

As the US trade representative (USTR), Carla Hills was in charge of US trade policy during the administration of President George Herbert Walker Bush. She too emphasizes the importance of nonpartisanship in the work of the Institute:

Today there seems to be perhaps less harmony, more polarization, less capacity to listen, and therefore I suppose one might say greater need for the Institute to bridge the gap because the Institute is nonpartisan, apolitical, and doesn't run into the allegation that it represents one party or the other party.

Business leaders who support the work of the Institute also see its nonpartisanship as essential to its success. James Owens is the CEO of Caterpillar and a member of the Institute's Board of Directors:

Caterpillar is keenly interested in global free trade. We've been a strong champion for many, many years. But if we are lobbying on that subject, we're seen as having a huge vested interest. If we can support the Institute and its economic analysis and thoughtful assessments of trade policy, and they come to the same conclusions that trade liberalization benefits our citizenry, they are much more effective at reaching the Congress . . . and helping get good legislation. . . . They have established themselves as a highly credible, independent, and nonpartisan think tank in that area.

George David, CEO of United Technologies Corporation and vice chairman of the Institute's board, expresses similar sentiments:

To me the glorious thing about this Institute is it is decidedly . . . nonpartisan. . . . It produces simply first-class analysis, not biased left or right, and therefore we can really believe and rely on it.

The impression that the Institute is professional and nonpartisan in its analyses is reinforced by the care that is taken in recognizing that trade liberalization (and globalization more generally), despite its overall benefits, can have harmful effects on some parties. The Institute's continuing work on trade adjustment assistance—a field in which Fred Bergsten is a pioneer—is particularly notable in this regard. Stuart Eizenstat comments:

Fred and the Institute are at the forefront of trying to stress the positive aspects of globalization, why it's actually a good thing, but also to recognize that unless governments put in place programs . . . to build a safety net for those who would otherwise fall through, that we're going to lose public support for the kind of flexible, open policies we need to succeed in a globalized world.

Of necessity, the Institute's work concerns not just the United States and its economy but the rest of the world as well. Indeed, a major and continuing focus of Institute work has been on other important economies in Europe, Asia, and the developing world (most recently China)—including but not limited to the interaction of these economies with the United States. This work is widely read and influential around the world because of its professionalism and because, although it comes from a US-based institution, it takes a broad internationalist view of economic problems and their solutions.

Paul Volcker, who was chairman of the Federal Reserve Board from 1979 to 1987 and who knows Fred and the Institute well, comments on the growing importance of the Institute's internationalist orientation under Fred's direction:

> You know, right now a challenge for the Institute, a challenge for all of us, is a tendency for the United States [to be] rather unilateral, aggressive, almost arrogant toward the rest of the world. . . .
>
> And whether it's deliberate or not, I think it's a matter of pure instinct, the Institute has always been international if they're nothing else. Their whole purpose is international and getting some harmonious consensus around the world, particularly about the economic system and how the adjustments are going to be made. And whether or not you're successful in the specifics and whether or not all the particular suggestions make sense or not—I think that [this international] focus is absolutely critical for the country.

The Happy Cassandra

One of Fred Bergsten's enduring characteristics is his proclivity to forecast economic calamities. When the foreign exchange value of the US dollar was very strong in the early 1980s, the US and world economies were, according to Fred and Steve Marris, threatened with the imminent prospect of a "hard landing" for the dollar. With the dollar once again very strong, the global economy now faces the significant risk of a "dollar crash." Although trade liberalization has made fairly consistent, and cumulatively very substantial, progress throughout the postwar era, the world economy is increasingly threatened by wholesale regression into protectionism. Indeed, as discussed in the chapter by Mac Destler and Marcus Noland, according to Bergsten's famous "bicycle theory," if trade liberalization does not maintain sufficient forward momentum, it will not simply fall over like a bicycle but will start rolling backward.

Despite such gloomy predictions, I always find it surprising that Fred maintains a fundamentally optimistic outlook. Max Baucus, the senior senator from Montana and ranking Democratic member of the Senate Finance Committee, has long been concerned with issues of international trade and finance; he has known Fred and valued his work and that of the Institute for many years. Using his shrewd politician's instinct, he sizes up Fred Bergsten as follows:

> Well, Fred is quite a guy. He's a pistol. Fred's got more energy than about 10 other people I can think of. He's always excited, he's always positive, he's always

upbeat, and he's trying to find, you know, a solution to a problem. He's not a downer, he's not pessimistic, he's not dour. I think the world of Fred.

Thus although Fred is, among international economists, a leading Cassandra, he is a very happy Cassandra. How does he square his often gloomy forecasts with the fact that they typically fail to materialize? In a recent conversation, he explained:

> Academic theoreticians and even some market practitioners pooh-pooh the risk of international financial crises. They kind of half assume that the rest of the world will finance the United States forever and that good logic will prevail and [we will] avoid the application of protectionist trade measures. The problem with that reasoning is that past history shows that it can actually happen.
>
> It is true that when past crises have loomed or even appeared—in 1971, 1978, 1979, the middle 1980s . . . those crises were managed in ways to avoid the worst. The United States never did suffer a catastrophic hard landing or depression. The global trading system staggered through. The exchange rate system managed to survive, more or less untrammeled. But in all cases, it was a very close call and only through official action and a lot of international economic cooperation was the deluge avoided.

As someone who publicly argued that the dollar was too strong in the mid-1980s and would need to depreciate substantially, but who also publicly doubted the "hard landing" scenario, I do not entirely subscribe to this explanation. There is something to be said for getting the forecast right.

Nevertheless, I concede that Fred is also right that in seeking to motivate constructive action, or avoid destructive action, there is often some value in "responsible excess" in characterizing the risks of inaction or inappropriate action—at least as long as what you are arguing for is unlikely to be worse than what you are arguing against. Moreover, many share Fred's view that emphasizing the risks of potential crises is valuable in motivating actions that can help prevent them. Paul Volcker, for example, has a range of experience that makes him particularly well qualified to remark on this issue:

> [I]n the eighties when we did have a balance of payments problem and the dollar had gotten very high for a while, . . . there was a lot of concern articulated: most clearly, repeatedly, and forcefully by Steve Marris, who was a leading member of this Institute for International Economics. . . . And I think [it] had a constructive influence because it brought to the policymakers' attention that there was a danger. . . . [W]hile it never happened and we learned that markets could adjust, I think that policies in the later part of the eighties helped prevent [a crisis].
>
> I used to argue with Fred because I thought it [the dollar] would come down anyway; we didn't need his help. But however that may be, I think it is true that the concern—particularly the later concern—about operating in cooperation to maintain some stability in exchange rates was influenced by Fred and John [Williamson] and others who were centered . . . in the Institute.

Concerning the threat of protectionism, one may also question whether the "bicycle theory" is perhaps somewhat overdone. But the fact is that both congressional and public support for open policies toward international trade (and capital flows) have been eroding in the United States, and the situation is hardly better in Europe and elsewhere. Outside the Institute, many well-informed observers are increasingly worried.

One of them is Phil English, who was elected to Congress from Pennsylvania in 1994 and was the first freshman Republican to be appointed to the House Ways and Means Committee since George H.W. Bush in the 1960s. As a leading congressional expert on international trade matters (who expresses great appreciation for the work of the Institute), Congressman English worries,

> What I find is there is a rising fear within the public, within the business community, within workers' organizations—fear of unfair trade. And this is evolving, I think, potentially [into] a backlash that could move us away from international engagement. I'm afraid that in terms of international economic policy there's a great deal of pressure for us to disengage from the world trading system, to pull back on ourselves. And the fact is, no country has ever done that successfully and maintained its standard of living.

Carla Hills, who has remained very actively involved with international trade issues (and with the Institute) since leaving the office of the USTR, shares similar worries:

> I'm very concerned that we are experiencing creeping protectionism. I worry that although tariffs have come down, dumping actions, safeguard actions, and particularly actions over domestic regulations like standards are creeping in to keep foreigners' products out. . . .That will have an adverse effect on the growth of the global economy and on the well-being of our national economy.

Star Player, Team Leader

When you enter the Institute's new building on Massachusetts Avenue and walk past the reception area, you come to the large room where the Institute holds its book release luncheons, conferences, and other public functions—invariably with C. Fred Bergsten as the designated "host." This room is about 30 feet wide and over 100 feet long. In view of Fred's parentage, some might think that it resembles a modern church. More appropriately, I believe that it resembles a basketball court. Because Fred Bergsten is in fact a bit of a basketball fiend.

Les Gelb reflects on the importance of basketball in the career of his long-time friend:

> Fred and I have known each other since I was ten and he was eight, and it had to do with basketball. His father was the pastor of St. John's Methodist Church in New Rochelle, New York. And St. John's sported the only indoor gymnasium in the city that you could use on Saturdays. So on Saturdays I became a Methodist and went over there to play basketball. Fred was always there. And he and I had this passion for that game which we share to this day. . . . Fred and Jenny, and my wife Judy, we even had season tickets to the Washington Bullets basketball games for many, many years.

Fred . . . had a certain basketball skill that was directly transferable to his success at the IIE, namely luck. Those balls that he shot up, he couldn't have even seen the basket on half those shots. He was just heaving them up all the time, and . . . all sorts of them actually went in. . . .

Whenever you run a place like the IIE . . . some things you can attribute to your skill, but you're making calls all the time between this program [or] that program, this senior fellow or that senior fellow, and . . . Fred Bergsten had an awfully high percentage of right calls. . . .

Fred has a very consistent personality. If you took a vote among foreign policy people who have known him over the years, they would vote Fred the most unchanged. In basketball he used to take the most shots . . . whoever was playing on his team, somehow or other Fred ended up taking 50 percent of the shots. Fred still has the knack now for getting attention to what he says. He's still taking a lot of good shots.

I hasten to add that not everyone who knows Fred and was important in his career was overly impressed with his performance on the basketball court. Stuart Eizenstat observes,

Fred is wise in many ways, and one of his greatest acts of wisdom was not asking me to play basketball, because I was a high school all-American basketball player and I might have shown him up too much.

Paul Volcker is even more succinct:

I don't play basketball with him, no. . . . He's too short. I don't play basketball with short guys with beards.

Despite these doubts about Fred's basketball prowess, I think Les Gelb is fundamentally right in attributing significance to basketball in forecasting and shaping key aspects of Fred's later career. It is true that in the work of the Institute, Fred is the leading shooter—and probably the leading scorer. Even more important, as a basketball player, Fred clearly learned that championships are won by great teams, not merely by highly talented individual players.

Richard N. Cooper, the Maurits Boas Professor of Economics at Harvard University and chairman of the Institute's Advisory Committee, has known Fred for nearly 40 years, since Fred first worked for him at the State Department as well as when they were both officials in the Carter administration. He emphasizes Fred's skill in recruiting a great team:

Fred Bergsten . . . has an outstanding way of drawing in excellent people and he has established an absolutely first-class team. It is easier to do once an institution has developed a reputation, but he started out at the beginning with an extremely good core of senior staff members, some of whom are still with the Institute.

Lawrence Summers, former US treasury secretary and former president of Harvard University, makes much the same point, while also noting Fred's performance as the Institute's leading shot taker:

Fred is irrepressible. He doesn't get discouraged—ever. He keeps coming back on his ideas. He listens, and he responds to the questions people ask, rather than simply the concerns that he has, and he assembles remarkable people together as a team and he allows them to each pursue their initiative.

And so Fred has undoubtedly written more books than anyone else at the Institute. Fred has surely given more interviews than anyone else at the Institute, but a great part of what he has accomplished is the set of people that he has brought together at the Institute who have made his work better and who have made enormous contributions to international economic thinking.

Pete Peterson reflects more broadly on the key qualities that have made Fred such a great leader for the Institute:

One thing that's unique about the Institute is its director. . . . Fred Bergsten is a statistical anomaly. . . . It's extremely rare to find in one person at least three qualities that you dream about in a director.

First, you want someone who is very good about defining policy issues and implementing them and selling them and reaching out and telling the world about them. I think Fred is one of the best in that area.

Second, you want an executive director who can attract top talent. And I know I may be called prejudiced, but I know quite a lot about a lot of think tanks; I think it's the best group of economists in the world I've ever seen.

And third, . . . we use the euphemism "development" . . . for reaching deep into other people's pockets. I've got to tell you, every time I see Bergsten, I put both hands in both pockets, but somehow he reaches down and finds the money anyway.

Jessica Einhorn, the dean of Johns Hopkins University's School of Advanced International Studies (SAIS) and a long-time friend of Fred Bergsten, holds somewhat different but not inconsistent views:

There are a couple of qualities about Fred that make him the best possible choice to head the Institute. One, I think, is the brilliance and passion that he brings to international economics. . . .

The second one is, and it's only grown with the years, his total sense of security intellectually, which may make him a very strong debater but also only makes him happy if somebody can prove him wrong because what Fred is interested in is learning and then getting the right answers. . . .

And the third great thing about Fred is Jenny. And the fact that we have Jenny as part of the Institute, from the aesthetic touch to the emotional intelligence to the ability to manage Fred in the best possible way, that's another great thing about Fred. He chose a great wife.

Observations: C. Fred Bergsten, the Man and His Institute

"I think the Institute exceeded our expectations. If you're in the grant-making business and you bat .500, which is pretty good baseball, you think you're doing terrifically. The Institute is a home run. The Institute did exactly what we hoped it would do—that is, provide analysis to policymakers that needed it in a timely fashion."

—*Frank Loy*

"Has it met our objectives of 25 years ago? I could not have imagined the Institute being this successful. Every time I look at this wonderful building and meet all of the great fellows and spend a few hours there listening to their work, I could not have imagined this kind of aggregation of talent 25 years ago."

—*Peter G. Peterson*

"I think the Institute certainly exceeds my expectations and the expectations of many people who were involved at the beginning. . . . It met the goals and it went well beyond that. The Institute has established itself much more firmly than I think anyone would have guessed 25 years ago. . . . There's no more laudatory comment on the Institute than the desire today of the Europeans to emulate the Institute for International Economics, and they have just last year created a new institute, Bruegel, which is expressly modeled on the Institute for International Economics."

—*Richard N. Cooper*

"The Institute, as I always say, is a national treasure."

—*Jessica Einhorn*

"Fred . . . has a knack of combining a solid economic framework and . . . an obsession about practical policy problems. And his conception of the Institute from the beginning was to combine good economic analysis with practical and timely application to policy problems, and I think on that score you have to say he has been very successful."

—*Paul Volcker*

"My impression of the Institute over the last 25 years is if it weren't there, somebody would have had to invent it because it's really in the last 25 years that the reality of interdependence, or now more often called globalization, has come home to roost with the policy world. . . . I think we're very lucky that Fred was the one who invented [the Institute]."

—*Marina von Neumann Whitman*

"I don't think there have been many institutions outside the government, if any, that have had the same kind of impact on global economic thinking and, through their impact on global economic thinking, on the global economy as the Institute for International Economics. As an American and as a citizen of the world, I feel we're lucky to have the Institute for International Economics."

—*Lawrence Summers*

"I think the Institute has been one of the most important factors in shaping US trade policy, and, indeed, I could go beyond that. . . . The Institute is the very best in international economics. It has a stable of scholars and deep thinkers who are number one on anybody's list across the board, whether it be monetary policy, China, trade policy. The Institute just has the very best, and the work product that they put out is not only persuasive but [also] so well written that people who are not able to do the economic formulae for themselves can understand why trade is a benefit to the national interest.

I give Fred Bergsten huge credit for where the Institute is today. He is thinking about the future of the Institute 24/7, and he brings together diverse points of view. He accepts criticism and he listens carefully. I think he's just a superb director."

—*Carla Hills*

"Well, the Institute has helped us in Congress in many, many ways. One is with trade legislation . . . [and with] trade promotion authority. It's the basic trade legislation we have to have for this government to function in the world. But it's also . . . trade adjustment assistance [and] lots of other areas where the Institute is providing invaluable service. . . . I'm not exaggerating. I think the Institute is one of the best organizations that we have in this country in terms of helping the government—whether it's at one end of Pennsylvania Avenue or the other, Republicans or Democrats—[to] better understand trade and international financial policy in a way where we're making things happen in a positive way.

There are huge challenges out there in the world, huge, and they're getting more and more challenging. . . . The Institute for International Economics . . . is playing a very vital role, and I think that it will play an even more vital role as these issues become even more important than they already are."

—*Senator Max Baucus*

"[T]he Institute is enormously influential because it's a munitions factory. It produces real materiel in the war on ideas. And it will—for an individual like me that is trying to address complicated issues in a nuanced way—IIE has done a remarkable job of giving me options, giving me real research, . . . giving me the building blocks of real policies."

—*Representative Phil English*

"I think the Institute for International Economics has one of the most seasoned, experienced, and well-recognized staffs of economists in the world, with deep expertise . . . on trade and exchange rates, the economies of China, India. . . . It's a great resource to have the research that's being done here as we think through the business of how we do a better job serving those markets."

—*James Owens*

"[W]e have taken a great deal from the Institute in our own thinking at UTC [United Technologies]. This is our primary source of economic advice outside of our own company. We turn always to Fred, to the Institute. He just spoke at one of our conferences a couple of days ago. His thinking is influential for us looking at the two- to three-year time period ahead. . . . It covers the full range of topics, and I think the Institute could be even broader."

—*George David*

"There's no institute anywhere in the world, in my opinion, that comes close to having the broad impact that the Institute for International Economics does in capitals across the world in their economic thinking, in trying to promote an open trade environment, sound exchange rate policies, domestic economic reforms. It's really quite a remarkable impact, and there simply is no institute that comes close to it. If this Institute didn't exist, we'd have to create it overnight because it has filled such a vacuum and filled it so well that it really has become an essential part of policymaking all over the world."

—*Stuart Eizenstat*

"Twenty-five years from now, Fred Bergsten will even be more renowned as director of the IIE than he is today."

—*Leslie Gelb*

Amen!

2

Constant Ends, Flexible Means: C. Fred Bergsten and the Quest for Open Trade

I. M. DESTLER and MARCUS NOLAND

Over the past 25 years, C. Fred Bergsten has launched and institutional-ized a remarkable think tank. And beyond his role at the Peterson Insti-tute for International Economics, he has established himself as a front-rank public intellectual on a range of international economic policy issues. He has interpreted the past. He has lauded or decried the present. He has prescribed for the future. His voice and his pen have marked out a broad range of policy territory: money, trade, Europe, Japan, American compet-itiveness, the G-7, APEC—the list goes on.

Central to his work has been the goal of trade liberalization, which he has pursued throughout his professional career. His efforts began as a government official (at State, the National Security Council, and Treasury) and think tank analyst (at the Council on Foreign Relations and Brook-ings) from the late 1960s through 1980. They multiplied with the creation of the Institute in 1981. They combined recurrent themes with openness to new methods of attaining them as circumstances seemed to dictate.

I. M. Destler, visiting fellow, has been associated with the Institute since 1983. He is a professor at the School of Public Policy, University of Maryland. Marcus Noland, senior fellow, has been associ-ated with the Institute since 1985.

Bergsten's work has highlighted both economics and politics, addressing not just the welfare-enhancing benefits of trade expansion but how the political system might bring it about. This chapter summarizes and analyzes this impressive Bergsten record. It begins by highlighting recurrent themes and then moves to the historical record, centering particularly on the Institute and its work. The conclusion asks whether the same emphases are likely to be appropriate during the Institute's next 25 years.

Recurrent Themes

Core Commitment to Trade Liberalization

Central to the Bergsten worldview is the value of open trade. For the most part, trade's goodness is assumed rather than demonstrated, but there are recurrent references to the "welfare benefit of reducing present restrictions" (Bergsten 1973a, footnote 20). Moreover, as discussed later, Bergsten mandated and publicized the work of Gary Hufbauer and his colleagues to generate a "big number" estimate ($1 trillion annually) of trade's benefits to the US economy (Bradford, Grieco, and Hufbauer 2005). There is also recognition of a broad political economy rationale for barrier reduction: "the traditional foreign policy desire to use economic negotiations as a functional means for expanding global cooperation" (Bergsten 1973a). Presumably, he concurs—at least in spirit—with the view of Cordell Hull that "unhampered trade dovetailed with peace" and its opposite, "high tariffs . . . with war" (Hull 1948).

But Bergsten has been much more concerned with means: how to get free trade and how to resist new trade protection. Domestically, the threat comes from producers seeking restricted markets and hurt by foreign competition. The threat is intensified if the dollar becomes overvalued and the trade balance deteriorates, as this increases the range and depth of injury from imports. In recommending policy responses, Bergsten has consistently stressed three:

- international negotiations to reduce trade barriers (the "bicycle theory");

- macroeconomic policy balance and coordination (the overvalued dollar as "leading indicator" of protectionism); and

- compensating the trade losers (adjustment assistance).

And there is a corollary to the first: a theory of "competitive liberalization" holding that bilateral and regional barrier reduction stimulates market opening worldwide.

International Negotiations and the "Bicycle Theory"

Over 30 years ago, Bergsten declared trade policy to be "dynamically unstable," making "maintenance of the status quo . . . untenable. . . . Steady movement toward trade liberalization is necessary to halt the acceleration of the trend toward increasing trade restrictions" (Bergsten 1973a). By the early 1980s, if not earlier, he was giving it a now familiar name.[1]

> The hypothesis of "dynamically unstable trade policy" holds that the trade regime either moves forward toward liberalization or backward toward protection, and an MTN [multilateral trade negotiation] helps the trade policy "bicycle" keep its forward-moving momentum. . . . According to the "bicycle theory," trade policy must move ahead or it will topple. (Bergsten and Cline 1982, 18, 71)

> I'm fond of something called the bicycle theory, which says that trade policy has to either be moving ahead, toward greater liberalization, or it topples in the face of protectionist pressures from individual sectors. . . . To hold back the protectionist slide and curb restrictive pressures from vested parochial interests you need to couch trade policy in the broader context—the national interest in greater welfare for the consumer and the economy as a whole, and the benefits to export interests from opening markets worldwide. That, in turn, seizes the interest of a President, a Congress, a prime minister of another country and gets a political commitment made to proceed in the liberalizing direction. (Bergsten quoted in Cohen 1984, 241)

Once coined, the "bicycle theory" became standard Bergsten parlance:

> History demonstrates the validity of the "bicycle theory": if trade policy does not move toward the greater openness that is in the general interest, it will topple in the face of protectionist pressures. (Bergsten 1988, 137; see also 140 and 155)

> The history of trade policy teaches forcefully that failure to move steadily forward toward liberalization condemns the trading system to topple over or fall backward in the face of protectionist pressures—the "bicycle theory." (Bergsten 1996b, 108)

> The situation is very serious if, like me, you believe in the bicycle theory, which says you either move forward or you fall over. (Bergsten 2000)

As suggested by these quotes (and the more extensive analyses from which they are drawn), the logic of the theory is straightforward. Liberal trade policy is ever vulnerable to protectionist pressures from trade-impacted producers—if the agenda is left to them, the question will be not whether to impose new trade restrictions, but how much and on what. You can't beat something with nothing; there must be a liberalizing alternative. Since large-scale unilateral barrier reduction is seldom viable politically,

---

1. Concerning the "bicycle theory," Deardorff's "Glossary of International Economics" says, "the idea was suggested by Bergsten and named by Bhagwati (1988)." The latter is incorrect, as documented above. The 1982 quotation above was the earliest use of the term we could find, so it was likely "named by Bergsten."

the alternative must be negotiations with trade partner-competitors in which we offer to reduce our barriers in exchange for their reducing theirs. With them, the trade policy bicycle moves forward. Without them, it falls down. (Remember Smoot-Hawley!)

Negotiations keep the bicycle moving by affecting both *process* and *outcome*. There are at least two process effects. While talks are ongoing, US officials can deny protection to claimants on the grounds that it will undercut US bargaining at Geneva (or wherever).[2] And major negotiations engage the interest of presidents, prime ministers, and protrade members of Congress, adding weight to the antiprotectionist side. The outcome effect is straightforward: Successful negotiations leave the US market (and partner markets) more open than they were before. The bicycle thus moves forward.

The theory contains at least two propositions: first, that the bicycle will fall in the absence of negotiations (protection will increase); second, that during negotiations less protection is in fact provided than would be otherwise. And the latter proposition must prevail over a counterproposition: that successful negotiations require that certain potential opponents (textiles, steel) be "bought off" with protection.

> Every president who has wanted to obtain the domestic authority to conduct new international liberalizing negotiations has had to make concessions to the chief protectionist interests of the day. The entire history of U.S. postwar trade policy can be characterized as "one step backward, two steps forward." (Bergsten 2002, 92–93)

In general, recent US trade history appears to validate the bicycle theory—at least up to the mid-1990s. There were substantial surges in protectionist pressures after both the Kennedy and the Tokyo Rounds.

A Corollary: "Competitive Liberalization"

As the United States moved to negotiate preferential free trade agreements (FTAs) in the 1980s and 1990s, Bergsten embraced these as promoting liberalization overall. One reason was the "bicycle" phenomenon:

> One of the great advantages of the contemporary regional initiatives is that they have kept the bicycle moving after the conclusion of the Uruguay Round. (Bergsten 1996b, 108)

But he moved beyond this to develop a broader argument for "competitive liberalization."

---

2. As the emphasis shifted from import protection to export promotion in the 1980s, the existence of ongoing multilateral negotiations could be invoked to dissuade export interests from using potentially punitive unilateral measures such as Section 301. This was the case, for example, with respect to the demands for market opening in Japan by the USA Rice Millers' Association during the Uruguay Round negotiations.

[Why have] so many countries . . . headed in the same direction [of reducing trade barriers?] The overarching force . . . has been the process of competitive liberalization. [There has been a] dynamic interaction between regional and global initiatives to reduce trade barriers. . . . When the [Uruguay] Round faltered in the late 1980s, the three North American countries launched NAFTA and the Asians initiated APEC. When the Round almost failed to meet its final deadline in December 1993, APEC's initial summit in Seattle in November 1993 induced the Community to finally agree because, according to one top European negotiator, it "demonstrated that you had an alternative and we did not." (Bergsten 1996a)

In the George W. Bush administration, US Trade Representative Robert Zoellick embraced this strategy,[3] with Bergsten's strong endorsement.

US policy has been approaching that ultimate goal [global free trade] via three channels of negotiation: bilateral FTAs with individual countries or small groups thereof, megaregional FTAs with Latin America (and, though only rhetorically so far, with the Asia Pacific), and multilateral reductions to trade barriers at the global level through the WTO (currently via the Doha Round). The strategic underpinning of this threefold approach is the concept of "competitive liberalization," under which negotiations at each level create new incentives and pressures for nonparticipating countries to join the process. (Bergsten and the Institute for International Economics 2005, 32–33)

The case seems strong that US-Canada, NAFTA, and APEC helped spur the initiation and completion of the Uruguay Round. However, the FTAs completed under Bush have not had a comparable effect—both the global Doha Round negotiations and the regional FTA talks have broken down. Arguably, the countries involved in the preferential agreements of the 2000s have been too small. Successful completion of the US-Korea FTA negotiations could have an impact on Japan, however, spurring greater liberalization among the Asia-Pacific nations, if not globally.[4]

Indeed, the global and preferential approaches exist in a kind of symbiosis—as long as the multilateral system remains fundamentally strong, preferential agreements can be used tactically to spur competitive liberalization. The risk, of course, is that they come to be viewed as a genuine alternative to multilateral liberalization and ultimately contribute to a world characterized by greater fragmentation and economic and political rivalry

---

3. A representative Zoellick statement was an address delivered in Phoenix, Arizona, on April 30, 2002, where he spoke of a US-generated "competition in liberalization": we would "proceed with countries that are ready" to open their markets, and success would "create pressure on others" (Zoellick 2002, 81).

4. In a broadly skeptical critique of the Bush administration's "competitive liberalization" strategy, Simon J. Evenett and Michael Meier characterize Bergsten as "Perhaps the most consistent and high profile analyst in support of Competitive Liberalization." After surveying "literally hundreds of documents, press releases, and statements," they declare that "if there is a ferocious contest for better access to the large U.S. market then many [potential FTA partners] are being very quiet about it." Their "interim assessment" concludes that the policy "is almost certain to fall well short of its goals" (Evenett and Meier 2006).

between competing "blocs" than would have otherwise been the case. We return to this possibility below in the context of the contemporary trade policy agenda.

Trade and Macroeconomics: The Exchange Rate

A second recurrent theme sounded (and plausibly pioneered)[5] by Bergsten is the notion that an overstrong currency is the greatest generator of increased protectionism.

> The postwar history of trade policy in the United States, at least, reveals that the most accurate "leading indicator" of trade policy—on both the liberalizing and protectionist sides—is the degree of equilibrium in the dollar exchange rate. Dollar overvaluation clearly breeds protectionist pressures even when unemployment is low (as in 1970–1972), while dollar equilibrium supports liberalizing measures even in the face of high unemployment (as in 1974). This is because dollar overvaluation adversely affects the competitive position of stronger industries as well as those that are traditionally susceptible to foreign competition, and thus fosters much broader political coalitions in support of restrictive policies. (Bergsten 1981, 13)

> One [major risk] is further escalation of trade protectionism in the United States. Dollar overvaluation and the huge external deficits it spawns have traditionally been the primary precursors of such domestic political swings, which would carry large costs for both the US economy and foreign policy. (Bergsten and the Institute for International Economics 2005, 9)

> The history of U.S. trade policy amply demonstrates that dollar overvaluation, and the huge and growing trade deficits that it spawns, are by far the most accurate predictors of U.S. protectionism. When currency misalignments provide sizable advantages to their competitors, more industries look for relief from imports. When their goods and services are priced out of global markets, meanwhile, fewer exporters are credibly able, or even willing, to fight for liberalization. (Bergsten 2005, 17)

A stronger dollar confers greater price competitiveness to imports, resulting in economic pressure on producers of domestic goods. A stronger dollar demoralizes exporters as well, since it renders them less price competitive overseas. Hence it not only unbalances trade but generates a political imbalance as well.

This critique is typically followed by an argument for greater exchange rate stability, through target zones or some other stabilizing arrangement.

---

5. Since the authors have not undertaken a comprehensive intellectual history of the field of trade policy analysis, we cannot reach definitive conclusions on whether this or any specific concept *originated* with Bergsten. But we know of no other expert who has given comparable emphasis to this relationship or who highlighted it earlier insofar as US trade is concerned.

> What is needed . . . is some kind of synthesis between the excessive rigidity of the fixed rate regime under Bretton Woods and the excessive flexibility . . . of the past ten years. . . . My own preference is for a target zone system. . . . (Bergsten quoted in Cohen 1984, 234–35)

So stated, this relationship seems elementary, important to stress only because it was long underrecognized. What gives Bergsten's thesis bite, however, is the argument that the strong dollar is a more powerful generator of protectionism than the traditional suspect, high unemployment. And for the 1962–95 period, this argument seems valid. The most intense protectionism came in strong-dollar periods (1969–71, 1981–85), not in the years of deepest recession (1974–75, 1982–83), though there is some obvious overlap between the two.

Compensating the Trade "Losers"

A third constant theme has been the need to respond to the distributional hurt caused by trade with programs to compensate the losers. Bergsten did not originate the idea of trade-related adjustment assistance, of course,[6] but he has been active in developing and promoting the idea. His most detailed exposition came early in his career, when he chaired a Chamber of Commerce Task Force on Adjustment Assistance.

> The Chamber [supports] a program of economic adjustment that will enable the United States to pursue a liberal trade policy in the 1970s. . . . It believes that such a program must compensate those whose skills are rendered unprofitable by trade for their losses and, more importantly, help them adjust into new endeavors. (US Chamber of Commerce 1973)

This introductory language was supported by more than 20 pages detailing the components of such a program. Trade adjustment assistance (TAA) was in fact expanded by the Trade Act of 1974 but then curtailed by the Reagan administration in 1981. Bergsten has continued to advocate strengthened adjustment programs—through that decade and up to the present (building on TAA program reforms enacted in 2002).

> The rapid pace of global economic change will continue to threaten industries in the United States (and elsewhere). . . . The challenge is to achieve adjustment in the most efficient and humane manner, avoiding excessive costs both to the individuals involved and to the economy as a whole.
> The basic goal of such a program should be to provide a wide array of financial assistance and adjustment services to displaced workers, thereby reducing the interest of labor in trade protection. (Bergsten 1988, 145)

---

6. It dates from a Council on Foreign Relations planning paper drafted during World War II and was given prominence by United Steelworkers President David J. McDonald in 1953 (Destler 2005, 23–24).

When portions of society are harmed by policy choices taken in the general interest, there is a strong case for providing equitable compensation. [Moreover, t]he domestic backlash against globalization has become so powerful, especially over the past decade, that it has severely limited US foreign economic policy throughout that period. The case for mounting an effective program of domestic assistance to workers, and perhaps entire communities, disadvantaged by globalization, is very strong. (Bergsten and the Institute for International Economics 2005, 39)

Politically, TAA has in fact proved useful in deflecting protectionism—in particular, it has given protrade Democrats a rationale for supporting new negotiations *and* helping those who are hurt by the process. And it has aided a modest proportion of those Americans whose jobs have been casualties of trade expansion. The program has yet to fulfill its full substantive or political potential, however, in part because of the reluctance of organized labor to fully support it.

Bergsten as Policy Entrepreneur

In addition to his consistency in substantive themes, Bergsten has been consistent tactically in promoting free trade and global openness. He has been an exponent of "responsible excess," exaggeration of dangers in order to win attention. Thus he predicted that many commodity cartels would follow OPEC (Bergsten 1973b) and that the United States and Europe risked a trade war (Bergsten 1999). He sponsored and endorsed Stephen Marris's (1985) apocalyptic "hard landing" scenario for the world economy and has employed somewhat comparable language about the even greater imbalances that have emerged 20 years later (Bergsten and the Institute for International Economics 2005).

He has also encouraged "responsible apostasy" by others, sponsoring studies that diverged from free trade and proglobalization orthodoxy. Examples are Tyson's (1992) advocacy of aggressive trade activism and Rodrik's (1997) focus on globalization's costs.

When predicted calamities did not occur on schedule, Bergsten has claimed credit for heading them off—"the self-denying prophecy." The threat of Third World–based cartels was averted because Secretary of State Henry A. Kissinger changed policy and responded to Third World concerns. Likewise, a hard landing was averted in the 1980s because—prodded in part by the writings of Marris and Bergsten—Secretary of the Treasury James Baker III mobilized his counterparts at the September 1985 Plaza meeting and drove the dollar downward. Bergsten has recently urged Secretary of the Treasury Henry Paulson to undertake a similar initiative.[7]

Bergsten's promotion of open-trade policies has also been a constant throughout his professional career. It was on display during his work as a

---

7. C. Fred Bergsten, "What's a Treasury Secretary to Do? An Agenda for Henry Paulson, Here and Abroad," *The Washington Post*, July 26, 2006.

fellow at the Council on Foreign Relations (1967–69, 1971–72) and the Brookings Institution (1972–77). As senior assistant for international economic affairs at the National Security Council (1969–71), he promoted TAA and the launch of new trade negotiations and sought compromise in the festering US-Japan textile dispute that was undermining protrade initiatives. As assistant secretary for international affairs (and acting under secretary) of the Treasury (1977–81), he continued to pursue this agenda. He saw his bicycle and exchange rate theories vindicated as protectionism surged in 1967–71, then receded with dollar decline and the launch of the Tokyo Round.

Most important, however, Bergsten's mix of intellectual and practical skills was such that when the German Marshall Fund of the United States made the landmark strategic decision to launch the Institute, he was a (perhaps *the*) natural choice for its director. And it was there that he found an ideal platform for his substantive, managerial, and promotional talents.

The Institute Years

The Institute for International Economics was formed in 1981, and it soon became evident that the relationship between the institute and its director was symbiotic: Bergsten would have a central influence on the Institute's agenda; at the same time, the work produced by Institute-affiliated analysts would affect his own thinking.

The Institute's founding coincided with the accession to the presidency of Ronald Reagan, whose two administrations would mix continuity with, and departure from, previous practice. From the standpoint of Bergsten and the Institute, the Reagan administration's combination of tight monetary policy and profligate fiscal policy predictably resulted in rising real interest and exchange rates, widening trade and current account deficits, and pressures on trade policy emanating from the resulting squeeze on import competing sectors:

> The sharp tax cuts combined with massive defense expenditures will continue to produce large budget deficits. . . . To fight inflation, which will be promoted by its fiscal stance, the administration is relying solely on monetary policy, thus insuring that interest rates will remain quite high for the indefinite future. This level of interest rates—unprecedented in real terms in modern history and stemming primarily from the faulty policy mix of the administration—has badly distorted and undermined all major components of the world economy . . . the unprecedented overvaluation of the dollar caused by the policy mix will produce huge U.S. trade deficits and retard U.S. growth . . . the policies set in motion seem almost certain to revive strong protectionist efforts. The postwar record reveals that an overvalued dollar is by far the greatest single threat to a liberal trade policy in the United States. (Bergsten 1981, 24–30)

He concluded, "Continued malign neglect of the impact of U.S. economic policy on other countries would devastate U.S. foreign policy and U.S. domestic prosperity" (Bergsten 1981, 36).[8]

In Bergsten's distinctive view, the irresponsible macro policies threatened the gains to trade as well as broader foreign policy interests. Alteration in the macro policy mix could be justified in terms of protecting the gains from trade, domestic prosperity, and ultimately, the United States' standing in the world. In the policy realm, this is an unusual view, subordinating *macroeconomic* policymaking to a political economy imperative of maintaining the sanctity of the liberal, rules-based *microeconomic* international trade regime. Analytically, exchange rate overvaluation and current account deficits are interpreted as leading indicators of subsequent demands for international trade protection—which, once incorporated into law and practice, can have long-lived adverse welfare effects.

Bergsten and the Institute offered a multifaceted response to these challenges during the first half of the 1980s. The centerpiece of the critique of Reagan macroeconomic policies was Stephen Marris's analysis of the possibilities of a dollar crash created by the stresses of the Reagan macroeconomic policy mix, a campaign that culminated in the publication of *Deficits and the Dollar* (Marris 1985), released just after the Plaza Agreement. For the remainder of the decade, the Institute continued to support international initiatives to manage the global process of payments adjustment through the Louvre Agreement (Funabashi 1988), claiming credit for a "self-denying prophecy" with respect to Marris's jeremiad and continuing to warn of the adverse trade policy implications of an overvalued dollar (see also Destler and Henning 1989).

While Marris and others addressed the underlying macroeconomic causes of the worsening trade environment, invoking the "bicycle theory," Bergsten called for a new round of multilateral trade negotiations under the General Agreement on Tariffs and Trade (GATT) (Bergsten 1983, 12). In addition, the Institute strongly supported the launch of what became the Uruguay Round, which was to represent a constructive outlet for political pressures for trade policy activism (e.g., Hufbauer and Schott 1985, Hathaway 1987, and Miner and Smith 1988).

Multilateral trade negotiations are protracted affairs, and the Uruguay Round proved to be no exception. As a consequence, the tactic of offering

---

8. These expressions were not atypical by any stretch: Later, in congressional testimony, Bergsten would argue that, "The substantial overvaluation of the dollar in the exchange markets . . . is by far the most critical trade problem now faced by the United States" (Bergsten 1982, 1) and that industry and labor groups demanding such protection, however ill advised, "are really asking only for policy intervention to correct the distortions generated by other policy intervention (e.g., loose fiscal policy and very high interest rates) and nonintervention (e.g., in the exchange markets)" (Bergsten 1982, 5). In response Bergsten called for a macroeconomic package that would amount to "a reversal of almost 180 degrees from the approach of the past two years" (Bergsten 1983, 6).

multilateral liberalization as a constructive alternative to protection was only partly successful—it deflected traditional demands for protection more effectively than the growing demands for export activism backed by threats of market closure. Clearly, the results would have been worse had there been no GATT negotiations. Nevertheless, the decade of the 1980s saw increasing pressure in the United States for discriminatory and GATT-inconsistent trade protection such as the "voluntary export restraints" (VERs) on products such as steel, machine tools, and automobiles, negotiated with Japan, South Korea, Taiwan, and other countries (Destler and Odell 1987).

The Institute response was threefold: first, establish the linkage between macroeconomics and the political economy of trade policy; second, make explicit the costs of protectionist measures; and third, support TAA for those adversely affected by international trade. Making the costs of protection explicit initially took the form of analyses of the impact of protection in particular US industries or sectors (Hufbauer, Berliner, and Elliott 1986; Cline 1987), a research program that eventually broadened to produce economywide estimates of the costs of protection in the United States and other major participants in the international trade system (Hufbauer and Elliott 1994; Sazanami, Urata, and Kawai 1995; Kim 1996; Zhang, Zhang, and Wan 1998; Messerlin 2001). And if quantitative nontariff protection was to be granted, it would be better to do it in the form of "auction quotas," which would reduce the attractiveness of quantitative restrictions to both importers and exporters and ensure that the resulting quota rents were captured by the public treasury, not private interests (Bergsten 1975b, Bergsten et al. 1987). At the same time the Institute was making the costs of protection explicit, it was also producing proposals to aid the adjustment of those adversely affected by the expansion of international trade (Hufbauer and Rosen 1986).

In addition to this four-pronged approach—address the underlying macroeconomic issues, provide a constructive multilateral alternative to protection, publicize the costs of protection, and advocate support for those adversely affected by trade—the 1980s saw the launching of a new development that arguably shaped the subsequent evolution of the international trade system profoundly.

Throughout the postwar period, US trade policy, with the GATT as its centerpiece, had been fundamentally global and nondiscriminatory in its orientation. Exceptions were relatively minor: The United States and Canada had a special agreement with respect to automobile trade, the United States maintained a modest program of duty-free access for some developing-country exports (under the GATT's generalized system of preferences), and it had occasionally imposed special, discriminatory protection, most often in textiles and apparel or against Japanese exports.

In the 1980s, however, the US concluded free trade agreements with Israel (1985) and Canada (1988). The Israel agreement was driven primarily by foreign policy considerations (Rosen 1989). The negotiations with Canada were launched in the wake of a failed 1982 GATT ministerial, partly as a gambit to spur the launch of what became the Uruguay Round (Bergsten 1991), and the Institute published studies supportive of the FTA (Wonnacott 1987, Schott and Smith 1988).

Arguably, neither the Israel nor the Canada deals had major systemic implications (though the trade negotiations agenda was expanded with the inclusion of services in the Canadian agreement). The picture began to change, however, when the US-Canada agreement was expanded to include Mexico. The initiative came from the Mexican side, and the receptive US response was justified as much or more by foreign policy interests as by economic considerations per se. Yet the North American Free Trade Agreement (NAFTA) was precedent setting inasmuch as it represented the first free trade agreement between large developed and developing countries, and thereby greatly broadened the realm of possible preferential deals. Again, the Institute published generally positive evaluations of the prospective NAFTA agreement (e.g., Hufbauer and Schott 1992, 1993; Martin 1993) and its subsequent performance (e.g., Hufbauer et al. 2000, 2005). This favorable finding was to be replicated when additional preferential agreements came onto the US trade policy agenda, with Institute studies typically concluding that the free trade agreement under consideration would contribute positively to US and global welfare (Schott 1989a, 1989b, 2004).

On the US side, NAFTA was partly motivated by frustration over the slow pace of the Uruguay Round negotiations (Schott 1990). It was hoped that the demonstration that the US could pursue preferential arrangements as an alternative to the GATT system would encourage a more forthcoming negotiating stance on the part of its Uruguay Round partners, most importantly the European Union. When NAFTA did not have the intended strategic effect, Bergsten seized on the embryonic Asia Pacific Economic Cooperation (APEC) forum as a means of upping the ante. Chosen to head its newly minted "Eminent Persons Group" in 1992, Bergsten presented the group's first report to the region's assembled heads of government at Blake Island, WA, in October 1993 and effectively authored APEC's "Bogor Declaration," establishing a commitment the following year to a phased freeing of trade under the organization's "open regionalism" mantra (Bergsten 1995). The sight of the leaders of countries representing nearly half of world output meeting in the US undoubtedly concentrated European minds, and the Uruguay Round agreement was concluded in December 1993 and signed the following year. APEC has subsequently failed to live up to its initial promise, at least in terms of trade liberalization.[9]

---

9. Although the members of APEC do not appear likely to achieve the Bogor goals of trade liberalization, the organization has played a useful role in facilitating trade. Among the Institute publications addressing these issues have been Funabashi (1995), Wilson (1996), Bergsten (1997), Dua and Esty (1997), and Mann and Rosen (2002).

The Reagan-era macro policy mix had set in motion the mobilization of protectionist interests in the United States that the Reagan administration and its successors resisted with mixed success, and the repercussions were felt beyond the ambit of traditional trade negotiations, global or preferential. One such development was the increasing transpacific orientation of US trade and investment patterns, primarily centered on Japan but also including economies such as South Korea and Taiwan (together with Hong Kong and Singapore dubbed the newly industrializing countries or NICs). The shift away from the traditional transatlantic focus of US trade policy was important, in that a number of these economies were pursuing distinctive development strategies embodying a high degree of state intervention, conducted in a legal and cultural milieu that presented new challenges to US policymakers used to operating in the more familiar European environment (Noland and Pack 2003).

Bergsten's initial response to the increasingly acrimonious US trade relations with Japan was to emphasize the macroeconomic roots of America's trade deficit, both globally and with Japan, and to resist demands for protection (Bergsten and Cline 1985). But this stance was inadequate to deal with the growing demand for trade policy activism aimed at opening foreign markets—as distinct from import relief—and the growing US-Japan rivalry in a number of high-technology industries. As the decade wore on, Institute studies beginning with Balassa and Noland (1988) started examining Japan's economy in greater depth, highlighting the possible impediments to market access for foreign suppliers that its distinctive institutions might pose and providing some of the intellectual bedrock for the George H. W. Bush administration's Structural Impediments Initiative negotiations with Japan.

This reexamination reached its apotheosis in the early 1990s, with three Institute studies. One was by Laura Tyson (1992), who would head the Council of Economic Advisers and then the National Economic Council in the first Clinton administration, on trade policies for high-technology industries. Then followed the studies of US-Japan relations by Bergsten and Noland (1993) and of the roles of reciprocity and retaliation in US trade policy by Bayard and Elliott (1994). Commissioning the first study could be interpreted as an attempt to reach out to heterodox thinkers in the profession whose ideas, such as voluntary import expansions, while untested, were finding a receptive audience among policymakers, and to subject these analyses to more rigorous examination. The second represented a growing realization that in certain respects the Asian countries did pose new challenges calling for new thinking, while the third attempted to assess in greater specificity US experience with aggressive export promotion, finding resonance in the 1993 Framework Agreement between the United States and Japan. Bergsten himself embraced the old verities (macroeconomic policy adjustment), the emerging new "behind-the-border" orthodoxy (the need for international antitrust policies, harmonization of tax policies), and even the new "managed trade" solutions (infelicitously dubbed in congressional testimony "involuntary import expansions" or IIEs) in a quest to manage the relationship to forestall protection and maintain competitive markets (Bergsten 1990, 1993). As he explained it,

> When neither of the preferred options [removing explicit barriers or applying antitrust policy] is available and it can be demonstrated persuasively that access to the Japanese market is artificially hindered, it may be necessary to seek Japanese agreement to temporary use of quantitative measures of increased penetration—to manage the trade in a way that will unmanage the market. I have no philosophical problem with such efforts: they expand trade, expand the number of participants in the targeted market, increase competition, reduce prices and reduce cartel activity. They bear no resemblance to traditional protection—which closes markets, reduces the availability of the product, raises prices and creates or shores up cartels. (Bergsten 1993, 6–7)

Eight years later, Bergsten, Ito, and Noland (2001) closed this cycle, after a decade of considerable policy reform in both the United States and Japan, a period of strong US and weak Japanese economic performance (in stark contrast to Japan's strong performance during the prior decade of the 1980s), and at least some degree of institutional convergence in the two economies. The title of their book, *No More Bashing*, signaled the abandonment of extraordinary asymmetrical measures to force the opening of Japanese domestic markets. Bergsten would eventually propose a free trade agreement between the two countries (Bergsten 2004).

Although much of the focus was on Japan, during the second half of the 1980s Bergsten and the Institute began to grapple with the NICs, publishing Balassa and Williamson's (1987) examination of their exchange rate policies, followed by Noland (1990) examining the economic prospects not only of the NICs but of the rising economies of Southeast Asia as well. The Institute hosted prominent visitors from South Korea, and the research program began delving more deeply into Asian regional integration, with Bergsten offering a steady stream of commentary (e.g., Bergsten 1989).[10] Since then the Institute has published a multitude of Korea-related publications and easily has the most active Korea-related program of any think tank outside that country.[11]

---

10. One of the visiting scholars, Cho Soon, returned to South Korea and became the deputy prime minister and later governor of the central bank; as deputy prime minister he established a government think tank, the Korea Institute for International Economic Policy, modeled on the Institute for International Economics. Another South Korean visitor, Il SaKong, founded a private institution, the Institute for Global Economics, also inspired by the Institute.

11. A partial recitation of this output would include Bayard and Young (1989), SaKong (1993), Cho (1994), Bergsten and SaKong (1995, 1996, 1997), Noland (1998, 2000, 2004), Choi and Schott (2001), Bergsten and Choi (2003), and Graham (2003).

Plus Ça Change, Plus C'est la Même Chose?

A well-known witticism variously attributed to both Karl Marx and Oliver Wendell Holmes (!?) alleges that history repeats itself, first as tragedy, then as farce. In certain respects, the current international economic situation resembles that facing Bergsten during the Institute's early years. The second Clinton administration saw a lapse in presidential "fast-track" trade negotiating authority (Destler 1997) and a surge in antiglobalization sentiment. At the same time, the inclusion of environmental (Esty 1994, Hufbauer et al. 2000) and labor (Elliott and Freeman 2003) considerations, and the option of pursuing trade liberalization on a preferential basis, lengthened and complicated the trade liberalization agenda (Destler and Balint 1999, Destler 2005).

In a number of respects, the reactions of Bergsten and the Institute (Bergsten 2000, Bergsten and the Institute for International Economics 2005) echoed their responses to similar situations two decades earlier. A primary response was once again to get the bicycle rolling, supporting the launch of the Doha Development Round of trade negotiations under the auspices of the World Trade Organization, the successor to the GATT created by the Uruguay Round Agreement (Schott 1998, 2000; Bergsten 2002; Elliott 2006; Hufbauer and Schott 2006). In this connection, to publicize the magnitude of the accomplishments to date, and to flag the potential future gains that remained to be harvested, Bergsten commissioned research by Institute scholars to estimate the impact of globalization on the US economy. This effort yielded an estimate of approximately $1 trillion in annual benefits to the US economy and a "conservative" estimate of another half trillion dollars in potential additional gains (Bradford, Grieco, and Hufbauer 2005). Meanwhile, analyses of globalization in information technology by Catherine L. Mann responded to anxieties about offshoring of jobs (concerns that peaked during the 2004 presidential campaign) and highlighted potential US gains from further liberalization of markets for services (Mann 2005, 2006).

A second response was to focus on the underlying macroeconomic roots of politically sensitive balance of payments disequilibria, as well as the recurrent financial crises of the 1990s that were fueling antiglobalization sentiment in many parts of the world (Bergsten and Williamson 2003, 2004; Cline 2005). As was the case 20 years earlier, these imbalances centered on the United States and a rising Asian power—in this instance, China. In policy terms, addressing the issue required macroeconomic adjustments, including changes in exchange rate policies, and analytically it meant devoting resources to the examination of an institutionally distinct economy (Lardy and Goldstein 2004, Lardy 2005, Bergsten 2006, Bergsten et al. 2006).

A third tack was to again deal constructively with domestic adjustment issues created by trade, this time as part of a broad "globalization balance sheet" project directed by J. David Richardson (Richardson 2005, forthcoming; see also Kletzer 2001, Scheve and Slaughter 2001, Kletzer and Rosen 2005). Another response familiar from the earlier period was to bring heterodox thinkers into the big tent (e.g., Rodrik 1997).

One big difference this time around was the availability of the preferential (and/or regional) alternative to global liberalization. In Bergsten's eyes, the attraction of the preferential alternative was purely instrumental: Such agreements took less time to negotiate and permitted bolder action than obtainable through the global system (Bergsten 1996a). Yet he also acknowledged the "fundamentally superior" nature of the global approach, potential tension between the two alternatives, and the need to harness regionalism to constructive multilateral ends. Used constructively, this "creative tension" and "dynamic interaction" could be used to propel the global system forward. However, without "determined leadership" to move forward on the global front, "then regionalism will not only fill the vacuum . . . but it will take place in the absence of any effective multilateral framework and that could lead to fears that many have expressed over the years that regionalism will drive the world apart rather than move it together" (Bergsten 2000, 5). The Institute would subsequently produce a plethora of mostly supportive analyses of preferential arrangements, while continuing to support the successful completion of the Doha Round.

Echoing the endgame tactics of the previous Uruguay Round, Bergsten argued that credible movement toward "megaregional" integration (probably via APEC) was a necessary catalyst to bring the Doha Round negotiations to a successful close; indeed "it may be the only tool available to bring Doha back to life" (Bergsten 2005, 23).[12] Failing that, the United States could try to force the issue through promiscuous invitations to bilateral preferential integration.[13]

Complementing this expanding substantive agenda were innovations in outreach, principally through the increased use of the Internet and shorter publication forms. In 1998 the Institute inaugurated a "policy brief" series, publishing approximately nine per year, along with a similar number of more technical "working papers." In addition, Institute scholars are widely cited in the press and continue to testify before Congress, as they have throughout the organization's existence. Bergsten himself is perennially the most widely cited think tank economist in the United States, and other Institute scholars regularly place in the upper reaches of the citation counts (Trimbath 2005).

---

12. A partial listing of these publications would include Feinberg (1997), Frankel (1997), Choi and Schott (2001), Pastor (2001), Schott (2001), Scollay and Gilbert (2001), Lardy and Rosen (2004), Schott (2004), Galal and Lawrence (2005), and Hufbauer and Baldwin (2006).

13. C. Fred Bergsten, "Plan B for World Trade: Go Regional," *The Financial Times*, August 16, 2006.

Looking Ahead: Will the Same Patterns Persist?

As the Institute celebrates its 25th birthday, and Bergsten his 65th, both can look back with pride. The relationship has been serious and comprehensive, both in intellectual and practical terms. The impact has been impressive, indeed enviable.

Will the same themes prove appropriate for the next quarter century? At present, the United States is in the midst of a natural experiment testing Bergsten's two signal theses—the trade bicycle and the exchange rate. The global Doha Round talks have adjourned without agreement and with dubious future prospects. The US trade imbalance (driven in part by exchange rate misalignment) is at an astronomical level, with the nation importing over $9 in goods for every $5 it sells overseas. These should be generating, by the logic set forth here, an enormous protectionist backlash.

Thus far, this backlash has not occurred. There is, to be sure, heightened concern over China—the persistent 6-to-1 bilateral trade imbalance and its undervalued exchange rate. There have been some import safeguards imposed, and a bilateral textile agreement negotiated—both within the framework of that nation's WTO accession agreement. And there is a broad antiglobalization movement. But the latter is rooted in social concerns as much as economic interests. Most important, the business-generated protectionism that characterized the early 1970s and the early and mid-1980s in the United States is conspicuously absent, though organized labor is still as, or even more, protectionist and resistant to globalization.

This could be a long-term change. One of us has argued elsewhere that the globalization of US business has made a pure protectionist position very difficult for the great majority of firms and sectors to sustain—they are simply too dependent on trade (needing imports for inputs as much as or more than exports, in many cases). For example, the once formidable textile-apparel coalition has crumbled as apparel makers moved offshore and cloth producers concluded that they could not build their futures on the US market alone. Rent-seeking demands on trade policy continue to exist, but they have taken different forms. So, for example, the mills shifted from protectionism (the Multi-Fiber Arrangement, which expired in 2005) to bilateral FTAs with rules of origin requiring lower-wage clothing producers in partner nations to use US cloth as a condition for barrier-free access to the US market—in effect a local content requirement for imports (Destler 2005, chapter 9)!

Labor cannot, by definition, globalize to the same degree, and open trade policy remains vulnerable to the charge that the gains have not been broadly shared. Still, it was business firms producing at home with domestic inputs for the home market, not organized labor, that were the backbone of historic US protectionism. The overall movement of US business into the internationalist camp is thus an important, arguably durable structural shift that may render the trade bicycle less unstable and the trade-political balance less vulnerable to exchange rate misalignment. These trends may have been further reinforced by the currency hedging strategy implicit in the global dispersion of production facilities by multinational corporations.

However, this relatively benign outcome is facilitated by two conditions—one political, one economic, and both subject to change. Today's congressional acquiescence on trade policy is a product, in part, of Republican control of both the presidency and both Houses of Congress. If the country were to return to the "divided government" that characterized the 1980s, partisanship could contribute to an intensification of congressional intervention (though it also could drive the administration to take the Democrats' concerns seriously).

The other condition that may well have contributed to the relatively benign outcome observed to date has been the generally robust macroeconomic performance of the US economy. Should the US economy experience a noticeable slowdown or recession—especially if associated with external disruptions such as a hard landing of the dollar—then pressures for trade restrictions could multiply. Once again, Bergsten dramatizes the threat:

> It's not pretty to contemplate US trade policy, and hence the global trading system, in a year or two if US growth slows sharply and joblessness rises while our global trade deficit exceeds $1 trillion and the bilateral imbalance with China rises to $300 billion to $400 billion. The fact is that the US external deficits are unsustainable, and they would be even if the rest of the world were willing to finance us indefinitely. (Bergsten 2006a)

If this scenario eventuates, we will enter terra incognita, political as well as economic.

The potential downside risk embodied in this scenario is reinforced, as earlier noted, by the official July 2006 "suspension" of the Doha Round negotiations and the possibility that it will be the first global trade negotiation since the establishment of the GATT to fail. Such an outcome could lead to an erosion of multilateral discipline, a drift toward greater trade discrimination, and the formation of competing rival blocs.

If the world does move in that direction, we hope Bergsten will conjure up ways to limit the damage.

References

Balassa, Bela, and Marcus Noland. 1988. *Japan in the World Economy*. Washington: Institute for International Economics.

Balassa, Bela, and John Williamson. 1987. *Adjusting to Success: Balance of Payments Policy in the East Asian NICs*. POLICY ANALYSES IN INTERNATIONAL ECONOMICS 17. Washington: Institute for International Economics.

Bayard, Thomas O., and Kimberly Ann Elliott. 1994. *Reciprocity and Retaliation in US Trade Policy*. Washington: Institute for International Economics.

Bayard, Thomas O., and Soogil Young, eds. 1989. *Economic Relations Between the United States and Korea: Conflict or Cooperation?* Special Report 8. Washington: Institute for International Economics.

Bergsten, C. Fred. 1973a. Future Directions for U.S. Trade. *American Journal of Agricultural Economics* (May): 280–88.

Bergsten, C. Fred. 1973b. The Threat from the Third World. *Foreign Policy* (Summer).

Bergsten, C. Fred. 1975a. *Toward a New International Economic Order: Selected Papers of C. Fred Bergsten, 1972–1974*. Lexington, MA: D. C. Heath and Co.

Bergsten, C. Fred. 1975b. On the Non-Equivalence of Import Quotas and "Voluntary" Export Restraints. In *Toward a New World Trade Policy: The Maidenhead Papers*, ed. C. Fred Bergsten. Washington: Brookings Institution.

Bergsten, C. Fred. 1981. The Costs of Reaganomics. *Foreign Policy* 44: 24–36.

Bergsten, C. Fred. 1982. The Dollar, the Yen and US Trade. Testimony before the Subcommittee on Trade, House Ways and Means Committee, Washington, November 30.

Bergsten, C. Fred. 1983. Can We Prevent a World Economic Crisis? *Challenge* (January-February): 4–13.

Bergsten, C. Fred. 1988. *America in the World Economy: A Strategy for the 1990s*. Washington: Institute for International Economics.

Bergsten, C. Fred. 1989. Currency Manipulation? The Case of Korea. Testimony before the Subcommittee on International Trade, Senate Finance Committee, Washington, May 12.

Bergsten, C. Fred. 1990. The United States and Japan: Forging a New Economic Relationship. Paper prepared for the first meeting of the US-Japan Leadership Council, Ojai, California, November 16–18.

Bergsten, C. Fred. 1991. Policy Implications of Trade and Currency Zones. Paper presented at a symposium sponsored by the Federal Reserve Bank of Kansas City, Jackson Hole, Wyoming, August 23.

Bergsten, C. Fred. 1993. United States–Japan Economic Relations. Testimony before the Subcommittee on Trade, Committee on Ways and Means, US House of Representatives, Washington, July 13.

Bergsten, C. Fred. 1995. *APEC: The Bogor Declaration and the Path Ahead*. Working Paper 95-1. Washington: Institute for International Economics.

Bergsten, C. Fred. 1996a. *Competitive Liberalization and Global Free Trade: A Vision for the 21st Century*. Working Paper 96-12. Washington: Institute for International Economics.

Bergsten, C. Fred. 1996b. Globalizing Free Trade. *Foreign Affairs* (May/June).

Bergsten, C. Fred, ed. 1997. *Whither APEC? The Progress to Date and Agenda for the Future*. Special Report 9. Washington: Institute for International Economics.

Bergsten, C. Fred. 1999. America and Europe: Clash of the Titans? *Foreign Affairs* (March/April).

Bergsten, C. Fred. 2000. The Backlash Against Globalization. Speech given before the Trilateral Commission, Tokyo, Japan, May 9. Available at www.iie.com (accessed July 21, 2006).

Bergsten, C. Fred. 2002. A Renaissance for U.S. Trade Policy? *Foreign Affairs* (November/December).

Bergsten, C. Fred. 2004. The Resurgent Japanese Economy and a Japan-United States Free Trade Agreement. Paper presented to the Foreign Correspondents' Club of Japan, Tokyo, Japan, May 12. Available at www.iie.com (accessed July 21, 2006).

Bergsten, C. Fred. 2005. Rescuing the Doha Round. *Foreign Affairs*, special edition (December): 15–24.

Bergsten, C. Fred. 2006. The US Trade Deficit and China. Testimony before the hearing on US-China Economic Relations Revisited, Committee on Finance, US Senate, March 29. Available at www.iie.com (accessed July 21, 2006).

Bergsten, C. Fred, and Inbom Choi, eds. 2003. *The Korean Diaspora in the World Economy*. Special Report 15. Washington: Institute for International Economics.

Bergsten, C. Fred, and William R. Cline. 1982. *Trade Policy in the 1980s*. POLICY ANALYSES IN INTERNATIONAL ECONOMICS 3. Washington: Institute for International Economics.

Bergsten, C. Fred, and William R. Cline. 1985. *The United States–Japan Economic Problem*. POLICY ANALYSES IN INTERNATIONAL ECONOMICS 13. Washington: Institute for International Economics.

Bergsten, C. Fred, Kimberly Ann Elliott, Jeffrey J. Schott, and Wendy E. Takacs. 1987. *Auction Quotas and United States Trade Policy*. POLICY ANALYSES IN INTERNATIONAL ECONOMICS 19. Washington: Institute for International Economics.

Bergsten, C. Fred, Bates Gill, Nicholas R. Lardy, and Derek Mitchell. 2006. *China: The Balance Sheet—What the World Needs to Know Now About the Emerging Superpower*. New York: Public Affairs.

Bergsten, C. Fred, and the Institute for International Economics. 2005. *The United States and the World Economy: Foreign Economic Policy for the Next Decade*. Washington: Institute for International Economics.

Bergsten, C. Fred, Takatoshi Ito, and Marcus Noland. 2001. *No More Bashing: Building a New Japan–United States Economic Relationship*. Washington: Institute for International Economics.

Bergsten, C. Fred, and Marcus Noland. 1993. *Reconcilable Differences? United States–Japan Economic Conflict*. Washington: Institute for International Economics.

Bergsten, C. Fred, and Il SaKong. 1995. *The Political Economy of Korea–United States Cooperation*. Washington: Institute for International Economics.

Bergsten, C. Fred, and Il SaKong, eds. 1996. *Korea–United States Cooperation in the New World Order*. Washington: Institute for International Economics.

Bergsten, C. Fred, and Il SaKong, eds. 1997. *Korea–United States Economic Relationship*. Washington: Institute for International Economics.

Bergsten, C. Fred, and John Williamson, eds. 2003. *Dollar Overvaluation and the World Economy*. Special Report 16. Washington: Institute for International Economics.

Bergsten, C. Fred, and John Williamson, eds. 2004. *Dollar Adjustment: How Far? Against What?* Special Report 17. Washington: Institute for International Economics.

Bhagwati, Jagdish. 1988. *Protectionism*. Cambridge: MIT Press.

Bradford, Scott C., Paul L. E. Grieco, and Gary Clyde Hufbauer. 2005. The Payoff to America from Global Integration. In *The United States and the World Economy*, C. Fred Bergsten and the Institute for International Economics. Washington: Institute for International Economics.

Cho, Soon. 1994. *The Dynamics of Korean Economic Development*. Washington: Institute for International Economics.

Choi, Inbom, and Jeffrey J. Schott. 2001. *Free Trade between Korea and the United States?* POLICY ANALYSES IN INTERNATIONAL ECONOMICS 62. Washington: Institute for International Economics.

Cline, William R. 1987. *The Future of the World Trade in Textiles and Apparel*. Washington: Institute for International Economics.

Cline, William R. 2005. *The Case for a New Plaza Agreement*. Policy Brief 05-4. Washington: Institute for International Economics.

Cohen, Benjamin J. 1984. The World Economy: An Interview with C. Fred Bergsten. *The Fletcher Forum* (Summer). The Fletcher School of Law and Diplomacy, Tufts University.

Destler, I. M. 1986. *American Trade Politics: System Under Stress*. Washington: Institute for International Economics and Twentieth Century Fund.

Destler, I. M. 1997. *Renewing Fast-Track Legislation*. POLICY ANALYSES IN INTERNATIONAL ECONOMICS 50. Washington: Institute for International Economics.

Destler, I. M. 2005. *American Trade Politics*, 4th ed. Washington: Institute for International Economics.

Destler. I. M., and Peter J. Balint. 1999. *The New Politics of Trade, Labor, and the Environment.* POLICY ANALYSES IN INTERNATIONAL ECONOMICS 58. Washington: Institute for International Economics.

Destler, I. M., and C. Randall Henning. 1989. *Dollar Politics: Exchange Rate Policymaking in the United States.* Washington: Institute for International Economics.

Destler, I. M., and John S. Odell. 1987. *Anti-Protection: Changing Forces in United States Trade Politics.* POLICY ANALYSES IN INTERNATIONAL ECONOMICS 21. Washington: Institute for International Economics.

Dua, André, and Daniel C. Esty. 1997. *Sustaining the Asia Pacific Miracle: Environmental Protection and Economic Integration.* Washington: Institute for International Economics.

Elliott, Kimberly Ann. 2006. *Delivering on Doha: Farm Trade and the Poor.* Washington: Institute for International Economics and Center for Global Development.

Elliott, Kimberly Ann, and Richard B. Freeman. 2003. *Can Labor Standards Improve Under Globalization?* Washington: Institute for International Economics.

Esty, Daniel C. 1994. *Greening the GATT: Trade, Environment, and the Future.* Washington: Institute for International Economics.

Evenett, Simon J., and Michael Meier. 2006. An Interim Assessment of the U.S. Trade Policy of "Competitive Liberalization." Available at www.evenett.com (accessed September 26, 2006).

Feinberg, Richard E. 1997. *Summitry in the Americas: A Progress Report.* Washington: Institute for International Economics.

Frankel, Jeffrey A. 1997. *Regional Trading Blocs in the World Economic System.* Washington: Institute for International Economics.

Funabashi, Yoichi. 1988. *Managing the Dollar: From the Plaza to the Louvre.* Washington: Institute for International Economics.

Funabashi, Yoichi. 1995. *Asia Pacific Fusion: Japan's Role in APEC.* Washington: Institute for International Economics.

Galal, Ahmed, and Robert Z. Lawrence. 2005. *Anchoring Reform with a US-Egypt Free Trade Agreement.* POLICY ANALYSES IN INTERNATIONAL ECONOMICS 74. Washington: Institute for International Economics.

Graham, Edward M. 2003. *Reforming Korea's Industrial Conglomerates.* Washington: Institute for International Economics.

Hathaway, Dale E. 1987. *Agriculture and the GATT: Rewriting the Rules.* POLICY ANALYSES IN INTERNATIONAL ECONOMICS 20. Washington: Institute for International Economics.

Hull, Cordell. 1948. *The Memoirs of Cordell Hull.* New York: Macmillan.

Hufbauer, Gary Clyde, and Richard E. Baldwin. 2006. *The Shape of a Swiss-US Free Trade Agreement.* POLICY ANALYSES IN INTERNATIONAL ECONOMICS 76. Washington: Institute for International Economics.

Hufbauer, Gary Clyde, Diane E. Berliner, and Kimberly Ann Elliott. 1986. *Trade Protection in the United States: 31 Case Studies.* Washington: Institute for International Economics.

Hufbauer, Gary Clyde, and Kimberly Ann Elliott. 1994. *Measuring the Costs of Protection in the United States.* Washington: Institute for International Economics.

Hufbauer, Gary Clyde, Daniel Esty, Diana Orejas, Luis Rubio, and Jeffrey J. Schott. 2000. *NAFTA and the Environment: Seven Years Later.* POLICY ANALYSES IN INTERNATIONAL ECONOMICS 61. Washington: Institute for International Economics.

Hufbauer, Gary Clyde, and Howard R. Rosen. 1986. *Trade Policy for Troubled Industries.* POLICY ANALYSES IN INTERNATIONAL ECONOMICS 15. Washington: Institute for International Economics.

Hufbauer, Gary Clyde, and Jeffrey J. Schott. 1985. *Trading for Growth: The Next Round of Trade Negotiations.* POLICY ANALYSES IN INTERNATIONAL ECONOMICS 11. Washington: Institute for International Economics.

Hufbauer, Gary Clyde, and Jeffrey J. Schott. 1992. *North American Free Trade: Issues and Recommendations.* Washington: Institute for International Economics.

Hufbauer, Gary Clyde, and Jeffrey J. Schott. 1993. *NAFTA: An Assessment*. Washington: Institute for International Economics.

Hufbauer, Gary Clyde, and Jeffrey J. Schott. 2006. *The Doha Round after Hong Kong*. Policy Brief 06-2. Washington: Institute for International Economics.

Hufbauer, Gary Clyde, and Jeffrey J. Schott, assisted by Paul L. E. Grieco and Yee Wong. 2005. *NAFTA Revisited: Achievements and Challenges*. Washington: Institute for International Economics.

Kim, Namdoo. 1996. *Measuring the Costs of Visible Protection in Korea*. Washington: Institute for International Economics.

Kletzer, Lori G. 2001. *Job Loss from Imports: Measuring the Costs*. Washington: Institute for International Economics.

Kletzer, Lori G., and Howard Rosen. 2005. Easing the Adjustment Burden on US Workers. In *The United States and the World Economy*, C. Fred Bergsten and the Institute for International Economics. Washington: Institute for International Economics.

Lardy, Nicholas R. 2005. China: The Great New Economic Challenge? In *The United States and the World Economy*, C. Fred Bergsten and the Institute for International Economics. Washington: Institute for International Economics.

Lardy, Nicholas R., and Morris Goldstein. 2004. *What Kind of Landing for the Chinese Economy?* Policy Brief 04-7. Washington: Institute for International Economics.

Lardy, Nicholas R., and Daniel H. Rosen. 2004. *Prospects for a US-Taiwan Free Trade Agreement*. POLICY ANALYSES IN INTERNATIONAL ECONOMICS 73. Washington: Institute for International Economics.

Mann, Catherine L. 2005. Offshore Outsourcing and the Globalization of US Services: Why Now, How Important, and What Policy Implications? In *The United States and the World Economy*, C. Fred Bergsten and the Institute for International Economics. Washington: Institute for International Economics.

Mann, Catherine L., with Jacob Funk Kirkegaard. 2006. *Accelerating the Globalization of America: The Role for Information Technology*. Washington: Institute for International Economics.

Mann, Catherine L., and Daniel Rosen. 2002. *The New Economy and APEC*. Washington: Institute for International Economics.

Marris, Stephen. 1985. *Deficits and the Dollar: The World Economy at Risk*. POLICY ANALYSES IN INTERNATIONAL ECONOMICS 14. Washington: Institute for International Economics.

Martin, Philip L. 1993. *Trade and Migration: NAFTA and Agriculture*. POLICY ANALYSES IN INTERNATIONAL ECONOMICS 38. Washington: Institute for International Economics.

Messerlin, Patrick A. 2001. *Measuring the Costs of Protection in Europe: European Commercial Policy in the 2000s*. Washington: Institute for International Economics.

Miner, William M., and Murray G. Smith, eds. 1988. *World Agricultural Trade: Building a Consensus*. Washington: Institute for International Economics.

Noland, Marcus. 1990. *Pacific Basin Developing Countries: Prospects for the Future*. Washington: Institute for International Economics.

Noland, Marcus, ed. 1998. *Economic Integration of the Korean Peninsula*. Special Report 10. Washington: Institute for International Economics.

Noland, Marcus. 2000. *Avoiding the Apocalypse: The Future of the Two Koreas*. Washington: Institute for International Economics.

Noland, Marcus. 2004. *Korea after Kim Jong-il*. POLICY ANALYSES IN INTERNATIONAL ECONOMICS 71. Washington: Institute for International Economics.

Noland, Marcus, and Howard Pack. 2003. *Industrial Policy in an Era of Globalization*. Washington: Institute for International Economics.

Pastor, Robert A. 2001. *Toward a North American Community: Lessons from the Old World for the New*. Washington: Institute for International Economics.

Richardson, J. David. 2005. Uneven Gains and Unbalanced Burdens? Three Decades of American Globalization. In *The United States and the World Economy*, C. Fred Bergsten and the Institute for International Economics. Washington: Institute for International Economics.

Richardson, J. David. Forthcoming. *Global Forces, American Faces: US Economic Globalization at the Grass Roots.* Washington: Institute for International Economics.

Rodrik, Dani. 1997. *Has Globalization Gone Too Far?* Washington: Institute for International Economics.

Rosen, Howard F. 1989. The US-Israel Free Trade Area Agreement: How Well Is It Working and What Have We Learned? In *Free Trade Areas and US Trade Policy,* ed. Jeffrey J. Schott. Washington: Institute for International Economics.

SaKong, Il. 1993. *Korea in the World Economy.* Washington: Institute for International Economics.

Sazanami, Yoko, Shujiro Urata, and Hiroki Kawai. 1995. *Measuring the Costs of Protection in Japan.* Washington: Institute for International Economics.

Scheve, Kenneth F., and Matthew J. Slaughter. 2001. *Globalization and the Perceptions of American Workers.* Washington: Institute for International Economics.

Schott, Jeffrey J. 1988. *United States–Canada Free Trade: An Evaluation of the Agreement.* POLICY ANALYSES IN INTERNATIONAL ECONOMICS 24. Washington: Institute for International Economics.

Schott, Jeffrey J., ed. 1989a. *Free Trade Areas and US Trade Policy.* Washington: Institute for International Economics.

Schott, Jeffrey J. 1989b. *More Free Trade Areas?* POLICY ANALYSES IN INTERNATIONAL ECONOMICS 27. Washington: Institute for International Economics.

Schott, Jeffrey J., ed. 1990. *Completing the Uruguay Round: A Results-Oriented Approach to the GATT Trade Negotiations.* Washington: Institute for International Economics.

Schott, Jeffrey J., ed. 1998. *Launching New Global Trade Talks: An Action Agenda.* Special Report 12. Washington: Institute for International Economics.

Schott, Jeffrey J., ed. 2000. *The WTO after Seattle.* Washington: Institute for International Economics.

Schott, Jeffrey J. 2001. *Prospects for Free Trade in the Americas.* Washington: Institute for International Economics.

Schott, Jeffrey J., ed. 2004. *Free Trade Agreements: US Strategies and Priorities.* Washington: Institute for International Economics.

Schott, Jeffrey J., and Murray G. Smith, eds. 1988. *The Canada–United States Free Trade Agreement: The Global Impact.* Washington: Institute for International Economics.

Scollay, Robert, and John P. Gilbert. 2001. *New Regional Trading Arrangements in the Asia Pacific?* POLICY ANALYSES IN INTERNATIONAL ECONOMICS 63. Washington: Institute for International Economics.

Trimbath, Susanne. 2005. Think Tanks: Who's Hot and Who's Not. *The International Economy* (Summer): 10–47.

Tyson, Laura D'Andrea. 1992. *Who's Bashing Whom? Trade Conflict in High-Technology Industries.* Washington: Institute for International Economics.

US Chamber of Commerce. 1973. *Economic Adjustment to Liberal Trade: A New Approach.* Prepared by the Task Force on Adjustment Assistance, C. Fred Bergsten, Chairman. Reprinted in Bergsten (1975a).

Wilson, John Sullivan. 1996. *Standards and APEC: An Action Agenda.* POLICY ANALYSES IN INTERNATIONAL ECONOMICS 42. Washington: Institute for International Economics.

Wonnacott, Paul. 1987. *The United States and Canada: The Quest for Free Trade.* Appendix by John Williamson. POLICY ANALYSES IN INTERNATIONAL ECONOMICS 16. Washington: Institute for International Economics.

Zhang, Yansheng, Wan Zhongxin, and Zhang Shuguang. 1998. *Measuring the Costs of Protection in China.* Washington: Institute for International Economics.

Zoellick, Robert. 2002. *Remarks by Ambassador Robert B. Zoellick in Phoenix, Arizona, April 30, 2002.* Washington: Office of the US Trade Representative.

3

Trade Policy at the Institute: 25 Years and Counting

GARY CLYDE HUFBAUER and JEFFREY J. SCHOTT

The Institute for International Economics opened its doors in 1981, a pivotal time for the world trading system. Only two years after the conclusion of the Tokyo Round of multilateral trade negotiations (1973–79),[1] world trade was buffeted by a second oil shock that precipitated the deepest global recession since the 1930s. Growing protectionist pressures threatened to stall or reverse the freshly minted commitments to trade liberalization. Debt crises in developing countries and currency misalignments further complicated the political economy of trade. Calls for fresh trade negotiations to address these manifold challenges fell victim to increasingly fractious transatlantic trade disputes over steel and agriculture, the proliferation of orderly marketing agreements and voluntary export restraints, and US extraterritorial sanctions seeking to block construction of Soviet gas pipelines. The "twilight of the GATT"—the General Agreement on Tariffs and Trade—seemed a real possibility.

The travails of world trade, linked integrally to problems with international debt, finance, and exchange rates, became prime targets of Institute analysis and the focus of one of its first major conferences, in June 1982, leading to the publication of *Trade Policy in the 1980s*, edited by William

Gary Clyde Hufbauer has been the Reginald Jones Senior Fellow at the Institute since 1992. Jeffrey J. Schott, senior fellow, has been associated with the Institute since 1983.

1. The Tokyo Round, like its six predecessors and its immediate successor (the Uruguay Round), was conducted under the auspices of the General Agreement on Tariffs and Trade (GATT).

Cline (1983). Globalization was then a fresh term, if not a new phenomenon. Trade negotiations were no longer narrowly focused on border restrictions. Policy analysis required an understanding of the interactions between domestic and international economic policies and of how these interactions obstructed or encouraged international flows of trade and investment. Such multifaceted issues were made to order for the experienced team that founded the Institute.

Trade Mavens on Board. The Institute's initial complement of fellows, advisers, and board members brought an array of trade experience from executive departments and congressional halls. Prior to launching the Institute, the director, C. Fred Bergsten, and the chairman of the advisory board, Richard Cooper, had both engineered key accords in the Tokyo Round from their perches at Treasury and State. The chairman of the board of directors, Peter G. Peterson, served as secretary of commerce during the Nixon administration, and his fellow board member Anthony Solomon dealt with trade issues and other economic matters as a senior official in both the Johnson and Carter administrations. At the Institute's founding, Bergsten lured three Treasury colleagues with trade backgrounds: William Cline, Gary Hufbauer, and Jeffrey Schott. I. M. Destler came to the Institute with trade experience from Capitol Hill. Among the other research staff from that era, Kimberly Elliott, Joanna Shelton Erb, and Howard Rosen brought a wealth of trade expertise. As the Institute grew and thrived, other talented scholars with an interest in trade and investment policy joined the staff permanently or as visitors: Edward M. Graham, Jeffrey Frankel, Robert Z. Lawrence, Catherine Mann, Marcus Noland, J. David Richardson, and Matthew Slaughter.

Armed with this array of talent, the Institute was well positioned to grapple with the big trade debates that emerged in the 1980s, 1990s, and 2000s. In this chapter, we highlight three megathemes: rampant globalization, multitrack trade strategy, and the splintering US trade coalition.[2] Following a short preview in this introduction, we turn to the meat of the Institute's work in these areas.

Globalization Steals the Show. Economists are fond of pointing out that globalization finds ample precedent in the golden decades between 1871 and 1914. What is undeniably new, however, is public fascination and debate, which enables a handful of authors to make an excellent living (exemplified by Thomas Friedman), boosts a few neo-isolationist politicians (Ross Perot and Patrick Buchanan), and provides a theme for certain TV personalities (notably Lou Dobbs). It also presents a special challenge to

---

2. As a result, we skip lightly over several trade policy debates that engaged the Institute in its first quarter century. Our tread is light both because "trade policy" has expanded well beyond tariffs and because each issue has its own complex dimensions.

the Institute, since much of the public debate questions the value of traveling the globalization road.

One of the reasons the globalization debate is so strident—whether in the United States, Europe, or in developing countries—is that advocates and critics often focus on gross gains or losses. It is easier to cast blame (especially against foreigners) than to address the nuanced distributional consequences resulting from global competition. Harder still is to prescribe responsible domestic policy reforms that redistribute gains or losses via taxes or subsidies from one group to another.

Yet globalization inevitably creates winners and losers in each society. While many Institute volumes published in the 1980s and early 1990s addressed the costs of protection and the benefits of liberalization, the first Institute book featuring globalization in its title, *Has Globalization Gone Too Far?* by Dani Rodrik (1997), struck a skeptical note. So, too, did Laura Tyson (1992) in *Who's Bashing Whom? Trade Conflict in High-Technology Industries*, which was published shortly before she was named to lead President Clinton's Council of Economic Advisers. Later that decade, the Institute launched the Globalization Balance Sheet (GBS) project, directed by J. David Richardson. Since its inception, the GBS project has provided an umbrella for more than a dozen books and monographs, covering the pluses and minuses of trade, investment, labor, environment, and other dimensions. Institute studies have offered pioneering analyses of electronic commerce (Mann, Eckert, and Knight 2000), worker adjustment (Kletzer 2001), worker perceptions (Scheve and Slaughter 2001), labor standards (Elliott and Freeman 2003), the gains from globalization (Bradford and Lawrence 2004; Bradford, Grieco, and Hufbauer 2005), and other themes. As this chapter is written, Richardson is tying the whole GBS project together in his capstone volume, *Global Forces, American Faces*.

Multitrack Strategy: Flavor du Jour.   Soon after the Institute opened its doors, US Trade Representative William Brock radically shifted US trade strategy from its historic "single-track" approach, centered on multilateral GATT negotiations, to a "multitrack" approach, which eventually featured bilateral and regional agreements alongside GATT talks. The provocation was foot-dragging by the European Community, Japan, and others over the launch of a new GATT round; Brock turned to the multitrack strategy after the failed GATT ministerial meeting in November 1982. The United States tested the waters with a free trade agreement (FTA) with Israel in 1985; shortly after, the US-Canada FTA was signed in 1988, covering a hundred times more commerce.

President George H. W. Bush then started the United States down the regional track, not only opening NAFTA negotiations with Mexico in 1991 and signing the pact in 1992 but also proposing at the same time the Enterprise for the Americas Initiative to deepen US trade and investment ties with, and help address the debt problems of countries in Latin America and the Caribbean. President Bill Clinton proved equally enthusiastic, augmenting the NAFTA with side agreements on labor and environment before securing congressional ratification in 1993. The following year, Clinton pushed summit initiatives in the Western Hemisphere and the Asia-Pacific regions that called for the Free Trade Area of the Americas (FTAA) and free trade and investment across the Asia-Pacific, under the auspices of the Asia-Pacific Economic Cooperation forum (APEC). All the while, the Uruguay Round of GATT negotiations, launched at Punta del Este in 1986, was grinding to a finale at Marrakesh in April 1994. In retrospect, these multiple trade initiatives, playing off one another, created the golden age of "competitive liberalization," to use the phrase later coined by Bergsten (1996).

Each of these trade initiatives was both anticipated and then analyzed in Institute books, articles, and policy briefs. Wonnacott (1987) examined the US-Canada quest for free trade, and Schott and Smith (1988) assessed the subsequent US-Canada FTA; in Hufbauer and Schott (1992, 1993, 1994) we anticipated and then analyzed the North American Free Trade Agreement (NAFTA) as well as the prospective Western Hemisphere accord; and Schott (1990, 1994) evaluated the Uruguay Round both in prospect and in retrospect. Last but certainly not least, Bergsten developed the "vision" of free trade and investment in the Asia-Pacific region in the three annual reports issued during his tenure as chairman of APEC's Eminent Persons Group. Bergsten (1995) then prescribed options for implementation of the ambitious goals set out by APEC leaders in their 1994 Bogor Declaration.

After Marrakesh, US trade officials were constrained by the absence of "fast track" negotiating authority: It expired in June 1994 and was not renewed for the duration of the Clinton administration. Consequently, the United States only entered into compacts that required little change in existing US policies and practices. World Trade Organization (WTO) bargains were reached in two sectors, telecommunications (Petrazzini 1996, Hufbauer and Wada 1997) and financial services (Dobson and Jacquet 1998), but otherwise multilateral liberalization was stalled (Schott 1998b). The collapse of the WTO ministerial in Seattle in December 1999 confirmed both the overarching importance of US negotiating authority and the impasse among WTO members. The collapse also emboldened antiglobalization activists to demonize trade officials for killing turtles and forcing "Frankenstein" foods on unwitting consumers, among other offenses.

In the aftermath of Seattle, the WTO needed new direction, and the Institute offered an extensive blueprint for recasting the trade agenda to address the myriad challenges confronting the trading system in *The WTO after Seattle* (Schott 2000). The erstwhile "Seattle Round" evolved into the Doha Development Agenda, launched in November 2001 in the wake of the terrorist attacks two months earlier. But these talks too followed a familiar pattern: The 2003 ministerial in Cancún failed and negotiators consistently missed deadlines (Jeffrey J. Schott, "Unlocking the Benefits of World Trade," *The Economist*, US edition, November 1, 2003; Hufbauer and Schott 2006). During this period, FTAA and APEC talks also faltered (Schott 2001, Bergsten 2001), and US trade policy came to rely on a single rail, bilateral FTAs. These developments reflected our third megatheme, the splintering coalition for free trade.

Splintering Coalition: Trade Beware! When President Eisenhower wrested control of the Republican Party from Senator Taft and aligned the Republican Party with the trade philosophy of Franklin Roosevelt, he created a bipartisan coalition for freer trade that endured until the early 1990s. Destler (1986) documented these trends in his classic study, *American Trade Politics*, now in its fourth edition. The coalition eventually splintered both because organized labor pictured international commerce as an engine for destroying US jobs and suppressing blue-collar wages and because critics at both extremes of the political spectrum came to view trade agreements as feathering the nest of multinational corporations but not improving the lives of ordinary people. Consequently, Howard Rosen's (2002) analysis of nine major trade bills between 1974 and 2002 found a particularly sharp drop in the likelihood of "yes" votes among House Democrats—falling from a probability of 89 percent in the 1970s to only 52 percent in the 1990s (though 2002). Given this trend, it is not surprising that US trade promotion authority (TPA)—formerly known as "fast track"—initially cleared the House by one vote in 2002 (and finally passed with only a three-vote margin) and that Central American Free Trade Agreement–Dominican Republic (CAFTA-DR) passed the House by a bare two-vote margin in 2005.

The causes and consequences of the splintering coalition inspired numerous Institute studies over the past six years: Graham (2000) on the virtues and vices of multinational corporations, Scheve and Slaughter (2001) on the perceptions of American workers, Kletzer (2001) on worker adjustment, Baldwin (2003) on the role of US trade unions, and Elliott and Freeman (2003) on global labor standards. In addition, the fourth edition of Destler's classic study, *American Trade Politics* (2005), added new sections on these contentious topics.

Rampant Globalization

Global forces swept across all dimensions of the world economy between 1980 and 2005, as depicted in table 3.1. Initially, these forces were broadly welcomed, not repelled. But the fractious US debate over the ratification of the NAFTA—which put a spotlight on the challenges involved in economic integration with developing countries—shifted public opinion dramatically. Strident opponents of a trade pact with Mexico warned of a

Table 3.1   Economic globalization: Sharp acceleration since the mid-1980s

Indicator	Before	After
Ratio of growth in merchandise trade to growth in global GDP	1.2 (1974–84)	3.3 (1990–2004)
FDI stock as a percentage of global GDP	5.9 (1980–85)	13.8 (1990–2004)
Royalty and licensing fees paid to US companies from foreign sources	$7 billion (1985)	$53 billion (2004)
International telephone traffic minutes	38 billion (1990)	145 billion (2004)
Foreign exchange transactions (daily)	$60 billion (1983)	$1.9 trillion (2004)
Worldwide number of Internet users	26 million (1995)[a]	1 billion (2005)

FDI = foreign direct investment

a. The World Wide Web did not exist prior to 1991.

Sources: Preeg (2003); UNCTAD *World Investment Report 2005*; Bank for International Settlements (2005), www.bis.org; Internet World Stats, Usage and Population Statistics, www.internetworld stats.com; International Telecommunication Union, www.itu.int.

"sucking sound" of jobs and investment seeking low wages and a pollution haven. By the time China joined the WTO at the end of 2001, amid slowing growth worldwide, the critics of trade and globalization were firmly joined at the hip.

While commercial negotiations focused on merchandise trade through the late 1980s, the General Agreement on Trade in Services (GATS) became a centerpiece of the Uruguay Round. Meanwhile, awareness grew among trade policy officials that service and merchandise trade flows are both closely linked to foreign direct investment (FDI). In fact, "Mode 2" of the GATS dealt explicitly with market access via foreign commercial presence, while other WTO agreements addressed the connection between FDI and merchandise trade. Throughout the 1990s, international finance exploded and electronic commerce blossomed.

Along with Hollywood, 24-hour news, and migration, these trends became the economic face of globalization—an uplifting and inevitable force to Thomas Friedman and a nationalist rallying cry to Lou Dobbs. If the Institute had been launched in 2001 rather than 1981, it might have been named the Institute for Global Economics.[3] Yet, while "global" was not in the name, it was very much in the substance of the Institute's work.

---

3. In fact, in the early 1990s, former Korean Finance Minister and Institute Visiting Fellow Il SaKong gave this name to his own institute in Seoul, patterned after the Institute.

The Costs of Protection

In the 1980s, most journalists who wrote about trade were oblivious to the fact that barriers take money from domestic consumers. They penned wrenching accounts of farm and factory workers who lost their jobs to cheap imports, but the fourth estate had a hard time putting poetry to higher prices at the checkout counter. To provide a better balance, the Institute launched its "Cost of Protection" series, starting with *Trade Protection in the United States* (Hufbauer, Berliner, and Elliott 1986) and later updated and extended in separate monographs to Japan, Korea, China, and the European Union. The headline number, consistent across all studies, was the staggering cost per job saved in protected industries—figures upwards of $100,000 per job per year characterized the United States and Europe. Almost as noteworthy was the finding that protected firms, not workers, garner the lion's share of benefits. Indeed, Cline (1990, 251) calculated that US protection of textiles and clothing imposed a heavy burden on low-income US families, reducing the income of the poorest 20 percent of US households by almost 4 percent. These facts undergird the economic case for trade adjustment rather than trade protection to answer the disruption caused by globalization.

The cost-per-job-saved calculations have been most effectively used by a handful of firms that, in particular episodes, mounted coalitions against protection. Early examples were documented by Destler, Odell, and Elliott (1987), along with internal crosscurrents that hobble associations such as the Business Roundtable. More recently, distributors of luxury autos (such as Lexus cars), industrial users of steel (such as Caterpillar), and some clothing chains (such as Gap) have effectively reversed or limited the extent of ad hoc quotas. But on the whole, antiprotection coalitions are a story of the dog that didn't bark: Major sugar consumers (such as Coca-Cola), major clothing distributors (such as Wal-Mart), and major home builders (such as Toll Brothers) have not successfully or even conspicuously reversed high barriers that raised the prices of their wares.[4]

Benefits of Foreign Investment

In the late 1960s and early 1970s, fierce debate waged in the US Congress over "runaway plants" erected by multinational corporations. However, after the Burke-Hartke bill died in the House Ways and Means Committee in 1973, the issue was crowded off the US agenda by the first oil shock

---

4. Toll Brothers and other home builders paid the penalty of antidumping and countervailing duties on softwood lumber imports from Canada for more than 25 years, until a ceasefire was negotiated in 2006. These duties amounted to hundreds of millions of US dollars annually.

and rising inflation. For most of the 1960s and 1970s, the greatest criticism of multinational corporations emanated from developing countries, generally with a Marxist flavor. This was soon to change, as the forces of globalization turned the United States into the largest host country for FDI in the 1980s. Arguments were voiced in this country that foreign multinationals would depress American wages, skimp on research, and on the whole act as poor corporate citizens. Graham and Krugman (1989) turned such arguments on their head in *Foreign Direct Investment in the United States*, a book that saw its third edition in 1995.

After that, Graham and his colleagues tilted at FDI windmills at five-year intervals. Graham (2000) severely criticized antiglobalization activists for derailing the Multilateral Agreement on Investment. Graham and Marchick (2006) examined the national security threat of inward FDI in the wake of the US rejection of China National Offshore Oil Corporation's bid for Unocal and the Dubai Ports World bid for Peninsular and Oriental Steam Navigation Company's terminal leases. Meanwhile, Moran, Graham, and Blomström (2005) edited a comprehensive volume bringing together fresh work on the linkages between FDI and development.

Payoff from Globalization

These days, the old argument that protection takes money from Peter to pay Paul, with waste along the way, no longer enlists much support for globalization. Taxing Peter to pay Paul is an old game in Washington and every other capital city. The case for globalization must therefore be stated in positive terms to gain policy traction. In stating the positive case, the Institute has made four noteworthy contributions.

Jeffrey Frankel's (1997) pioneering study of regional trade agreements revived the gravity model as a working tool of trade analysis. While Frankel's analysis, based on data from the 1980s and earlier, estimated weak coefficients for the trade augmentation effect of FTAs, subsequent work by Rose (2004) and DeRosa and Gilbert (2005) arrived at much larger and more robust coefficients. Trade liberalization apparently sparks two-way commerce to a far greater extent than standard elasticity coefficients might suggest.

Drawing on econometric estimates of the relation between trade intensity and GDP growth, Cline (2004) estimated that total free trade, practiced by developed and developing countries alike, could lift an astonishing 500 million people out of poverty by 2015. If trade ministers revive and conclude a robust Doha Development Round, they could do far more for the world's poor than bilateral aid and multilateral development bank programs combined. Using a different methodology, Bradford and Lawrence (2004) calculated that integration of the markets for goods alone among just eight advanced countries (Australia, Canada, Germany, Italy, Japan,

Netherlands, United Kingdom, and the United States) would raise the GDP of all Organization for Economic Cooperation and Development (OECD) nations by $450 billion annually (1997 dollars), with a spillover to developing countries of another $100 billion.

Bradford, Grieco, and Hufbauer (2005) assembled a range of methodologies, including the approaches just mentioned, to calculate US gains from more intense trade with the rest of the world—an important dimension, though not the only dimension, of globalization. Greater trade intensity since the Second World War—merchandise imports plus exports rose from 9 percent of US GDP in 1950 to 24 percent in 2003—reflects the combined forces of dramatic policy liberalization and rapidly falling transportation and communication costs. The centered calculation of resulting US GDP gains, drawing on five different methodologies, is about $1 trillion annually, about $10,000 per household each year. Future US gains, if the United States and the rest of the world complete the march to zero tariffs and quotas (not counting any future fall in transportation or communication costs), could be another $500 billion annually, about $5,000 per household.

Globalization Balance Sheet

As mentioned, in 1998 the Institute launched the multiyear, multiproduct GBS project under the direction of J. David Richardson. To date, the project has authored or inspired some 13 books and numerous articles by resident and nonresident fellows, and Richardson himself is working on a capstone volume, *Global Forces, American Faces*, which integrates the studies into current research along the same lines. Here is a sampler of headlines from the GBS project:

- American manufacturing plants that export continuously grow 0.5 to 1.5 percent faster per year than otherwise comparable plants that are locally focused. Globally engaged American firms in general, including services firms, grow up to 2 percent faster per year and enjoy 1 to 2 percent higher annual survival rates than otherwise comparable local firms.

- In American manufacturing as a whole, worker wages are about 10 percent higher at plants that export. Moreover, wages average up to 7 percent higher at plants with an equity stake from a foreign multinational corporation (MNC) and up to 15 percent higher at plants owned by an American MNC, compared with worker wages at comparable manufacturing plants that are not globally engaged.

- American workers at plants linked to either foreign or US-owned MNCs maintained these higher wages *even though* their MNC employers "offshored" 1.5 to 2 times as many intermediate input purchases as comparable non-MNC plants.[5] More precisely, MNC plants imported—i.e., outsourced from offshore sources—11 to 16 percent of their supplies and components, whereas comparable non-MNC plants imported only 6 to 8 percent.

- In American service firms, wages are 6 percent higher in tradable (export- and import-oriented) subsectors than in comparable sectors that are locally insulated. Premiums in high-technology services are even larger: American wages are 15 percent higher in high-tech tradable professional and business service firms than wages for otherwise comparable workers.

- In sum, globally valued and high-technology occupational skills create additive worker benefits. Workers' investment in the skills required to find employment in high-technology, tradable occupations pays premiums *above and beyond* garden-variety investments in education and experience.

- But globalization creates losers as well as winners (Kletzer 2004). In 2000–2001, a recession period, workers in broad import-sensitive sectors (roughly 30 percent of manufacturing jobs) experienced dislocation rates that were more than double those facing other manufacturing workers (6.1 percent compared with 2.8 percent). American workers in tradable services likewise faced dislocation rates that were twice as high as workers in nontradable services (10.6 percent versus 5.4 percent).

- In their new jobs, workers dislocated from import-sensitive manufacturing sectors in 2000–2001 suffered mean losses in earnings that were twice as high compared with the late 1990s. Almost one-third of recently dislocated workers suffered earnings losses above 25 percent.

- The American backlash to globalization is widespread, not just the vocal objection of a small fringe (Scheve and Slaughter 2001). Many Americans oppose further immigration, trade integration, and liberalization of investment barriers. The backlash grew in the 1980s and 1990s in close correlation with the flattening out of labor market prospects for American workers with median skills. Scheve and Slaughter estimate that every extra year's education in their cross section of voters makes an American 5 to 6 percent less likely to support higher import barriers and 2 to 3 percent less likely to oppose immigration. Americans recognize the benefits from globalization, but give much

---

5. Offshore outsourcing is the substitution of imported inputs for inputs formerly produced by a firm's own workers. This is part of the general trend toward outsourcing, which substitutes inputs from arm's-length suppliers for inputs formerly produced internally by a vertically integrated firm.

more weight to the perceived cost of volatile jobs and sluggish wage growth.

- In brief, the patterns revealed by the GBS project suggest an expanding array of *both* benefits and burdens from America's global trends, but also an expanding *scope* for both benefits and burdens across the American workforce and American firms.

- While the political split between proglobalization and antiglobalization sentiment is roughly 50-50 in the United States, the economic balance between national gains and dislocation losses is hugely lopsided. Estimates by Bradford, Grieco, and Hufbauer (2005) indicate that annual US gains from globalization since the Second World War are about $1 trillion, whereas annual dislocation losses are around $50 billion—a ratio of 20 to 1.

Multilateral Trade Negotiations

Until the failed GATT ministerial of November 1982, postwar US trade policy had focused exclusively on multilateral trade negotiations in the GATT. The rejection by other countries of US initiatives to prepare for a new round of GATT talks—due to both protectionist concerns and the lack of readiness to add trade in services to the negotiating agenda—led then US Trade Representative Bill Brock to pursue bilateral free trade agreements (FTAs) with Israel and Canada. These talks were regarded as complements to, not substitutes for, the GATT process; US officials maintained their efforts to launch what became the Uruguay Round in 1986. Over the two decades since, the United States has followed a multitrack trade strategy—involving a mix of bilateral, regional, and multilateral negotiations—to address the unfinished and new international trade agenda and to propel economic growth. Institute studies have tracked these efforts and sometimes presaged new initiatives. In particular, Institute authors have undertaken

- strategic planning for multilateral trade negotiations (MTNs), starting with a blueprint for the prospective Uruguay Round (Hufbauer and Schott 1985) and then for the first trading round in the WTO (Schott 1996, 1998b, 2000).

- assessment of MTN results, starting with Hufbauer and Erb (1984) on subsidies in the Tokyo Round, then Schott's 1994 *Uruguay Round: An Assessment*, and Dobson and Jacquet (1998) on financial services. More recently, in Bergsten (2005) and Hufbauer and Schott (2006), the Institute has contributed journal articles and policy briefs on progress and problems in the Doha Round.

- analysis of traditional sectors resistant to reform in the postwar era, notably studies on agriculture by Hathaway (1987) and Elliott (2006) and on textiles and clothing by Cline (1990, rev. ed.).

- analysis of "new" issues on the GATT/WTO agenda, including Graham and Richardson (1997) on competition policy, Graham and Krugman (1989) and Graham (2000) on investment, Maskus (2000) on intellectual property rights, Esty (1994) on *Greening the GATT* (1994), and Elliott and Freeman (2003) on labor standards.

Bilateral and Regional Trade Negotiations

Throughout the GATT/WTO era, the United States has given priority to Geneva negotiations. At the same time, however, FTAs have been pursued with increasing vigor, particularly in periods when Geneva talks have drifted, to maintain momentum for trade liberalization, to forge alliances in favor of new liberalization both bilaterally and multilaterally, and to catalyze other major trading nations to work more diligently in the GATT/WTO. The United States has concluded bilateral FTAs with a variety of its trading partners and launched complementary regional initiatives in the Western Hemisphere, Southeast Asia, and the Middle East North Africa region. Apart from NAFTA, however, US trade negotiations with its main trading partners—the European Union, China, and Japan—have been conducted primarily through multilateral channels.

Institute work has focused on the United States, given the influence of US initiatives on the multilateral trading system and the fact that Europe already had its network of preferential trading arrangements. Institute conference volumes documented the evolution of US policy, first in the late 1980s when the collapse of the "mid-term review" of the Uruguay Round (1988) sparked interest in an FTA between the United States and Canada. *Free Trade Areas and US Trade Policy*, edited by Schott (1989), examined the objectives and prospects for bilateral US pacts with countries in Latin America and East Asia.

Institute studies have assessed both the role of FTAs in US trade policy and the benefits and costs of pursuing specific accords. In some cases, Institute analyses provided a blueprint for prospective negotiations; in others, Institute findings were cited in subsequent ratification debates in the partner countries. Because Institute studies exposed either potential problems that would have to be addressed or warts and blemishes in the negotiated outcomes, they provided an objective antidote to the "pep rally" press releases of the partner governments. Indeed, in one instance, governments decided not to pursue FTA talks after reading the detailed Institute assessment of the negotiating requirements (Hufbauer and Baldwin 2006). In another, Taiwan rejected the bottom line Institute conclusion not to proceed with a bilateral FTA and has continued to push, so far unsuccessfully, for a FTA with the United States (Lardy and Rosen 2004). Since the initial FTA with Israel in 1985, the United States has actively engaged in bilateral negotiations with countries across the globe. Current and prospective US FTA partners number around 30 and account for almost 44 percent of total US trade and more than half of US merchandise exports (see table 3.2).[6] Institute studies have examined both the broad policy implications of regional and bilateral agreements and the application of an FTA policy to prospective US partners (Schott 1989 and 2004).

Because of its path-breaking role in linking two developed and one developing country in a comprehensive FTA and its impact on subsequent US trade pacts, Institute studies have focused special attention on NAFTA (Hufbauer and Schott 1992, 1993, 2005). Our initial studies examined the issues and problems in pursuing deeper North American economic integration and then assessed the negotiated outcome. More recently, in Hufbauer and Schott (2005), we assessed the decadal experience of NAFTA and examined the key challenges to North American economic integration that still confront the three trading partners.

NAFTA set the precedent for a series of initiatives that followed in Latin America and East Asia, as US trading partners queued up for NAFTA-like negotiations. The Institute's NAFTA trilogy established a baseline for analyzing new ventures with other countries. Institute studies have assessed the costs and benefits of entering FTA negotiations with individual countries, starting with Korea (Choi and Schott 2001) and followed by Taiwan, Egypt, Switzerland, Pakistan, Colombia, and Indonesia. An overall study of a US–Middle East FTA will soon be published. In addition, Bergsten has written numerous articles on prospects for a US-Japan accord and a monograph on a prospective free trade deal with New Zealand.

Has all this activity undercut US support for ongoing WTO negotiations? The experience to date argues that it has not—though the answer with regard to the Doha Round is not completely written. Bilateral and regional talks have often advanced during lulls or breakdowns in multilateral negotiations. For example, the NAFTA talks were launched at a time when US-European differences on agriculture had put the Uruguay Round in a deep freeze; then in late 1993, APEC initiatives helped propel the final compromises needed to conclude the round. The FTAA negotiations began in the 1990s as the WTO struggled in its first years to develop consensus for new efforts to advance multilateral trade liberalization.

---

6. These data do not include countries or regions participating in the FTAA talks but not in separate free trade talks with the United States (the main exclusions are Mercosur, Venezuela, and Caricom).

Table 3.2   Bilateral FTA partners of the United States as of June 2006
(billions of dollars)

| Country/region | 2005 GDP | US merchandise trade, 2005 | | | | FTA status[c] |
		US exports to[a]	US imports from[b]	Trade balance	Total trade	
Canada	1,130.2	183.2	287.5	−104.3	470.8	A
Mexico	768.4	101.7	169.2	−67.5	270.9	A
Korea	793.1	26.2	43.2	−16.9	69.4	C
Malaysia	130.8	9.5	33.7	−24.2	43.2	C
Singapore	117.9	18.7	15.1	3.6	33.8	A
Thailand	168.8	6.6	19.8	−13.2	26.4	C
CAFTA-5	77.3	11.5	13.4	−1.9	24.9	A/B
Israel	123.5	6.5	16.9	−10.4	23.4	A
Australia	708.0	14.6	7.4	7.3	22.0	A
Indonesia	276.0	3.0	11.9	−8.9	14.9	D
Colombia	122.3	5.0	8.8	−3.8	13.7	C
Chile	114.0	4.7	6.7	−2.1	11.4	A
SACU-5[d]	258.3	3.8	6.8	−2.9	10.6	C
United Arab Emirates	133.8	7.9	1.4	6.5	9.3	C
Dominican Republic	29.2	4.4	4.6	−0.3	9.0	B
Ecuador	33.1	1.7	5.9	−4.1	7.6	C
Peru	78.6	2.0	5.1	−3.1	7.2	B
Egypt	93.0	3.1	2.1	1.1	5.2	D
Panama	15.2	2.0	0.3	1.7	2.3	C
Jordan	12.9	0.6	1.3	−0.7	1.9	A
Oman	30.3	0.6	0.5	0.1	1.0	B
Morocco	52.0	0.5	0.5	0.0	1.0	A
Bahrain	12.9	0.3	0.4	−0.1	0.7	B
Subtotal (FTA partners)	5,279.5	418.1	662.3	−244.2	1,080.4	
United States (world trade totals)	12,485.7	804.0	1,662.4	−858.4	2,466.4	

CAFTA-5 = Central American Free Trade Agreement (Costa Rica, El Salvador, Guatemala, Honduras, and Nicaragua)

SACU-5 = Southern African Customs Union (Botswana, Lesotho, Namibia, South Africa, and Swaziland)

a. US domestic exports.
b. US imports for consumption.
c. A = in effect; B = signed; C = under negotiation; D = under consideration
d. Suspended in April 2006.

Sources: GDP: IMF's *World Economic Outlook* database, September 2005; trade data: USITC Dataweb.

Importantly, however, the FTAA talks did not distract US officials from taking the lead in launching the Doha Round in November 2001.

The US Free Trade Coalition Splinters

When I. M. Destler authored the first edition of *American Trade Politics* in 1986, a bipartisan coalition for free trade dominated the US Congress. To be sure, during the Reagan era, autos, steel, and a few other industries grumbled loudly, as they were buffeted by international competition and a strong dollar. But after the Plaza Accord, congressional dissent was limited to jawboning with foreign governments, using the malleable "crowbar" of Super 301 to launch unfair trade complaints, and invoking minor provisions of the Omnibus Trade Act of 1988 such as advance notification prior to a plant shut down.

In the 1990s, with globalization rampant, US trade policy became a salient feature of the domestic economy and thus more contentious. The fractious congressional debate over NAFTA stoked partisan fires. As the trade agenda broadened to cover a large array of domestic subsidy and regulatory policies and as trade pacts were used to pursue foreign policy as well as economic objectives, more members took a keen interest. Maintaining a protrade coalition became increasingly complex. Fast-track authority lapsed, and Congress rebuffed attempts to renew the authority in 1994, 1997, and 1998. As noted in the Institute volume *Restarting Fast Track* (Schott 1998a), some Democratic members held fast track hostage in retaliation for Republican opposition to their favored domestic programs.

By the time Destler authored the fourth edition of *American Trade Politics* in 2005, the bipartisan free trade coalition had almost totally fractured. Major trade legislation could be passed only with the overwhelming support of House Republicans because House Democrats were almost unified in opposition. Five years after fast track failed to pass congressional muster, the rebranded TPA passed by a 3-vote margin (25 Democrats and 190 Republicans) in the Trade Act of 2002, while CAFTA-DR passed by only two votes in 2005 (15 Democrats and 202 Republicans). Protrade Democrats such as Calvin Dooley (D-CA) became a vanishing breed. The free trade coalition fractured for multiple reasons, but the underlying forces were information technology and global competition. As information technology diffused through the economy, it not only boosted average productivity growth (from a meager 1.5 percent between 1973 and 1995 to 3 percent between 1996 and 2005) but also sharply raised the salaries of the highest quintile of the workforce (1.6 percent annually in real terms between 1990 and 2004) while the lowest quintile experienced stagnant wages (0.2 percent annually). Armed with IT, each skilled American could do the work of several unskilled Americans at higher wages per employee but lower costs per unit of output.

At the same time, global competition put enormous pressure on blue-collar factory workers and white-collar office workers alike. In the ensuing drama of wage dispersion and job disruption, the global economy made a more obvious and politically attractive target than information technology. Highly polarized politics, clashing congressional personalities, bitter disagreement about social safety nets, and genuine concerns about the impact of market forces on labor and environmental conditions abroad added to the underlying forces that fractured the free trade coalition. Being both analytical and constructive, the Institute's fellows, starting with Destler, not only diagnosed the break but also offered solutions.

Labor Practices at Home and Abroad

The "pauper labor argument" is a durable myth that originated with 19th century trade between England and India and today contends that trade between the United States and China will inevitably drag US wages down to the Chinese level. The myth has a surface similarity to the famed Stolper-Samuelson factor price equalization theorem, but the theorem depends on highly restrictive assumptions that are seldom fulfilled: the same technological menu available to rich and poor countries alike, the massive exchange of labor-intensive goods for capital-intensive goods, and fixed stocks of capital.

In fact, research finds little connection between widening income disparities in the United States and the growth of merchandise trade. Trade flows are highly concentrated in manufactured goods; manufacturing technology differs vastly between the United States and developing countries; on balance, the capital intensity of imports is about the same as exports; stocks of manufacturing capital are highly elastic to the real rate of return; and in any event, the lowest-paid workers in American society are concentrated in nontraded services such as gardening, home care, restaurants, public transportation, and janitorial services.

Like other economists, Institute authors have tried to drive a stake in the pauper labor argument, but contemporary political debates suggest that the challenge remains. Indeed, the offshore outsourcing controversy, discussed in a moment, can be viewed as a modern version of the pauper labor argument.

The second strand of the labor debate concerns the danger of exploitation abroad, particularly in developing countries, whatever the impact might be on wages in the United States or the European Union. Social champions argue that US commercial policies should aim for grander goals than income gains accruing to American workers and firms. Elliott and Freeman (2003) developed this theme, illustrated by approaches such as labeling, ISO 15000 standards, and voluntary codes that might become a central component of US trade policy under a Democratic president.

Offshore Outsourcing

Through articles, press, and TV, Catherine Mann (2003, 2005) fast became an acknowledged expert on "offshore outsourcing"—the delivery of services through electronic means from workers abroad to large US firms, such as Dell, Microsoft, JPMorgan, and American Airlines. As offshore outsourcing became an antiglobalization rallying cry, Mann highlighted several inconvenient facts. Estimates of US jobs actually displaced are small (under 0.5 million relative to a US workforce of 140 million) and projections are highly speculative. Most of the impact is on lower-skilled service work, exemplified by call centers. The US workforce benefits from a large amount of "onshore insourcing" as skilled lawyers, doctors, accountants, and investment bankers provide services to foreign clients. Finally, and perhaps most significantly, Mann contends that outsourcing certain IT functions boosts the productivity of US firms, in much the same channels as the diffusion of IT over the past two decades. Her broad conclusion is that the United States gains more than it loses from outsourcing and that one answer to competitive pressure is a tax credit for corporate training programs that upgrade the skills of American workers.

Trade Adjustment

Struck by the huge costs of retaining jobs in declining industries through trade protection—upwards of $70,000 per job per year in the 1980s—Hufbauer and Rosen (1986) proposed that quantitative restrictions be converted to degressive ad valorem tariffs. They proposed that the revenue thereby raised be devoted to generous worker adjustment measures. The idea of recapturing quota rents from producers and distributors, here and abroad, was further developed in *Auction Quotas and United States Trade Policy* by Bergsten et al. (1987). Whatever its economic merits, the idea was anathema to those enriched and never gained political traction in the United States (though it was adopted to unravel protection in Australia and New Zealand and other countries).

The core idea of trade adjustment assistance had its own difficulties. It ran into the principled opposition of Secretary George Shultz, who objected to special benefits for workers dislocated by imports. It ran into entrenched Republican opposition to *any* enlargement of the social safety net. Retrospective evaluation of trade adjustment assistance (TAA) programs showed little positive effect in shifting dislocated workers to new careers. Finally, organized labor derided TAA as burial insurance. By the time NAFTA was debated, in 1993, TAA was only marginally effective in garnering political support for trade pacts.

Against this background, Kletzer and Litan (2001) came up with a novel approach: assistance for dislocated workers contingent on getting a new job, not staying unemployed. "Wage insurance" was to compensate in part for the difference between a dislocated worker's wage in the old job and the new job. This idea was embraced as a pilot program along with a tripling of overall appropriations for TAA programs (as a quid pro quo for Democratic support for TPA) in the Trade Act of 2002.

Environmental Awareness

Starting with NAFTA, then the "greenest trade agreement ever," environmental issues began to make an appearance in trade policy. They grew from concerns about a form of "social dumping"—the fear that environmentally destructive firms would take advantage of weak standards and lax enforcement in developing countries and move production abroad. The connection with trade policy thus had a much more mercantile flavor than the "big picture" environmental issues—global warming, ozone holes, and endangered species. Although the Montreal Protocol and the Convention on International Trade in Endangered Species (CITES) both invoked trade measures, and although commercial instruments were an intended part of the Kyoto Protocol, these international accords were not first and foremost about trade policy. Much more in focus were practices that might cut the costs of affected industries and spur their relocation. Against this background, Daniel Esty (1994) authored a call for a Global Environmental Organization (GEO) as a sister institution to the GATT.

The Next 25 Years

What do the next 25 years hold for trade policy? Since our crystal ball is not particularly clear, we write this final section more to throw out provocative questions than to provide speculative answers. Our successors at the Institute's 50th anniversary party can decide whether we asked the right questions and enjoy a good laugh over our predictions.

- In our view, the biggest question is whether the march toward more intense international integration—trade, investment, even migration—will grind to a halt. Will global powers attempt to "corner" energy supplies? Will episodes of terrorism and disease drive up the security tax on trade in goods and services? Will insistent nationalism interrupt the expansion of global MNCs? Will a resurgence of populism, fueled by the seemingly skewed distribution of global growth, stop the show? Our guess is that the advance of communications and transportation technology, coupled with the gains reaped as billions of newcomers enter the market economy, will prove more powerful than the forces of isolation. Nations will deal with the unequal distribution of wealth and income by national measures, not by closing their borders. The march will go on.

- A follow-up question: What will be the contribution of policy-driven liberalization by comparison with privately driven globalization? Private markets, working within static rules and barriers, have greatly increased economic activity across borders—not only "good commerce" but also, alas, "bad commerce," exemplified by drug trafficking, money laundering, and illegal migration (Naím 2005). Private markets will continue to drive international activity in the future, owing to the rise of e-commerce, the integration of capital markets, and the fall of transportation and communication costs. Our guess is that, even if the Doha Round, the FTAA, and APEC all flop, merchandise trade will still expand at 2 to 4 percent per year faster than world GDP, and that e-commerce, direct investment, and financial capital will grow at a much faster clip. That said, it would certainly help if public policy provided a tailwind, not a headwind, for the integration of world markets.

- Finally, will the WTO sputter as an engine of liberalization and take a long slumber, reminiscent of the ILO between 1930 and 1990? Admittedly, our view is heavily influenced by the difficulty in bringing the Doha Development Round to a robust conclusion. We foresee that the mantle of leadership in the globalization agenda will increasingly be borne by bilateral and regional agreements. But we do not foresee exclusive economic blocs centered on China, the European Union, and the United States. Rather, we predict a crisscross network of agreements. Messy, to be sure, but sufficiently flexible that clever firms will circumvent discriminatory barriers by locating the right slices of their global operations in just the right places.

References

Baldwin, Robert E. 2003. *The Decline of US Labor Unions and the Role of Trade.* Washington: Institute for International Economics.
Bergsten, C. Fred. 1995. *APEC: The Bogor Declaration and the Path Ahead.* Working Paper 95-1. Washington: Institute for International Economics.
Bergsten, C. Fred. 1996. *Competitive Liberalization and Global Free Trade: A Vision for the Early 21st Century.* Working Paper 96-15. Washington: Institute for International Economics.
Bergsten, C. Fred. 2001. *Brunei: A Turning Point for APEC?* International Economics Policy Brief 01-1. Washington: Institute for International Economics.
Bergsten, C. Fred. 2002. A Renaissance for United States Trade Policy? *Foreign Affairs* (November/December).
Bergsten, C. Fred. 2004. Foreign Economic Policy for the Next President. *Foreign Affairs* (March–April).
Bergsten, C. Fred. 2005. Rescuing the Doha Round. *Foreign Affairs*, WTO Special Edition (December).

Bergsten, C. Fred, Kimberly Ann Elliott, Jeffrey J. Schott, and Wendy E. Takacs. 1987. *Auction Quotas and United States Trade Policy*. POLICY ANALYSES IN INTERNATIONAL ECONOMICS 19. Washington: Institute for International Economics.

Bradford, Scott C., and Robert Z. Lawrence. 2004. *Has Globalization Gone Far Enough? The Costs of Fragmented Markets*. Washington: Institute for International Economics.

Bradford, Scott C., Paul L. E. Grieco, and Gary C. Hufbauer. 2005. The Payoff to America from Global Integration. In *The United States and the World Economy: Foreign Economic Policy for the Next Administration*, C. Fred Bergsten and the Institute for International Economics. Washington: Institute for International Economics.

Choi, Inbom, and Jeffrey J. Schott. 2001. *Free Trade Between Korea and the United States?* POLICY ANALYSES IN INTERNATIONAL ECONOMICS 62. Washington: Institute for International Economics.

Cline, William R., ed. 1983. *Trade Policy in the 1980s*. Washington: Institute for International Economics.

Cline, William R. 1990. *The Future of World Trade in Textiles and Apparel,* revised edition. Washington: Institute for International Economics.

Cline, William R. 2004. *Trade Policy and Global Poverty*. Washington: Institute for International Economics.

DeRosa, Dean, and John Gilbert. 2005. The Economic Impacts of Multilateral and Regional Trade Agreements in Quantitative Economic Models: An Ex Post Evaluation. Draft paper prepared for the Institute. Washington: Institute for International Economics.

Destler, I. M. 1986. *American Trade Politics.* Washington: Institute for International Economics.

Destler, I. M., John S. Odell, and Kimberly Ann Elliott. 1987. *Anti-Protection: Changing Forces in United States Trade Politics*. POLICY ANALYSES IN INTERNATIONAL ECONOMICS 21. Washington: Institute for International Economics.

Dobson, Wendy, and Pierre Jacquet. 1998. *Financial Services Liberalization in the WTO*. Washington: Institute for International Economics.

Elliott, Kimberly Ann. 2006. *Delivering on Doha: Farm Trade and the Poor*. Washington: Institute for International Economics and Center for Global Development.

Elliott, Kimberly Ann, and Richard B. Freeman. 2003. *Can Labor Standards Improve under Globalization?* Washington: Institute for International Economics.

Esty, Daniel C. 1994. *Greening the GATT: Trade, Environment, and the Future.* Washington: Institute for International Economics.

Frankel, Jeffrey A. 1997. *Regional Trading Blocs in the World Economic System*. Washington: Institute for International Economics.

Graham, Edward M. 2000. *Fighting the Wrong Enemy: Antiglobal Activists and Multinational Enterprises.* Washington: Institute for International Economics.

Graham, Edward M., and Paul R. Krugman. 1989. *Foreign Direct Investment in the United States.* Washington: Institute for International Economics.

Graham, Edward M., and David M. Marchick. 2006. *US National Security and Foreign Direct Investment.* Washington: Institute for International Economics.

Graham, Edward M., and J. David Richardson. 1997. *Competition Policies for the Global Economy*. POLICY ANALYSES IN INTERNATIONAL ECONOMICS 51. Washington: Institute for International Economics.

Hathaway, Dale E. 1987. *Agriculture and the GATT: Rewriting the Rules*. POLICY ANALYSES IN INTERNATIONAL ECONOMICS 20. Washington: Institute for International Economics.

Hufbauer, Gary Clyde, and Richard E. Baldwin. 2006. *The Shape of a Swiss-US Free Trade Agreement*. POLICY ANALYSES IN INTERNATIONAL ECONOMICS 76. Washington: Institute for International Economics.

Hufbauer, Gary Clyde, and Joanna Shelton Erb. 1984. *Subsidies in International Trade*. Washington: Institute for International Economics.

Hufbauer, Gary Clyde, and Howard R. Rosen. 1986. *Trade Policy for Troubled Industries*. POLICY ANALYSES IN INTERNATIONAL ECONOMICS 15. Washington: Institute for International Economics.

Hufbauer, Gary Clyde, and Jeffrey J. Schott. 1985. *Trading for Growth: The Next Round of Trade Negotiations*. POLICY ANALYSES IN INTERNATIONAL ECONOMICS 11. Washington: Institute for International Economics.

Hufbauer, Gary Clyde, and Jeffrey J. Schott. 1992. *North American Free Trade: Issues and Recommendations*. Washington: Institute for International Economics.

Hufbauer, Gary Clyde, and Jeffrey J. Schott. 1993. *NAFTA: An Assessment,* revised edition. Washington: Institute for International Economics.

Hufbauer, Gary Clyde, and Jeffrey J. Schott. 1994. *Western Hemisphere Economic Integration.* Washington: Institute for International Economics.

Hufbauer, Gary Clyde, and Jeffrey J. Schott. 2005. *NAFTA Revisited: Achievements and Challenges*. Washington: Institute for International Economics.

Hufbauer, Gary Clyde, and Jeffrey J. Schott. 2006. *The Doha Round after Hong Kong*. International Economics Policy Brief 06-2. Washington: Institute for International Economics.

Hufbauer, Gary Clyde, and Erika Wada. 1997. *Unfinished Business: Telecommunications after the Uruguay Round*. Washington: Institute for International Economics.

Hufbauer, Gary Clyde, Diane E. Berliner, and Kimberly Ann Elliott. 1986. *Trade Protection in the United States: 31 Case Studies*. Washington: Institute for International Economics.

Kletzer, Lori G. 2001. *Job Losses from Imports: Measuring the Costs*. Washington: Institute for International Economics.

Kletzer, Lori G. 2004. Trade-Related Job Loss and Wage Insurance: A Synthetic Review. *Review of International Economics* 12, no. 5.

Kletzer, Lori G., and Robert E. Litan. 2001. *A Prescription to Relieve Worker Anxiety*. International Economics Policy Brief 01-2. Washington: Institute for International Economics.

Lardy, Nicholas R., and Daniel H. Rosen. 2004. *Prospects for a US-Taiwan FTA*. POLICY ANALYSES IN INTERNATIONAL ECONOMICS 73. Washington: Institute for International Economics, December.

Mann, Catherine L. 2003. *Globalization of IT Services and White Collar Jobs: The Next Wave of Productivity Growth*. International Economics Policy Brief 03-11. Washington: Institute for International Economics.

Mann, Catherine L. 2005. Offshore Outsourcing and the Globalization of US Services: Why Now, How Important, and What Policy Implications. In *The United States and the World Economy: Foreign Economic Policy for the Next Decade*, C. Fred Bergsten and the Institute for International Economics. Washington: Institute for International Economics.

Mann, Catherine, Sue E. Eckert, and Sarah Cleeland Knight. 2000. *Global Electronic Commerce: A Policy Primer*. Washington: Institute for International Economics.

Maskus, Keith. 2000. *Intellectual Property Rights in the Global Economy*. Washington: Institute for International Economics.

Moran, Theodore, Edward M. Graham, and Magnus Blomström, eds. 2005. *Does Foreign Direct Investment Promote Development?* Washington: Institute for International Economics.

Naím, Moisés. 2005. *Illicit: How Smugglers, Traffickers and Copycats Are Hijacking the Global Economy*. New York: Doubleday.

Petrazzini, Ben A. 1996. *Global Telecom Talks: A Trillion Dollar Deal*. Washington: Institute for International Economics.

Preeg, Ernest H. 2003. *From Here to Free Trade in Manufactures: Why and How*. Arlington, VA: Manufacturers Alliance/MAPI.

Richardson, J. David. Forthcoming. *Global Forces, American Faces: US Economic Globalization at the Grass Roots*. Washington: Institute for International Economics.

Rodrik, Dani. 1997. *Has Globalization Gone Too Far?* Washington: Institute for International Economics.

Rose, Andrew K. 2004. Do We Really Know That the WTO Increases Trade? *American Economic Review* 94, no. 1: 98–114.

Rosen, Howard F. 2002. Reforming Trade Adjustment Assistance: Keeping a 40-Year Promise. Paper presented at Institute conference on Trade Policy in 2002. Washington: Institute for International Economics.

Scheve, Kenneth F., and Matthew J. Slaughter. 2001. *Globalization and the Perceptions of American Workers*. Washington: Institute for International Economics.

Schott, Jeffrey J., and Murray G. Smith, ed. 1988. *The Canada–United States Free Trade Agreement: The Global Impact*. Washington: Institute for International Economics.

Schott, Jeffrey J., ed. 1989. *Free Trade Areas and US Trade Policy*. Washington: Institute for International Economics.

Schott, Jeffrey J., ed. 1990. *Completing the Uruguay Round: A Results-Oriented Approach to the GATT Trade Negotiations*. Washington: Institute for International Economics.

Schott, Jeffrey J. 1994. *The Uruguay Round: An Assessment*. Washington: Institute for International Economics.

Schott, Jeffrey J. 1996. *The World Trading System: Challenges Ahead*. Washington: Institute for International Economics.

Schott, Jeffrey J., ed. 1998a. *Restarting Fast Track*. Special Report 11. Washington: Institute for International Economics.

Schott, Jeffrey J., ed. 1998b. *Launching New Global Trade Talks: An Action Agenda*. Washington: Institute for International Economics.

Schott, Jeffrey J. 2000. *The WTO after Seattle*. Washington: Institute for International Economics.

Schott, Jeffrey J. 2001. *Prospects for Free Trade in the Americas*. Washington: Institute for International Economics.

Schott, Jeffrey J., ed. 2004. *Free Trade Agreements: US Strategies and Priorities*. Washington: Institute for International Economics.

Tyson, Laura D'Andrea. 1992. *Who's Bashing Whom? Trade Conflict in High-Technology Industries*. Washington: Institute for International Economics.

Wonnacott, Paul. 1987. *The United States and Canada: The Quest for Free Trade*. POLICY ANALYSES IN INTERNATIONAL ECONOMICS 16. Washington: Institute for International Economics.

4

Economic Sanctions and Threats in Foreign and Commercial Policy

KIMBERLY ANN ELLIOTT

Analysis of the costs and benefits of manipulating economic flows to influence policies abroad has been an interest of C. Fred Bergsten's and a topic of research at the Peterson Institute for International Economics from the professional beginnings of both. Bergsten launched his career as assistant for international economic affairs to National Security Adviser Henry Kissinger (1969–71), whom he advised on export control issues, inter alia, while Kissinger was crafting his détente policies for the Soviet Union and China. Leaving government in 1971 for the think tank world (at Brookings), Bergsten wrote widely about international economic issues, including implications of the Arab use of oil as a weapon, East-West relations, and possible tensions in the Western alliance arising from increasing economic interdependence. After returning to government in 1977 as assistant secretary of the Treasury for international affairs in the administration of President Jimmy Carter, Bergsten again played a role in US sanctions policy vis-à-vis the Soviet Union as well as South Africa and Iran, among others (with assistance from Treasury colleagues Gary Hufbauer and Jeffrey Schott). In public statements, he generally opposed restrictions on US

Kimberly Ann Elliott is a senior fellow jointly at the Institute and the Center for Global Development. She has been associated with the Institute since 1982.

trade or investment flows as ineffective, with the costs likely to outweigh the benefits.[1]

But in a statement to the Senate Committee on Banking, Housing, and Urban Affairs in March 1979, Bergsten noted a telling exception to the economic undesirability of using trade sanctions: "Controls over either exports or imports can be an appropriate measure if they are used as a lever to gain access for U.S. products to foreign markets that are unfairly restricting entry of U.S. exports" (Bergsten 1980, 204). This was just a few years after Congress had approved section 301 of the Trade Act of 1974, which authorizes the president to retaliate against foreign unfair trade practices by restricting US imports in cases where a satisfactory market-opening agreement cannot be reached.

Bergsten also recommended that President Carter respond aggressively to the subsidies that the European Community was providing to upstart aircraft manufacturer Airbus to enable it to compete with Boeing. Eastern Airlines had announced the first-ever purchase of Airbus planes by an American airline, and Bergsten wanted the Treasury Department to retaliate by imposing countervailing duties equal to the value of the subsidies received by Airbus. His recommendations were overruled, however, after Eastern CEO Frank Borman convinced the White House that the airline might not survive deregulation and increased competition if it was prevented from purchasing the planes at the subsidized price. As Bergsten predicted, disputes over subsidies to Airbus remain a problem in US-European trade relations to this day.[2] This incident is indicative of the pragmatic, and aggressive, approach to trade policy and politics that is Bergsten's hallmark (see chapter 2 by I. M. Destler and Marcus Noland).

At the Institute, Bergsten and colleagues tackled issues related to economic sanctions and trade threats immediately. One of the first projects launched after the Institute's creation in late 1981 was *Economic Sanctions Reconsidered*, led by Senior Fellow Gary Hufbauer. He was soon joined by Jeffrey Schott and me, and we all remain on the "sanctions team" as the third edition of the study is now being completed. Bergsten foresaw the utility of a case study approach to this issue as early as 1973 when he was asked by the Ford Foundation to prepare a report on the most important international economic issues in need of further research: "There have been a number of efforts in recent history to use economic leverage for political reasons, running from the League of Nations sanctions against Italy through the U.S. export embargoes toward Communist countries to the United Nations sanctions against Rhodesia, from which we should be able to learn much about such possibilities in the future" (Bergsten 1973, 32).

---

1. See, for example, the chapters in Bergsten (1980) on export controls, international economic conflict, and sanctions against South Africa.

2. Private conversation with C. Fred Bergsten, August 25, 2006.

On the trade side, a decade after Assistant Secretary Bergsten had endorsed the idea, Thomas O. Bayard and I adapted the case study methodology to analyze the effectiveness of trade threats and sanctions in opening foreign markets to US exports. In addition to these core studies of sanctions, other authors have studied various aspects of the political economy of using economic leverage to manage trade policy, including Bergsten himself on several occasions, especially with respect to Japan and now China.

This chapter begins with a description of the Institute's major and ongoing project on economic sanctions for foreign policy goals, which has been a staple of Institute research for 25 years. It also discusses other Institute research into the costs and benefits of using economic tools to pursue noneconomic goals. It then turns to the use of threats and sanctions in commercial policy.

Economic Sanctions for Foreign Policy Goals

The Institute's research on economic sanctions was launched in the wake of the grain embargo of the Soviet Union after its invasion of Afghanistan and in the midst of President Ronald Reagan's sanctions campaign against Poland and the Soviet Union over the crackdown on the Solidarity trade union. The conventional wisdom at the time was that "sanctions never work." As the sanctions aimed at political repression in Poland morphed into secondary sanctions against the United States' European allies over their decision to pursue development of a pipeline to import Soviet natural gas, views of the costs and benefits of sanctions grew even more negative. Using an empirical approach based on more than 100 case studies from 1914 to the early 1980s, in Hufbauer, Schott, and Elliott (1983, 1985) my colleagues and I were able to show that the conventional wisdom was mistaken and that sanctions had achieved at least partial success in about a third of the cases studied (table 4.1).[3]

The second edition of *Economic Sanctions Reconsidered* was released in late 1990, in the midst of the comprehensive United Nations sanctions designed to coerce Iraqi President Saddam Hussein to withdraw from Kuwait. This was a time when it was hoped that the end of the Cold War would restore the United Nations' role as a mechanism for international peace and collective security. Because Iraq was heavily dependent on oil

---

3. Two things about the definition of success in this context are important. First, the goals against which effectiveness are assessed are instrumental foreign policy goals—changes in target country behavior, policies, or leadership—and do not include goals of deterring third parties or signaling toughness to allies, nor do they include domestic political goals of satisfying constituent demands for action. Second, the standard for success does not require total achievement of goals nor do sanctions have to be the decisive element in the outcome. We allow partial achievement of goals with sanctions as a substantial factor but not necessarily the one determining the outcome.

Table 4.1   Use and effectiveness of US economic sanctions and threats

Overall result	Total number of cases	Number of successes	Success rate (percent)
Foreign policy cases			
All cases, 1914–2000	204	70	34
Unilateral US cases	82	22	27
1945–69	19	10	53
1970–89	52	10	19
1990–2000	11	2	18
US section 301 cases			
All cases, 1975–94	87	45	52
All cases, 1985–94	62	38	61
Worker rights and GSP			
All cases, 1985–94	32	15	47
Goals matter			
Foreign policy cases, 1914–2000			
Modest goals	43	22	51
All other goals	163	48	29
US section 301 cases, 1975–94			
Border measures	25	19	76
Other market barriers	47	16	34
Worker rights and GSP, 1985–94			
Forced or child labor	14	4	29
Subminimum working conditions	15	7	47

GSP = generalized system of preferences

Sources: Hufbauer, Schott, and Elliott (1990, forthcoming); Bayard and Elliott (1994); and Elliott (2000).

exports and because it was nearly landlocked and had few transportation outlets for the oil, the UN sanctions imposed an unprecedented cost on Iraq's economy. At the same time, prewar analysis indicated that American and allied casualties could run into the thousands. The Institute analysis, which suggested that the Iraqi case had many of the elements associated with success, was cited in the Senate debate over the joint resolution authorizing the use of force, which passed by just two votes. A competing resolution, sponsored by Senator Sam Nunn (D-GA), did not rule out the use of force in the future but called on President George H. W. Bush to continue to try to resolve the situation with sanctions and diplomatic measures. It failed by just 4 votes.[4]

---

4. Roll call results are available at www.senate.gov.

These hopes for sanctions as an alternative to war echoed earlier cycles of optimism (beginning with Woodrow Wilson's hopes for the League of Nations after World War I), but they were dashed even more quickly. By the time the second edition of *Economic Sanctions* came out in November 1990, President Bush had already concluded that sanctions would not be sufficient. The following January, he ordered American troops into action in the first Gulf War.

Disillusion with UN sanctions grew as the decade wore on. Moreover, with a dozen new cases from the 1980s, the second edition of the sanctions book modified the conclusions about the effectiveness of sanctions to note that unilateral US sanctions in the 1970s and 1980s were far less effective than they had been earlier in the postwar period. While the overall success rate for all countries using sanctions across all periods remained at about one in three, the proportion of unilateral US cases that achieved at least modest success dropped from one in two in the early post–World War II period to less than one in five from 1970 to 1989 (table 4.1).

There has been a long lag between the second and third editions, but the increment of new cases is also much larger, with the number of observations nearly doubled to more than 200. This increase reflected the unsettling forces released by the collapse of the Soviet Union and the end of the Cold War as well as the initial optimism regarding the potential for UN sanctions with the strong collective response to the Iraqi invasion of Kuwait. In the first half of the 1990s, the Soviet Union and then Russia imposed sanctions six times in an effort to protect its interests in the newly independent countries emerging from former Soviet republics. This contrasts with no Soviet sanctions in the previous 20 years. Similarly the United Nations mandated economic sanctions only twice during the Cold War (broad sanctions against Rhodesia when it declared independence and an arms embargo against South Africa over apartheid), but on twelve occasions in the decade following 1990.[5]

It was only after it became clear that American policymakers had no intention of lifting the sanctions against Iraq as long as Saddam Hussein remained in power and that the "oil-for-food" program was more likely to be used by Hussein to enrich himself and his cronies than to mitigate the humanitarian costs of the sanctions that a backlash against comprehensive UN embargoes took hold. The backlash peaked with the embargo that was intended to restore democracy in Haiti: Instead it unleashed streams of impoverished Haitians desperately trying to get to the United States in unseaworthy vessels. From 1994 to 2000, the United Nations imposed only limited sanctions and participated in just two new episodes.

---

5. The UN General Assembly recommended sanctions in at least two other cases documented in *Economic Sanctions Reconsidered*—an arms embargo against North Korea and China during the Korean War and broad sanctions against Portugal over its refusal to grant independence to its African colonies in the 1960s—but the Security Council never acted in either case.

Figure 4.1 Trends in the use of economic sanctions, 1914–99

number of cases

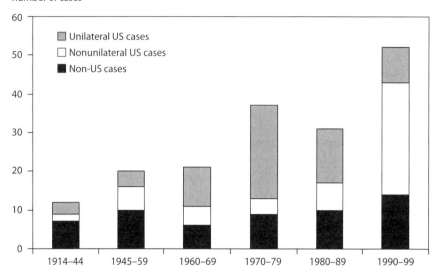

The first half of the 1990s was also a time of angst for the US business community, which feared that a perceived explosion of new *unilateral* US sanctions would undercut its competitive advantage at a time when international trade and investment flows were growing rapidly. Once again, however, empirical research from the Institute was able to show that the conventional wisdom was exaggerated. While existing sanctions against Cuba, Iran, and Libya were expanded and codified in legislation, a worrying trend to be sure, new uses of unilateral sanctions by the United States declined overall, as shown in figure 4.1.

The conclusion that emerges from this research is that the correct question to ask is not whether sanctions work but when and under what circumstances. In simple terms, sanctions are more likely to be effective when the costs of defying the sanctioner's demands exceed the costs of complying with them. The problem for the analyst is that, while the costs of defiance can be relatively easily identified and measured, it is far harder to assess the costs that a target might bear by acquiescing to pressure to forgo weapons of mass destruction or to hold free and fair elections. In addition, while Hufbauer, Schott, and I are interested in whether sanctions have contributed toward foreign policy goals, such as changes in behavior or regimes, we recognize that sanctions are often used for other purposes, including to mollify domestic constituents outraged by a target country's behavior. Sanctions that are designed primarily to respond to domestic political demands may not be effective in achieving foreign policy goals. Thus it has proved difficult to come to robust conclusions about the factors that contribute to effective sanctions. Econometric testing of the data conducted for the third edition of *Economic Sanctions* has not identified many variables that are statistically significant, and the variables included account for only a small share of the variation in outcomes.

Still, the data compiled for this project do show clear correlations between certain variables, and these patterns, while they are no guarantee of success, can offer useful lessons for policymakers. Just a few examples are discussed here, illustrating both how the data support the conventional wisdom and where they raise questions about it.

Some of the conclusions are fairly straightforward. For example, it is surely no surprise that more modest foreign policy goals, such as Arab League sanctions to deter Canada from moving its embassy in Israel to Jerusalem, are more achievable with economic measures than more ambitious ones, such as inducing Iraq to withdraw its forces from Kuwait prior to the first Gulf War. Overall, Hufbauer, Schott, and I judged half of sanctions cases with modest goals to have been at least partially successful, compared to less than one in three for more difficult ones (table 4.1). Also not surprisingly, sanctions are on average more effective the higher the economic cost they impose on the target. The average cost to the target as a share of GNP is more than 50 percent higher in successful cases than in failed ones, even when outliers such as the UN sanctions against Iraq are excluded. And the more difficult the goal, the higher the cost imposed generally must be to achieve a positive outcome.

Other patterns in the data are less intuitive, however. For example, a staple of the sanctions literature is that multilateral sanctions should be more effective than unilateral ones, because the costs imposed should be higher. The Institute database paints a more nuanced picture. Multilateral cooperation can certainly be helpful, but that cooperation can be difficult and time-consuming to organize, and so a sanctioner with modest goals may not bother to seek cooperation from others. In other cases, cooperation may be necessary but still not sufficient if the costs of compliance are higher than the costs of defiance, even when the latter are quite high.

Overall in the data, there is no relationship between the degree of international cooperation with a sanctions effort and the probability of a successful outcome, and there is even a negative relationship with respect to cases involving relatively modest goals, such as release of a political prisoner or demands for regime change. Positive outcomes in cases involving more ambitious goals, including efforts to disrupt a relatively minor military adventure, to impair the military capability of another country, or to achieve other major goals such as the surrender of territory, are positively correlated with higher degrees of international cooperation. But the probability of success in cases with more ambitious goals, even if they involve a relatively high degree of cooperation, generally remains low because economic pressure is usually inadequate to achieve goals that could threaten a target country's national security.

Concerns about the Costs of Economic Sanctions

Because the United States has been by far the major user of sanctions over the past several decades and because they have been relatively ineffective since the 1970s in achieving US foreign policy goals, a recurring theme in the policy debate is that the economic costs to American firms usually outweigh the foreign policy benefits. The first Institute entry in this debate was J. David Richardson's *Sizing Up US Export Disincentives* (1993). Richardson used a variety of quantitative methods to assess the impact on US exports of national security export controls and economic sanctions as well as tax and regulatory policies. He concluded that US export losses in 1989 due to government policies were probably around $20 billion. He also found that export controls accounted for most of the forgone exports, with other economic sanctions accounting for perhaps $3 billion (the effects of tax and regulatory policies were inconsequential) (Richardson 1993, 127–32).

In addition to these results, Richardson's research contributed the idea of using a "gravity model" of trade to assess the impact of sanctions on exports. The gravity model has performed well in predicting bilateral trade flows based on the size and wealth of two trading partners and the distance between them. Not surprisingly, the countries with the largest estimated shortfalls between actual and predicted imports from the United States were the Soviet Union and the Eastern European countries subject to sanctions and export controls as well as a number of other countries that were the subject of US sanctions (Richardson 1993, chapter 5).[6]

In Hufbauer et al. (1997), an extension of the gravity model approach, we used the foreign policy sanctions database and created a dummy variable indicating the relative severity of sanctions imposed by the United States against trading partners (limited, moderate, or extensive). This paper was updated by Hufbauer and Oegg in 2003 using Andrew Rose's version of the gravity model, which included several additional variables that might affect trade between two parties. Both efforts incorporated variables not used by Richardson to reflect common borders, languages, or membership in various types of trade blocs, and both found a lower impact on trade from economic sanctions—$15 billion to $17 billion in Hufbauer et al. and $5 billion to $10 billion in Hufbauer and Oegg. Of course, these estimates, unlike Richardson's, were after the end of the Cold War and after export controls against the former Soviet bloc had been loosened. Even more interesting, these papers raised questions about the long-held business complaint that the costs of sanctions linger long after they are

---

6. Collins and Rodrik (1991) also analyzed the global effects on both trade and capital flows of the broader changes in Eastern European and former Soviet economic policies and of their integration into the world economy.

lifted because of reliability and reputational effects. This concern was not supported by the results in either paper.

Still, the impact on costs has been frequently cited by US-based businesses and others who are interested in trying to reform the process by which sanctions are imposed and who wish to see more cost-benefit analysis in the process. Thus far, these efforts have had only limited success. One reform that was adopted in a few cases of legislatively imposed sanctions was an automatic sunset provision so that they would not go on for years with no resolution, as has the embargo of Cuba. The reform has not had the hoped-for effect, however, as legislation imposing sanctions against Iran and Burma have been repeatedly extended, most recently this year.

Other Studies Exploring Uses of Economic Leverage for Foreign Policy Purposes

Hufbauer, Schott, and I have applied the general framework and data from the sanctions project to particular cases or functional questions in Institute working papers and policy briefs, testimonies, and other articles and papers. The issue of targeted sanctions attracted a great deal of attention in the late 1990s from scholars in as well as outside the Institute. Concerns about the humanitarian impact of the broad sanctions against Iraq and Haiti led to a search for "smart" sanctions that could be targeted against rogue regime leaders while sparing innocent civilians. These include travel bans and financial asset seizures targeted against individuals as well as arms embargoes. Both Hufbauer and Oegg (2000) and I (Elliott 2002) concluded that targeted sanctions could be useful in certain situations, particularly to serve symbolic or political goals, but that they were unlikely to be effective in achieving most foreign policy goals.

This analysis proved useful when attention turned to disrupting financial support for terrorists and their operations after the September 11, 2001, attacks. Within weeks, Hufbauer, Schott, and Oegg released a policy brief summarizing past cases where sanctions had been used to influence state sponsors of terrorism, including Iran, Iraq, Libya, and Syria, and drawing lessons from that experience for squeezing terrorist finances. The authors noted that sanctions had not been very effective in bringing state sponsors of terrorism to heel, though sanctions and international isolation did eventually convince Libya's Muammar Gaddhafi to moderate his support for terrorist groups and give up aspirations for weapons of mass destruction. The authors also surveyed US government efforts to disrupt financial flows to individual terrorists and groups (and drug traffickers) and found even more limited effectiveness. They concluded that the financial sanctions adopted after September 11 were likely to play at best an "auxiliary role" in the war on terror.

In 2004, Edwin M. Truman, in collaboration with University of Maryland economist Peter Reuter, completed a comprehensive study of American and international anti–money laundering strategies. In *Chasing Dirty Money*, the authors analyzed how anti–money laundering and other enforcement tools available to the US government could be used to disrupt terrorist financing. The book also analyzed how these same tools could be used to deny corrupt dictators the fruits of their illicit activities or to seize stolen assets and return them to the home country. The Truman and Reuter analysis of what can be expected of these tools and how to make them more effective is clearly relevant to the debate over "targeted" economic sanctions, which include the freezing of assets held abroad by individuals in rogue regimes. In particular, Truman and Reuter identify obstacles to seizing "kleptocratic" assets that also underscore the limitations of using targeted sanctions to vanquish the bad guys without hurting innocent civilians.

One rogue nation that has attracted repeated attention from Institute scholars over the past decade or so is North Korea. During the 1993–94 crisis over Kim Il-sung's efforts to acquire nuclear weapons, I applied the sanctions framework to what was publicly known at the time about the North Korean economy and then revisited the case when concerns about North Korea's nuclear activities flared up again early in the administration of President George W. Bush.[7] I concluded that a carrot-and-stick strategy, including economic sanctions, could contribute to resolution of the crisis *if* key countries—China, Japan, and South Korea—cooperated and *only* if Kim viewed nuclear weapons as a bargaining chip rather than as essential to his regime's survival. The framework agreement reached between the United States and North Korea in 1994 initially seemed to support the bargaining chip hypothesis, but subsequent cheating on the agreement by North Korea raised questions about the regime's motives.[8]

Marcus Noland, one of a handful of experts on the North Korean economy, analyzed various scenarios for reform or collapse in *Avoiding the Apocalypse* (2000), as well as how to handle North Korea's challenge to regional and global stability, including via the use of economic leverage. In *Korea after Kim Jong-il*, Noland explicitly modeled a scenario involving comprehensive economic sanctions and concluded that it would raise the probability of regime change in that country to nearly 50 percent (Noland 2004, 39–41). Most recently, he testified before the US Senate Committee on Homeland Security on how the North Korean regime fi-

---

7. A version of the paper originally prepared in the midst of the 1993–94 crisis was ultimately published in Elliott (1997), while the output in the second round was an Institute policy brief (Elliott 2003).

8. By this time Kim Il-sung had died and been succeeded by his son, Kim Jong-il.

nances itself through illicit activities and what US policymakers might be able to achieve by disrupting those flows.[9]

Use of Trade Threats and Sanctions in Managing Trade Policy

In the mid-1980s, a great deal of research focused on the US trade deficit and the role of trade policy in addressing it. Destler's various editions of *American Trade Politics* cover this period well. Responding to the Japan bashers in Congress and elsewhere, Bergsten and Cline (1985) and Balassa and Noland (1988) emphasized the macroeconomic and structural sources of the deficit. These studies focused on the need to bring down the overvalued dollar and reduce the large government budget deficit in the United States as well as address structural obstacles to domestic consumption, imports, and more balanced growth in Japan. But recognizing that the effects of these policies would be seen only over the long run, attention also turned to how trade policy could be used to dampen rising pressures to protect US firms and workers from import competition (see chapter 3 by Hufbauer and Schott and chapter 2 by Destler and Noland).

In 1985, the Reagan administration implemented a dual-track strategy. First, newly appointed Secretary of Treasury James Baker joined with European and Japanese allies at the Plaza Hotel in New York in September 1985 to engineer a decline in the value of the dollar. Second, knowing that dollar devaluation would take time to work through to trade balances, the Office of the US Trade Representative shifted trade policy to the offensive, adopting an "aggressively unilateral" approach to opening foreign markets by bringing down "unfair" trade barriers to US exports. A year later, the administration also succeeded in getting trading partners to agree to launch a new multilateral round of trade negotiations to reduce trade barriers globally. Several years later, President Bill Clinton adopted a more explicitly "managed trade" policy toward Japan, which was still viewed as the major problem in US trade relations.

Aggressive Unilateralism in US Trade Policy

Building on the model of the sanctions work, I joined with Thomas O. Bayard and adopted a similar case-study methodology to analyze the costs and benefits associated with the use of threats of trade retaliation to beat back protectionist pressures in the United States by opening up markets abroad. In this case, in Bayard and Elliott (1994), we used the "data-

---

9. This testimony is posted on the Institute's Web site at www.iie.com.

base" provided by US experience with section 301 of the Trade Act of 1974, which authorizes the president to retaliate against unfair trade practices by US trading partners. In addition to statistical analysis of 72 section 301 cases, and with contributions from Charles Iceland and Amelia Porges, we also analyzed seven case studies in depth. Later, I worked with David Richardson to update and extend the statistical analysis (Elliott and Richardson 1997).

These analyses again raised questions about the conventional wisdom of the time. Bayard and I found that US trade policy in this period was less aggressive than often alleged—the US Trade Representative repeatedly threatened trade sanctions but seldom imposed them—and also less unilateral—US officials took care to act consistently with the spirit if not always the letter of international rules under the General Agreement on Tariffs and Trade (GATT).[10] Also in contradiction to frequently expressed concerns, US trade sanctions in commercial disputes seldom resulted in counterretaliation by trading partners and never in tit-for-tat trade wars with escalating sanctions. Nor was there much evidence that US negotiators used threats to conclude discriminatory deals that benefited US exporters at the expense of others.

Bayard and I concluded that section 301 investigations were most likely to result in market opening abroad when the practice targeted was a traditional—and visible and measurable—border measure. We also found that the target country's degree of dependence on the US market (exports to the United States as a share of total exports) and the bilateral trade balance were statistically significant correlates with successful outcomes. Richardson and I subsequently added several new cases and variables to the analysis but generally confirmed the conclusions of the original. Noland (1997) used evidence from the annual *National Trade Estimate Report on Foreign Trade Barriers* as well as section 301 cases and other formal US trade actions to examine similar issues regarding the political economy of US trade policy. He concluded that the bilateral trade balance was the most reliable predictor of US trade policy attention and, like the studies above, also found that the target country's dependence on the US market offered the best explanation of success in bilateral trade initiatives.

In a conference paper (Elliott 2000, also summarized in Elliott and Freeman 2003), I again used the case-study method to assess the effectiveness of using conditionality under the generalized system of preferences (GSP)—which grants developing countries duty-free access to the US market for eligible exports—to improve respect for worker rights. I concluded

---

10. GATT rules required a consensus before a member could be authorized to retaliate against another member's violation of the rules. Bayard and I found that the US Trade Representative was more likely to behave aggressively if implementation of a GATT panel ruling had been blocked by the "defendant" or if the dispute was in an area not covered by GATT rules, such as services or intellectual property.

that threats to revoke GSP eligibility if worker rights were not improved had a success rate similar to that for modest foreign policy goal cases and for commercial goals in section 301 cases—that is, they were effective about 50 percent of the time. Within that overall average, such threats were more likely to achieve demands to improve technical working conditions, such as raising the minimum wage, than to change more socially entrenched practices, such as the use of child or forced labor. And as with the section 301 cases, countries that were more dependent on the US market appeared to be more vulnerable.

Japan and Managed Trade

With respect to Japan (and Korea), where suspected trade barriers were rooted in "ways of doing business," or bureaucratic discretion, problems in enforcing market-opening agreements led to demands for quantitative benchmarks and "measurable results." The first such agreement was in 1986 with Japan, requiring that it import a minimum quantity of semiconductors from the United States. The seeming success of this agreement resulted in demands for similar deals in other sectors, culminating in the Clinton administration's proposal for a "framework agreement" that included negotiations on a number of structural and sectoral issues and that sought to expand the use of quantitative indicators (Bergsten, Ito, and Noland 2001, chapter 5).

Revisionist arguments and nontraditional policy proposals for dealing with Japan (and Korea) have been analyzed by several Institute scholars, including Fred Bergsten. One of the most prominent of these analyses was authored by visiting fellow Laura D'Andrea Tyson (and published by the Institute), which helped lay the foundation for the Clinton approach. Her *Who's Bashing Whom? Trade Conflict in High-Technology Industries* (1992) was released just before her appointment to head Clinton's Council of Economic Advisers. This and related studies in this period did not focus on sanctions per se but addressed the uses of economic leverage by the United States to influence commercial policies abroad. Tyson's report was particularly strong in arguing for the renewal of "Super 301," which was originally passed by Congress in 1988 to force the administration to be more aggressive in tackling barriers to US exports and to identify unfair trading *countries* as well as individual unfair practices.[11] She was especially concerned about protecting US competitiveness in high-tech sectors

---

11. The 1988 trade act required the US trade representative to identify trade negotiation priorities, including both unfair foreign practices and those that would have the most positive effect on US exports. The 1988 legislation authorized this so-called Super 301 provision for only two years but it was revived by executive order in 1994 under President Clinton (Bayard and Elliott 1994, chapter 2).

that she concluded were important to American economic health and national security.

Bergsten and Noland (1993) refined the Tyson arguments, examining in more detail the potential costs as well as benefits of a more aggressive approach in responding to Japan's industrial and trade policies in high-tech and other sectors. The authors did not rule out the use of aggressive tactics in some cases, but they did oppose renewing Super 301 and developed stringent criteria for resorting to managed trade tactics to penetrate the Japanese market. In general, the authors favored using the international rules under the GATT whenever possible to address unfair foreign trade barriers.

In 1995 those rules—and the costs of pursuing an aggressively unilateral trade policy—changed significantly with the creation of the World Trade Organization (WTO). It prohibited the use of trade sanctions by one member against another unless authorized by a WTO dispute settlement panel finding that a member country had failed to correct a violation of WTO rules.[12] That the WTO would in fact constrain US policy was confirmed not long after its creation when US negotiators backed down from a threat to retaliate against alleged Japanese barriers to imports of autos and auto parts. Japan announced that it would file a complaint in the WTO if the United States imposed unauthorized sanctions and US negotiators settled for a face-saving agreement that did little to change Japanese policy or to increase US exports of auto parts. With the creation of the WTO, and after a decade of economic stagnation, Japan-specific policies faded. Bergsten, Ito, and Noland (2001) recommended that there be "no more bashing" and that US policymakers formally bury the Japan-specific economic policies that had been followed by successive presidents for the previous 20 years.

Around the same time, attention turned to China, which has since replaced Japan as the country with the largest bilateral trade surplus with the United States. Most of the Institute research on China, like that on Japan earlier, emphasizes the role of macroeconomic factors—the exchange rate, an unbalanced growth strategy in China, and, again, the fiscal deficit in the United States. But out of concern that continued large trade imbalances could trigger a protectionist backlash, and despite the fact that China joined the WTO in 2001, Bergsten testified in March 2006 that passage of legislation imposing a surcharge on Chinese exports might be necessary if China did not allow its currency to appreciate. Bergsten's preferred course if China did not revalue the renminbi was for the Trea-

---

12. In a major reform of the old GATT rules, the WTO Dispute Settlement Understanding allowed retaliatory sanctions to be imposed by a consensus minus one member, meaning that a country in violation of the rules could no longer block enforcement measures against it. Note, however, that these constraints do not apply to foreign policy sanctions, which are generally exempted under Article XXI allowing trade restrictions for national security reasons.

sury Department to label the country a currency manipulator under existing legislation, to seek international cooperation in pressuring China from US allies and the International Monetary Fund, and, if China still did not respond, to have the administration drop opposition to and Congress expeditiously pass legislation introduced by Senators Chuck Grassley (R-IA) and Max Baucus (D-MT) to impose lesser sanctions on any country, notably China, whose currency was in "fundamental misalignment." But in testimony before the Senate Finance Committee in March 2006, Bergsten cautioned:

> *If the first four steps in the strategy fail to produce the necessary results in the near future, Congress should pass the Schumer-Graham legislation to impose an across-the-board surcharge on imports from China.* Such a step would be highly regrettable but must be envisaged as a last resort if all else fails to resolve the issue.[13] (emphasis in original)

Summary and Conclusions

As illustrated here, the use of economic leverage to achieve both foreign and commercial policy goals has been a theme of Institute research from the beginning. The emphasis in this area, as in most Institute research, has been on providing rigorous empirical analysis to illuminate the costs as well as benefits of different policy approaches, including the option of doing nothing. A continuing concern of Director Bergsten is that *not* taking action may be more costly over time if imbalances and protectionist pressures reach the breaking point than breaking some crockery with trade threats and sanctions if doing so contributes to resolving the problem.

A thorough, integrated analysis of the data across both the foreign policy and commercial policy fields remains to be done. One lesson seems to come through clearly, however. Economic threats and sanctions appear to work best when the demand is not only limited but clearly defined so that compliance can be monitored and more readily enforced. The broader and more vague the demands, such as demanding that a country "effectively enforce" its laws protecting intellectual property or worker rights, the harder it is to specify when a violation of any agreement has occurred and therefore the harder it is to make credible threats to retaliate against violations. Thus, in table 4.1, as noted above, modest foreign policy goals are more likely to be achieved than more ambitious ones. In the commercial policy area, section 301 cases were more likely to result in market opening abroad when they involved traditional border measures than when they involved less tangible and behind-the-border barriers such as services regulations or enforcement of rules protecting intellectual property. GSP

---

13. C. Fred Bergsten, The US Trade Deficit and China, Testimony before the hearing on US-China Economic Relations Revisited, Committee on Finance, United States Senate, March 29, 2006.

conditionality on worker rights also tended to work better to achieve limited changes in policy, such as an increase in the minimum wage, than to rectify broader problems, such as child labor.

References

Balassa, Bela, and Marcus Noland. 1988. *Japan in the World Economy*. Washington: Institute for International Economics.

Bayard, Thomas O., and Kimberly Ann Elliott. 1994. *Reciprocity and Retaliation in US Trade Policy*. Washington: Institute for International Economics.

Bergsten, C. Fred. 1973. *The Future of the International Economic Order: An Agenda for Research*. A Report to the Ford Foundation. Lexington, MA: Lexington Books.

Bergsten, C. Fred. 1980. *The International Economic Policy of the United States: Selected Papers of C. Fred Bergsten, 1977–79*. Lexington, MA: Lexington Books.

Bergsten, C. Fred, and William R. Cline. 1985. *The United States–Japan Economic Problem*. POLICY ANALYSES IN INTERNATIONAL ECONOMICS 13, updated in 1987. Washington: Institute for International Economics.

Bergsten, C. Fred, and Marcus Noland. 1993. *Reconcilable Differences? United States-Japan Economic Conflict*. Washington: Institute for International Economics.

Bergsten, C. Fred, Takatoshi Ito, and Marcus Noland. 2001. *No More Bashing: Building a New Japan–United States Economic Relationship*. Washington: Institute for International Economics.

Collins, Susan, and Dani Rodrik. 1991. *Eastern Europe and the Soviet Union in the World Economy*. POLICY ANALYSES IN INTERNATIONAL ECONOMICS 32. Washington: Institute for International Economics.

Destler, I. M. 2005. *American Trade Politics*, 4th ed. Washington: Institute for International Economics.

Elliott, Kimberly Ann. 1997. Will Economic Sanctions Work Against North Korea? In *Peace and Security in Northeast Asia: The Nuclear Issue and the Korean Peninsula*, ed. Young Whan Kihl and Peter Hayes. New York: M. E. Sharpe.

Elliott, Kimberly Ann. 2000. Preferences for Workers? Worker Rights and the Generalized System of Preferences. Paper prepared for Calvin College, Globalization Seminar. Grand Rapids, Michigan.

Elliott, Kimberly Ann. 2002. Analyzing the Effects of Targeted Sanctions. In *Smart Sanctions: Targeting Economic Statecraft,* ed. David Cortright and George A. Lopez. Lanham, MD: Rowman and Littlefield Publishers, Inc.

Elliott, Kimberly Ann. 2003. *Economic Leverage and the North Korean Nuclear Crisis*. International Economics Policy Brief 03-3. Washington: Institute for International Economics.

Elliott, Kimberly Ann, and Richard B. Freeman. 2003. *Can Labor Standards Improve Under Globalization?* Washington: Institute for International Economics.

Elliott, Kimberly Ann, and J. David Richardson. 1997. Determinants and Effectiveness of "Aggressively Unilateral" U.S. Trade Actions. In *The Effects of U.S. Trade Protection and Promotion Policies,* ed. Robert C. Feenstra. Chicago: University of Chicago Press for the National Bureau of Economic Research.

Hufbauer, Gary Clyde, and Barbara Oegg. 2000. Targeted Sanctions: A Policy Alternative? *Law and Policy in International Business* 32, no. 1 (Fall).

Hufbauer, Gary Clyde, and Barbara Oegg. 2003. *The Impact of Economic Sanctions on US Trade: Andrew Rose's Gravity Model*. International Economics Policy Brief 03-4. Washington: Institute for International Economics.

Hufbauer, Gary Clyde, Jeffrey J. Schott, and Kimberly Ann Elliott. 1983. *Economic Sanctions in Support of Foreign Policy Goals*. POLICY ANALYSES IN INTERNATIONAL ECONOMICS 6. Washington: Institute for International Economics.

Hufbauer, Gary Clyde, Jeffrey J. Schott, and Kimberly Ann Elliott. 1985. *Economic Sanctions Reconsidered*. Washington: Institute for International Economics.

Hufbauer, Gary Clyde, Jeffrey J. Schott, and Kimberly Ann Elliott. 1990. *Economic Sanctions Reconsidered*, 2nd ed. Washington: Institute for International Economics.

Hufbauer, Gary Clyde, Jeffrey J. Schott, and Kimberly Ann Elliott. Forthcoming. *Economic Sanctions Reconsidered*, 3rd ed. Washington: Institute for International Economics.

Hufbauer, Gary Clyde, Kimberly Ann Elliott, Tess Cyrus, and Elizabeth Ann Winston. 1997. *US Economic Sanctions: Their Impact on Trade, Jobs, and Wages*. Special Working Paper. Washington: Institute for International Economics.

Hufbauer, Gary Clyde, Jeffrey J. Schott, and Barbara Oegg. 2001. *Using Sanctions to Fight Terrorism*. International Economics Policy Brief 01-11. Washington: Institute for International Economics.

Noland, Marcus. 1997. *Chasing Phantoms: The Political Economy of USTR*. Institute for International Economics Working Paper 97-1, published in *International Organization* 51, no. 3: 365–87.

Noland, Marcus. 2000. *Avoiding the Apocalypse: The Future of the Two Koreas*. Washington: Institute for International Economics.

Noland, Marcus. 2004. *Korea after Kim Jong-il*. POLICY ANALYSES IN INTERNATIONAL ECONOMICS 71. Washington: Institute for International Economics.

Richardson, J. David. 1993. *Sizing Up US Export Disincentives*. Washington: Institute for International Economics.

Truman, Edwin M., and Peter Reuter. 2004. *Chasing Dirty Money: The Fight Against Money Laundering*. Washington: Institute for International Economics.

Tyson, Laura D'Andrea. 1992. *Who's Bashing Whom? Trade Conflict in High-Technology Industries*. Washington: Institute for International Economics.

5

Trade Adjustment Assistance: The More We Change the More It Stays the Same

HOWARD ROSEN

Throughout his career, Fred Bergsten has demonstrated deep appreciation for the domestic consequences of international economic developments and the need to address them in order to promote and sustain efforts toward international economic liberalization. In particular, he has consistently and vigorously called for assistance to workers, firms, and communities adversely affected by changes in international trade and investment.

His views on this issue are most clearly represented in a report he drafted for the Chamber of Commerce in 1973, calling for a significant expansion of the adjustment assistance program that was established in 1962 (a summary of the report is in appendix 5A).[1] The report sets out a critique of the 1962 program and proposes a series of detailed recommendations for expanding adjustment assistance.

In an unfortunate twist, the report is more relevant today than when it was written 33 years ago. This relevance is disconcerting because most of

Howard Rosen is a visiting fellow at the Institute and executive director of the Trade Adjustment Assistance Coalition, a nonprofit organization that provides assistance to workers, firms, and communities facing dislocations as a result of increased imports and shifts in investment.

1. *Economic Adjustment to Liberal Trade: A New Approach*, prepared by the Task Force on Adjustment Assistance, US Chamber of Commerce. The report was also published in Bergsten (1973, 1975a, 1975b).

the recommendations have yet to be adopted, despite the rising importance of international trade to the US economy and the extent of worker, firm, and community dislocations. It is also troublesome that despite an increase in import competition and shifts in investment—and the economic dislocations associated with those developments—the Chamber of Commerce appears to have weakened its support for assisting those adversely affected by changes in international trade and investment.

Origins of Trade Adjustment Assistance

David J. McDonald, president of the United Steelworkers from 1952 to 1965, first floated the idea of assisting workers adversely affected by imports in 1954, as part of the minority report of the Commission on Foreign Economic Policy. McDonald's idea was to provide financial assistance to workers, firms, and communities instead of imposing border measures as stipulated under the existing escape clause procedure. Under his proposal, workers would receive training and relocation assistance in addition to unemployment compensation, technical and financial assistance would be provided to firms, and communities would be given preferential treatment in competing for government contracts.

Although Senators John Kennedy, Hubert Humphrey, and Paul Douglas supported McDonald's initial idea of assisting workers hurt by imports, it did not become law until 1962, with congressional approval of the Trade Expansion Act. The inclusion of worker assistance appears to have been a factor in winning the AFL-CIO's support for the act; indeed, the United Steelworkers, the United Auto Workers, and the Electrical Workers' unions all supported passage of the act (Mitchell 1976).

In keeping with its long-standing support for trade liberalization, the business community for the most part supported the Trade Expansion Act, although some business groups opposed the adjustment assistance provisions. In its testimony before the Senate Finance Committee during hearings on the act, the National Association of Manufacturers (NAM) raised four areas of concern that have remained part of the debate over trade adjustment assistance for the last 40 years:[2]

- Adjustment assistance seems to imply that there is something wrong with the operation of the free market. . . .

- Business enterprises and their employees are continuously affected, for better or for worse, by all sorts of events beyond their control. . . .

---

2. US Congress, Senate Finance Committee, *Trade Expansion Act of 1962*, 1630–31.

We . . . oppose singling out any one of these possibilities as a basis of a special program of Federal assistance.

- It is impossible to trace out all the effects of any given tariff change. . . . Judgments as to which firms or persons would be entitled to special assistance would inevitably be arbitrary. . . .

- All experience warns that programs of this type inevitably expand and proliferate.

On January 25, 1962, in a Special Message to Congress on Foreign Trade Policy, President Kennedy wrote,

> Those injured by trade competition should not be required to bear the full brunt of the impact. Rather, the burden of economic adjustment should be borne in part by the federal government. . . . [T]here is an obligation to render assistance to those who suffer as a result of national trade policy. (Kennedy 1963)

This statement itself is not surprising—except for the context in which it was made: In 1962 imports accounted for less than 3 percent of GDP compared with over 13 percent in 2005; GDP growth was running at 6 percent in 1962 versus 3.5 percent in 2005; and the trade balance was in surplus in 1962 as opposed to a deficit of 6 percent of GDP in 2005.

The Trade Expansion Act of 1962, including the provisions establishing the adjustment assistance program, passed in the House by a vote of 298 to 125 and in the Senate by a vote of 78 to 8.

Given the economy's robust growth, the limited importance of imports to the economy, and tough eligibility criteria, no workers received assistance under the new program between 1962 and 1969.[3] This was due in large part to the strict eligibility requirement that injury be directly and demonstrably linked to a US trade concession.

In 1973, as the policy community was preparing the most far-reaching trade legislation in years, Bergsten and others began to appreciate the prospect of an increase in the importance of international trade to the US economy. Recognizing the importance of *preparing* the economy for this development, Bergsten understood that this would require major changes in trade adjustment assistance. The Chamber of Commerce established the task force on adjustment assistance to review the existing program's track record and propose detailed recommendations for reforming and expanding the effort. Bergsten served as chairman of that task force.[4]

The task force's major criticisms of the existing adjustment assistance program were (Bergsten 1973):

---

3. The 25 petitions filed during this period were all denied (Storey 1999).

4. The Chamber of Commerce did not formally adopt the task force's recommendations, although Bergsten was afforded the rare opportunity to present them to the chamber's board.

- It enables little real adjustment to economic change for dislocated workers, providing only temporary supplements to unemployment compensation.

- Its assistance commences long after dislocation has occurred, and it delivers this long-delayed assistance far too slowly.

- Its level of compensation to workers for their loss of jobs is inadequate and frequently amounts to less than half of their previous earnings.

- The program provides no help whatsoever for communities.

- There is no high-level governmental attention to the program and no central direction to it.

Based on these criticisms, the report presented a long list of detailed recommendations for expanding and improving the adjustment assistance program (see appendix 5A for the complete list).

The Trade Act of 1974 is probably the most important piece of trade legislation passed by Congress since World War II. In addition to establishing the "fast track" process, making it possible for the United States to participate in multilateral trade negotiations, the act permanently established the Office of the US Trade Representative (USTR), transformed the Tariff Commission into the International Trade Commission (ITC), and formally established the enhanced trade adjustment assistance (TAA) program.

The reinvigorated TAA program liberalized eligibility criteria and expanded the assistance package. Among the important features of the program were the following:

- The explicit link to a US trade concession was removed. The trade test was changed to acknowledge that "imports contributed importantly" to a decline in output and employment.

- Certified workers received 26 weeks of income maintenance payments, called trade readjustment allowance (TRA), set at half the average manufacturing weekly earnings.

- Workers enrolled in training were eligible to receive an additional 26 weeks of TRA payments.[5]

Two Steps Forward, One Step Back

Between 1974 and 1981, US imports grew on average 15 percent a year and from 6 percent of GDP in 1975 to 8.5 percent of GDP in 1981. Although

---

5. Affected workers were thus entitled to 26 weeks of UI, 26 weeks of TRA, and an additional 26 weeks of TRA if enrolled in training.

manufacturing employment was relatively flat over this period, its share of total employment was beginning to fall. The US economy was entering a new phase, marking both a structural shift from manufacturing to services and the increasing importance of international trade to the economy.

TAA petitions increased significantly as a result of the increase in imports and the liberalization of eligibility criteria. The number of workers covered by petitions—most of them in the auto, steel, and textile and apparel industries—soared from 73,373 in 1975 to 874,968 in 1980, with the Department of Labor (DOL) certifying, on average, two-thirds of the petitions. The number of workers receiving TRA increased tenfold—from fewer than 50,000 in 1975 to more than a half million workers in 1980. Accordingly, outlays for TAA rose from $71 million in 1975 to $1.6 billion in 1980.

The number of petitions filed, the percent certified, the number of workers receiving TRA payments, and the TAA budget all increased significantly in 1980 from their levels even the year before. These increases were only partly explained by the fact that the growth in imports that year was above average for the period (a rise of 18 percent over the previous year) or by the fact that manufacturing employment declined by 700,000 workers in 1980 and its share of total employment fell by almost one percentage point, the largest decline in 5 years.

There were allegations that the large increase in TAA certifications proved that the Carter administration was using the program for political purposes during the 1980 election. There were reports that workers employed in the auto and steel industries were receiving TRA payments during periods of temporary shutdowns, thereby reducing the need for the unions to provide supplemental short-term assistance. The large increase in petitions placed a considerable strain on the DOL, causing lengthy delays in determinations. As a result, eligible workers received lumpsum instead of weekly payments, feeding the criticism that TAA did not facilitate adjustment.

To no one's surprise, TAA was high on the Reagan administration's "hit list" of programs to be eliminated when it came into office. Despite the administration's efforts, however, the program was not eliminated but instead reformed. Among the major reforms adopted, the amount of TRA payments was reduced to the unemployment insurance (UI) level and TRA payments, capped at 52 weeks, were made conditional on enrollment in training.

The outset of the Reagan administration also witnessed a dramatic decline in the percent of workers covered by certifications. On average 32 percent of workers covered by petitions were certified for TAA between 1976 and 1979. This rate reached a program high of 81 percent in 1980, before falling to an average of 20 percent between 1981 and 1984. By the end of the 1980s, the number of workers covered by petitions, the number of workers receiving TRA payments, and the program's budget had returned to their pre-1980 levels. But TAA appeared to have lost its ability to win support for trade liberalization from the prolabor community—unions opposed liberalization and congressional Democrats' support for it also began to weaken.

The vote margin in the Senate in favor of major trade legislation has fallen from a high of 96 votes in 1984 to 30 votes in the most recent Trade Act of 2002. The decline in the House is much more pronounced—from a high of 388 votes in 1979 to only 3 votes on the Trade Act of 2002. Much of this change can be explained by the decline in Democratic support for major trade legislation. The percent of Senate Democrats voting in favor of major trade legislation fell from an average of 94 percent in the 1970s and 1980s to 37 percent in 2002. The decline in support for trade legislation is much more pronounced in the House, falling from an average of 85 percent in the 1970s and 1980s to just 12 percent in 2002 (Rosen 2003).

Critics argued that TAA was no longer meeting its initial objectives of promoting worker adjustment and winning support for trade liberalization. The prolabor community began referring to TAA as "burial insurance"—an inadequate quid pro quo for trade liberalization.[6] Despite these claims, efforts to eliminate the program were unsuccessful.

In the early 1990s, the United States embarked on one of its most ambitious trade policy initiatives to date, the North American Free Trade Agreement (NAFTA). Unlike previous multilateral agreements, NAFTA was the first regional agreement between the United States and a low-wage country, Mexico. This fact conjured up the fear of competing against cheap imports, symbolized by Ross Perot's prediction that NAFTA would create "the great sucking sound" of US jobs into Mexico.

Despite considerable opposition, Congress passed NAFTA in 1993. The Clinton administration and Congress called for a separate program for workers who lost their jobs due to increased imports from and/or shifts in production to Canada and Mexico as part of the NAFTA implementing legislation. The NAFTA–Transitional Adjustment Assistance (NAFTA-TAA) program provided almost identical assistance to that provided under the general TAA program, with the exception of some differences in the scope of coverage. In addition to workers who lost their jobs in import-competing industries, NAFTA-TAA provided assistance to workers who

---

6. It has never been clear to what extent TAA "buys" congressional support for trade liberalization. Although organized labor strongly endorsed the establishment of adjustment assistance, it would probably have supported the Trade Expansion Act of 1962 even without the program. Since then, despite modest expansions in TAA, organized labor has opposed efforts at trade liberalization in 1974, 1988, 1993, and 2002. There are no detailed studies of the link between the TAA program and support for trade liberalization; even if there were, it is not clear that members of Congress would be able or willing to admit how important TAA was in determining their vote on trade liberalization.

lost their jobs due to shifts in production. The DOL also provided assistance to some "secondary workers," people who worked for suppliers or downstream producers of firms that faced increased import competition from Canada or Mexico.[7] Given the overlap in the two programs, NAFTA-TAA created considerable confusion and arbitrary discrimination between workers.

Between 1994 and 2000 the US economy experienced robust growth, growing on average almost 4 percent annually. At the same time, US import growth averaged 11 percent per year, raising the import penetration ratio from 9.5 percent of GDP in 1994 to 12.5 percent in 2000. TAA enrollment during this period continued to be lackluster, at best. The number of workers receiving TRA payments, under both TAA and NAFTA-TAA, between 1994 and 2000 averaged 32,600 per year, a comparatively modest increase from an average of 27,100 a year between 1982 and 1993. By contrast, budget outlays for TRA payments plus training more than doubled, from an annual average of $143.8 million per year in 1982–93 to a $318.4 million per year in 1994–2000. This increase was primarily due to a significant increase in the average duration of benefits, from an average of 23.8 weeks in 1982–93 to 52.7 weeks in 1994–2000, an increase that is especially noteworthy given the economy's strong performance during the 1990s.

During the 1990s TAA provided up to 52 weeks of TRA payments, at a worker's UI level, for as long as a worker was enrolled in training.[8] The average weekly TRA payment in fiscal 2000 was a little over $200 per week, less than half the total average weekly earnings ($474) and barely a third of the average weekly earnings in manufacturing ($598). Stipends for job search and relocation assistance were also provided.

The 2002 Reforms

Despite robust economic growth, congressional support for trade liberalization continued to erode through the 1990s, and the Clinton administration was unable to win congressional approval for fast-track trade negotiating authority. Upon coming into office, the Bush administration placed a high priority on getting congressional approval for fast track. In 2001, in an effort to capitalize on the administration's efforts to obtain trade negotiating authority (by that point renamed trade promotion authority, TPA),

---

7. Under NAFTA-TAA, a downstream producer was defined as "a firm that performs additional, value-added production processes, including a firm that performs final assembly, finishing, or packaging of articles produced by another firm" (Public Law 103-182).

8. Beyond the 26 weeks of UI.

Senators Max Baucus and Jeff Bingaman introduced legislation to significantly reform and expand TAA.

The Trade Act of 2002, which Congress passed in July and President Bush signed into law in August, incorporated most of the provisions introduced by Senators Baucus and Bingaman, including the following:[9]

- TAA and NAFTA-TAA were merged—eligibility criteria and the assistance package under both programs were harmonized and unified in one program.

- Eligibility criteria were expanded to include workers who lost their jobs from plants producing inputs for goods that face significant import competition. Some of these workers were already covered under NAFTA-TAA.[10]

- Eligibility criteria were also expanded to include workers who lost their jobs due to shifts in production to countries with bilateral free trade agreements with the United States and "where there has been or is likely to be an increase in imports. . . ."[11]

- A health coverage tax credit (HCTC) was added to the assistance package, allowing eligible workers a 65 percent advanceable, refundable tax credit to offset the cost of maintaining health insurance for up to two years.

- A wage insurance program was established. Workers over 50 years old and earning less than $50,000 a year may be eligible to receive half the difference between their old and new wages, subject to a cap of $10,000, for up to two years. In order to qualify, workers must find a new full-time job and enroll in the alternative trade adjustment assistance (ATAA) program (i.e., wage insurance) within 26 weeks of job loss, and they cannot receive assistance from the TAA program, except the HCTC.

- The cap for the program's total training appropriation was increased from $110 million to $220 million.

- TRA payments were extended by 26 weeks so that workers can be enrolled in training and receive income maintenance for up to two years.

- The amounts provided for job search assistance and relocation assistance were increased to keep up with inflation.

---

9. The bill passed in the House of Representatives by a vote of 215 to 212 and in the Senate by a vote of 64 to 34.

10. The General Accounting Office (GAO 2000) estimates that this provision could add between 2,000 and 149,000 new participants each year.

11. Public Law 107-210, Section 113(a).

Table 5.1   Trade adjustment assistance program, 2000–2005

Item	2000	2001	2002	2003	2004	2005
Petitions						
Number filed	1,379	1,635	2,627	3,095	2,687	2,298
Number certified	845	1,029	1,647	1,885	1,733	1,545
Number denied	534	606	980	1,210	954	753
Percent denied	38.7	37.1	37.3	39.1	35.5	32.8
Number of workers covered						
by certifications	98,007	139,587	235,072	197,264	147,956	117,904
By denials	53,433	59,028	94,564	82,658	n.a.	38,213
Certifications						
Based on imports	845	1,029	1,594	1,158	n.a.	846
Based on shifts in productions	0	0	0	565	n.a.	611
Based on secondary workers	0	0	0	157	n.a.	88
Coverage						
New income support						
recipients	32,808	34,698	42,362	47,992	84,048	55,293
New training recipients	22,665	29,941	45,771	47,239	53,295	37,774
New on-the-job training						
recipients	304	194	292	386	n.a.	n.a.
New alternative trade						
adjustment assistance	0	0	0	42	n.a.	n.a.
Training waiver recipients	19,858	19,169	20,947	30,138	n.a.	52,336
Income support take-up rate						
(percent)	33.5	24.9	18.0	24.3	56.8	46.9

n.a. = not available

Source: US Department of Labor.

The 2002 provisions resulted in the most extensive expansion and reform of TAA since its establishment in 1962. In particular, the HCTC and ATAA programs were significant innovations in assisting unemployed workers.[12]

From 2001 to 2002 TAA petitions increased by more than 60 percent (see table 5.1). Some of this growth may have been due to the slowdown in the economy as well as increased attention to the program during the congressional debate over TPA. The number of workers receiving assistance under the program rose from approximately 35,000 in 2001 to just over

12. In the early 1990s, Canada ran a wage insurance demonstration program (Bloom et al. 1999) and in 2003 Germany instituted a wage insurance program similar to the US program.

42,000 in 2002.[13] In 2003, following implementation of the 2002 reforms, the number of petitions filed rose by 18 percent and the number of workers receiving assistance by 13 percent. Although the number of petitions filed fell in both 2004 and 2005, the number of workers receiving assistance rose 75 percent in 2004, to 84,000, before falling to 55,000 in 2005.[14]

It is particularly noteworthy that TAA participation over the last several years has been low despite the overall weak performance of the US labor market, the continued growth in the import penetration ratio, the important expansion in eligibility criteria, including shifts in production and secondary workers, and no major change in the rate of petition denials.

One of the ongoing mysteries of TAA is the low percentage of certified workers who receive assistance, known as the "take-up" rate.[15] Contrary to the expectation that this rate would be higher during times of economic slowdown, it actually fell from 33.5 percent in 2000 to 24.9 percent in 2001, before hitting a low of 18 percent in 2002. The take-up rate seems to have recovered since the implementation of the 2002 reforms, reaching almost 57 percent in 2004 before falling to about 47 percent in 2005.[16]

At less than 50,000 workers per year, the take-up rate for TAA is significantly lower than for UI.[17] Discussions with workers and state and local

---

13. Data for 2000 to 2002 are for TAA only and exclude petitions for NAFTA-TAA. For fiscal 2003, petitions are for the combined TAA. The DOL has not provided a complete set of data in order to make the appropriate comparisons.

14. The increase in the number of workers receiving assistance despite the decline in the number of petitions filed can be explained by the increase in the "take-up" rate. Similar to the increase in the number of the petitions filed after the 2002 reforms, the increase in the take-up rate may have been due to improved awareness of the program. It is unclear why the take-up rate fell in 2005.

15. One potential explanation for the low take-up rates is that workers find employment without needing assistance. Although finding a new job is a desirable outcome, studies reveal both a need for reemployment assistance and large earnings losses even with reemployment. Kletzer (2001) reports reemployment rates in the range of 60 to 65 percent for trade-displaced workers, with the average reemployed trade-displaced worker experiencing an earnings loss of 13 percent. For a sample of displaced workers in Pennsylvania, Jacobson, LaLonde, and Sullivan (1993) report average earnings losses on the order of 25 percent five to eight years following job loss. Another possible explanation is that workers are not willing to enroll in training in order to receive income support.

16. Analysis of the impact of the 2002 reforms on the TAA program are seriously handicapped by the Department of Labor's refusal to make data publicly available—except for some limited data for 2003, the DOL has not made available data concerning the wage insurance program. It has also been difficult to get data from the Internal Revenue Service about the HCTC.

17. Information from the DOL's Employment and Training Administration shows that approximately 21 million workers made an initial claim for UI in 2003. See www.doleta.gov.

Table 5.2   Federal budget outlays for trade adjustment assistance, 2000–2005 (millions of dollars)

Assistance	2000	2001	2002	2003	2004	2005
Trade readjustment allowance	275	275	286	348	513	646
Training	129	132	131	222	258	259
Total	404	407	417	570	771	905

Source: Budget of the United States (various years), Office of Management and Budget.

service providers repeatedly confirm that insufficient knowledge about TAA helps explain its low take-up rates.[18]

However, as a result of the 2002 reforms, total outlays for TAA more than doubled between 2002 and 2005 (see table 5.2). Adding shifts in production and secondary workers to the eligibility criteria expanded the potential number of workers eligible for TAA. The reforms also enlarged the package of assistance available to workers—for example, by extending the period for receiving TRA and establishing the HCTC and ATAA programs.

Programs like TAA often face the criticism that government-financed labor-market adjustment programs do not work. Although there is evidence that some government labor market adjustment programs fall short of meeting the goals of reducing the period of unemployment and the size of permanent wage losses, there is considerable literature on the effectiveness of displaced-worker adjustment programs (Kletzer and Koch 2004). The arguments in favor of government-supported assistance for trade-related dislocated workers presented in this chapter are based on the premise that every effort should be made to design and implement effective programs that deliver meaningful assistance. From a political perspective, the question is: What would be the alternative to TAA? Political pressures suggest that doing nothing is highly unlikely (Rosen 2003). So the challenge is not whether to intervene but how to design the most effective interventions.

Running in Place

Despite significant changes in the US economy over the last 30 years (including both a large increase in import penetration and outward shifts in investment), as well as adaptations to the TAA program since its establishment in 1962 (see table 5.3), assistance to workers, firms, and communities

---

18. DOL performs virtually no public outreach to inform employers, workers, and communities of the existence of TAA.

Table 5.3 Legislative history of trade adjustment assistance

Legislation	Eligibility criteria	Trade readjustment allowance (TRA)	Training outlays	Other assistance
Trade Expansion Act of 1962	Increase in imports resulting from tariff reduction or other US trade concessions	65 percent of a worker's average wage for up to 52 weeks, additional 13 weeks for workers over 60. Unemployment insurance deducted from TRA.	Vocational education and training assistance	Relocation assistance
Trade Act of 1974	Imports "contributed importantly" to decline in production and employment	26 weeks at 70 percent of average weekly wage, not to exceed average manufacturing wage; additional 26 weeks if enrolled in training	Rose from $2.7 billion in fiscal 1976 to $13.5 billion in fiscal 1979, before falling to $6 billion in fiscal 1980	Job search assistance (capped at $500) and job relocation assistance (capped at $500)
Omnibus Budget Reconciliation Act of 1981	No change	TRA payments reduced to upto 52 weeks at the unemployment insurance level, if enrolled in training	Rose from $2.4 billion in fiscal 1981 to $80 billion in fiscal 1993	Job search assistance ($800) and job relocation assistance ($800)
NAFTA Implementation Act	Imports from and/or shifts in production to Canada and/or Mexico "contributed importantly" to decline in production and employment	No change	$30 million in addition to training funds under general trade adjustment assistance program	No change
Trade Act of 2002	Imports and/or shift in production "contributed importantly" to decline in production and employment; upstream and downstream "secondary workers"	Up to 78 weeks at the unemployment insurance level, if enrolled in training	Capped at $220 million	Health coverage tax credit (65 percent), wage insurance (50-50-50), job search assistance ($1,250), and job relocation assistance ($1,500)

**Figure 5.1 Manufacturing share of total employment
and import penetration ratio, 1960–2005**

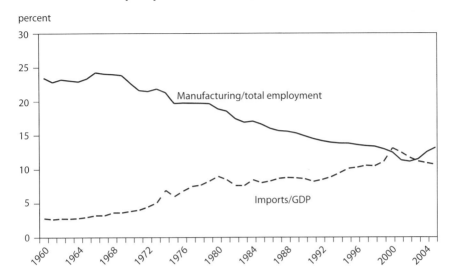

Sources: Bureau of the Census; Bureau of Labor Statistics.

adversely affected by changes in international trade and investment remains far from the program Bergsten envisioned in the report he drafted for
the US Chamber of Commerce in 1973.

From 1975 to 2005, the import penetration ratio more than doubled,
from 6 percent in 1975 to 13.2 percent in 2005 (figure 5.1). At the same
time, manufacturing employment as a share of total employment fell by
half, from close to 22 percent in 1975 to 10.7 percent in 2005. Despite these
developments, the number of workers enrolled in TAA remained fairly
consistent, except in 1979–81 when there was a spike in enrollment associated with the 1980 presidential election (figure 5.2).

With the exception of the 1979–81 period, TAA budget expenditures
were relatively flat from 1975 to the mid-1990s (figure 5.3). Two developments have contributed to the rise in expenditures over the past decade.
First, there has been an increase in the duration of benefits, correlating
with an overall increase in the duration of unemployment experienced
throughout the workforce (Kletzer and Rosen 2006). Second, the 2002 reforms, primarily the expansion of eligibility criteria, help explain the more
recent increase in expenditures.

Bergsten's 1973 report proposed that income maintenance be set at 75
percent of a worker's previous wage. But the Trade Act of 1974 set the
amount of TRA payments at 70 percent of a worker's average weekly
wage, not to exceed the national average manufacturing wage. Then in
1981 TRA payments were reduced to a worker's UI level, about half of

Figure 5.2 Participants in trade adjustment assistance, 1975–2005

thousands of workers

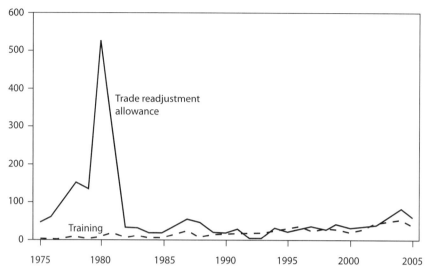

Source: Storey (1999).

Figure 5.3 Trade adjustment assistance budget expenditures, 1975–2005

millions of dollars

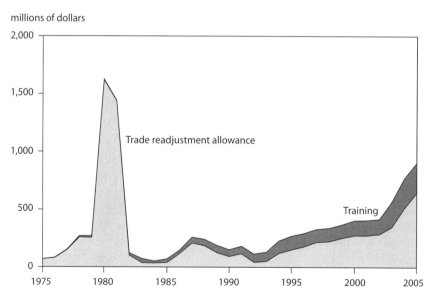

Source: Storey (1999).

average weekly earnings. Thus, despite recent increases in the program's total expenditures and in the number of workers enrolled in the program, the amount of assistance each worker receives is actually moving in the opposite direction.

Chamber of Commerce Support for TAA

Another disturbing development in the history of TAA over the last 30 years is the business community's lukewarm support of the program, of which the Chamber of Commerce is just one example. In the early years the chamber led the business community in supporting assistance to workers adversely affected by import competition.[19] This support appears to have continued through the 1990s. In a letter addressed to all members of the US Senate on October 13, 1999, R. Bruce Josten, the chamber's executive vice president for government affairs, wrote: [20]

> As for TAA, it is true that far more jobs have been created by expanded trade in the 1990s than have been lost, *but this mechanism still plays an essential role in assisting those who need retraining* [emphasis added]

By 2002, despite a significant increase in import penetration and a dramatic decline in manufacturing employment, the chamber once again led the business community, but this time in opposing the TAA reforms proposed by Senators Baucus and Bingaman. In a letter to members of Congress dated February 13, 2002, Josten wrote: [21]

> The Chamber of Commerce has traditionally been a strong advocate of TAA. Unfortunately, the Senate bill contains several troubling provisions and bears little resemblance to prior TAA legislation. . . .

The chamber opposed the inclusion of the HCTC, claiming that it would "inflate employers' health benefit spending" and "extend the government-run Medicaid program." The chamber also opposed expanding eligibility to cover secondary workers on the grounds that it would "greatly expand (theoretically to virtually incomprehensible bounds) the eligibility provisions of the TAA. . ."

But the chamber's comments on the proposed wage insurance program were the most troublesome. Josten wrote:

> We must also express our concern with the so-called "wage insurance program" which provides a government wage subsidy of up to 50 percent of the difference

---

19. Although the chamber supported adjustment assistance and later TAA, the organization did not formally endorse Bergsten's 1973 report.

20. See appendix 5B for the complete text of the letter.

21. See appendix 5C for the complete text of the letter.

between the wages received by a worker in his or her new job and the wages received at the time of separation for up to two years, capped at $10,000. While the current eligibility criteria are targeted, the program raises many administrative concerns and sets a precedent for government intervention into employer wage structures, which will likely be extended to other government programs. Though immediate costs may be modest, the ultimate outlay for the government could potentially be enormous.

Contrary to Josten's assertion, providing eligible workers with wage insurance rather than up to 104 weeks of TRA payments and training would *significantly reduce* total outlays. As Josten acknowledges, assistance under wage insurance is capped at $10,000 over two years, which is much less than the average cost of 104 weeks of TRA payments.[22]

Unfinished Business

Despite significant changes made in 2002, the current TAA program remains less ambitious than the program envisioned by the Chamber of Commerce's 1973 report (table 5.4).

For the most part, the 2002 reforms were "fighting the last battle" and did not fully address recent economic developments such as the phenomenon of international outsourcing of services. In addition, there are several technical problems that were discovered while implementing the 2002 reforms.

The following is a list of the major issues that in my view still need to be addressed.[23]

- *Service Workers.* The DOL follows a narrow interpretation of TAA eligibility, denying assistance to thousands of workers laid off from the service sector. According to the law, workers must prove that they lost their job to a firm that makes a product that is "similar or like an imported good." Although the law does not specifically restrict TAA eligibility to workers employed in manufacturing industries per se, over the years the DOL's interpretation of the law has de facto resulted in such a restriction. In response to several appeals brought before the Court of International Trade, the DOL recently partially reversed its position and announced that software workers who met the general eligibility criteria could receive assistance under TAA.

- *Industry Certification.* Petitions for TAA eligibility are currently filed according to firm-related layoffs, meaning that the DOL can receive

---

22. $260 a week for 78 weeks (104 minus 26) equals more than $20,000.

23. See Kletzer and Rosen (2005) for additional recommendations.

Table 5.4   Comparison of Chamber of Commerce's task force proposals with current trade adjustment assistance program

	1973 task force proposals	Current trade adjustment assistance program
Eligibility	Decline in output and increase in imports of a likely or directly competitive product; workers of firms whose output declined and 50 percent of whose output represented inputs to product lines that met the overall injury test; other supplying firms could become eligible if they could demonstrate that their own problems were substantially due to the effect of import competition on their customers. There would thus be a presumption that injury existed and eligibility for assistance established when rising imports and reduced output coincided	Any group of 3 or more workers laid off from a company for which an increase in imports or shift in production "contributed importantly" to a decline in output and employment. Secondary workers also covered
Income maintenance	75 percent of earnings, up to $12,000 ($53,000 adjusted for inflation) for 26 weeks. Those enrolled in training would be eligible for an additional 52 weeks	State unemployment insurance level (current national average is $262 per week, $13,624 per year)
Early retirement	Workers 55 or older would be eligible for early retirement, receiving benefits at the level otherwise available at age 62 for those retiring before 60, and at the level available at age 65 for those retiring at 60 or over, under their private pension plans and the Social Security and Medicare systems. The additional costs of such early retirement would be reimbursed to the private firm or Social Security system by the new government assistance program	No provision; workers within 2 years of being eligible for Social Security or a private pension can waive the training requirement

(table continues on next page)

Table 5.4   Comparison of Chamber of Commerce's task force proposals with current trade adjustment assistance program *(continued)*

	1973 task force proposals	Current trade adjustment assistance program
Insurance	Pay 100 percent of whatever premiums the companies had previously been paying, at the group rate prevailing before the worker was laid off, to enable all dislocated workers to maintain in full their insurance plans. Workers not covered could join the insurance plans for state government employees	65 percent health care tax credit; no provision for maintaining life insurance
Other forms of assistance	Job search and relocation assistance	Job search and relocation assistance; wage insurance
Firms	Firms are eligible for technical assistance from the government, on both a grant and reimbursable basis, if it is determined that they face a "threat of serious injury" from imports. Government guarantees should be extended—for a fee—to enable eligible firms to obtain credit from private sources	Firms eligible for technical assistance; no government loan guarantees
Farmers	No provision	Farmers who experience a 20 percent drop in the national average price from the average price of the previous 5 years can receive 50 percent of the difference; farmers must participate in technical assistance seminars
Communities	Base assistance on the program administered by the Office of Economic Adjustment in the Department of Defense	No provision

Source: Information obtained from Bergsten (1973).

multiple petitions from workers employed in the same firm as well as in the same industry. In an effort to streamline the petition process and remove arbitrary discrimination between workers from the same firm and industry, industry-wide certification should be added to the existing firm-related layoff certification. For example, if the apparel industry was found to experience a decline in employment related to an increase in imports, then any worker laid off from the industry, regardless of cause, would be immediately eligible for TAA without filing a petition.

Current eligibility criteria require documentation of an increase in imports, but for the most part these data do not exist for the service sector. Industry certification would therefore also facilitate eligibility determinations for workers displaced from service industries.

■ *Training Appropriations.* Many states exhaust the funds available for training before the end of the fiscal year. In fiscal 2003, it quickly became clear that the appropriation cap included in the Trade Act of 2002, $220 million, was insufficient to cover the potentially significant expansion in participation due to the expanded eligibility criteria. The funding cap should be raised to at least $300 million and eventually linked to an estimate of how much money would be necessary to provide adequate training to all TAA participants.

■ *Health Coverage Tax Credit (HCTC).* Under the new law, workers must receive income maintenance, which means that they must be enrolled in training in order to be eligible to receive the HCTC. This restriction severely limits the number of displaced workers who can receive the credit. A recent GAO report (GAO 2004a) found that this requirement has forced workers to enroll in training and to request income maintenance payments. Some argue that requiring a worker to undertake training promotes "real adjustment," while others contend that it results in workers getting expensive assistance that they may not need or want. One proposal would be to provide the HCTC to all TAA-certified workers for up to two years or until the worker finds a new job, regardless of enrollment in training.

Other technical issues concerning the HCTC, such as the waiting period before enrollment, require immediate attention. Some members of Congress have called for increasing the tax credit above the current 65 percent.

■ *Wage Insurance (ATAA).* The current program is restricted to workers over the age of 50. Although there is some evidence that older workers may have a harder time finding a new job, ATAA can benefit all workers. It is a cost-effective means of encouraging workers to find and take a new job, which should be the goal of any labor-market adjustment program. The age requirement for ATAA should be lowered so that all workers are eligible.

- *Self-employed.* The current program discourages workers from pursuing self-employment. One option would be to continue providing TRA payments and training to workers starting their own businesses.

- *Outreach.* Another recent GAO report (GAO 2004b) found that many workers are unaware of TAA although they are eligible to receive assistance. This may help explain why program take-up rates are so low. To date, the DOL has not performed any significant outreach to make employers and employees aware of the program. More resources need to be devoted to informing workers about TAA and other forms of assistance for dislocated workers.

- *Community Adjustment.* One of the lessons learned from large layoffs due to plant closings is that local economic and social conditions can exacerbate the adjustment process. Providing temporary financial assistance and training to workers is not enough to restore economic stability to the region.

  One possible model for assisting communities under pressure from large plant closings would be to borrow from the Defense Department's experience in facilitating economic adjustment in response to military plant closings. It is interesting to note that this recommendation was also put forth in Bergsten's 1973 report.[24]

- *Data Reporting.* Over the last decade, the DOL, under both Democratic and Republican leadership, has been extremely reluctant to release data related to TAA, despite the fact that these data, which were widely available in prior years, do not appear to include any sensitive information. Participation data are crucial to determining how well TAA is working and which aspects of the program need to be improved, eliminated, or expanded. Public access to TAA program data is therefore critical to monitoring and evaluating the program.

- *TAA for Firms.* The current program provides technical assistance to firms facing significant international competition, but the program is small—total outlays were $16 million in 2005. Better coordination with other government-sponsored technical assistance efforts (such as the Manufacturing Extension Program and small business programs) could strengthen the program.

- *TAA for Farmers.* Cash payments under this program are very small under the current program, making it unattractive to farmers. The formula for determining cash assistance needs to be modified. Enroll-

---

24. A limited Adjustment Assistance for Communities program was initiated as part of the Trade Act of 1974 (Public Law 19 USC 2371) but was later repealed.

ment in technical assistance seminars has been encouraging, although it is too early to measure their effectiveness.

TAA as a Model for Assistance to All Displaced Workers

The US labor market is remarkably fluid (Kletzer and Rosen 2006). Nearly one of every five workers is expected to lose and/or gain a job in any given year.[25] In my view the extent of this turnover highlights a number of shortcomings in the country's existing labor-market adjustment programs.

Despite calls to customize labor-market programs to the needs of individual workers, the US UI system continues to operate on the "one-size-fits-all" model. States determine the amount of assistance independent of the reason for dislocation or a worker's difficulty in finding a new job. The triggers for extended UI are ineffective, as evidenced during the last recession. Access to government-financed training is similar to playing the lottery—funds allocated to states have little connection to actual need, and the demand for training funds is always greater than the amount budgeted.[26]

Pressures on the US labor market due to technological change, productivity improvements, and international competition suggest the need for significant reform and expansion of all US labor-market adjustment programs. Unfortunately, the only area in which Congress and the president have been willing to even consider reform is TAA, and those reforms have been accepted only to achieve congressional approval of trade negotiating authority. Given the lack of political will to reform, redesign, and expand programs that would better meet the needs of US workers and their families, the second-best strategy appears to be to continue incrementally expanding TAA. Recent attention to service outsourcing further underscores the need to consider comprehensive expansion and reform. But although service outsourcing is receiving more attention than traditional trade-related job loss, concern over job losses in general is clearly broadening.[27]

The phenomenon of outsourcing once again reveals the limits of targeted labor-market adjustment programs. Many workers adversely affected by outsourcing are not eligible for TAA. This has further fueled calls to expand TAA eligibility to cover service-sector workers. But this change alone will not be sufficient to address the problem, because of difficulties associated with clearly identifying the causes of job loss—an issue that is central to TAA.

---

25. This includes voluntary and involuntary job separations.

26. See Kletzer and Rosen (2006) for a more detailed discussion of the current UI system.

27. It is difficult to determine the extent of service outsourcing as existing data do not accurately capture this activity.

Another group of workers left out of TAA's reach are those employed in export-related industries. From 2000 to 2002 US exports fell by 11 percent, most likely contributing to job losses in related industries.[28] Although export-related job losses do not occur as frequently as those from import competition and/or shifts in production, they are no less painful or disruptive to workers and their families. Despite this fact, workers who lose their jobs due to a fall in exports are not eligible for assistance under TAA.

In order to address these administrative difficulties, one option would be to precertify large groups of workers, possibly by industry, occupation, or region. Another proposal would be to provide more assistance to all displaced workers, regardless of industry or cause of dislocation.[29] Providing TAA-type assistance to all dislocated workers would also require a major reform in the country's UI system, including the UI trust fund. But as with health care and social security, building a coalition to reform the country's UI system would be difficult to do. In the meantime, incremental changes may be easier to achieve.

An immediate reform would be to provide the HCTC to all displaced workers, a measure that would reduce the discrimination between workers who specifically lost their jobs due to changes in international trade and investment and all other displaced workers. This reform would also have the added benefit of reducing the growing number of uninsured.

Another option would be to provide wage insurance for a larger set of, or even perhaps all, displaced workers. Wage insurance encourages workers to accept a new job more rapidly, thus addressing one of the criticisms of UI. It also offers targeted assistance for an important aspect of involuntary job loss, potentially lower earnings on the new job.

Cost Estimates for Reform Proposals

Table 5.5 presents cost estimates for several proposals to expand coverage of the existing TAA program.[30] The first option would be to automatically

---

28. See Kletzer (2002) for an analysis of the link between changes in exports and job loss.

29. An immediate problem with this proposal is that it would break the link between TAA and trade policy. Although in reality the relationship has been evident only in periodic legislation, some policymakers may be opposed to weakening that link.

30. Estimates of the number of potential recipients are derived from the Displaced Worker Survey, a biennial supplement to the Current Population Survey. Data for 1998–2001 were initially analyzed. Impact and cost estimates for 2001 were significantly different from those for the earlier three years because of the recession. Estimates presented in table 5.5 are based on averages for 1998–2000. The average cost for income maintenance and training under TAA is approximately $10,000 per worker per year. Because current training funds continue to be inadequate, an average of $100 per worker per month was used in these estimates. The average cost for the HCTC is approximately $200 per month per worker. Workers can receive the credit for up to 24 months.

Table 5.5   Estimated budget costs for trade adjustment assistance expansion

Item	Number of potentially eligible participants	Spending estimate (millions of dollars)				
		Trade readjustment allowance	Training	Alternative trade adjustment assistance	Health coverage tax credit	Total
Average fiscal 2004 and fiscal 2005	70,000	600	260	10	n.a.	870
Industry certification	165,000	1,900	750	100	375	3,125
All dislocated workers	575,000	7,000	2,800	900	1,400	12,100

n.a. = not available

Source: Author's calculations from the 2000 and 2002 Displaced Worker Surveys, Current Population Survey, Bureau of Labor Statistics.

certify all workers employed in industries facing significant pressure from imports and shifts in production. To receive assistance, workers would only have to prove that they worked in one of these industries. Approximately 83,000 workers would be displaced annually from the 27 industries determined to be "high import" industries.[31] In addition, GAO (2000) estimates that there is a 1:1 relationship between the number of direct trade-displaced workers and secondary workers. Thus, approximately 165,000 workers per year could be expected to receive assistance under this reform proposal. It is estimated that covering all of these workers would cost a little over $3 billion per year.

A second option would be to provide TAA to all dislocated workers. This would not only remove any remaining discrimination between workers but also significantly reduce the burden of administering a targeted program with specific eligibility criteria. Under this proposal, all dislocated workers, regardless of cause of dislocation or industry, would be eligible to receive the entire package of assistance currently provided under the TAA program.[32] There would be no petition process. As with current TAA participants, all dislocated workers enrolled in training would be eligible for up to 104 weeks of income support, the HCTC, and wage insurance (ATAA), as well as job search and relocation assistance.

---

31. See Kletzer (2001) for the "highly import-competing" classification scheme.

32. Dislocation (displacement) is commonly understood to be the involuntary loss of a job, without regard to an individual worker's performance. Dislocation does not include voluntary quits or firing due to reasonable cause.

Approximately 575,000 workers could potentially receive assistance under this proposal. Program costs for enrolling these workers in TAA, with the complete set of benefits, would be approximately $12 billion per year.[33]

Table 5.5 also presents costs estimates for providing just the HCTC and/or enrollment in wage insurance to the two groups of workers listed above. Providing the HCTC to all dislocated workers would cost approximately $1.4 billion per year. Providing wage insurance, under the current structure, to the approximately 70,000 potentially eligible workers would cost a little less than $1 billion per year.[34]

Currently, UI is primarily financed through a complicated web of federal and state payroll taxes.[35] TAA is financed through general revenues, without any dedicated revenue offset.[36] One proposal would be to dedicate custom duties to finance a further expansion of TAA. In fiscal 2005, total custom duties equaled approximately $23.4 billion, and they are projected to rise to $34 billion by the end of the decade (OMB 2006). Since funds collected from custom duties are considered general revenue, diverting them to finance these proposals would contribute to the federal budget deficit. A more limited proposal would be to dedicate only the *increase* in custom duties over the next few years to offset the costs associated with expanding adjustment programs. This would also exacerbate the fiscal deficit and might not be sufficient to cover the total costs of the more ambitious proposals outlined above. Nonetheless, it might be a good way to jump-start the reform process.[37]

Another option would be to increase the UI payroll tax, which is extremely modest—0.8 percent on the first $7,000 of taxable income. For the vast majority of workers, this amounts to only $56 per year. The ratio of taxable wages to total wages has fallen from 98 percent in 1938, when the UI trust fund was established, to 33 percent in 1997.[38] A simplistic, straight-line calculation suggests that each $1,000 increase in the taxable wage base would generate approximately $800 million in additional revenue each year.[39]

---

33. Based on these estimates, trade-related displaced workers account for 14 percent of all dislocated workers.

34. In order to be eligible to participate in ATAA, workers must find a job within 26 weeks of the job loss. Thus ATAA participants are *not* included in the number of workers potentially eligible for income maintenance, training, and the HCTC. Kletzer and Rosen estimate that removing the minimum age requirement would raise the number of potential participants to approximately 450,000, at an estimated cost of $4 billion per year.

35. The federal payroll tax accounts for approximately one-quarter of the UI trust fund.

36. Section 245 of the Trade Act of 1974 called on the Department of Treasury to establish a trust fund, financed by all custom duties, from which to finance TAA, but this trust fund has not been established.

37. It should be noted that there is long-standing opposition among economists to dedicated funding schemes.

38. The DOL has not published more recent data because of technical problems.

39. This estimate does not consider any income or substitution effects.

Obviously, a third option would be to finance these reforms the same way TAA is currently financed: through general revenues with no direct revenue offset.

Recent Congressional Activity

Several pieces of legislation aimed at further expanding and reforming TAA were introduced in the 109th Congress. Senator Baucus, Congressmen Smith and Rangel, and Congressman English introduced the most prominent bills. Table 5.6 presents a comparison of these bills.

Congressional support for TAA is not strong enough to enable both houses of Congress to pass stand-alone legislation implementing the changes outlined above. All previous changes in the program have been part of broader trade legislation—primarily legislation granting the president trade negotiating authority and implementing multilateral trade negotiations. There is no evidence that this pattern will change in the near future.

TPA expires in mid-2007. If enough progress is made on the WTO negotiations, Congress will be asked to consider implementing legislation. If not, the president will likely ask Congress to consider an extension or renewal of TPA in order to complete the negotiations. Either one of these scenarios would provide an opportunity for Congress to consider the more ambitious TAA reform agenda outlined above.

Conclusion

Bergsten has been one of the most outspoken economists acknowledging the domestic consequences of international economic developments and advocating assistance to workers, firms, and communities adversely affected by those developments.

Although the labor community initially embraced the concept of adjustment assistance as part of its support for the Trade Expansion Act of 1962, its support for trade liberalization has diminished to the point that the community currently opposes almost all efforts to further liberalize trade. Labor unions have long ceased considering TAA as a quid pro quo for trade liberalization, referring to it instead as "burial insurance." But TAA provides assistance to those facing probably the greatest financial crisis of their lives.

Support for TAA in the business community also appears to have waned. The decline in TAA's ability to "buy" support for trade liberalization and a general skepticism over government-sponsored labor-market programs have combined to undermine the business community's support for TAA. The recent apparent reversal in the Chamber of Commerce's views on TAA serves as a prime example of this phenomenon.

Table 5.6 Comparison of proposed changes in the existing trade adjustment assistance program: Bills introduced in the 109th Congress

Congressman	Eligibility criteria	Coverage	Training appropriations	Other assistance
Senator Max Baucus (D-MT) S 1309, S 365, S 1444, and S 1963	Automatic certification for any industry subject to trade remedy under antidumping, countervailing duties, or safeguards; US Department of Labor can certify any industry or occupation from which three or more petitions have been filed within six months or which Senate Finance Committee or House Ways and Means requests	Include service workers	Replace cap with formula	Lower wage insurance threshold age to 40
Representative Adam Smith (D-WA) and Representative Charles Rangel (D-NY) HR 4156	Same as Baucus	Same as Baucus	Increase cap from $220 million to $660 million by 2012	Increase health coverage tax credit to 80 percent
Representative Phil English (R-PA) HR 6208	Same as Baucus	Same as Baucus	Replace cap with formula	Increase health coverage tax credit to 75 percent; lower wage insurance threshold age to 40

Source: Information obtained from Trade Adjustment Assistance Coalition, www.taacoalition.com.

Despite significant changes in the US economy over the last 30 years, including an increase in the import penetration ratio and a decline in manufacturing employment as a share of total employment, efforts to assist workers adversely affected by increases in imports and shifts in production have remained modest at best. In fact, the current TAA program continues to fall short of the recommendations in Bergsten's report, written more than 30 years ago.

Several pieces of legislation have recently been introduced to continue the efforts begun in 2002 to reform and expand TAA. These proposals include extending eligibility criteria to cover workers who lose their jobs from service industries, establishing a process for certifying entire industries, increasing the budget cap on training expenditures, and expanding the HCTC and wage insurance programs. These proposals are likely to be considered as part of any congressional effort to extend or renew trade promotion authority in 2007.

It would seem that increased importance of international trade to the US economy and the growing concern over economic dislocations would make assistance to workers, firms, and communities facing these pressures more relevant in 2006 than it was in 1973. Yet despite public support for this kind of assistance and election year rhetoric on the need to increase worker training, policymakers have been reluctant to expand labor market adjustment programs like TAA. It remains unclear if expanding programs like TAA can save the remaining support in Congress for trade liberalization. The link between further trade liberalization and assistance to workers, firms, and communities adversely affected by increases in imports and shifts in production is likely to be tested over the coming years.

Appendix 5A

Summary of Recommendations in *Economic Adjustment to Liberal Trade: A New Approach*, **Report of the Task Force on Adjustment Assistance, US Chamber of Commerce**

1. Eligibility

   a. Workers employed continuously by a firm for more than six months should be presumed to be eligible for assistance if lay-offs affect a significant share (perhaps 5 percent) of those engaged in producing a product in which total domestic output and the output of their particular firm have declined, and imports of a likely or directly competitive product have increased, over a representative period of time (perhaps the latest twelve months for which data are available compared with either of the two previous twelve month periods, or an average of those two periods).

   b. Firms would be presumed eligible if their own output and total national output of the product declined while imports rose, and for certain forms of assistance when there was serious threat of such developments, if the product represented a substantial share of the total output of the firms, unless imports were generated by the firm itself.

   c. Firms, and workers thereof, whose output declined and 50 percent of whose output represented inputs to product lines that met this new injury test themselves would be eligible; other supplying firms could become eligible if they could demonstrate that their own problems were substantially due to the effect of import competition on their customers.

   d. Communities would automatically be eligible when a significant share (perhaps 5 percent) of their total workers has been declared eligible for the program themselves. Communities could qualify in any event by demonstrating that their own problems were substantially due to the effects of import competition.

   e. In all of these cases, there would thus be a presumption that injury existed and eligibility for assistance established when rising imports and reduced output coincided. The presumption could be challenged by the administering authority in cases where it felt that imports were not a substantial cause of the dislocation, as could often be the case for firms where poor management (including failure to anticipate competition from imports) was the crucial factor.

2. Speed of Delivery

    a. The government should actively contact firms (and trade associations) to keep abreast of their judgments concerning trade trends, and inform firms of problems that appear to be developing.

    b. Firms should actively consult the government to check out their own individual views as they make their future investments and marketing plans.

    c. The Chamber also recommends that firms be eligible for technical assistance from the government, on both a grant and reimbursable basis, when the administering authority determines in advance of the actual manifestation of any injury that they face a "threat of serious injury" from imports.

    d. The Chamber views it as the responsibility of the US firms to give the maximum possible advance notice to workers whom they will be laying off and to provide them with full information concerning the available benefits under the proposed program. It urges all firms to comply with this principle.

3. Compensation Benefits for Workers

    a. The Chamber believes that 75 percent is a reasonable level of compensation and recommends that it replace the present level (with a ceiling of an annual rate of $12,000 for any individual worker).

    b. There should thus be no alternative calculation based on the national average.

    c. For those few workers affected by imports who are not covered by unemployment insurance, the assistance program would have to finance all benefits.

    d. The Chamber thus recommends that the government assistance program pick up whatever premiums the companies had previously been paying, at the group rate prevailing before the worker was laid off, to enable all dislocated workers to maintain in full their insurance plans.

    e. In cases where workers were enrolled in local plans that could not be maintained, if they moved elsewhere to train or pursue jobs, they could join the insurance plans for employees of the government of the states to which they had moved for the temporary period in question.

4. Adjustment by Workers

    a. Workers would thus have to be actively seeking employment to receive any of the compensation benefits just described.

b. Workers would also have to apply for retraining programs to qualify them for suitable jobs, that were identifiable as available, to use the skills when they were trained for them, and join those training programs as soon as openings developed.

c. The Chamber therefore recommends that the full compensation benefits as outlined above be paid for the duration specified in the present act, except that the extension period for workers in training programs be increased from 26 to 52 weeks.

d. Workers 55 or older would be eligible to receive the same benefits. The Chamber therefore recommends that older workers be offered the alternative early retirement, with immediate commencement of benefits (at the level otherwise available at age 62 for those retiring before 60, at the level available at age 65 for those retiring at 60 or over) under their private pension plans and the Social Security and Medicare systems.

e. The additional costs of such early retirement would be reimbursed to the private firm or Social Security system by the new government assistance program.

f. To utilize effectively both the on-the-job and institutional programs, sharp improvements are needed in the federal-state employment service and computerized job-worker matching, including better statistics on "jobs available" and continuous updating of job definitions.

g. All dislocated workers should receive sharply improved counseling services to bring workers and jobs together.

h. Workers should be authorized to use private counseling services approved by the government, but under it's continuing surveillance, and be reimbursed for the costs thereof.

i. Trade-dislocated workers should be eligible to participate in all present programs, and the new counseling programs must assure that workers will be aware of all alternatives available to them.

j. The costs of such moves should be completely financed by the trade adjustment program.

k. All dislocated workers, not just heads of families, should be made eligible for relocation expenses.

5. Adjustment by Firms

a. Government guarantees should be extended—for a fee—to enable eligible firms to obtain credit from private sources.

b. The interest rate on guaranteed loans should not be tied to the borrowing rate of the Treasury.

c. Guarantees should cover 100 percent of the private loans (instead of the present 90 percent ceiling) if they were arranged sufficiently early in the adjustment process to provide high promise of saving the firm.

d. Technical assistance, including consideration of mergers and sales of a firm's assets, should be expanded through additional use of private consultants approved by the government and under its continuing surveillance, at the earliest instances made possible by the new system of early warning, the new criteria, and the improved administration.

6. Adjustment by Communities

a. Eligible communities should then receive attention of the type carried out successfully by the Office of Economic Adjustment in the Department of Defense, in recent years on behalf of the President's Inter-Agency Adjustment Committee, for over 160 large and small communities (including entire counties) impacted by changes in defense spending since 1961.

b. Financing from ongoing government programs should be available under the new trade adjustment program as well.

7. Administration

a. A single agency is needed to administer the adjustment program under tight time limits specified in the authorizing legislation.

b. The Chamber recommends the creation of a new government agency independent of all existing departments.

c. In view of the long run and continuing nature of the adjustment problem the new government agency should operate under a multi-year authorization.

d. The policy director of the agency, within the framework legislated by the Congress, should be set by a mixed board comprising the relevant government officials and representatives from the private sector.

Source: *Economic Adjustment to Liberal Trade: A New Approach*, prepared by the Task Force on Adjustment Assistance, US Chamber of Commerce. The report was also published in Bergsten (1973, 1975a, 1975b).

Appendix 5B

October 13, 1999

To All Members of the United States Senate,

The Senate is expected to consider soon bipartisan legislation to boost American trade. The U.S. Chamber of Commerce urges your support for the trade package embracing the African Growth and Opportunity Act, Caribbean Basin Initiative (CBI) enhancement, and legislation to renew the Generalized System of Preferences (GSP) and Trade Adjustment Assistance (TAA).

Passage of the Africa and Caribbean Basin bills would open markets to U.S. investors and exporters by encouraging improved intellectual property protection, reduced trade barriers, and market reforms in these countries. This legislation would encourage economic reform while offering a helping hand rather than a hand-out. For Central America and the Caribbean, a positive vote would expand on a trade initiative with a 15-year record of success. U.S. exports to the Caribbean Basin have quadrupled since CBI became law, and the American economy will continue to benefit from this dynamic trade relationship if CBI Enhancement is passed.

Renewal of GSP and TAA is also essential. Recent lapses in GSP have threatened to destabilize commercial relationships that depend on the program. The U.S. Chamber has long argued that the competitiveness of U.S. companies should not be undercut by the uncertainty that has already resulted from lapses in the GSP program. As for TAA, it is true that far more jobs have been created by expanded trade in the 1990s than have been lost, but this mechanism still plays an essential role in assisting those who need retraining.

As the world's largest business federation, representing more than three million businesses, the U.S. Chamber of Commerce believes that American workers, consumers, and businesses will benefit greatly from passage of this trade package. We urge you to cast a favorable vote.

Sincerely,

R. Bruce Josten
Executive Vice President
Government Affairs

Appendix 5C

February 13, 2002

MEMBERS OF THE UNITED STATES SENATE:

On behalf of the U.S. Chamber of Commerce, the world's largest business federation, representing over three million businesses and organizations of every size, sector and region, I am writing to urge the Senate to take prompt action on a critical priority, Trade Promotion Authority (TPA).

Last fall, the House of Representatives took the important first step of doing what should have been done years ago. The House passed TPA legislation that will help put American businesses, workers and consumers back in the game of international trade. Since TPA expired in 1994, the U.S. has sat helpless on the sidelines while other countries have woven a spider web of preferential trade agreements that put American companies at a competitive disadvantage. Of over 130 regional free trade agreements in force today, the U.S. is party to just three.

American small business owners and workers have been assured repeatedly that the Senate is listening to their pleas for action on TPA. Support for the TPA bipartisan compromise legislation is strong, yet the Senate has still failed to take up the TPA bill this Congress.

Now we are advised that TPA cannot move ahead in the Senate unless and until it is attached to separate legislation on Trade Adjustment Assistance (TAA). The Chamber of Commerce has traditionally been a strong advocate of TAA. Unfortunately, the Senate bill contains several troubling provisions and bears little resemblance to prior TAA legislation or even to the TAA reauthorization bill that passed the House of Representatives last year by an overwhelming vote of 420-3.

The TAA legislation (S. 1209) now pending before the Senate includes provisions that will inflate employers' health benefits spending beyond the current record increases, and extend the government-run Medicaid program for the poor to individuals with potentially far greater means. While individuals who participate in COBRA health coverage pay the full premium, plus a two percent administrative fee, employers' actual cost of COBRA benefits average 154 percent of the cost of their general employee pool. Further, because S. 1209 directs the 75 percent subsidy for COBRA benefits to group health plans rather than to the individual, employers face significant administrative requirements and issues, including financial liability for the individual's enrollment until funds from the U.S. Treasury are transmitted to the plan. We are greatly concerned that adding people to the Medicaid rolls when state budgets are so constrained will force program payments to providers to shrink even further, sending some of our most essential safety net providers to the breaking point. We urge you to reconsider the impact of this proposal on employers and pursue alternative health care financing arrangements that empower the individual to select a health plan that best meets his or her needs.

S. 1209 also includes a section that grants adjustment assistance to secondary workers at "downstream" producers and suppliers. Downstream producers, as defined in the bill, are firms that perform "additional value-added production processes" such as finishing or packaging of articles produced at a firm whose employees are "adversely affected." The bill defines supplier to include providers of services. These provisions greatly expand (theoretically to virtually incomprehensible bounds) the eligibility provisions of the TAA, especially in light of the change in eligibility criteria from decreases in sales or production to increases in volume of imports and shifts in production to foreign countries.

We must also express our concern with the so-called "wage insurance program" which provides a government wage subsidy of up to 50 percent of the difference between the wages received by a worker in his or her new job and the wages received at the time of separation for up to two years, capped at $10,000. While the current eligibility criteria are targeted, the program raises many administrative concerns and sets a precedent for government intervention into employer wage structures, which will likely be extended to other government programs. Though immediate costs may be modest, the ultimate outlay for the government could potentially be enormous.

Clearly, the current Senate version of TAA legislation raises serious questions that should be addressed through hearings and modifications to the bill. One alternative, which is receiving growing support, would be to pass legislation similar to the House-passed TAA bill. That would enable the Senate to act quickly on TAA while releasing the current stranglehold on TPA. We believe this approach provides the best solution with the greatest likelihood of prompt action and strong bipartisan support in the Senate.

We hope that we can count on you and your colleagues in the Senate to do the right thing by moving forward on a non-controversial version of TAA and allowing TPA to come to the floor soon for a vote.

Sincerely,

R. Bruce Josten
Executive Vice President
U.S. Chamber of Commerce

References

Bergsten, C. Fred. 1973. Economic Adjustment to Liberal Trade: A New Approach. In *Trade Reform*, Hearings before the House Ways and Means Committee, May 1973, Part 3: 894–906.

Bergsten, C. Fred. 1975a. Economic Adjustment to Liberal Trade: A New Approach. In *Toward a New International Economic Order: Selected Papers of C. Fred Bergsten, 1972–1974*. Lexington, MA: Lexington Books, D. C. Heath and Company.

Bergsten, C. Fred, ed. 1975b. *Toward a New World Trade Policy: The Maidenhead Papers*. Lexington, MA: Lexington Books, D. C. Heath and Company.

Bloom, Howard, Saul Schwartz, Susanna Lui-Gurr, with Jason Peng and Wendy Bancroft. 1999. *Testing a Re-employment Incentive for Displaced Workers: The Earnings Supplement Project*. Ottawa, Canada: Social Research and Demonstration Corporation (May).

Frank Jr., Charles R. 1977. *Foreign Trade and Domestic Aid*. Washington: Brookings Institution.

GAO (US General Accounting Office). 2000. *Trade Adjustment Assistance: Trends, Outcomes, and Management Issues in Dislocated Worker Programs*. GAO-01-59. Washington: General Accounting Office.

GAO (US General Accounting Office). 2002. *Workforce Investment Act: Better Guidance and Revised Funding Formula Would Enhance Dislocated Worker Program*. GAO-02-274. Washington: General Accounting Office.

GAO (US Government Accountability Office). 2004a. *Health Coverage Tax Credit: Simplified and More Timely Enrollment Process Could Increase Participation*. GAO-04-1029. Washington: Government Accountability Office.

GAO (US Government Accountability Office). 2004b. *Reforms Have Accelerated Training Enrollment, but Implementation Challenges Remain*. GAO-04-1012. Washington: Government Accountability Office.

Jacobson, Louis, Robert Lalonde, and Daniel Sullivan. 1993. *The Costs of Worker Dislocation*. Kalamazoo, MI: W. E. Upjohn Institute for Employment Research.

Kennedy, John F. 1963. *Public Papers of the Presidents of the United States, 1963*. Washington: Government Printing Office.

Kletzer, Lori G. 2001. *Job Loss from Imports: Measuring the Costs*. Washington: Institute for International Economics.

Kletzer, Lori G. 2002. *Imports, Exports, and Jobs: What Does Trade Mean for Employment and Job Loss?* Kalamazoo, MI: W. E. Upjohn Institute for Employment Research.

Kletzer, Lori G., and William L. Koch. 2004. International Experience with Job Training: Lessons for the U.S. In *Job Training Policy in the United States*, ed. C. O'Leary, R. Straits, and S. Wandner. Kalamazoo, MI: W. E. Upjohn Institute for Employment Research.

Kletzer, Lori G., and Howard Rosen. 2005. Easing the Adjustment Burden on US Workers. In *The United States and the World Economy: Foreign Economic Policy for the Next Decade*, ed. C. Fred Bergsten and the Institute for International Economics. Washington: Institute for International Economics.

Kletzer, Lori G., and Howard Rosen. 2006. *Reforming Unemployment Insurance for a Twenty-First Century Workforce*. Washington: Brookings Institution.

Mitchell, Daniel J. B. 1976. *Labor Issues of American International Trade and Investment*, Policy Studies in Employment and Welfare 24. Baltimore: Johns Hopkins University Press.

OMB (US Office of Management and Budget). 2006. *Budget of the United States Government, FY 2007*. Washington: Government Printing Office.

Rosen, Howard. 2001. A New Approach to Assist Trade-Affected Workers and Their Communities: The Roswell Experiment. *Journal of Law and Border Studies* 1:1.

Rosen, Howard. 2003. *Congress and Trade: End of an Era*. Washington: Center for National Policy.

Storey, James. 1999. *Trade Adjustment Assistance Programs for Dislocated Workers*. Washington: Congressional Research Service.

6

Fred Bergsten as an Early Architect of an International Regime for Foreign Direct Investment

EDWARD M. GRAHAM

Of the many achievements of C. Fred Bergsten, one of the less heralded has been his role as an early advocate of an international regime for foreign direct investment (FDI) and his related efforts to launch the process that has resulted in at least some components of such a regime. The objective of this chapter is, first, to review Bergsten's role as an early advocate of an international investment regime and, second, to examine why a full-blown international investment regime does not yet exist despite the positive role it would serve.

An international regime in this context comprises both a set of rules for governments in the conduct of international commerce and a mechanism for enforcing these rules. The World Trade Organization (WTO) is an example of such a regime for international trade. Under the WTO rules, it is recognized that nations are sovereign and therefore cannot be compelled to obey the rules. Enforcement is therefore limited to dispute settlement procedures: If a WTO member nation believes it has suffered harm due to another nation's refusal to abide by the rules, the dispute can be settled by mutual consultation or, failing that, an arbitral procedure. In the end, however, "enforcement" depends on the noncompliant nation's voluntary implementation of remedial measures recommended by arbitral "panels," with the possibility of sanctions imposed by the aggrieved party if the vio-

---

Edward M. Graham has been a senior fellow at the Institute since 1990.

lator nation refuses to implement the measures. Bergsten has advocated a "regime" for FDI—a set of rules and an enforcement mechanism—along the lines of those now embodied in the WTO.

At the outset, it is useful to outline what an international regime for FDI would comprise and what use it would serve. FDI is, technically, the equity supplied by an investor to a foreign country where the investor exercises managerial control over the investment. In practice, such an investor is most often a firm rather than an individual, and the investment most often is also a firm (a subsidiary of the parent firm). The ensemble consisting of the investor firm and its overseas subsidiaries is variously termed a multinational corporation or multinational enterprise (MNE). The investor firm is considered the parent company, the country in which it is headquartered is the home country of the MNE, and the country in which the investment is located is the host country. Most of the world's largest business enterprises can be classified as MNEs.

An international regime for investment would create a set of obligations for governments with respect to how they treat MNEs and their economically valuable output, especially the output created by their overseas subsidiaries. Thus, in this context, FDI is shorthand for various aspects of MNEs, including most importantly their operations outside their home countries. Bergsten recognized early on that an international investment regime would be more like the existing regime for international trade than the rules pertaining to international capital movements.

But his work in this area tends to be underappreciated for two reasons. First, efforts by governments to create such a regime have not met with full success, or at least not yet. Indeed, two major efforts to negotiate a fully developed international investment regime have been aborted: One at the Organization for Economic Cooperation and Development (OECD) was terminated in 1999, and another at the WTO was terminated in 2004. Second, Bergsten's role was largely played out during the 1970s, when he was a scholar at the Brookings Institution and later assistant secretary of the US Treasury, well before the two efforts just noted were undertaken. Thus his role was that of pioneer, not architect of a final product. Nonetheless, some components of an international investment regime have been successfully implemented, one of which (the WTO Agreement on Trade-Related Investment Measures, or TRIMs) achieves some, but not all, of what Bergsten laid out as the priority goals of a policy regime for FDI.

Bergsten as Early Advocate of an International Regime for Investment

By the late 1960s and early 1970s it was widely recognized that production by overseas subsidiaries of multinational corporations had become an important component of international commerce. Indeed, during those years a number of sometimes flamboyantly titled books, such as Jean-Jacques Servan-Schreiber's *Le Défi Americain (The American Challenge)*, Raymond Vernon's more scholarly *Sovereignty at Bay*, and Richard Barnett and Ronald Müller's left-leaning *Global Reach*, addressed the growing spread of multinational business activity and the problems and benefits created by this activity. These books were widely read. Moreover, there were a number of calls by prominent international economists for new multilateral rules that would apply to FDI and to government policies affecting it; notable among these were Goldberg and Kindleberger (1970), Safarian and Bell (1973), and Bergsten (1974).

Goldberg and Kindleberger (1970) focused on whether there should be a multilateral approach to curbing the monopoly powers of MNEs. Concern over the market power of MNEs was common during the 1970s, especially in developing nations. One consequence was that two intergovernmental discussions were undertaken at the United Nations Conference on Trade and Development (UNCTAD) during the 1970s (and persisted into the 1980s). One of these centered on developing a code of conduct for MNEs and the other on developing a code—largely directed toward MNEs—to address restrictive business practices. But these discussions wound up producing very little, in large measure because neither the Carter nor the Reagan administrations would agree to codes that might be binding on states or US-based firms. Indeed, the sense in the US government was that any measures resulting from these discussions would likely be discriminatory against US-based firms because, at that time, the majority of MNEs were based in the United States.

Moreover, the US position was that any international rules that pertained to MNEs and were binding on governments should be centered on a principle of nondiscrimination. This principle, sometimes called the principle of national treatment for foreign-owned enterprises, can be succinctly stated as follows: Government measures should in general not act to discriminate against foreign-owned business activity, subject to a limited and specific set of exceptions (e.g., measures undertaken to protect national security).

Whereas the Goldberg and Kindleberger proposal was for an international regime that would restrict the power of the MNE, both the Safarian and Bell and the Bergsten proposals called for new rules that would restrict government measures to promote the establishment of MNE activities in the government's jurisdiction, especially if such measures might cause harm to other nations. Thus, these proposals were more along the lines of the existing GATT rules pertaining to trade than was the Goldberg and Kindleberger proposal. Safarian and Bell believed that measures such as government tax incentives granted to an MNE in exchange for the enterprise locating plants or other economic activity in the jurisdiction of the government might have distorting effects on domestic and international commerce. They also worried that measures such as value-added requirements imposed by governments on local operations, or requirements that a certain amount or percent of output be exported, would be tantamount to import restrictions or export subsidies.

Bergsten, employing an approach he would use to address other issues as well as FDI, went further, arguing that proliferation of such measures was leading the world toward investment wars that would not be unlike the devastating trade wars of the 1930s. He was not the only person raising such fears. John Dunning (1974), who arguably was the "dean" of scholars of FDI and the activities of MNEs,[1] worried along similar lines, as did a student of his, David Robertson (1975). Although the concerns of Bergsten and Dunning in retrospect were exaggerated in the sense that no investment wars came about, they were nonetheless justifiable. Studies done for the US Treasury Department during the late 1970s indicated that measures such as investment incentives (including tax incentives) or performance requirements (including most especially value-added, or "local-content," requirements and export requirements) were proliferating and that this proliferation could generate welfare-reducing economic distortions. Thus, Bergsten was right to believe that negotiated rules to restrict the use of such measures were warranted.[2]

Unlike other analysts who had written on these issues, Bergsten was soon in a position actually to do something about them. He became assistant secretary for international affairs at the US Treasury in 1977, where one agenda he pursued was an effort to launch a US government initiative to negotiate and implement rules limiting the use of investment incentives and performance requirements. It was an uphill battle. Other US government agencies involved in international economic affairs were not convinced that negotiating such rules should be a US priority, and it is safe to say that during his first three years in the position, one of the only things that Bergsten was able to do was to keep the issue alive.[3] However, during his final year, some progress was made.

The Task Force on International Direct Investment

In the fall of 1979 a Task Force on International Direct Investment was formed under the aegis of the Joint Development Committee of the Inter-

---

1. Dunning (1974) is considered to be the first major, seminal work on these issues.

2. This view was most strongly stated in a book that Bergsten coauthored with Thomas Horst and Theodore Moran (Bergsten, Horst, and Moran 1978), written prior to but published more than two years after Bergsten became assistant secretary for international affairs at the US Treasury Department.

3. After leaving the Treasury Department, in 1981 Bergsten talked about these issues and the progress made on them (but not about the uphill nature of the battle) in testimony before the US Senate Committee on Foreign Relations, Subcommittee on International Economic Policy, reprinted as Bergsten (1983).

national Monetary Fund and the World Bank. As official representative of the United States, Bergsten chaired the task force, which included representatives of the governments of Australia, Brazil, France, Germany, Mexico, and the United Kingdom. The mission of this task force was to determine whether any new rules pertaining to FDI would serve global economic interests and, if so, the nature of those rules and in what institution they would be sited. Bergsten was able to convince the other representatives that the task force should seriously investigate the desirability of rules to restrict governments from either imposing performance requirements or granting investment incentives or other subsidy-like measures. He did not, however, convince all the members of the task force that they should *endorse* such rules.

A senior member of the World Bank staff, Dale Weigel, was assigned to work more or less full time on the task force and to draft its final report. I participated in the project as a US Treasury Department economist. The task force representatives, all of whom were quite senior representatives of their respective governments,[4] eventually gave Weigel and me considerable latitude to explore the economic case for and against rules of the sort proposed by Bergsten and to identify the political factors that influence bringing such rules to fruition. We commissioned studies of these issues by John Dunning and Steven Guisinger, both acknowledged experts in the field of MNEs and FDI. The Australian representative to the task force, David Robertson, had been an academic researcher prior to his government service and was also a recognized expert in this field. Consequently, he effectively became a consultant to the task force, as well as a member of it, and helped draft the final report.

This team of experts soon became convinced that there were different cases to be made for international rules to restrict investment incentives and to restrict performance requirements.

First, for investment incentives, it quickly became clear that the economic case against these incentives was not unequivocal. The counter case based on empirical evidence accumulated during the 1970s indicated that FDI, via the local subsidiaries of MNEs, can create positive externalities in host nations.[5] These externalities (also called positive spillovers into the local economy) create a positive economic rationale for subsidies to the activity that generates them. But the evidence for such externalities was ambiguous—while some studies suggested that they do exist, others did not.

---

4. The representative of Mexico, Bernardo Sepúlveda, for example, would become finance minister of that country a few years later, and the French representative, Michel Camdessus, later became managing director of the International Monetary Fund.

5. The relevant literature, including studies conducted since the 1970s, is reviewed in Lipsey and Sjöholm (2005). The positive case for public subsidies to FDI to stimulate externalities is laid out in some detail in Blalock and Gertler (2005).

The consultants to the task force thus were asked to determine if there was evidence that investment incentives to MNEs increased their activity in the countries in which they operated. They found that investment incentives did not seem to cause direct investors to undertake more activity internationally than they would have in the absence of the incentives. However, there was considerable evidence that investment incentives could affect the specific location of a direct investment. For example, if an MNE based outside the United States decided to create a US subsidiary, the availability of investment incentives from particular states might influence the choice of location for the subsidiary. Thus it could be worthwhile for state governments to offer incentives, although for all states to do so would be a negative-sum game,[6] resulting in a "bidding war" that would improve the lot of the MNE's shareholders at the expense of taxpayers in the states offering the subsidies.[7]

The above considerations would also hold for nations competing for investments by MNEs. Indeed, the consultants found that investment incentives were quite commonly offered to MNEs by state or provincial governments as well as by national governments. A clear implication was that any rules restricting the use of government incentives would be effective only if they applied to subnational as well as national governments.

Alas, enthusiasm for such rules among government officials and political leaders, including most members of the task force, was meager.[8] Rather, the view was that national and subnational governments should retain the option of granting investment incentives. Behind this view was considerable skepticism that, if rules were established, they would be followed. It would be difficult to sanction governments that offered incentives in violation of the rules. (It must be remembered that these discussions took place in 1979, when the dispute settlement procedures in the GATT were quite weak.) Moreover, for obvious reasons, MNEs themselves had no enthusiasm for international rules to limit investment incentives.

Thus, whatever the substantive case for international rules to limit investment incentives, there simply was no constituency in favor of such rules—and there were constituencies against them. Accordingly, it is no surprise that the task force members could not agree to language in the final report recommending new rules to curb investment incentives. They did agree, however, that incentives represented bad policy and that further study of the issue was needed. At its September 1980 meeting, the task force remanded the issue to the World Bank Executive Board, which

---

6. States sought to attract FDI during the 1970s and, indeed, state officials seemed to understand that positive externalities could be generated by such investment, although it is doubtful that many of these officials could have articulated this understanding.

7. This outcome is easily modeled using the "prisoner's dilemma" from game theory.

8. This sentiment was held particularly strongly among the US state government officials that we contacted.

took no action. Indeed, although there have since been a number of agreements or rules established that pertain to international investment at both multilateral and regional levels, they do not cover investment incentives (with the exception of TRIMs).[9]

Rules to limit performance requirements were a different matter, on which action would prove feasible. The difference reflects an important economic reality. In the case of investment incentives, subsidies can create net costs for the global economy, but these are borne by the community (nation or regional unit) that grants the subsidy. Thus the only constituency that might be expected to favor international rules to limit the subsidy should be the community that grants them. If there is no real enthusiasm among subsidy-granting communities for such rules, the negotiation of such rules is a nonstarter. But in the case of performance requirements (or at least some of them), the costs they generate can extend beyond the community served by the government entity imposing the requirements. Thus constituencies may favor rules to limit them.

The typical example is a value-added (or local content) requirement, which obligates an MNE subsidiary to substitute locally produced inputs for imported ones. The locally produced inputs might be supplied internally by the subsidiary or, in most cases, by locally owned, unrelated suppliers. The effect of the requirement is equivalent to the combination of a protective tariff and a production subsidy (Graham and Krugman 1990). There might be some positive rationale for such a performance requirement from the point of view of the host government, such as appropriation of some of the MNE's excess return. (MNEs necessarily operate in imperfect markets that enable excess returns.) However, even if there is a potential gain to be had from such an appropriation, if all nations seek such gain, the collective result will be distortions that are globally welfare reducing. Moreover, rational calculation of potential national gain in practice does not seem to be the main motivation behind value-added requirements; rather, the motivation is of the standard mercantilist sort—that is, to reduce imports and substitute local production, even if there is a net cost to the economy of doing so. The main international objection to such a performance requirement is also typically mercantilist: Other nations oppose local-content requirements because they lose exports, not because they expect a global welfare loss. Nevertheless, economic analysis indicates that there usually is an overall welfare loss, and the countries whose mercantilist thinking leads them to believe that there are net losses form a potential constituency to support international rules to restrict value-added requirements.

---

9. The most comprehensive investment agreement currently in place is that of chapter 11 of the North American Free Trade Agreement, and trade policy experts believe that this chapter might serve as a model for a multilateral agreement. But chapter 11 does not provide disciplines on investment incentives and, to the best of my knowledge, no bilateral investment treaty or agreement does. The only such disciplines in existence are in the WTO's Agreement on TRIMs but, as discussed later in the chapter, they are very limited in scope.

Moreover, MNEs themselves can be expected to oppose value-added requirements; from their point of view, unlike an investment incentive, which grants them a subsidy, a value-added requirement effectively imposes a tax.[10]

Other types of performance requirements raise issues similar to those raised by value-added requirements. For example, host countries have imposed export performance requirements on local MNE subsidiaries that call for the export of a specified amount of the subsidiary's output. Such a requirement is tantamount to an export subsidy, except that the subsidy is financed by the MNE itself rather than by the host government. Host governments favor these requirements for reasons that are largely mercantilistic. As is the case for value-added requirements, export performance requirements are all of the following: (a) collectively world welfare reducing; (b) likely to be opposed by countries other than that which imposes the requirement, which it likely does for mercantilist reasons; and (c) opposed by the MNEs themselves.

Thus in considering the feasibility of a negotiated set of rules to regulate or eliminate performance requirements, it is important to recognize that two potentially strong constituencies would favor such rules: governments of nations that are adversely affected by these requirements (even if in the mercantilist sense) and MNEs.

As with investment incentives, the final report of the task force indicated that performance requirements can have adverse consequences but did not recommend what action, if any, might remedy them. Rather, again, the report remanded the issue to the executive board of World Bank. However, unlike the case of investment incentives, the issue did not stop there. In 1981, at the behest of the Treasury Department, the US government, represented by the US trade representative (USTR), formally introduced the subject of possible trade-distorting effects of government measures on FDI at a meeting of the GATT Consultative Group of 18. In doing so, government representatives drew on the task force's finding that performance requirements can have trade-distorting effects and recommended that the GATT Secretariat compile a list of investment measures that might distort trade, with a focus on performance requirements. Developing countries at the meeting did not support this recommendation, and while representatives of the European Community and Japan supported the recommendation in principle, they also indicated that the GATT Secretariat had higher priorities at the time than the recommended compilation. Consequently, the GATT Secretariat did not act on the recommendation. That would change, however, the following year.

---

10. Why then have MNEs often accepted value-added requirements imposed by host nations without raising objections? As Bergsten (1974) himself noted, most often value-added or other performance requirements are imposed as a condition for receipt of investment incentives. Clearly then, in many instances, the firms have calculated that the value of the incentives exceeds the cost of the performance requirements.

Action in the GATT

In 1982, the United States launched a complaint in the GATT against the government of Canada, arguing that performance requirements imposed by the Canadian Foreign Investment Review Agency (FIRA, an agency that no longer exists) on Canadian subsidiaries of US firms were in violation of a number of GATT obligations. A GATT panel subsequently ruled that one type of performance requirement (value-added or local-content requirement) was indeed in violation of a GATT article (on national treatment) but other types were not. The panel muddied the water by noting that a value-added requirement might not be in violation of the GATT if it were used "to promote economic development" in conformity with GATT Article XVIII, section C.

The United States then argued for the next three years that its 1981 proposal should be accepted and urged the GATT to examine an enlarged set of investment-related measures for possible trade distortions. In 1986, these efforts bore fruit in the preparatory meetings for the launching of what was to become known as the Uruguay Round of multilateral trade negotiations. The ministerial declaration of the meeting at which this round was launched included language establishing a Negotiating Group on TRIMs. This group was to consider the possible trade-distorting effects of such measures, to identify violations of existing GATT articles that might be created by such measures, and to negotiate "further provisions that may be necessary to avoid such adverse effects on trade."[11]

During the negotiations that ensued (and lasted for nine years), the United States enumerated eight types of performance requirements that might have trade-distorting effects: (1) value-added or local-content requirements, (2) export performance requirements, (3) local manufacturing requirements, (4) trade balancing requirements, (5) production mandates, (6) mandatory technology transfer, (7) foreign exchange balancing requirements, and (8) limits on equity participation and remittances. In the end, the negotiating group agreed that items (1), (4), and (7) were both trade distorting and in violation of existing GATT articles but could not agree that this was true of any of the remaining items. The negotiating group went on to produce the TRIMs agreement, which effectively banned value-added or local-content requirements, trade balancing requirements, and foreign exchange balancing requirements, and required GATT contracting parties (now known as WTO member countries) first to list such requirements as they might have in place and subsequently to phase them out. Developed countries were given two years to phase out these requirements, and developing countries were given five years.

---

11. Quoted wording is from the Ministerial Declaration of the Punta del Este meeting of the GATT establishing the Uruguay Round, as quoted in Graham and Krugman (1990).

The United States also succeeded in persuading the Uruguay Round Negotiating Group on Subsidies and Countervailing Measures to consider as "actionable" subsidies to direct investment (i.e., investment incentives) that are granted on condition that the recipient agree to performance requirements of types (1), (4), or (7).

Thus, the Uruguay Round eventually brought about implementation of a partial set of rules to limit government measures directed at MNEs that might have trade-distorting effects, as Fred Bergsten had proposed early on and toward which he worked very hard during his tenure as assistant secretary of the US Treasury. But this implementation hardly represented a towering victory for Bergsten. Rather, in the words of trade policy expert Jeffrey Schott, "the Uruguay Round accord on TRIMs represents only a small first step toward international discipline on the nexus of trade and investment issues" (Schott 1994, 113). However, Bergsten did succeed in planting a seed that sprouted and grew at least into a sapling.

Bergsten and the Early Days of the Committee on Foreign Investment in the United States

As assistant secretary of the Treasury from early 1977 to early 1981, Fred Bergsten acted as working chairman of the Committee on Foreign Investment in the United States (CFIUS). The secretary of the Treasury formally chairs the CFIUS, but in practice the working chairman oversees most of the committee's activity. The CFIUS was established in 1975, during the administration of Gerald Ford, in response to growing concern about foreign investment, especially from OPEC nations, in the United States. Original members of the committee included the secretaries of the Treasury (chair), Commerce, Defense, and State departments, the US attorney general, the chairman of the Council of Economic Advisers, the USTR, and the director of the Office of Management and Budget. Later, representatives of other federal agencies (most recently, the secretary of Homeland Defense) were added. In practice, the cabinet and subcabinet officers themselves attend CFIUS meetings only under exceptional circumstances (e.g., to recommend a block of a foreign takeover of a US firm); instead, their designated representatives attend on their behalf.

The mission of the CFIUS, according to the executive order that established it, was to monitor the impact of foreign investment in the United States and to coordinate the implementation of policy on such investment. In particular, the CFIUS was to (1) analyze trends and significant developments in foreign investment in the United States; (2) provide guidance on arrangements with foreign governments with respect to any investment these governments might hold in the United States; (3) review particular investments in the United States that, in the judgment of the committee, might have major implications for US national interests; and (4) consider proposals for new legislation or regulation relating to foreign investment in the United States, as necessary. However, the Ford administration left office before the CFIUS had much time to function or to define its role beyond the parameters established by the executive order. Thus defining the specifics of the role of the CFIUS fell largely to the incoming Carter administration.

In 1977, shortly after the Carter administration took office, the Economic Policy Group, the administration's top officials involved in setting economic policy, conducted a formal review of US policy on inward investment. The group subsequently did something that had never been done before: It issued a formal statement articulating US policy concerning inward investment. The statement included the following language:

> The fundamental policy of the U.S. Government toward international investment is to neither promote nor discourage inward or outward flows or activities.... The Government therefore should normally avoid measures that would give special incentives or disincentives to investment flows or activities and should normally not intervene in the activities of individual companies regarding international investment. Whenever such measures are under consideration, the burden of proof is on those advocating intervention to demonstrate that it would be beneficial to the national interest.... [The Government] should not discriminate against established firms on the basis of nationality or deprive such firms of their rights under international law.[12]

In other words, the US government should grant national treatment to US subsidiaries of foreign-owned firms and should grant to both these subsidiaries and their parent organizations all protections afforded to international investors under international law. Such protections include an assurance that investments will not be nationalized or subjected to measures tantamount to nationalization, except for a public purpose (e.g., national security), in which case nationalization will be executed under due process of law and subject to rapid and full compensation. National treatment and rights accorded under international law should form the core principles of an international regime for FDI, and the Economic Policy Group's statement in effect expressed the United States' willingness to abide by these core principles.

During most of Bergsten's tenure as working chairman of the CFIUS, the committee was not highly active, in part because the major reasons for its creation—OPEC investment in the United States and fear and suspicion of this investment among members of Congress—diminished after 1976. But in 1979 the committee, under Bergsten's leadership, did act to address concerns about the acquisition of American Motors by the French firm Renault. Because Renault was partly owned by the French government, the committee worried that, as a subsidiary of Renault, American Motors might somehow be used by the French government to advance

---

12. Reprinted in Bergsten (1983).

French national objectives of a noneconomic nature. That concern was mitigated when the CFIUS sought and received an assurance from the French government that Renault would operate American Motors purely as a commercial entity.[13] This case established the precedent for the CFIUS to undertake a formal review, if the chairman deemed it advisable, of any investment in the United States in which a foreign government had a stake. If the CFIUS determined that the investment might have a major adverse implication for US national interests, the committee would convey its finding to the Economic Policy Group and the National Security Council; then if these bodies concurred, the relevant government would be asked either to refrain from making the investment or to modify it to make it acceptable to the CFIUS.

In the wake of the 1979 oil price increase, there was renewed suspicion and fear of OPEC investment in the United States and, with it, calls from Congress for a more activist role for the CFIUS, as well as new powers congressionally granted to the president to regulate foreign investment in the United States. In official testimony before the House of Representatives Subcommittee on Commerce, Consumer, and Monetary Affairs in late July of that year, Bergsten argued against new legislative authority, claiming that it could discourage foreign investment in the United States. He argued that such investment, and international investment on the whole, "will generally result in the most efficient allocation of economic resources if it is allowed to flow according to market forces" (Bergsten 1979). He further argued that there was no basis for concluding that FDI harmed US national interests.

No legislation to create a more activist CFIUS was passed at that time. However, nine years later, in the wake of renewed fears of FDI (from Japan rather than OPEC), new legislation was passed, the Exon-Florio Amendment to the Omnibus Trade and Competitiveness Act of 1988. This amendment, later made part of permanent law, authorized the president to block foreign acquisition of a US firm if the president determined that the acquisition "impaired or threatened to impair" US national security. The president subsequently delegated to the CFIUS implementation of so-called Exon-Florio reviews of acquisitions of US firms by foreign investors. Under current procedure, the CFIUS need not fully review every such acquisition but may review any acquisition. A 1992 amendment to the law makes such reviews mandatory if the foreign investor is a foreign government (or an entity under the control of a foreign government) and if the CFIUS determines in a preliminary review that there may be a connection between the acquisition and US national security. The outcome of a review is that the CFIUS recommends to the president whether or not to

---

13. This matter is recalled in C. Fred Bergsten, "Avoiding Another Dubai," *The Washington Post*, February 26, 2006.

block a particular acquisition; to date, the president has followed the CFIUS recommendations.

In practice, since the passage of the Exon-Florio amendment, the CFIUS has recommended blocking only one foreign acquisition of a US firm for national security reasons. However, about a dozen proposed acquisitions have been cancelled because of an investor's expectation that the acquisition likely would be blocked (for details, see Graham and Marchick 2006). The small number (13 or 14) of formal or de facto blocks by the CFIUS must be compared with the number of successful foreign acquisitions of US firms, which total more than 3,000 since enactment of the Exon-Florio authority.

At the time of this writing, bills are pending in both the US Senate and the House of Representatives to modify the Exon-Florio authority to make it more likely that any acquisition of a US firm by a foreign investor will be subject to an Exon-Florio review or for the CFIUS to recommend to block the acquisition. Fervor in the Congress to "tighten" Exon-Florio was fomented first by the (failed) effort of the China National Offshore Oil Corporation (CNOOC) to acquire the US oil firm Unocal and subsequently by the acquisition of US port operations (via takeover of a British firm that operated certain US port facilities) by Dubai Ports World, a firm under the control of the Emir of Dubai. However, it is not clear that either bill will actually be acted upon.

Since the furor in 2006 over Dubai Ports World, a number of other countries—most prominently, China and Russia (for details, see Graham and Marchick 2006)—have enacted or are considering measures that could restrict FDI activity. These developments come after 15 years during which numerous countries took significant steps to liberalize law and policy for foreign investment in their economies.[14] Given that this trend toward liberalization might be reversing itself, it is worth reconsidering whether Bergsten was correct in calling for some sort of international rules pertaining to government treatment and regulation of international investment and MNEs.

Does the Case for an International Regime for Investment Still Stand?

In order to answer this question in the affirmative, we should be able to demonstrate two things: (1) FDI yields a net gain for the global economy,

---

14. Developments in international law and policy pertaining to FDI have been documented since 1991 in the *World Investment Report*, published annually by the United Nations Conference on Trade and Development (UNCTAD); since that year, about 80 percent of the reported changes have been in the direction of liberalization of treatment for foreign investors.

and (2) international rules pertaining to such investment would enable even greater gains. While it is not possible to unequivocally demonstrate either of these conclusions, I would argue that both are likely true.

The first point—that FDI yields a net gain for the global economy—is easier to argue. Operations enabled by FDI generate positive externalities that can be empirically measured, and although empirical evidence is mixed as to whether these externalities actually exist, recent evidence tilts in their favor. Moreover, if FDI does generate gains of this sort, it should also raise the overall rate of growth of the economy (through, for example, more rapid transfer and diffusion of technology). A number of studies attempt to measure the effect of FDI on growth, and all but one concludes that FDI is positively and robustly associated with growth. Among these are results reported by Blomström, Lipsey, and Zejan (1994), who find that FDI positively affects growth if and only if a national wealth threshold is reached. By their finding, FDI does not positively affect growth if a country is quite poor. Balasubramanyam, Salisu, and Sapsford (1996) also find a positive relationship but only if the country is open to international trade. This result is not inconsistent with Blomström, Lipsey, and Zejan because, in recent history, poorer countries have tended to be less open to trade than richer countries. Borzenstein, de Gregorio, and Lee (1998) also find a positive relationship but only if a country meets a threshold level of education. Again, this finding is generally consistent with the earlier results, because poorer countries tend to have less well-educated populations than do richer ones. It should be noted, however, that Blomström, Lipsey, and Zejan did consider education as a conditioning variable but found it not to be significant. Alfaro et al. (2003) again find a positive relationship but only in countries with well-developed financial markets; this is (roughly) consistent with earlier findings, because richer countries have better developed financial markets than do poorer ones. Finally Blonigen and Wang (2005) find, using a later and larger dataset than Blomström, Lipsey, and Zejan, that FDI affects growth more strongly in developing (poorer) countries than in rich ones. This lattermost finding is of course not consistent with the other and earlier ones and might be explained by a number of factors, including that the data is more recent and hence affected strongly by growth in China. Moreover, it is possible that because a majority of FDI in rich countries in recent years has been created by cross border merger and acquisition, as opposed to "greenfield" FDI, the former type of FDI simply generates less growth than the latter.[15] By contrast, the majority of FDI in certain developing countries, most especially China, has been of the "greenfield" variety. Kumar and Pradhan (2005) use instead of an ordinary

---

15. "Greenfield" FDI occurs when the foreign investor creates an affiliate, which then creates plant and equipment, as opposed to the foreign investor acquiring an extant, ongoing operation from local investors.

least squares (OLS) estimator an "Arellano-Bond" (modified General Method of Moments) estimator to test whether FDI in south Asia has had a positive impact on growth. They conclude in the affirmative. This study is notable because an Arellano-Bond estimator is now accepted as a more appropriate tool with which to analyze panel data than the more commonly used OLS estimator.

In addition to studies based on panel data, there have been studies of individual nations based on time series. We note an unpublished study in particular (Dayal-Gulati and Husain 2001) focusing on China. Comparisons of regions within China reveal that, in the years subsequent to China becoming more open to FDI in 2001, there was an acceleration of economic growth in those regions that received significant amounts of FDI. By contrast, this acceleration in economic growth was not observed in those regions where such FDI did flow. The findings thus are consistent with a claim that FDI does accelerate economic growth. Carkovic and Levine's analysis (2005), which includes a critical review of other studies, does not support this claim. Carkovic and Levine's analysis indicates that there is a positive relationship between FDI and growth but that it is not robust. The authors also find that FDI is positively and robustly associated with growth unless a variable for trade openness is included in the specification, in which case the association between FDI and growth becomes nonrobust. In a commentary on Carkovic and Levine, Melitz (2005) concludes that their finding should be reinterpreted as follows: Trade openness and FDI jointly are positively and robustly associated with growth.

As with the empirical evidence regarding FDI and growth, there is an empirical literature on FDI and externalities, and the reported results are mixed. A recent survey of the rather extensive literature (Lipsey and Sjöholm 2005), however, notes a curious fact: Whereas older studies tend both to support and not support the hypothesis that FDI does create positive externalities, newer studies more consistently find in favor of this hypothesis than do the older ones. The authors conclude that one of two possibilities is correct: Either, in recent times, the externalities themselves are more prevalent and perhaps stronger than in earlier times, or methodologies have improved such that externalities that have long existed but once escaped detection are now more readily discerned than in the past. Either way, the recent evidence does seem to point towards the likely existence of positive, and mostly technology-based, externalities being generated by FDI.

Despite the fact that the studies just cited do not unequivocally support that FDI creates gains to the host or world economies, the evidence is quite strong that such gains do occur. Moreover, there is no empirical evidence whatsoever that FDI does harm. Thus, I would argue that the case for FDI is quite strong. But is this case supportive of a call for new international rules on investment? Would such rules increase gains from FDI?

In the absence of such rules, it is difficult to answer this last question. The closest thing to a comprehensive set of such rules is chapter 11 of the North American Free Trade Agreement (NAFTA). With respect to this agreement, Hufbauer and Schott (2005, 30) argue that, since NAFTA came into effect, Mexico has realized "an FDI boom," which presumably has benefited Mexico, although the authors do not attempt to quantify this benefit. But, assuming that Mexico does benefit from accepting the rules on investment of NAFTA chapter 11, would similar benefits be realized by other countries from a multilateral version of these rules? In the absence of experience, it is difficult to answer "yes"—but equally or more difficult to claim that the answer is "no."

Subject to such qualification as offered in the previous paragraph, let me nonetheless offer an opinion with respect to this last question: Bergsten and others noted earlier in this chapter, who called for such rules more than 30 years ago, were right then and remain right now. Government measures certainly can have the effect of diminishing the gains from investment or creating "beggar thy neighbor" outcomes whereby some nations are advantaged by investment at the expense of others and to the likely detriment of global economic welfare.

Having said this, my own view is that Bergsten might only have gotten the priorities wrong when he stressed as a first priority to develop rules to regulate investment incentives and performance requirements. He was right in stressing that certain government measures can lead to distortions that reduce global economic welfare. But surely the worst such distortions are not caused by incentives and performance requirements but rather by measures that discourage FDI altogether. Thus NAFTA provides for rules ensuring the right of entry of multinational firms to the three NAFTA nations (subject to a number of reservations) and for postestablishment national treatment of operations of foreign investors. And the same priority was at the heart of the (failed) Multilateral Agreement on Investment. Moreover, as recognized by practitioners of trade policy and trade negotiations, international rules on any aspect of commerce are useful only if they are enforceable; thus NAFTA created a dispute settlement procedure meant to increase enforceability of the chapter 11 rules, and such a procedure would be an important element of any effective multilateral rules on investment.

But maybe the big question is not whether international rules pertaining to investment would be a good idea, but rather will such rules ever come into being? At the moment, the picture is not encouraging. In the Cancun meeting of the WTO, the "trade and investment" negotiations were taken off the table. Thus, whatever the case for such rules, they are unlikely to come about in the near future. History will judge whether this proves to be a major or simply a minor failing of whatever comes out of the Doha Round. But, in any event, Bergsten surely was right to begin; a full set of these rules does need to come into existence.

References

Alfaro, L., C. Areendam, S. Kalemil-Ozcan, and S. Selin. 1999. FDI and Economic Growth: The Role of Local Financial Markets. *Journal of International Economics* 61: 512–33.

Balasubramanyam, V. N., M. Salisu, and D. Sapsford. 1996. Foreign Direct Investment and Growth in EP and IS Countries. *Economic Journal* 106: 92–105.

Bergsten, C. Fred. 1974. Coming Investment Wars? *Foreign Affairs* 53: 136–39.

Bergsten, C. Fred. 1979. US Policy Toward Foreign Direct Investment in the United States: The Committee on Foreign Investment in the United States. In *The International Economic Policy of the United States: Selected Papers of C. Fred Bergsten, 1977–1979*, ed. C. Fred Bergsten. Lexington, MA: Lexington Books.

Bergsten, C. Fred. 1983. International Investment: The Need for a New US Policy. In C. Fred Bergsten. *The United States in the World Economy: Selected Papers of C. Fred Bergsten, 1981–1982*. Lexington, MA: Lexington Books.

Bergsten, C. Fred, Thomas Horst, and Theodore H. Moran. 1978. *American Multinationals and American Interests*. Washington: Brookings Institution.

Blalock, Garrick, and Paul J. Gertler. 2005. Foreign Direct Investment and Externalities: The Case for Public Intervention. In *Does Foreign Direct Investment Promote Development?* ed. Theodore H. Moran, Edward M. Graham, and Magnus Blomström. Washington: Institute for International Economics.

Blomström, Magnus, Robert Lipsey, and Mario Zejan. 1994. What Explains Developing Country Growth? In *Convergence and Productivity: Gross National Studies and Historical Evidence*, eds. William Baumol, Richard Nelson, and Edward Wolff. Oxford: Oxford University Press.

Blonigen, Bruce A., and Miao Grace Wang. 2005. Inappropriate Pooling of Wealthy and Poor Countries in Empirical FDI Studies. In *Does Foreign Direct Investment Promote Development?* eds. Theodore H. Moran, Edward M. Graham, and Magnus Blomström. Washington: Institute for International Economics.

Borzenstein, E. J. de Gregorio, and J. W. Lee. 1998. How Does Foreign Investment Affect Growth? *Journal of International Economics* 45: 115–72.

Carkovic, Maria, and Ross Levine. 2005. Does Foreign Direct Investment Accelerate Economic Growth? In *Does Foreign Direct Investment Promote Development?* eds. Theodore H. Moran, Edward M. Graham, and Magnus Blomström. Washington: Institute for International Economics.

Dayal-Gulati, A., and A. M. Husain. 2000. *Centripetal Forces in China's Economic Take-off*. International Monetary Fund Working Paper 0086. Washington: International Monetary Fund. Available at www.imf.org.

Dunning, John H. 1974. The Future of the Multinational Enterprise. *Lloyd's Bank Review* 113: 15–32.

Goldberg, Paul M., and Charles P. Kindleberger. 1970. Toward a GATT for Investment: A Proposal for the Supervision of the Multinational Corporation. *Law and Policy in International Business* 2, no. 2: 295–325.

Graham, Edward M., and Paul R. Krugman. 1990. Trade-Related Investment Measures. In *Completing the Uruguay Round: A Results-Oriented Approach to the GATT Trade Negotiations*, ed. Jeffrey J. Schott. Washington: Institute for International Economics.

Graham, Edward M., and David M. Marchick. 2006. *US National Security and Foreign Direct Investment*. Washington: Institute for International Economics.

Hufbauer, Gary C., and Jeffrey J. Schott. 2005. *NAFTA Revisited: Achievements and Challenges*. Washington: Institute for International Economics.

Kumar, Nagesh, and Jaya Prakash Pradhan. 2005. Foreign Direct Investment, Externalities, and Economic Growth in Developing Countries: Some Empirical Explorations. In *Multinationals and Foreign Investment in Economic Development*, ed. Edward M. Graham. London: Palgrave MacMillan.

Lipsey, Robert E., and Fredrik Sjöholm. 2005. The Impact of Inward FDI on Host Countries: Why Such Different Answers? In *Does Foreign Direct Investment Promote Development?* eds. Theodore H. Moran, Edward M. Graham, and Magnus Blomström. Washington: Institute for International Economics.

Melitz, Mark J. 2005. Comment. In *Does Foreign Direct Investment Promote Development?* eds. Theodore H. Moran, Edward M. Graham, and Magnus Blomström. Washington: Institute for International Economics.

Robertson, David. 1975. International Regulations for Multinational Enterprises. *Pacific Community* 6: 300–13.

Safarian, A. E., and Joel Bell. 1973. Issues Raised by National Control of the Multinational Corporation. *Columbia Journal of World Business* 21, no. 4: 16.

Schott, Jeffrey J. 1994. *The Uruguay Round: An Assessment*. Washington: Institute for International Economics.

7

The International Monetary System in the Work of the Institute

MORRIS GOLDSTEIN

The search for ways to improve the operation of the international monetary system and, in particular, to prevent and manage crises in emerging economies—including through the work of the International Monetary Fund (IMF)—has been an enduring theme in the research agenda of the Peterson Institute for International Economics. It has likewise been a topic close to the heart of its director, C. Fred Bergsten, who has made a number of valuable contributions to this long-running debate.

A review of the Institute's work in this area amply demonstrates both the wide range of issues covered and their importance among the broad range of international economic policy issues that are the métier of the Institute. This review provides the foundation for more extensive discussions of key policy issues that are at the heart of the debate over the functioning of the international monetary system and the role of its central international institution, the IMF. Several of these issues are taken up in the following chapters.

John Williamson reexamines the continuing debate over the appropriate nature of the exchange rate regime, both from the perspective of individual countries and from a more systemic viewpoint. Edwin Truman then takes up a question that is a logical precursor to the analysis of target zone proposals for major currency exchange rates, long advocated by Fred

Morris Goldstein has been the Dennis Weatherstone Senior Fellow at the Institute since 1994.

Bergsten and John Williamson—namely, whether large variations in the real effective exchange rate of the US dollar over the past three decades provide useful messages concerning desirable adjustments in economic policies or other efforts to influence the exchange rate of the dollar. Martin Baily and Robert Lawrence then analyze the much discussed issue of whether the United States is losing international "competitiveness." They propose a way to measure fundamental shifts in a country's underlying trade performance in terms of shifts in the schedule relating a country's terms of trade (or real effective exchange rate) to its trade balance. Next, William Cline reviews and updates his landmark work on the problems of emerging-market debt and the functioning of the international financial system in light of recent experience with emerging-market financial crises and debt restructurings.

These discussions are followed by three chapters on the role of the IMF in the international monetary system. The first, by Michael Mussa, takes up two recent controversies concerning the role of the IMF in providing financial assistance to countries with balance of payments difficulties: (1) the widely expressed concern that IMF financial assistance generates substantial moral hazard by inducing emerging-market countries and their external investors to undertake undue risks, and (2) the controversy over very large-scale IMF assistance packages that began with assistance to Mexico in 1995. Next comes my chapter on the issue of exchange rates and specifically on the role that the IMF needs to play as the global umpire of exchange rate policies under its clear mandate to "exercise firm surveillance over the exchange rate policies of members." The chapter by Randall Henning takes more of a political science perspective on the role of the international financial institutions (IFIs), particularly the IMF, and disagrees to some extent with my prescription for the IMF.

The Institute's very first publication, *The Lending Policies of the International Monetary Fund* (1982) by John Williamson, presented the conclusions of an Institute conference that examined the Fund's role in the international financial intermediation process, its cooperation with the World Bank, and the appropriate design and monitoring of IMF adjustment programs.[1] This was soon followed by a set of studies on the developing-country debt crisis of the early to mid-1980s authored by Fred Bergsten, Bill Cline, Donald Lessard, and John Williamson (see Cline 1983, 1984, 1987; Williamson 1983c, 1988; Lessard and Williamson 1985, 1987; Bergsten, Cline, and Williamson 1985).[2] In Bergsten, Cline, and Williamson

---

1. The papers presented at that conference appeared in Williamson (1983a).

2. In 1995, the Institute published Cline's comprehensive reexamination of the international debt problem (Cline 1995). The bulk of these studies dealt with the middle-income developing countries (now typically known as "emerging" economies). The Institute has also done some analysis of debt problems in low-income developing countries; see, for example, Lancaster and Williamson (1986), Lancaster (1991), and Williamson and Birdsall (2002).

(1985) the authors focused on the nature and terms of past and future bank loans to debtor countries and evaluated a large set of policy proposals based on their prospects for averting a costly collapse of the international banking system, sustaining the economies of the debtor countries, facilitating a return to voluntary lending by banks, and preventing future crises.

During the 1990s and extending into this decade, the Institute focused on many of the hot "crisis issues" facing emerging economies, including, inter alia, how to minimize the costs for transition economies following the collapse of the Soviet Union, how to design better currency regimes for the area's emerging economies, how to reduce the frequency and severity of future emerging-market banking crises, what policy lessons to draw from the most prominent emerging-market financial crises of the past dozen years—i.e., Mexico in 1994–95, the Asian financial crises of 1997–98, and the Argentinian crisis of 2001–02, and how to strengthen what has come to be known as the international financial architecture (IFA).[3]

Recognizing the importance of the political dissolution and economic collapse of the Soviet Union, in the early 1990s the Institute launched a set of studies on its main implications—for the countries in the region as well as others. In *Currency Convertibility in Eastern Europe* (1991a), John Williamson brought together the main lessons from an Institute conference on this topic, soon followed by other studies that analyzed the external aspects of the economic policies adopted by the transition economies (Williamson 1991b); the likely impact of developments in Eastern Europe and the Soviet Union for the United States, the European Community, Japan, and the developing countries (Collins and Rodrik 1991); the prospects for establishing an Eastern economic community that would promote the preservation of trade links within the region (Havrylyshyn and Williamson 1991); and options for maintaining a payments system to finance interrepublic trade (Williamson 1992).

The collapse of the Mexican peso in late 1994 ushered in a wave of currency and banking crises in emerging economies that subsided only in 2003 (see Bergsten and Williamson 1994; Bergsten, Davanne, and Jacquet 1999; Bergsten 2005).[4] Not surprisingly, the Institute offered a menu of

---

3. In Goldstein (2001) I defined the IFA as the institutions, policies, and practices associated with the prevention and resolution of banking, currency, and debt crises, primarily but not exclusively in emerging economies.

4. In addition to analyzing currency regimes in emerging markets, the Institute kept up its tradition of evaluating currency regimes for the major reserve currencies and making recommendations for improving those regimes. In this connection, Fred Bergsten has long been an advocate of "target zones" for the major reserve currencies—a view he first outlined in Bergsten and Williamson (1983) and that he has continued to espouse with only minor modifications ever since; see, for example, C. Fred Bergsten, "How to Target Exchange Rates: G-7 Countries Should Allow Their Currencies to Fluctuate within Agreed EMS-Style Ranges," *Financial Times*, November 20, 1998; C. Fred Bergsten, Alternative Exchange Rate Systems and Reform of the International Financial Architecture, Testimony before the Committee on

policy recommendations. On the currency front, John Williamson assessed the pros and cons of currency boards (Williamson 1995), identified the lessons from the experiences of Chile, Colombia, and Israel with crawling band currency regimes (Williamson 1996), and completed the trilogy (Williamson 2000) by endorsing an "intermediate" currency regime for many emerging economies that has subsequently come to be known as the "BBC" regime (for currency *basket*, currency *band*, and *crawling* peg) (Williamson 1995, 1996, 2000). In Goldstein (2002), I focused on emerging economies that are heavily involved with private capital markets and argued for a currency regime of "managed floating plus," where "plus" is shorthand for a framework that includes inflation targeting and aggressive measures to combat currency mismatching.[5]

As discussed further in the next chapter, a host of Institute publications have also explored the methodology for estimating equilibrium exchange rates and have calculated exchange rate misalignments, increasingly including the currencies of prominent emerging economies (Williamson 1994; Wren-Lewis and Driver 1998; Bergsten and Williamson 2003; Goldstein 2004, 2006; Cline 2005; Bergsten and Williamson 2004). Fred Bergsten, whether in Institute publications, congressional testimony, or in numerous op-eds in the financial press, has been a leading participant in the ongoing debate about which currencies are most out of line and what needs to be done to reduce those misalignments (Bergsten 2005; Bergsten and Williamson 1994, 2003, 2004).[6]

It has been estimated that the fiscal costs of banking crises in developing countries over the past 25 years have exceeded $1 trillion (Honohan and Laeven 2005); in addition the lost output costs of banking crises are substantial, and banking crises have proved to be one of the better performing leading indicators of currency crises in emerging economies. In Goldstein (1997) I laid out the case for an international banking standard, identified the main elements that such a standard should contain, and discussed the operational issues involved. Many of these proposals were subsequently included in the Basel Core Principles of Effective Banking

---

Banking and Financial Services, May 21, 1999 (Washington: US House of Representatives). Other notable Institute work on currency regimes for the major industrial countries includes Williamson (1983b), McKinnon (1984), Bergsten (1988, 1991), Marris (1985), Goldstein (1995), Williamson and Miller (1987), Funabashi (1988), Cline (1989), Krugman (1991), Dominguez and Frankel (1993), Kenen (1994), Henning (1994), Bergsten and Henning (1996), Mann (1999), Bergsten and Williamson (2003, 2004), and Posen (2005).

5. More recently, Goldstein and Lardy argued for "two-stage" currency reform in China, while Williamson (2005a) has spelled out the advantages of an East Asian currency basket. See Morris Goldstein and Nicholas Lardy, "Two-Stage Currency Reform for China," *Asian Wall Street Journal*, September 12, 2003.

6. See, for example, C. Fred Bergsten, "Let the Dollar Fall," *Financial Times*, July 17, 2002; C. Fred Bergsten, The IMF and Exchange Rates, Testimony before the Committee on Banking, Housing, and Urban Affairs, May 19, 2004 (Washington: US Senate).

Supervision (the official international banking standard). Liliana Rojas-Suarez (2001a) evaluated whether international capital standards alone could be expected to strengthen banks in emerging markets.

More often than not, when there has been a major emerging-market financial crisis, the Institute has analyzed it to uncover the lessons for crisis prevention and management. The implications of the Mexican peso crisis—particularly for private capital flows to emerging economies—were analyzed in Calvo, Goldstein, and Hochreiter (1996). President Clinton characterized the Asian financial crisis as "the greatest financial challenge facing the world in the last half century." The Institute published a trio of studies on that crisis: I examined its origins, policy prescriptions, and systemic implications (Goldstein 1998); Marcus Noland and several colleagues, using a general equilibrium model, estimated the effects on the rest of the world from the large currency devaluations experienced by the Asian crisis countries (Noland et al. 1998); and Stephen Haggard (2000) studied the political aspects of the crisis in the countries most affected.[7] John Williamson (2002) and Morris Goldstein (Goldstein 2003) also offered perspectives on Brazil's currency and debt crisis of 2002, while Michael Mussa (2002) investigated what went wrong in Argentina's catastrophic crisis of 2001–02 and what important errors the IMF may have made either in supporting inappropriate policies or in failing to press for alternatives that might have avoided catastrophe.[8]

After the Mexican peso crisis, efforts to improve crisis prevention and resolution in emerging economies began to be grouped under the heading of IFA. Here, too, Institute management and staff have been very active. In 1998 the Council on Foreign Relations (CFR) convened a blue-ribbon task force on the future IFA. Institute Board Chairman Peter G. Peterson and board member Carla Hills cochaired the task force; I served as project director and drafted the report, and both Fred Bergsten and Nicholas Lardy served as task force members.[9] The task force's report (Council on Foreign

---

7. In addition to these studies, Noland (2000) explored how the Philippines avoided falling into a more serious crisis at the time of the wider Asian financial crisis; Fratzscher (2000) looked at the contagion of currency crises; Graham (1999) proposed a workable restructuring plan for South Korea; Posen (1999) laid out the policy measures Japan needed to take to implement a recovery; and Bergsten, in several shorter pieces, examined the policy actions needed to exit from the Asian financial crisis as well as the case for a revival of the Asian Monetary Fund. See C. Fred Bergsten, The International Monetary Fund and the National Interests of the United States, Testimony before the Joint Economic Committee, February 24, 1998 (Washington: US Congress); C. Fred Bergsten, "How to Target Exchange Rates: G-7 Countries Should Allow Their Currencies to Fluctuate within Agreed EMS-Style Ranges," *Financial Times*, November 20, 1998.

8. Gelpern (2005) also examined the implications of Argentina's approach to debt default and restructuring.

9. It is a testimony to Fred Bergsten's powers of persuasion that he was able to convince 10 of the other 28 members of the CFR task force to support a dissenting view calling for the establishment of target zones for the G-3 currencies.

Relations 1999), published jointly by the Institute and the Council, included recommendations on, inter alia, access limits on IMF lending, collective action clauses, and emerging-market currency regimes. Fred Bergsten was also at the time a member of the International Financial Institutions Advisory Committee (IFIAC)[10] and, when the IFIAC submitted its report to Congress in 2000, he was the principal author of a minority dissenting report. Bergsten[11] criticized the IFIAC report (2000) for painting a very misleading (negative) picture of the IFIs over the past 50 years, for failing to include appropriate monetary and fiscal policy elements in its prequalification criteria for IMF loans, and for prohibiting Fund support for countries that were of systemic importance but had not met the prequalification criteria.

Given the controversy over the use of the US Treasury's Exchange Stabilization Fund in the Mexican crisis, Randall Henning (1999) conducted an appraisal of its usefulness for future international financial support operations. Barry Eichengreen (1999) rejected radical reform and offered in its place a practical, post-Asian crisis agenda for the IFA that emphasized changes in private loan agreements, in emerging-market exchange rate policies, and in policies toward the capital account. In Goldstein (2000, 2001) I presented a comparison and evaluation of proposals for reform of the IFA and also made the argument for streamlining IMF structural conditionality. Henning (2002) put forward the case for and against regional financial arrangements in East Asia.

Morris Goldstein, Graciela Kaminsky, and Carmen Reinhart (2000) provided a comprehensive battery of empirical tests on early warning indicators of emerging-market currency and banking crises, and Liliana Rojas-Suarez (2001b) demonstrated and explained why indicators of individual bank failure that worked well in industrial countries did not perform as well in emerging markets.

Reflecting the view that there cannot be excessive borrowing from international capital markets without excessive lending, Wendy Dobson and Gary Hufbauer (2001) recommended a range of supervisory reforms in G-10 countries that would (via changes in both the Basel II framework and in official safety nets for G-10 banks) lower the incentives to offer emerging economies short-term, cross-border debt finance. John Williamson (2005b) argued that the boom-bust cycle in private capital flows to emerging markets could be tamed by undertaking a set of reforms in both creditor and debtor countries, including forward-looking provisioning by banks, retention of capital controls in some cases, and introduction of new financial instruments.

---

10. The IFIAC, created by the US Congress in 1988, was chaired by Allan Meltzer and came to be known as the Meltzer Commission.

11. C. Fred Bergsten, Reforming the International Financial Institutions: A Dissenting View, Testimony before the Committee on Banking, Housing, and Urban Affairs, March 9, 2000 (Washington: US Senate).

In the last five years, Institute work on the IFA—including reform of the IMF—again intensified. Peter Kenen (2001) reviewed progress on the IFA during the 1994–2000 period and concluded that there had been useful innovations but also that bolder efforts were needed: He recommended focusing more on IMF surveillance, narrowing the scope of IMF conditionality, and using IMF resources more effectively. Philip Turner and I (Goldstein and Turner 2004) developed a new measure for aggregate effective currency mismatches in emerging economies and put forward a set of proposals for controlling them. Nouriel Roubini and Brad Setser (2004) provided a comprehensive analysis of how the international community and the IMF should respond to financial crises in emerging economies; they argued that a return to low levels of access at the IMF was not realistic, that there has been too little differentiation in the official sector's response to crisis, and that the IMF should be willing to use its lending capacity to soften the flow during a debt restructuring. In Goldstein (2005b) I maintained that further reform of the IFA should place the highest priority on discouraging beggar-thy-neighbor exchange rate policies, controlling currency mismatches in emerging economies, giving debt sustainability a larger role in IMF surveillance and policy lending, improving the quality of compliance evaluation for international standards and codes, developing a better early warning framework for financial crises in emerging economies, and limiting extension of very large IMF loans to cases that are truly exceptional. And in Goldstein (2005a) I addressed the following question: If there was a new financial crisis in emerging economies, how would it start and spread, and which economies would be most affected? Ted Truman recently completed two studies on IMF reform. In the first (Truman 2006a) he contends that the IMF is under stress, that it risks declining into irrelevance, and that it must be reformed to restore its central role. He outlines a small set of key reforms, including those that would address the distribution of voting power in the Fund and representation on the IMF Executive Board, reaffirm the central role of the Fund in the resolution of external financial crisis, and upgrade its capacity to provide analysis and policy advice on members' internal and external financial sectors. The second study (Truman 2006b) brought together a set of papers on IMF reform presented at an Institute conference held in September 2005.

Throughout his career, Fred Bergsten has been both a strong supporter and a constructive critic of the IMF;[12] he also has been a champion of global governance reform—including replacing the G-7 with a steering committee for the global economy that would be more effective and more

---

12. See, for example, C. Fred Bergsten, The International Monetary Fund and the National Interests of the United States, Testimony before the Joint Economic Committee, February 24, 1998 (Washington: US Congress); C. Fred Bergsten, Alternative Exchange Rate Systems and Reform of the International Financial Architecture, Testimony before the Committee on Banking and Financial Services, May 21, 1999 (Washington: US House of Representatives);

consistent with changes in economic weight, particularly for the larger emerging economies.

Bergsten has emphasized consistently the positive long-term contribution that the Fund has made to the operation of the world economy, the ways in which Fund policies promote vital interests of the United States, the zero cost of the Fund to the American taxpayer and to the US economy, the need to ensure that the Fund has adequate financial resources to do its job, and the desirability and practicality of improving Fund policies and programs when there are shortcomings (rather than either shutting down the Fund or replacing or merging it with another institution). At the same time, he has frequently and vigorously prodded the Fund—for example, to promote the adjustment of external payments imbalances more, to enforce its guidelines against currency manipulation, to make the publication and management of equilibrium real exchange rates the fulcrum of international economic policy coordination, to invest more in early warning and early action systems for emerging-market financial crises, and to pay more attention to its comparative advantage vis-à-vis the World Bank (e.g., by transferring the Poverty Reduction and Growth Facility [PRGF] for low-income countries to the Bank).

On global governance reform, Bergsten has long argued (e.g., Bergsten and Henning 1996) that the G-7 has become increasingly ineffective and illegitimate. A mutual nonaggression pact essentially eliminates constructive peer pressure for policy reform, and today's international imbalances require substantial adjustment initiatives by countries outside (as well as inside) the G-7 (namely China and some other Asian economies) on exchange rates, key oil-producing countries (along with China and India) on global energy issues, and chief debtor countries (Brazil, Mexico, etc.) on debt problems. His latest proposal is to replace the G-7 with what he calls the "F-16" (that is, the finance G-20 countries, with the modification that there would be consolidated Euroland representation instead of representation by four individual European countries) (see Bergsten 2006).[13] The F-16 countries would account for about 80 percent of world output,

---

C. Fred Bergsten, Reforming the International Financial Institutions: A Dissenting View, Testimony before the Committee on Banking, Housing, and Urban Affairs, March 9, 2000 (Washington: US Senate); C. Fred Bergsten, Reforming the International Monetary Fund, Testimony before the Subcommittee on International Trade and Finance, Committee on Banking, Housing, and Urban Affairs, April 27, 2000 (Washington: US Senate); C. Fred Bergsten, The IMF and Exchange Rates, Testimony before the Committee on Banking, Housing, and Urban Affairs, May 19, 2004 (Washington: US Senate); C. Fred Bergsten, "An Action Plan to Stop the Market Manipulators Now," *Financial Times*, March 14, 2005.

13. C. Fred Bergsten, Reform of the International Monetary Fund, Testimony before the Subcommittee on International Trade and Finance, Committee on Banking, Housing, and Urban Affairs, June 7, 2005 (Washington: US Senate). Although Bergsten's criticism of the G-7 has been long running, he has at various times discussed steering committees for the global economy other than the F-16, including several versions of the G-2 or G-3.

would include the key players needed to address current systemic problems, and would represent, in Bergsten's view, the best compromise between legitimacy and efficiency.

References

Bergsten, C. Fred. 1988. *America in the World Economy: A Strategy for the 1990s*. Washington: Institute for International Economics.

Bergsten, C. Fred, ed. 1991. *International Adjustment and Financing: The Lessons of 1985–91*. Washington: Institute for International Economics.

Bergsten, C. Fred. 2005. A New Foreign Economic Policy for the United States. In *The United States and the World Economy: Foreign Economic Policy for the Next Decade*, ed. C. Fred Bergsten and the Institute for International Economics. Washington: Institute for International Economics.

Bergsten, C. Fred. 2006. A New Steering Committee for the World Economy? In *Reforming the IMF for the 21st Century*, ed. Edwin Truman. Washington: Institute for International Economics.

Bergsten, C. Fred, and Randall Henning. 1996. *Global Economic Leadership and the Group of Seven*. Washington: Institute for International Economics.

Bergsten, C. Fred, and John Williamson. 1983. Exchange Rates and Trade Policy. In *Trade Policy in the 1980s*, ed. William Cline. Washington: Institute for International Economics.

Bergsten, C. Fred, and John Williamson. 1994. Is the Time Ripe for Target Zones or the Blueprint? In *Bretton Woods: Looking to the Future*, Bretton Woods Commission, Washington.

Bergsten, C. Fred, and John Williamson, eds. 2003. *Dollar Overvaluation and the World Economy*. Washington: Institute for International Economics.

Bergsten, C. Fred, and John Williamson, eds. 2004. *Dollar Adjustment: How Far? Against What?* Washington: Institute for International Economics.

Bergsten, C. Fred, William Cline, and John Williamson. 1985. *Bank Lending to Developing Countries: The Policy Alternatives*. POLICY ANALYSIS IN INTERNATIONAL ECONOMICS 10. Washington: Institute for International Economics.

Bergsten, C. Fred, Olivier Davanne, and Pierre Jacquet. 1999. *The Case for Joint Management of Exchange Rate Flexibility*. Working Paper 99-9. Washington: Institute for International Economics.

Calvo, Guillermo, Morris Goldstein, and Eduard Hochreiter, eds. 1996. *Private Capital Flows to Emerging Markets after the Mexican Crisis*. Washington: Institute for International Economics.

Cline, William. 1983. *International Debt and Stability of the World Economy*. POLICY ANALYSIS IN INTERNATIONAL ECONOMICS 4. Washington: Institute for International Economics.

Cline, William. 1984. *International Debt: Systemic Risk and Policy Response*. Washington: Institute for International Economics.

Cline, William. 1987. *Mobilizing Bank Lending to Debtor Countries*. POLICY ANALYSIS IN INTERNATIONAL ECONOMICS 18. Washington: Institute for International Economics.

Cline, William. 1989. *United States External Adjustment and the World Economy*. Washington: Institute for International Economics.

Cline, William. 1995. *International Debt Reexamined*. Washington: Institute for International Economics.

Cline, William. 2005. *The United States as a Debtor Nation*. Washington: Institute for International Economics.

Collins, Susan, and Dani Rodrik. 1991. *Eastern Europe and the Soviet Union in the World Economy*. POLICY ANALYSIS IN INTERNATIONAL ECONOMICS 32. Washington: Institute for International Economics.

Council on Foreign Relations. 1999. *Safeguarding Prosperity in a Global Financial System*. Report of an Independent Task Force. Washington: Council on Foreign Relations and Institute for International Economics.

Dobson, Wendy, and Gary Hufbauer. 2001. *World Capital Markets: Challenge to the G-10*. Washington: Institute for International Economics.

Dominguez, Kathryn, and Jeffrey Frankel. 1993. *Does Foreign Exchange Intervention Work?* Washington: Institute for International Economics.

Eichengreen, Barry. 1999. *Toward A New International Financial Architecture: A Practical Post-Asia Agenda*. Washington: Institute for International Economics.

Fratzscher, Marcel. 2000. *On Currency Crises and Contagion*. Working Paper 00-9. Washington: Institute for International Economics.

Funabashi, Yoichi. 1988. *Managing the Dollar: From the Plaza to the Louvre*. Washington: Institute for International Economics.

Gelpern, Anna. 2005. *After Argentina*. International Economics Policy Brief 05-2. Washington: Institute for International Economics.

Goldstein, Morris. 1995. *The Exchange Rate System and the IMF: A Modest Agenda*. POLICY ANALYSIS IN INTERNATIONAL ECONOMICS 39. Washington: Institute for International Economics.

Goldstein, Morris. 1997. *The Case for an International Banking Standard*. POLICY ANALYSIS IN INTERNATIONAL ECONOMICS 47. Washington: Institute for International Economics.

Goldstein, Morris. 1998. *The Asian Financial Crisis: Causes, Cures, and Systemic Implications*. POLICY ANALYSIS IN INTERNATIONAL ECONOMICS 55. Washington: Institute for International Economics.

Goldstein, Morris. 2000. *Strengthening the International Financial Architecture: Where Do We Stand?* Working Paper 00-8. Washington: Institute for International Economics.

Goldstein, Morris. 2001. *IMF Structural Conditionality: How Much Is Too Much?* Working Paper 01-4. Washington: Institute for International Economics.

Goldstein, Morris. 2002. *Managed Floating Plus*. POLICY ANALYSIS IN INTERNATIONAL ECONOMICS 66. Washington: Institute for International Economics.

Goldstein, Morris. 2003. *Debt Sustainability, Brazil, and the IMF*. Working Paper 03-1. Washington: Institute for International Economics.

Goldstein, Morris. 2004. *Adjusting China's Exchange Rate Policies*. Working Paper 04-1. Washington: Institute for International Economics.

Goldstein, Morris. 2005a. *What Might the Next Emerging Market Financial Crisis Look Like?* Working Paper 05-7. Washington: Institute for International Economics.

Goldstein, Morris. 2005b. The International Financial Architecture. In *The United States and the World Economy: Foreign Economic Policy for the Next Decade*, ed. C. Fred Bergsten and the Institute for International Economics. Washington: Institute for International Economics.

Goldstein, Morris. 2006. Currency Manipulation and Enforcing the Rules of the International Monetary System. In *Reforming the IMF for the 21st Century*, ed. Edwin Truman. Washington: Institute for International Economics.

Goldstein, Morris, and Philip Turner. 2004. *Controlling Currency Mismatches in Emerging Markets*. Washington: Institute for International Economics.

Goldstein, Morris, Graciela Kaminsky, and Carmen Reinhart. 2000. *Assessing Financial Vulnerability: An Early Warning System for Emerging Markets*. Washington: Institute for International Economics.

Graham, Edward. 1999. *A Radical but Workable Restructuring Plan for South Korea*. International Economics Policy Brief 99-2. Washington: Institute for International Economics.

Haggard, Stephen. 2000. *The Political Economy of the Asian Financial Crisis*. Washington: Institute for International Economics.

Havrylyshyn, Oleh, and John Williamson. 1991. *From Soviet DisUnion to Eastern Economic Community*. POLICY ANALYSIS IN INTERNATIONAL ECONOMICS 35. Washington: Institute for International Economics.

Henning, C. Randall. 1994. *Currencies and Politics in the United States, Germany, and Japan.* Washington: Institute for International Economics.

Henning, C. Randall. 1999. *The Exchange Stabilization Fund: Slush Money or War Chest?* POLICY ANALYSIS IN INTERNATIONAL ECONOMICS 57. Washington: Institute for International Economics.

Henning, C. Randall. 2002. *East Asian Financial Cooperation.* POLICY ANALYSIS IN INTERNATIONAL ECONOMICS 68. Washington: Institute for International Economics.

Honohan, Patrick, and Luc Laeven. 2005. Introduction and Overview. In *Systemic Financial Crises: Containment and Resolution*, eds. Patrick Honohan and Luc Laeven. Cambridge, UK: Cambridge University Press.

IFIAC (International Financial Institutions Advisory Committee). *Report of the IFIAC.* Submitted to the US Congress and US Department of the Treasury, Washington, March 8, 2000.

Kenen, Peter, ed. 1994. *Managing the World Economy: Fifty Years After Bretton Woods.* Washington: Institute for International Economics.

Kenen, Peter. 2001. *The International Financial Architecture: What's New? What's Missing?* Washington: Institute for International Economics.

Krugman, Paul. 1991. *Has the Adjustment Process Worked?* POLICY ANALYSIS IN INTERNATIONAL ECONOMICS 34. Washington: Institute for International Economics.

Lancaster, Carol, and John Williamson, eds. 1986. *African Debt and Financing.* POLICY ANALYSIS IN INTERNATIONAL ECONOMICS 33. Washington: Institute for International Economics.

Lancaster, Carol. 1991. *African Economic Reform: The External Dimension.* Washington: Institute for International Economics.

Lessard, Donald, and John Williamson. 1985. *Financial Intermediation Beyond the Debt Crisis.* Washington: Institute for International Economics.

Lessard, Donald, and John Williamson. 1987. *Capital Flight and Third World Debt.* POLICY ANALYSIS IN INTERNATIONAL ECONOMICS 23. Washington: Institute for International Economics.

Mann, Catherine. 1999. *Is the US Trade Deficit Sustainable?* Washington: Institute for International Economics.

McKinnon, Ronald. 1984. *An International Standard for Monetary Stabilization.* POLICY ANALYSIS IN INTERNATIONAL ECONOMICS 8. Washington: Institute for International Economics.

Marris, Stephen. 1985. *Deficits and the Dollar: The World Economy at Risk.* POLICY ANALYSIS IN INTERNATIONAL ECONOMICS 14. Washington: Institute for International Economics.

Mussa, Michael. 2002. *Argentina and the Fund: From Triumph to Tragedy.* POLICY ANALYSIS IN INTERNATIONAL ECONOMICS 67. Washington: Institute for International Economics.

Noland. Marcus. 2000. *How the Sick Man Avoided Pneumonia: The Philippines in the Asian Financial Crisis.* Working Paper 00-5. Washington: Institute for International Economics.

Noland, Marcus, Ligang Liu, Sherman Robinson, and Zhi Wang. 1998. *Global Economic Effects of the Asian Currency Devaluations.* POLICY ANALYSIS IN INTERNATIONAL ECONOMICS 56. Washington: Institute for International Economics.

Posen, Adam. 1999. *Implementing Japanese Recovery.* International Economics Policy Brief 99-1. Washington: Institute for International Economics.

Posen, Adam, ed. 2005. *The Euro at Five: Ready for a Global Role?* Washington: Institute for International Economics.

Rojas-Suarez, Liliana. 2001a. *Can International Capital Standards Strengthen Banks in Emerging Markets?* Working Paper 01-10. Washington: Institute for International Economics.

Rojas-Suarez, Liliana. 2001b. *Rating Banks in Emerging Markets: What Credit Rating Agencies Should Learn from Financial Indicators.* Working Paper 01-6. Washington: Institute for International Economics.

Roubini, Nouriel, and Brad Setser. 2004. *Bailouts or Bail-Ins? Responding to Financial Crises in Emerging Economies.* Washington: Institute for International Economics.

Truman, Edwin. 2006a. *A Strategy for IMF Reform.* POLICY ANALYSIS IN INTERNATIONAL ECONOMICS 77. Washington: Institute for International Economics.

Truman, Edwin, ed. 2006b. *Reforming the IMF for the 21st Century*. Washington: Institute for International Economics.

Williamson, John. 1982. *The Lending Policies of the International Monetary Fund*. POLICY ANALYSIS IN INTERNATIONAL ECONOMICS 1. Washington: Institute for International Economics.

Williamson, John, ed. 1983a. *IMF Conditionality*. Washington: Institute for International Economics.

Williamson, John. 1983b. *The Exchange Rate System*. POLICY ANALYSIS IN INTERNATIONAL ECONOMICS 5. Washington: Institute for International Economics.

Williamson, John, ed. 1983c. *Prospects for Adjustment in Argentina, Brazil, and Mexico: Responding to the Debt Crisis*. Washington: Institute for International Economics.

Williamson, John. 1988. *Voluntary Approaches to Debt Relief*. POLICY ANALYSIS IN INTERNATIONAL ECONOMICS 25. Washington: Institute for International Economics.

Williamson, John, ed. 1991a. *Currency Convertibility in Eastern Europe*. Washington: Institute for International Economics.

Williamson, John. 1991b. *The Economic Opening of Eastern Europe*. POLICY ANALYSIS IN INTERNATIONAL ECONOMICS 31. Washington: Institute for International Economics.

Williamson, John. 1992. *Trade and Payments After Soviet Disintegration*. POLICY ANALYSIS IN INTERNATIONAL ECONOMICS 37. Washington: Institute for International Economics.

Williamson, John, ed. 1994. *Estimating Equilibrium Exchange Rates*. Washington: Institute for International Economics.

Williamson, John. 1995. *What Role for Currency Boards?* POLICY ANALYSIS IN INTERNATIONAL ECONOMICS 40. Washington: Institute for International Economics.

Williamson, John. 1996. *The Crawling Band as an Exchange Rate Regime: Lessons from Chile, Columbia, and Israel*. Washington: Institute for International Economics.

Williamson, John. 2000. *Exchange Rate Regimes for Emerging Markets: Reviving the Intermediate Option*. POLICY ANALYSIS IN INTERNATIONAL ECONOMICS 60. Washington: Institute for International Economics.

Williamson, John. 2002. *Is Brazil Next?* International Economics Policy Brief 02-7. Washington: Institute for International Economics.

Williamson, John. 2005a. *A Currency Basket for East Asia—Not Just China*. International Economics Policy Brief 05-1. Washington: Institute for International Economics.

Williamson, John. 2005b. *Curbing the Boom-Bust Cycle: Stabilizing Capital Flows to Emerging Markets*. POLICY ANALYSIS IN INTERNATIONAL ECONOMICS 75. Washington: Institute for International Economics.

Williamson, John. 2006. Revamping the International Monetary System. In *Reforming the IMF for the 21st Century*, ed. Edwin Truman. Washington: Institute for International Economics.

Williamson, John, and Nancy Birdsall. 2002. *Delivering on Debt Relief: From IMF Gold to a New Aid Architecture*. Washington: Institute for International Economics and Center for Global Development.

Williamson, John, and Marcus Miller. 1987. *Targets and Indicators: A Blueprint for International Coordination of Economic Policy*. POLICY ANALYSIS IN INTERNATIONAL ECONOMICS 22. Washington: Institute for International Economics.

Wren-Lewis, Simon, and Rebecca Driver. 1998. *Real Exchange Rates for the Year 2000*. POLICY ANALYSIS IN INTERNATIONAL ECONOMICS 54. Washington: Institute for International Economics.

8

Fred Bergsten and the Institute's Work on Exchange Rate Regimes

JOHN WILLIAMSON

When the Institute for International Economics started functioning in the second half of 1981, I recall being surprised at hearing Fred Bergsten predict that the dollar would continue appreciating and the United States would go into a big current account deficit. Personally, I don't believe in forecasting exchange rates, but I have to say that he was right on both counts. Those deficits have cumulated into a large net debtor position for the United States. Despite his love for the dramatic, Fred has never tried to imagine these debts away by postulating the existence of dark matter. Instead, he argued that deficits and debts posed a policy problem, to which we at the Institute sought a solution. A part of that solution (an important part, but he has always been clear that it is only a part) involved the exchange rate.

In this paper I trace the development of thought at the Institute on the exchange rate regime and the other arrangements that should complement it. I explain the intellectual background to these proposals and how they were related to other major intellectual developments of the period.

Perhaps I should say a word in this introductory section about the role of particular individuals and whether there is such a thing as an "Institute position" on such questions as the exchange rate regime. It is quite clear

---

John Williamson, a senior fellow at the Institute, has been associated with the Institute since 1981.

that there are no formal Institute positions; we have (mercifully) no vision statement to which new (or old) employees are required to subscribe. At the same time, it is difficult to imagine that a rabid protectionist, or someone who regarded the international financial institutions as either agents of imperialism or threats to the future of the United States, would feel comfortable applying for a job here, or would be likely to be appointed if he did. Within the ambit of a broad internationalist perspective, Fred has made a conscious effort to preserve a nonpartisan and eclectic reputation for the Institute. Not all of my colleagues subscribe to the views on exchange rate management that Fred or I (as the principal writers on this subject) have advanced: Indeed, Fred has not always endorsed my positions on these issues, as I will elaborate below. If Fred or I made more noise than anyone else about target zones, then it's possible the world identified the Institute with the target zone proposal. That is life, but it was not policy.

History

Fred Bergsten had been one of the leading advocates of moving to limited flexibility of exchange rates in the period prior to the breakdown of the Bretton Woods system (see Bergsten in Halm 1970). My own advocacy in that period had been focused exclusively on the crawling peg, rather than also embracing the wide band proposal. As it turned out, however, the world moved to floating rates rather than any form of limited flexibility. At the time, Fred and I both felt that the change to floating rates went too far and that the world would have been better off with an intermediate regime. The design of such a regime has been one of our continuing preoccupations since then.

The first venture of the Institute into the exchange rate issue was a joint paper that Fred and I wrote for the Institute's second conference, held in 1982, on Trade Policy in the 1980s (Bergsten and Williamson 1983). We argued that it was a mistake to analyze trade policy in isolation from the exchange rate issue: This mistake rested on an implicit but incorrect assumption that prolonged misalignments of exchange rates would not occur. In addition to their direct and obvious effect of fomenting trade imbalances, misalignments would widen the coalitions damaged by liberal trade and lend them some legitimacy and thus foster protectionist sentiment.

We distinguished three concepts of the equilibrium exchange rate: fundamental equilibrium (defined, with a glance over our shoulder at Bretton Woods, as the average rate over the cycle that would reconcile internal and external balance), current equilibrium (the fundamental rate modified to reflect cyclical forces), and market equilibrium (no intervention). Misalignments were defined as major and prolonged departures of the exchange rate from its fundamental equilibrium value. We discussed the role of the periodic yen/dollar misalignments in generating economic tensions between the United States and Japan. The climax of the paper was the enumeration of three strategies for exchange rate management intended to avoid misalignments: pegging with monetary policy subordinated to maintaining the peg, floating "with target zones or reference rates," and employing capital controls. In the first two cases it was envisaged that the nominal rate would crawl so as to maintain the real target constant. These strategies were not examined in detail, but one important additional point was made. It was acknowledged that an attempt to pursue a real exchange rate target could be destabilizing, in the same way that pursuit of a target for the real interest rate or unemployment could destabilize the economy. The key to avoiding such instability is to set a target consistent with stability and to adjust it promptly if evidence suggests it has been set wrongly.

Target Zones

As just noted, the pioneering paper by Fred and me did not focus on how a target zone system (or one based on reference rates) might function. But Fred recognized the importance of the issue and set me to work on it immediately. My first thoughts were published in September 1983, in one of the Institute's early Policy Analyses, or PAs (Williamson 1983, revised in 1985). I again drew the distinction between market, current, and fundamental equilibrium and defined misalignment (now sharply distinguished from volatility[1]) as prolonged departure of the exchange rate from its fundamental equilibrium. I attempted to measure the fundamental equilibrium exchange rates (FEERs) of the five major currencies of the day (US dollar, deutsche mark, yen, pound sterling, and French franc) and thereby to quantify misalignments. I diagnosed the costs of misalignments so as to build a case for managed exchange rates. But the heart of the paper was the first blueprint for a target zone system, which was laid out in a section called "Techniques of Exchange Rate Management." I concluded (page 72) that the "target zones" as I envisaged them would be characterized by

- soft margins, rather than a commitment to prevent the rate from straying outside the target zone;

- a zone perhaps 20 percent wide, outside of which rates would be considered "clearly wrong";

---

1. Incidentally, I am not sure whether Fred or I should claim any credit for the volatility/misalignment distinction, which became quite popular around 1983. I decided that it would be counterproductive to draw attention to any role we might have had in propagating the distinction, which might merely have prompted the fanatical floaters into denying a distinction that had caught on naturally because it responded to a widespread concern.

- a crawling zone, with the crawl reflecting both differential inflation and any need for balance of payments adjustment;

- publication of the target zone; and

- the partial direction of monetary policy (perhaps in the form of intervention that is not fully sterilized) to discourage the exchange rate from straying outside its target zone.

Fred was never happy with my support for the first of those features, the soft margins. He argued that speculators would be less inclined to enter the market in a stabilizing direction if they knew that the authorities had reserved the right to let the rate go outside any target zone. My reply was that the authorities were not in a position to guarantee that under no circumstances would they let rates deviate beyond the target zones they had named: The costs might simply be too great. He doubted that, because he always had more faith than I did in the power of intervention. (I eventually thought I had found a solution, which was to make fiscal policy a systematic part of the policy prescription, but he didn't like that either, as I will shortly recall.)

Fred had no difficulty with my suggestion that bands should be something like 20 percent wide. The remark about rates being "clearly wrong" outside the target zone was an attempt to respond to German critics like the late great Otmar Emminger, who had a habit of saying that while he had no idea what the right rate was he could certainly recognize a wrong rate. Well, I would say, tell me your wrong rate, then imagine that the problem is too weak/strong a currency rather than too strong/weak a currency, and tell me what the wrong rate is on that side too. I guessed that those rates would turn out to be about 20 percent apart, so this would give you a target zone. I fear I didn't persuade him!

The crawl feature was of course a carryover from what I had long argued: There is no point in abandoning a proposal just because it is old; the more relevant question is whether it is right. I thought of a crawl as being satisfied by a series of small steps, as a number of member countries were at that time organizing their European Monetary System (EMS) realignments.

I was always an emphatic supporter of publication. I could never understand how officials believed that transparency could harm them, but many did. On the other hand, while Fred also would prefer publication, he tended to see this as an area where one could compromise. If officialdom felt more comfortable with target zones that they kept secret, so be it.

I argued that the prime policy instrument used to defend target zones should be intervention, a part of which should be unsterilized. (At that time we were still recovering from a decade dominated in our field by the monetary approach to the balance of payments!) Fred had reservations regarding the idea that intervention should be left partially unsterilized, reflecting his greater optimism concerning the effectiveness of sterilized intervention. I did not categorically rule out other instruments, notably capital controls, but neither did I express enthusiasm for them.

Fred has argued that the greatest influence of the Institute on exchange rate policy arose in the subsequent period, on the basis of the unvarnished target zone proposal. The Plaza Agreement marked the return of the Reagan administration to concern about exchange rates. Several months before this the number two official in the Baker Treasury, Richard Darman, had lunch with several Institute scholars (Fred Bergsten, Stephen Marris, and me) to talk about how we envisaged a target zone system working. In due course the US Treasury decided that the dollar had fallen enough and needed to be stabilized, which led to the Louvre Agreement. This agreement can be regarded as endorsing some sort of target zones, although there are many important divergences from the proposals I had previously laid out. For example, there was no provision for a crawl to offset inflation differentials, *target zones* were called *reference ranges* and were defined in terms of dollar rates rather than effective rates, the ranges were provisional "until further notice" rather than containing provisions as to how they should be altered, they were unpublished but in fact centered on the rates prevailing on the date of the agreement, and they were much narrower. Their narrow width may explain why they had to be ditched unceremoniously after the stock market crash in late 1987. Perhaps the most important, though least obvious, difference is the fact that while policies leaned more heavily against exchange rate changes as long as they did not exceed 5 percent from the target, pressure was eased when the market rate deviated more from the center of the range. According to Funabashi (1988, 185), beyond 5 percent "the only obligation was consultation on policy adjustment and realignment."

While my own later work eschewed the terminology and has recognized some of the critical arguments, Fred has remained an unapologetic advocate of unvarnished target zones (Bergsten 1988, 1993, 1994, 1995; Bergsten and Henning 1996). In several respects those papers incorporated proposals articulated above, such as the size of the ranges and the means of determining their central rates, public announcement, frequent reappraisal of the appropriateness of the real zones, a crawl to offset inflation differentials, and a commitment to concerted intervention to defend the zones. Fred's 1993 and 1995 papers both suggested that the world had tried fixed rates, under Bretton Woods, and floating rates, during the subsequent nonsystem, and was now moving toward an intermediate regime. His 1995 paper also had a graphic depiction of how the dollar overvaluation of the first Reagan administration had nurtured protectionism that was still haunting the world (in particular, in the form of Super 301).

His article with Randy Henning also makes two major points that seem to me questionable. First, they argued that target zones should really be viewed as a variant of flexible rather than fixed exchange rates. Clearly the authors are right to argue that target zones are a form of intermediate regime rather than either extreme, but if one has to identify a cut-off between fixed and flexible rates, then my choice would be to ask whether at some rate there is a legal obligation to intervene to defend a margin, and on that test, target zones (at least with hard margins) are a form of fixed-rate system. More fundamentally, Fred and Randy attacked the consensus critique of policy coordination, which argues that monetary policy is already preempted by pursuit of the optimal combination of inflation and unemployment and therefore leaves no room to pursue an external target as well. They asserted that one will usually get a better *domestic* outcome by factoring *external* considerations into the decision. Logic says that it is not possible to improve on something that is already optimal, so the claim must be that the attempt to pursue what is domestically optimal is empirically prone to be inferior to the result achieved by looking at exchange rates. They give some telling examples, like US monetary policy in both the early and the late 1970s. Perhaps one could add current events in New Zealand as another instance where ignoring the external situation has led to an outcome that is distinctly suboptimal. So they may be right, but I confess that I am not yet persuaded of the general truth of this claim.

Be that as it may, it is surely not such considerations that have disappointed Fred's hopes of the early 1990s that the world was moving toward an intermediate regime based on target zones. On the contrary, the subsequent period witnessed the emergence of the "bipolar doctrine" (the notion that feasible exchange rate regimes are the two extremes, rigid fixity and free floating, and that all intermediate regimes are crisis prone and therefore undesirable). What are the reasons for the lack of appeal of anything like target zones?

The most important is probably the apparent difficulty that the world has in agreeing what equilibrium exchange rates are. Even in what seem to many of us to be absolutely unambiguous cases, like the renminbi peg, one finds economists with Nobel prizes and others paid inordinate sums by investment banks and at least part of the IMF staff prepared to assert that they do not know whether the renminbi is undervalued or not. If one then tries to take the analysis back a step, to search for exchange rates that will achieve an agreed set of current account targets, one finds that it is similarly impossible to secure agreement on what current account targets should be. Unless and until this sort of intellectual laissez-faire leads to the world ending up in a new depression, it seems hopeless to imagine that it can be changed.

A second important reason for the lack of support for target zones is the widespread belief in evidence of the absence of Krugmanesque stabilizing speculation (Krugman 1991) induced by such zones. To some of us the most important result is still the finding that the European Exchange Rate Mechanism (ERM) created a market expectation that the exchange rate would revert toward the center of the band (Svensson 1992). But Svensson's other findings, that Krugman's assumptions of perfect credibility and no intramarginal interventions are overwhelmingly rejected by the data, seem to have led to a general belief that zones have no stabilizing effect. Of course, no one doubts that a *credible* target zone would be stabilizing: The problem is that most target zones have apparently not been regarded as completely credible. After the ERM crises of 1992–93, or indeed the description of the reference ranges agreed at the Louvre as laid out above, it is not difficult to understand why. The world will clearly need to do better if it ever adopts a target zone regime.

A third reason cited by some is that inflation targeting seems to be proving a better basis for monetary policy than following an exchange rate target. This objection may not seem compelling to those of us who look to target zones to restrain markets from getting carried away on temporary errant paths, but there are still many economists who are unable to comprehend the possibility of misalignments and regard the only possible rationale for a fixed exchange rate as being to provide a guide for monetary policy.

The Blueprint

The next major development at the Institute on the question of managing the world economy, and the exchange rate regime that would facilitate this, was the "blueprint" for policy coordination (Williamson and Miller 1987), proposing rules for the coordination of fiscal and monetary policies among the G-7 countries. Monetary policy (interpreted as the short-term interest rate) was to be used to keep exchange rates within target zones around their FEERs, estimated as real effective exchange rates, as in the target zone proposal. The charge of critics that such a use of monetary policy might destabilize domestic demand was countered by introducing Keynesian fiscal policy. If, for example, an expansionary monetary policy designed to depreciate the domestic currency had an unwelcome by-product in expanding demand and thus stimulating inflation, then the answer posited was to tighten fiscal policy. Conversely, the implications for domestic demand of a tight monetary policy could be countered by an expansionary fiscal policy.

Since exchange rates are influenced by interest *differentials*, the proposed assignment left the world *average* interest rate indeterminate. (This is the old n–1 problem.) We argued that a symmetrical world system would provide that such a world variable should be determined by the needs of the world economy as a whole, rather than the needs of a particular country (as a dollar standard provides). In particular, we suggested that the world level of policy interest rates should be raised when the world was in a dangerously strong boom and lowered during a world recession. Concertation of such movements would be a responsibility of the G-7.

The other element of the blueprint was a proposal to vary fiscal policy in order to maintain "internal balance," which was defined in terms of a growth rate of domestic demand that would "promote the fastest growth of output consistent with a gradual reduction of inflation to an acceptable level and agreed adjustment of the balance of payments" (Williamson and Miller 1987, 2). The desired nominal demand growth was to be determined by something that looked rather like a Taylor Rule, and fiscal policy was then to be varied in the short-run manner advocated by the OECD in the 1960s in order to keep demand on track, given the interest rates that materialized jointly from world decisions and the need to keep the exchange rate within its target zone. Fred was highly skeptical of this approach, because he never thought the Congress would abandon its sovereign right to change taxes and expenditures without regard to the rest of the world.

Be that as it may, the blueprint created a lot of interest in the academic world (as opposed to the official community, which treated it with the same reservations as Fred). For the next several years I wrote a number of papers that elaborated on various aspects of the proposal and even found myself having to defend what became known as the "orthodox assignment" (monetary policy to the exchange rate and fiscal policy to internal demand) against proponents of the "heterodox assignment" (fiscal policy to manage the balance of payments and monetary policy to internal demand). Randy Henning and I wrote a paper that tried to explore the political economy implications of implementing the blueprint for the Institute conference that celebrated the 50th anniversary of the Bretton Woods conference (chapter 2 in Kenen 1994). We were vigorously attacked by Richard Cooper in his capacity as one of our discussants at the conference, on the grounds that, first, calculating the FEERs required as input a set of targets for current account balances and no one could agree what targets are appropriate and, second, that subjecting fiscal policy to supranational constraints is inconsistent with democracy.

Intervention

As already noted, one way in which Fred and I have disagreed over the years is in the power we attach to sterilized intervention in the foreign exchange market. The Institute's most impressive contribution to this perennial debate was the publication of *Does Foreign Exchange Intervention Work?* (Dominguez and Frankel 1993). In this work, the authors used previously unavailable daily data from the Fed and the Bundesbank to examine the effects of their sterilized purchases and sales of each other's currency for their own in the 1980s. They combined these data with foreign exchange rates, press reports of intervention, and surveys of foreign exchange traders about their expectations of future exchange rates and reached the following conclusions:

- Foreign exchange intervention can be an effective tool in influencing exchange rates, even when it is sterilized.

- Intervention is more effective when it is publicly known.

- Intervention may well work through some channel other than the traditional "signaling channel" (in which the central bank uses intervention to signal future changes in monetary policy) and "portfolio-balance channel" (in which it changes the relative supply of imperfectly substitutable bonds). In particular, it may work by pricking a speculative bubble. This is consistent with the greater effectiveness of publicly known intervention.

- They endorsed the previous finding that coordinated intervention is more effective than unilateral intervention.

At almost the same time, a conference in honor of Rinaldo Ossola heard a paper by three Banca d'Italia economists (Catte, Galli, and Rebecchini 1994) who also had access to daily data on intervention and also came to the conclusion that intervention had been an effective tool. They claimed that in about half of the 19 instances of intervention they identified, the course of the dollar had been definitively reversed, while in the other half the impact appeared to have been temporary. Discussants quibbled about whether some of the "definitive reversals" were really so definitive and whether many of the "temporary reversals" marked much of a reversal at all, but the general impression left by both this paper and the Dominguez-Frankel study was that sterilized intervention had been reinstated as a policy tool. However, both papers leave it open for Fred and me to maintain our individual views about whether intervention is a reliable tool that can be used in all circumstances and with reasonable assurance that it will work.

In a recent conference volume edited by Fred and me (Bergsten and Williamson 2004), two interesting papers reinforced themes that have been emerging in recent years. Chris Kubelec argued (and presented empirical evidence to support the thesis) that intervention was far more likely to be successful if it was attempting to reverse a large misalignment (which is consistent with the Dominguez-Frankel hypothesis that it may be particularly potent if it pricks a speculative bubble). In the other paper, Marcel Fratzscher treated intervention as not one but two policy instruments, one being trading in the foreign exchange market and the other "oral intervention" (a.k.a. jawboning). The fact that he finds a significant effect of oral intervention reinforces the suggestion that intervention should always be publicly announced.

Crawling Bands for Emerging Markets

In the 1990s the battle to persuade the G-7 countries to adopt more ordered exchange rate arrangements was lost. On the other hand, several emerging markets had adopted the sort of exchange rate arrangements that could have been described as target zones. But by then Paul Krugman had appropriated the term "target zone" to refer to the constant-nominal-rate bands of the EMS. Jacob Frenkel, soon after his appointment in 1991 as governor of the Bank of Israel, saved the day: He announced that the Israeli band would in future crawl according to the preprogrammed rate of deceleration of inflation, and that Israel's new system would be called a "crawling band." Hence (at least to some of us) target zones became crawling bands.

The two principal Institute publications that dealt with crawling bands were both by me (Williamson 1996, 2000). The first of these examined the operation of crawling bands in the three emerging markets that had the longest and most extensive experience with the regime and were still using it in the mid-1990s: Chile, Colombia, and Israel. In the event, in years subsequent to the book's publication, all three countries allowed their exchange rates to float. It is notable that in all three cases the shift to floating went rather smoothly: It was demonstrably less traumatic than in the many other countries that started to float in response to a crisis. If the role of the crawling band is only to enable countries to learn to float, it will still have served a worthwhile historical function.

The other of my two books was written after I emerged from my three years at the World Bank, as a response to the so-called bipolar thesis that became popular among economists after the Asian crisis. According to this thesis, the growth of capital mobility had narrowed the options for exchange rate policy to a choice between freely floating exchange rates and rates that were permanently and credibly fixed. (When the thesis was first expounded, there was an unfortunate tendency to take Argentina as the example par excellence of the second case; after the Argentinean implosion, it was quickly decided that Argentina had not had a real currency board and had therefore not deserved its star position.) My counterarguments were:

- There are other objectives besides avoiding crises, which may also be important for welfare, like avoiding excessively overvalued exchange rates.

- Even corner regimes may be subject to crisis (an argument that suddenly became more convincing the next year when Argentina abandoned its fixed rate in the midst of a horrendous crisis).

- There is nothing in the Impossible Trinity analysis that prevents countries from choosing an intermediate position, e.g., with limited capital controls, efforts to influence the exchange rate, and limited freedom for monetary policy. (An analysis of the Chilean experience with capital controls in the 1990s argued that there were serious defects in the literature that had dismissed their effectiveness.)

■ Even if countries might hesitate to commit themselves to defend an exchange rate target, they could usefully adopt a reference rate.

But that is a topic best discussed a little later.

Baskets

Under strong pressure from Fred to contribute to thinking about the problems of a part of the world that he perceived as critically important to the United States, I became interested in exchange rate policies in East Asia. Initially the interest focused on the policies of the newly industrialized countries, or NICs (as they were then called), especially Korea and Taiwan. Bela Balassa and I wrote a Policy Analysis that concluded that the NICs needed to revalue, and expand demand, as a contribution to the adjustment process (Balassa and Williamson 1987, revised edition 1990). This may have contributed to the decision of the US Treasury to cite them for currency manipulation. The current account surplus decreased notably in 1989, and in the second edition we argued—to the annoyance of the US Treasury—that both Korea and Taiwan (but not Singapore) had done enough to justify dropping the manipulation charge.

Shortly before I went on leave to the World Bank in 1996, Fred again urged me to address the currency issues of the region, this time more generally. I could see little logic in the fact that most of those economies[2] pegged their currencies to the US dollar as though we still lived in the 1960s. True, this had the advantage of avoiding intraregional exchange rate changes, but that could equally well be achieved by having them all peg to any other unit, as long as it was the same unit for all of them. In particular, it seemed natural to explore the conjecture that they would be better served by pegging to a common basket of currencies that reflected the average trade weights of the group.

Hence I endeavored to make a comparison of the merits of a dollar peg versus a common basket peg for a number of East Asian currencies. In the version of the paper that was presented to a conference in Seoul in November 1996 and in due course published (Williamson in Collignon, Pisani-Ferry, and Park 1999), I argued that at least six and possibly as many as nine East Asian currencies should peg to the same basket. The six

---

2. When on one occasion I carelessly wrote "countries" instead of "economies" in a paper presented in Beijing, I was chided by a student on the grounds that Hong Kong and Taiwan are not countries.

core members of the group, identified by the similarity in their trading patterns, were China, Hong Kong, South Korea, Malaysia, Taiwan, and Thailand. Both the Philippines and Singapore were marginal on one of my two criteria, while Indonesia was marginal on both[3], so I offered five comparisons. These involved actual policy; a unilateral peg to a basket of currencies with weights reflecting national trade patterns; a peg to a basket with weights reflecting the total trade of all nine economies; and similar baskets with weights reflecting the trade of eight and six economies, respectively. I showed that about 85 percent of the potential benefit of reducing instability of the nominal effective exchange rate to zero through using a unilateral basket peg could have been realized through (any of the) common basket pegs.

One of the issues that Fred wanted me to return to after I left the World Bank in 1999 was that of East Asian exchange rates. By now, after the East Asian crisis, a majority of the countries were nominally floating rather than pegging. In Williamson (2005), which appeared shortly after the much vaunted but de facto minimal change in Chinese policy in July 2005, I therefore referred to using a currency basket as the numeraire, a phrase sufficiently general to encompass not only a peg but also the measure of currency strength with reference to which authorities with a floating currency might intervene. A switch to a basket numeraire would still have the same basic effect of reducing instability of the effective exchange rate while avoiding any potential loss of competitiveness against other East Asian countries. And it would have resolved the collective action problem that seems to be a major factor explaining the fact that most of East Asia rode the dollar down when the dollar correction finally started in 2002.

The idea of pegging to a basket for countries with diversified trade had long been a part of my policy recommendations for emerging markets (at least since I surveyed the literature on the optimal peg, in Williamson 1982). I emphasized in my 1996 Policy Analysis that both Chile and Israel pegged (at that time) to baskets. But it was only after the East Asian analysis was developed, in 1996, that baskets achieved parity of esteem with bands and the crawl. It was then that Dornbusch and Park (in Collignon, Pisani-Ferry, and Park 1999) first referred to my proposals as the BBC system (basket, band, and crawl).

The System: Tinkering or Reference Rates?

For many years the Institute's monetary economists were effectively Fred Bergsten and me. Bill Cline did some valuable studies on debt and adjustment, and Steve Marris was here for a while, but I think it is fair to say

---

3. One criterion involved similarity in the geographical distribution of trade and the other that the countries be close competitors in world markets. Singapore was marginal on the first criterion and the Philippines on the second.

that we were the core staff interested in exchange rate regimes. That changed with the appointment of Morris Goldstein as a senior fellow in 1994. Since then it has changed even more dramatically as we have been joined by Martin Baily, Catherine Mann, Mike Mussa, Adam Posen, and Ted Truman. The new appointments have a distinctly less positive attitude toward attempts to redesign the global monetary system of the sort that have always appealed to Fred and me and are more inclined to search for modifications of present arrangements.

The future trend was trumpeted in the subtitle of Morris Goldstein's first publication for the Institute (Goldstein 1995): "A Modest Agenda." (No one remembers what the main title was, but everyone remembers that the Institute actually suggested something modest.) He proposed accepting the main features of the existing international monetary system but emphasizing the avoidance of large misalignments and having the main countries shift monetary policy away from purely domestic concerns in the event of a large misalignment, although keeping estimates of equilibrium exchange rates secret ("quiet"). Other proposals involved the IMF taking a more active role in diagnosing misalignments and prescribing policy adjustments and having the main industrial countries accept that the IMF ought to play such a role. The Fund needed to improve the flow of information to the private capital market (this was before the Special Data Dissemination Standard was invented). It also needed to reexamine the concepts of "exchange rate manipulation" and "unfair competitive advantage" to try and make them operationally useful.

His subsequent Policy Analysis, *Managed Floating Plus* (Goldstein 2002), was if possible even more emphatic in advocating the preservation of floating exchange rates. Most of the manuscript was in fact about the "plus," which consisted of inflation targeting and an effort to avoid currency mismatches. It always seemed to me that the less satisfactory part of the paper was about managed floating, specifically that it did not advocate the management of floating in any sense that I would recognize the word "management." He wrote (page 43):

> I call it "managed" floating to indicate that . . . the authorities could use various policies to counter some short-term movements in the exchange rate. They would be permitted . . . to intervene in the exchange market . . . to "smooth" what they regarded as excessive short-term fluctuations in exchange rates.

Later (page 44) he explains that the authorities would have no publicly announced exchange rate target and in a footnote emphasizes that, in contrast, most intermediate regimes do have a publicly announced target. This question of publication has increasingly struck me as the crux of the issue.

My own writing (e.g., Williamson 1998, 2006) has tended to accept that countries cannot be expected to commit themselves to defending any exchange rate target. In that sense, they float. However, the essence of management is that the authorities need to indicate when intervention is to be expected and to spell out their objectives and the criteria that could be used to judge their success. One possibility would be to announce a "leaning against the wind" strategy (Wonnacott 1958), but the objection to that is that it might oblige them to resist a change of which they approved (i.e., one that was tending to reduce a misalignment). If one thinks that misalignments are the problem, then the logical solution is to sanction intervention (or policies with the same objective) that would tend to reduce misalignments. That could be done either by prohibiting intervention (or other forms of management) that would tend to push the exchange rate away from a "reference rate," or by prohibiting all intervention inside a "monitoring zone" as well as any intervention that would push the rate away from that zone. But in either event there would be a need to identify and publish a target rate (i.e., the reference rate or the center of the monitoring zone). Fred regards this as less likely to be acceptable to officialdom than target zones because it involves the adoption of point estimates of equilibrium rather than ranges. (One way of meeting this difficulty would be to adopt the monitoring zone variant of the proposal.) The virtues (and vices, if there are any, apart from the unworthy desires of officials not to be held accountable) of publication need to be discussed. That is an assignment for the future.

Concluding Remarks

It is clear that Fred and I have not persuaded officialdom, or the economics profession, or the public, or even all our colleagues, that unmanaged (as I define them) floating exchange rates are not the best possible arrangement. Even if that remains true, there is perhaps some value in having helped to propagate regimes that have enabled countries to learn to float and so transition to floating without a crisis. Or else there would be value in having aided East Asia to move toward a regime that resolves the collective action problem that has so far caused it to ride the dollar down whenever there appeared to be a possibility of sufficient dollar adjustment to head off global economic crisis. And if we have helped develop thoughts toward the form that a backup regime might take if and when the nonsystem enters crisis, this too might justify our efforts.

References

Balassa, Bela, and John Williamson. 1987, rev. ed. 1990. *Adjusting to Success: Balance of Payments Policy in the East Asian NICs.* Washington: Institute for International Economics.
Bergsten, C. Fred. 1988. The Case for Target Zones. In *The International Monetary System: The Next Twenty-Five Years*, Symposium at Basle University to Commemorate Twenty-Five Years of Per Jacobsson Lectures.

Bergsten, C. Fred. 1993. Implications for International Monetary Reform. In *A Retrospective on the Bretton Woods System: Implications for International Monetary Reform*, ed. M. D. Bordo and B. Eichengreen. Chicago: University of Chicago Press.

Bergsten, C. Fred. 1994. Exchange Rate Policy. In *American Economics Policy in the 1980s*, ed. M. Feldstein. Chicago: University of Chicago Press.

Bergsten, C. Fred. 1995. The IMF and World Bank in an Evolving World. In *Fifty Years after Bretton Woods: The Future of the IMF and World Bank*, ed. J. M. Boughton and K. S. Lateef. Washington: International Monetary Fund and World Bank.

Bergsten, C. Fred, and C. Randall Henning. 1996. *Global Economic Leadership and the Group of Seven*. Washington: Institute for International Economics.

Bergsten, C. Fred, and John Williamson. 1983. Exchange Rates and Trade Policy. In *Trade Policy in the 1980s*, ed. W. R. Cline. Washington: Institute for International Economics.

Bergsten, C. Fred, and John Williamson, eds. 2004. *Dollar Adjustment: How Far? Against What?* Washington: Institute for International Economics.

Catte, Pietro, Giampaolo Galli, and Salvatore Rebecchini. 1994. Concerted Intervention and the Dollar: An Analysis of Daily Data. In *The International Monetary System*, ed. P. B. Kenen, F. Papadia, and F. Saccomanni. Cambridge, UK: Cambridge University Press.

Collignon, Stefan, Jean Pisani-Ferry, and Yung Chul Park. 1999. *Exchange Rate Policies in Emerging Asian Countries*. London and New York: Routledge.

Dominguez, Kathryn M., and Jeffrey A. Frankel. 1993. *Does Foreign Exchange Intervention Work?* Washington: Institute for International Economics.

Funabashi, Yoichi. 1988. *Managing the Dollar: From the Plaza to the Louvre*. Washington: Institute for International Economics.

Goldstein, Morris. 1995. *The Exchange Rate System and the IMF: A Modest Agenda*. Washington: Institute for International Economics.

Goldstein, Morris. 2002. *Managed Floating Plus*. Washington: Institute for International Economics.

Halm, George N., ed. 1970. *Approaches to Greater Flexibility of Exchange Rates: The Bürgenstock Papers*. Princeton: Princeton University Press.

Kenen, Peter B., ed. 1994. *Managing the World Economy: Fifty Years After Bretton Woods*. Washington: Institute for International Economics.

Krugman, Paul R. 1991. Target Zones and Exchange Rate Dynamics. *Quarterly Journal of Economics* 106, no. 3: 669-82 (August).

Svensson, Lars E. 1992. An Interpretation of Recent Research on Target Zones. *Journal of Economic Perspectives* 6, no. 4: 119–44.

Williamson, John. 1982. A Survey of the Emergent Literature on the Optimal Peg. *Journal of Development Economics* 11: 39–61.

Williamson, John. 1983, rev. ed. 1985. *The Exchange Rate System*. Washington: Institute for International Economics.

Williamson, John. 1996. *The Crawling Band as an Exchange Rate Regime*. Washington: Institute for International Economics.

Williamson, John. 1998. Crawling Bands or Monitoring Bands: How To Manage Exchange Rates in a World of Capital Mobility. *International Finance* 1, no. 1 (October): 59–79.

Williamson, John. 2000. *Exchange Rate Regimes for Emerging Markets: Reviving the Intermediate Option*. POLICY ANALYSIS IN INTERNATIONAL ECONOMICS 60. Washington: Institute for International Economics.

Williamson, John. 2005. *A Currency Basket for East Asia, Not Just China*. International Economics Policy Briefs PBO5-1. Washington: Institute for International Economics.

Williamson, John. 2006 (forthcoming). *Reference Rates and the International Monetary System*. POLICY ANALYSIS IN INTERNATIONAL ECONOMICS 82. Washington: Institute for International Economics.

Williamson, John, and Marcus H. Miller. 1987. *Targets and Indicators: A Blueprint for the International Coordination of Economic Policy*. Washington: Institute for International Economics.

Wonnacott, Paul. 1958. Exchange Stabilization in Canada 1950–54: A Comment. *Canadian Journal of Economics and Political Science* (May).

9

What Can Exchange Rates Tell Us?

EDWIN M. TRUMAN

My direct association with Fred Bergsten as a colleague at the Peterson Institute for International Economics is relatively recent, covering only 5 of the Institute's 25 years. While I was in government I benefited from many of the Institute's publications and pronouncements during its first two decades. Occasionally and understandably, I was dismayed by the critiques of policies that I helped to design and implement, in particular when those critiques tended to minimize some of the constraints I felt we faced or gloss over some aspects I thought were important. I was as perplexed as others when markets occasionally failed to discriminate between pronouncements by Fred Bergsten and those of high government officials.

Throughout his career, Fred Bergsten has advocated an activist approach to exchange rate policy. Over the past 25 years, these concerns have contributed to his advocacy of target zones or reference exchange rate ranges to provide more structure to the international monetary system.[1] In the Bergstenian framework, target zones are intended to disci-

Edwin M. Truman has been a senior fellow at the Institute since 2001. The author has benefited in this chapter's preparation from comments from Martin Baily, Randy Henning, Joe Gagnon, Morris Goldstein, Mike Mussa, Mark Sobel, and John Williamson as well as from C. Fred Bergsten himself and from excellent research assistance by Anna Wong and Doug Dowson. He was a close observer—and at times a co-conspirator—of the messages that movements in the US dollar conveyed to US policymakers through much of the period covered by this chapter. Thus, the reader should not look for a dispassionate analysis. For this reason, as well as the standard explanations for a disclaimer, he alone should be held responsible for any errors or specific interpretations.

pline macroeconomic policies and prevent sizable global imbalances from emerging, in particular those that contribute to the adoption of protectionist measures.[2]

In this chapter, I take a complementary approach to exchange rate movements. I focus not on using the regime to discipline specific economic polices; rather, my interest is in what movements in exchange rates can tell policymakers more broadly. From this perspective, I ask what US policymakers should have inferred from pronounced movements in the dollar during the floating rate period? Was the signal about the appropriateness of their macroeconomic policies? Was it a warning about protectionist pressures? Was it a bubble? I examine US economic history since 1972 with a view to discerning what exchange rates should, or should not, have told US policymakers about their policies.[3] In a substantial portion of this period, US policymakers thought that the dollar's movements were telling them to resist those movements via sterilized foreign exchange market intervention. For this reason, a subtheme of the description and analysis in this chapter is to consider whether these particular messages were appropriate as received.

In the next section, as is appropriate in a volume of this genre, I digress to describe briefly some of my interactions with Fred Bergsten over more than 30 years and to provide some background that motivated me to ask the central question of this chapter. The section that follows outlines the low-tech methodology I apply. The meat of the chapter in the section after that is an examination of seven episodes over the past 30-plus years to extract the messages that movements in the dollar were or were not sending US policymakers. Finally, I offer some concluding remarks. In brief, I conclude that while messages from US dollar exchange rate movements were not uniform or unambiguous, they were usually—and by implication still are—worth contemplating by analysts and policymakers to a greater degree than generally was the case.

---

1. See John Williamson's contribution to this volume on the evolution of his views about target zones and the exchange rate regimes that have been frequently, but not always completely, aligned with those of C. Fred Bergsten. See also Morris Goldstein's and Mike Mussa's contribution to this volume for an additional review.

2. As noted by Goldstein and Mussa, the high-water mark to date for Bergsten's championing of target zones was reached when he persuaded 10 of 28 members of a Council on Foreign Relations (1969) task force on the global financial system to support his dissent from the majority position and join him in calling for target zones.

3. A case can be made that the analysis should extend back to the mid-1960s because the deterioration of the US trade balance contributed not only to protectionist pressures in the United States at that time but also to the resulting breakdown of the Bretton Woods system of exchange rates. On the other hand, it was primarily the nonmovement of exchange rates during that period that was sending a message about economic policies rather than the movement of exchange rates, which is the focus of this chapter.

C. Fred Bergsten: Policymaker and Thinker

When Fred Bergsten was assistant secretary of the US Treasury for international affairs in the late 1970s, a position that I also occupied briefly in the late 1990s, I worked closely with him in my position as director of the Division of International Finance at the Federal Reserve Board on a number of projects in the international financial arena.

At the Federal Reserve in those days, we concentrated primarily on US policy interactions with industrial countries. When Fred Bergsten teamed up with Tony Solomon at the US Treasury, Fred paid relatively more attention to US economic, financial, and trade relations with nonindustrial countries, while Solomon was relatively more involved with the industrial countries, the G-5/G-7, and IMF issues. However, Fred was an active participant in interagency policy debates on all topics, in particular early in the Carter administration. Moreover, I was always impressed by how Solomon and Bergsten operated as a team, each with their area of principal responsibilities but each more than capable of not only covering for the other but also providing leadership in the other person's major area. In particular, I attended several meetings of the Organization for Economic Cooperation and Development's (OECD) Working Party Three, where the economic and financial policies of the major industrial countries were debated and discussed, when Fred headed the US delegation. He was a forceful and reasoned articulator of US views on the topics, which mostly dealt with the many poorly understood macroeconomic challenges of the day. In 1998, I was nominated to fill the position that Fred had occupied 20 years earlier. Tim Geithner, the undersecretary, and I followed the Solomon-Bergsten working model. I am presumptuous enough to believe that as a result we were the most effective team since Solomon and Bergsten.

One example stands out in my memory as illustrating Fred's qualities of responsible policymaking. After Tony Solomon left as Treasury undersecretary to become president of the Federal Reserve Bank of New York in April 1980, he was not replaced. Fred was the acting undersecretary, and he became more actively involved in exchange rate policy issues.[4] As the dollar strengthened in the final quarter of 1980, in particular after the election of Ronald Reagan, Fred strongly supported the decision that the US authorities (Treasury and Federal Reserve) aggressively purchase deutsche mark and a smaller amount of Swiss francs necessary to cover the US open position in those currencies that had been created by the earlier sale of part of the proceeds of Carter bonds, US foreign currency obligations issued as part of the November 1, 1978, dollar rescue package. The objective was to

---

4. Because of the heavy criticism of President Carter's economic policies at the time (in retrospect they were not so bad), he chose not to send to the Senate any nominations for economic policy positions during the last year of his term.

restore US balances of those currencies to pay off the Carter bonds (at a profit) when they matured and to leave behind no unfinished business. I was impressed with Fred's professionalism in managing the transition between administrations.[5] At the same time, Fred advocated building up a small "war chest" of foreign currency for future use. Subsequently, he justifiably was sharply critical of Under Secretary Beryl Sprinkel's wasting of a portion of the accumulated foreign exchange to finance the increase in the US quota in the IMF in 1984.

My first professional contact with Fred Bergsten, as best I can recall, was indirect and before he became assistant secretary. I was asked by the *Journal of Economic History* to review his 1975 magnum opus *The Dilemmas of the Dollar: The Economics and Politics of United States International Monetary Policy*.[6] The preface opened with characteristic Bergstenian overstatement: "The dollar had peaked as an international currency by 1968. It was decisively repudiated in 1973. Yet many noted economists continued to proclaim the international domination of the dollar and predict its perpetuation." Bergsten argued that a continuation of the dollar's dominance would be a mistake for the world and, in particular, for the United States. Therefore, he advocated a systemic reform of the international monetary system based on five principles (Truman 1977, 464):

> It must be managed internationally; it must accommodate diversity; it must be based on the SDR with holdings of other reserve assets permitted under rules to prevent adverse effects on the system; it must have an improved [exchange rate] adjustment process; and it must be based on real cooperation among countries.

This was an impressive agenda. I commented in my review that at least on paper the second amendment of the IMF Articles of Agreement, which was completed after *The Dilemmas of the Dollar* had been published but whose main outlines were clear by late 1973, came close to satisfying all but the third of his principles—an SDR-based system with rules governing other reserve asset holdings. In fact, I was guilty of excessive optimism, and I suspect that Fred would plead the same. He joined those deploring the international monetary "nonsystem" that subsequently evolved.[7]

Bergsten (1970, 63) earlier had addressed greater exchange rate flexibility for the dollar in the context of a rebalanced international monetary system: "Because of its broad objectives in economic and foreign policy, the

---

5. When I recently mentioned this episode to Fred, he demurred from taking principal responsibility for the policy; instead he credited the late Secretary G. William Miller and Deputy Secretary Robert Carswell.

6. My review (Truman 1977) appeared after Fred Bergsten had become assistant secretary of the Treasury, but I am quite confident that I completed the review before November 1976 and well before his nomination. I actually reviewed two other books as well, but the Bergsten tome accounted for well over half of the more than 1,000 pages that I covered in my review.

7. Although I understood their reasoning, I was never a member of this band.

United States has a major stake in the maintenance of an effective monetary system." His understated conclusion was that the United States should not oppose greater flexibility for the dollar, under appropriate rules encouraging a symmetrical adjustment process. The United States and the system as a whole would benefit.

I shared in the mid-1970s and share now many of Bergsten's concerns about the structure of the international monetary system. He argued (Bergsten 1975, 557) that under a more balanced and symmetric international monetary system the United States would be liberated from the "extra constraints" placed upon the country because the dollar had become the global reserve currency. Among those constraints he included:

> International political dominance, assumption of primary responsibility for the functioning of the monetary system, assured convertibility into all other assets (including gold) used as reserve assets in the system, maintenance of a ratio between reserve assets and liquid liabilities deemed "adequate" by the most conservative wing of opinion in the world financial spectrum, avoidance of exchange rate changes and comprehensive controls over international transactions, and probably a balance of payments comprised of current account surpluses plus net capital exports.[8]

As this quotation illustrates, Fred Bergsten's emphasis on the adjustment mechanism and exchange rates was motivated by considerations of external balance. In his role as a policymaker, thinker, and critic, Bergsten has frequently focused on the distorting effects of exchange rate misalignments not only on trade flows and global imbalances but also on domestic economies.[9]

Bergsten and Williamson (1983, 99), in one of the early publications of the Institute for International Economics on trade policy, motivated their argument with the following statement: "Relatively little attention has been paid to the impact of exchange rates on trade policy, despite widespread analyses by international monetary economists of their impact on trade flows." This has been a consistent refrain in Bergsten's writing. Not only did Bergsten and Williamson point to a number of instances in which exchange rate misalignments had induced the US political process to adopt protectionist measures, but they also argued (101–102), "If the exchange rate conveys price signals to producers and consumers which are incorrect reflections of underlying economic relationships, significant distortions can result for production, hence trade." Moreover, they noted that

---

8. In my review, I stated that Bergsten's analysis was in the tradition of Robert Triffin's *Gold and the Dollar Crisis* (1960). Bob Triffin had been my thesis adviser at Yale, and my comparison was intended as a compliment.

9. An early and recurrent theme of Bergsten's work and writings has been the importance of not separating domestic and international economic policies. When he was assistant secretary of the Treasury (Bergsten 1980, 4), he stated in April 1977, "The basic philosophy of the Carter administration has been that domestic and international economic issues are inextricably linked."

such distortions might outlive the exchange rate misalignment—witness Japan in the 1970s and 1980s and potentially China today. Therefore, in the Bergstenian view as presented with Williamson, benefits would accrue to a system focused on avoiding exchange rate "misalignments" and maintaining equilibrium exchange rates.

Bergsten and Williamson (1983) did not define exchange rate misalignment, but they implied that misalignments are prolonged departures from fundamental equilibrium.[10] They carefully described three concepts of equilibrium exchange rates: a "market equilibrium" that is produced by an absence of official intervention but that nevertheless might be distorted by other government policies and therefore is of limited empirical value; a "current equilibrium" produced by markets with full knowledge as well as by cyclical influences and, therefore, justified (by some) as reflecting economic fundamentals; and a "fundamental equilibrium" that they traced back to a similar concept in the original IMF Articles of Agreement. They maintained that this concept can have operational content as long as one is prepared to make judgments about such matters as internal balance, normal capital flows, cyclical positions, and trade elasticities.

They concluded that the international trading system would be improved by focusing on fundamental equilibrium exchange rates (and departures from them) in which monetary policy at least in part would be directed at supporting such exchange rates via (1) pegging (with a large degree of support from monetary policy in the form of *unsterilized* intervention), (2) floating with target zones or reference rates (but again backed up by monetary policy and *sterilized* intervention), or (3) capital controls, which was a distant third choice.[11]

The Bergstenian arguments about the links between trade policies and exchange rate misalignments and associated distortions are at least as valid today as they were 25 or 30 years ago. However, the possibility that a pegged rate for a major currency should be supported by subjugating monetary policy to an exchange rate objective never attracted me, perhaps because of my central banker background. Moreover, as was demonstrated by the crises of the exchange rate mechanism (ERM) of the European monetary system (EMS) in 1992–93, many doubt monetary policy is a feasible instrument to tightly manage exchange rates among major currencies with open capital markets, at least in part for reasons of political economy. Furthermore, even with floating exchange rates the lack of empirical support for the theoretical construct of uncovered interest parity (UIP) raises further questions about exchange rate policy prescriptions based on the use of monetary policy to achieve those objectives (see Isard

10. In Williamson (1983) this definition of misalignment was explicit.

11. Williamson (1983) combined the first two elements—pegging and reference rates—in his advocacy of crawling pegs. In the case of emerging-market economies, he later (Williamson 2000) linked those elements to a basket of currencies.

2006). Just as there is no simple link between budget positions and current account positions (Truman 2006), there is no simple link between differences in policy interest rates (the federal funds rate and the European Central Bank's repo rate) and exchange rates. In fact, the reasons are similar: Economies are too complex to generate empirical support for the use of such simple relationships to guide policy.

Bergsten has consistently argued that sterilized foreign exchange market intervention is an effective tool for managing exchange rates.[12] I am more skeptical about the sustained effectiveness of this instrument (Truman 2003). However, I would not discard sterilized intervention entirely from the toolkit. I have supported its use as a signaling device and in support of other policy adjustments. I merely doubt it is a reliable instrument to manage exchange rates on a day-by-day basis or to prevent prolonged misalignments. I have also argued (Truman 2003) that sterilized intervention may well be an inappropriate instrument in some economic and financial circumstances—for example, when monetary policy has an orientation that tends to push the exchange rate in the opposite direction.

Where does this leave me? I am left with the view that exchange rates matter and that exchange rate misalignments matter, but that care should be taken in interpreting the implications for economic *policies*, with an emphasis on the plural, of exchange rate movements and their possible misalignment. This view is not entirely at odds with Bergstenian doctrine. For example, Bergsten (1988, 34) states, "What is necessary is to view the whole range of domestic economic policies, macro and micro, through the lens of the exchange rate. If movements in the exchange rate suggest a need for policy action, steps should be taken on those policies which will effectively achieve the external and internal adjustment which is required." Moreover, Bergsten and Henning (1996, 102), in the context of making the case for target zones that are "quite wide (plus and minus 10 percent)," noted that one possible interpretation of exchange rate pressures "would be that the zone itself was incorrect and needed to be changed—an example of policy error by the authorities." These thoughts motivated me to undertake the examination that follows of the messages that US dollar movements were conveying to US policymakers over the past 30-plus years.

Methodology

Figure 9.1 displays in the heavy line the Federal Reserve Board staff's index of the real broad foreign exchange value of the dollar from January

---

12. In making his case for target zones for exchange rates Bergsten (1988, 34) argues that participating countries must accept a commitment to change their policies to protect the zones, starting with intervention and jawboning, using monetary policy next, and on occasion employing fiscal policy.

Figure 9.1 US dollar real effective exchange rate, average 1973Q1 to 2008Q2

index: January 1973 = 100

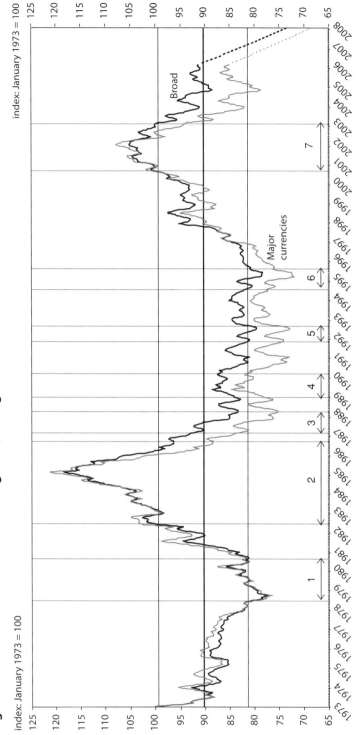

Source: Federal Reserve Board.

1973 (equal to 100) extended to March 2008, at which point I assume for purposes of this exercise that the dollar on this index will be 20 percent lower than it was in April 2006 as part of an international adjustment process that is well under way.[13] The figure also displays the average over the entire period and a band of plus or minus 10 percent around that average.[14]

Using the 10 percent bands as a crude statistical device serves to identify six episodes when the dollar's movements were sending potentially important messages about US economic policies: mid-1978 to late 1980 (dollar weakness); mid-1982 to late 1986 (dollar strength); most of 1992 (a short period of dollar weakness);[15] late 1994 to late 1995 (dollar weakness); late 2000 to early 2003 (dollar strength); and starting early in 2007 (prospective dollar weakness). If one were to perform the same exercise using the real major currency index for the dollar (the lighter line in figure 9.1), one period would be added (dollar weakness from late 1987 through 1988).[16] In addition, the period of dollar weakness in 1992 would be extended back to mid-1990 and forward to late 1993, the 1994–95 period of dollar weakness would also be stretched, and the recent period of dollar strength would be compressed somewhat.

One might reasonably observe that an average value for the real foreign exchange value of the dollar over 35 years is not an appropriate basis on which to identify periods of interest. One reason suggested by the analysis in Baily and Lawrence's chapter in this volume is that the value of the dollar consistent with US external balance has shifted down over time.[17]

An alternative statistical approach, shown in figure 9.2, is to look at a straight-line trend drawn from March 1973 to the hypothesized value in March 2008. After two devaluations of the dollar in 1971 and in early 1973 and the move to generalized floating of the major currencies in March 1973, the value of the dollar in March 1973 is a plausible estimate of the value that would have been associated with US external balance at that time. In contrast, the hypothesized value of the dollar in March 2008 is a

---

13. The precise value of the index in March 2008 is 73.6.

14. This bandwidth is consistent with that recommended by Fred Bergsten and John Williamson in their writings about target zones; see Bergsten and Henning (1996) and Williamson (1983).

15. The dollar touched the lower band as well in late 1990 and early 1991.

16. The average for the real major currency index for the dollar is 87.6 (not shown in figure 9.1), which is 3 percentage points below the average for the broad dollar, and the plus or minus 10 percent bands are comparably lower as well (also not shown).

17. This finding is consistent with one of the longest-standing empirical regularities in international economics: The aggregate income elasticity for US imports significantly exceeds that for US exports. It was first identified by Houthakker and Magee (1969) and has been frequently confirmed ever since; see for example Mann (2004).

Figure 9.2   US dollar real effective exchange rate, trend 1973Q1 to 2008Q2

index: January 1973 = 100

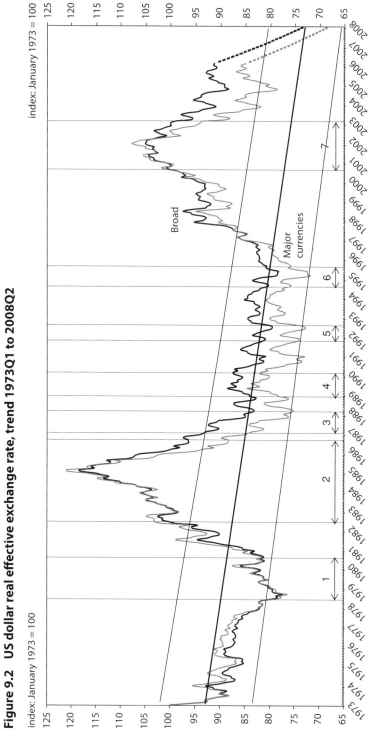

index: January 1973 = 100

Source: Federal Reserve Board.

plausible estimate of the value that would be associated with a US current account deficit in the range of 3 to 4 percent of GDP, which some might not consider to be external balance.

This second approach to identifying periods of interest based on the dollar's longer-term trend points to only three episodes for consideration: a short period of dollar weakness in 1978–79, a longer period of dollar strength in the mid-1980s, and a much longer period of dollar strength starting in the late 1990s and continuing into the "projection" period. It does not produce any new episodes for examination and eliminates two or three of the candidates suggested by the first approach.

In addition, at least through 1995, the intervention operations of the US monetary authorities in foreign exchange markets were more consistent with the implicit use of the historical average for the dollar than a downward sloping trend for the dollar as a guide. As noted above, a secondary theme of this chapter is to consider whether these operations were an appropriate response to the messages from the foreign exchange markets. In each of the six periods so far identified (not including the post-2007 period but including the 1987–88 period as indicated by use of the major currency index), there were significant net purchases or sales of dollars consistent with the view that the US authorities were concerned about an actual or potential misalignment of the dollar and were implicitly using a historical average to guide their judgments. In all cases the US authorities were not acting alone. In addition, during 1989 and early 1990, the US authorities bought almost $25 billion equivalent of foreign exchange in the largest sustained operations of the past 30-plus years. Consequently, in choosing episodes to examine to understand better what the dollar's movements might have been telling the US authorities, I have added the 1989–90 period and incorporated information about US intervention activities in my analysis.[18] The result is the following seven episodes.[19]

---

18. The analysis that follows is simplified in three respects. First, I relied primarily on the Federal Reserve Board staff's real broad index of the foreign exchange value of the dollar to pick episodes to examine. One might argue that the relevant exchange rates for the United States are not the 26 rates (treating the 12 members of the euro area as a single currency) now included in the FRB index. However, in the trade context, what is relevant is the dollar's value not against a particular currency but on an effective basis. Moreover, because the broad index depicted in figure 1 is based on moving-average weights, the importance of each currency rises as the importance of the country increases in the global trading system. For example, the seven "currencies" now included in the FRB staff's index of the dollar's value in terms of the major currencies accounted for 72 percent of the index in 1973 and only 53 percent today. Second, my choice of episodes to examine is only in part motivated by an effort to identify deviations from the average. Third, my principal concern is with US policies and US economic and financial conditions. The policies of other countries and global economic and financial conditions are relevant to a fuller analysis, but the focus in this chapter is on what the US dollar was telling US authorities about US policies.

19. I should emphasize that the episodes are more important than the precise dates used to identify them. However, it was necessary to use dates to assemble the associated information.

1. July 1978 to October 1980: Dollar Depreciation

2. July 1982 to October 1986: Soaring Dollar

3. March 1987 to April 1988: Arresting the Dollar's Decline

4. January 1989 to April 1990: Stabilizing the Dollar?

5. December 1991 to October 1992: The Dollar and the ERM Crises

6. September 1994 to October 1995: The Birth of the Strong Dollar

7. October 2000 to April 2003: Too Strong a Dollar?

The purpose of this volume is to honor C. Fred Bergsten, which justifies the following short, further digression examining the two representations of the US dollar over the past 30-plus years that I have employed to help identify episodes to consider. In writing about the potential greater exchange flexibility for the dollar as the Bretton Woods era was coming to a close, Bergsten (1970) identified two partially offsetting considerations for US policymakers: first, an improvement in the adjustment process from the standpoint of the United States and, second, the risk that excessive dollar weakness would undermine the dollar's role in the international monetary system. He noted that if the dollar on average were not allowed to decline sufficiently to achieve external adjustment on balance, the advantage of increased flexibility would be reduced if not eliminated, but the concern about the dollar's role would also be diminished.

We can use the data in figures 9.1 and 9.2 to perform a rough test of which tendency has predominated. In terms of the average value of the real broad index from March 1973 to April 2006, the dollar was more than 10 percent above the average (including the period extended to 2008) in 73 out of 398 months (18 percent of the time) and more than 10 percent below the average in only 32 months (8 percent). In terms of the trend for the broad index, the numbers are even more "unbalanced": in 163 months, more than 10 percent above the trend, and in only 8 months more than 10 percent below the trend. With respect to the real index in terms of the major currencies, the dollar was more than 10 percent above the average in 81 months (20 percent) and 10 percent below the average almost as often (73 months). However, in terms of the trend, the numbers are essentially the same as for the broad index: in 168 months more than 10 percent above the trend and in only 7 months more than 10 percent below.

On this basis, Bergsten appears to have been correct to be concerned that greater exchange rate flexibility for the dollar would not produce a substantial improvement in the global adjustment process in the absence of rules imposing greater symmetry in the operation of the adjustment mechanisms. By the metric of these exchange rate averages, the floating exchange rate system appears to have been associated with a US dollar whose value has been chronically overvalued, contributing to the deterioration of the US international investment position over the past 30 years.[20]

Returning to the analysis of the messages that US dollar movements were sending to US policymakers, for each of the seven identified episodes, I look at a number of indicators principally of US economic performance during the period (compared with periods immediately before and after the episode) and consider what the dollar's behavior might have been telling policymakers about US economic performance and whether they should have considered more seriously than they did the adjustment of policies including but not limited to US intervention policy, which may have been relied upon excessively or insufficiently. Among the candidate messages are the following:

1. US economic activity was too low, or too high, relative to trend, as indicated by the growth rate of real GDP, final sales to domestic residents, and the level of the unemployment rate. The dollar's movements were suggesting that macroeconomic policies should have been more, or less, stimulative.

2. Growth in the rest of the world was deficient or excessive as measured by a US export-weighted index. The dollar's movements were suggesting that the US authorities should press other countries to adjust their macroeconomic policies.[21]

3. US inflation was too high or too low, as indicated by the consumer price index (CPI) or the core CPI, excluding food and energy. The dollar's movements were suggesting that adjustments in US macroeconomic policies were appropriate.

4. US monetary policy was too easy or too tight, as indicated by the federal funds rate, the 10-year US Treasury bond yield, and real measures of these variables using contemporaneous CPI or core CPI inflation to construct them.[22] The dollar's movements were suggesting that this particular policy was inappropriate.

5. The US fiscal position was too easy or too tight, as indicated by the federal deficit or the general government deficit, as a percent of GDP.[23] The dollar's movements were suggesting that another particular policy should be modified.

---

20. Of course, some observers reject both metrics; see Richard N. Cooper (2005).

21. The Federal Reserve Board staff kindly provided the historical data incorporated in tables 9.1 to 9.7.

22. That is, inflation over the previous 12 months or four quarters.

23. A cyclically adjusted measure, or a measure of the structural deficit, would be more appropriate because in principle it strips out the endogenous cyclical influences of automatic stabilizers, but consistent series are not readily available.

6. The US trade (or current account) position, whether as represented by the US trade and current account position (as a percent of nominal GDP) and/or as proxied by the growth rates of real exports or imports of goods and services, pointed to a potential rise in US protectionism— a prominent Bergsten hypothesis. The dollar's movements were suggesting the adoption of policies to weaken the dollar.

7. There was a bubble in the foreign exchange market, and the dollar had little or no other information content because the market was wrong.[24] The dollar's movements were suggesting, perhaps, that foreign exchange market intervention would be appropriate.

To implement the analysis a number of quarterly indicators were assembled for each of the seven periods. In addition, the indicators were compared with similar information for periods eight quarters before and after the episode (see tables 9.1 to 9.7).[25] The potential messages are not mutually exclusive. Some people, including Fred Bergsten, would argue that the dollar's messages frequently called for heavier not lighter US foreign exchange market intervention, consistent with his advocacy of target zones for exchange rates. However, the theme of this chapter is that exchange rate movements can and do send more varied messages, including but not exclusively about the appropriateness of exchange market intervention.

The Evidence

For each of the seven episodes, I examine evidence bearing on the seven hypotheses. In some episodes, the evidence is ambiguous. I also incorporate information about US intervention activity during and surrounding the relevant periods.

July 1978 to October 1980: Dollar Depreciation

Following the US dollar's second devaluation in February 1973 and the grudging acceptance by the authorities of the major countries of moving

---

24. See Miller, Weller, and Williamson (1989) for a treatment of how target zones would help to limit such bubbles.

25. A quarter was included in the period even if it included only one month of the episode. In the case of growth rates four-quarter changes are used and the averages are for the relevant quarters, including the quarter containing the start and end of each episode. In a few cases, a portion of the episode overlaps with the prior or subsequent period. Of course, there are lags in the adjustment process. Issues of causality are involved as well. Finally, one might wonder what was going on more generally in the rest of the world. However, my purpose is to examine the broad-brush evidence about what the behavior of the dollar during each of these periods may have been signaling about US policy.

Table 9.1   July 1978–September 1980 episode (percent except as noted)

	Indicators	Episode	Episode less before[a]	Episode less after[b]
1	Growth of US real GDP	2.7	−2.1	2.2
2	Growth of US real gross domestic purchases	2.3	−2.7	1.8
3	US unemployment rate	6.3	−0.6	−2.1
4	Growth of world real GDP	4.2	−0.1	2.4
5	US CPI inflation	11.7	5.4	2.8
6	US core CPI inflation	10.5	4.1	1.0
7	US federal funds rate	11.3	5.4	−3.7
8	10-year US Treasury bond yield	9.9	2.3	−3.7
9	US federal budget[c]	−1.0	1.2	1.5
10	US general government[c]	−0.5	1.1	1.8
11	US trade balance[c]	−0.9	0.3	−0.4
12	US current account balance[c]	−0.1	0.5	−0.2
13	Growth of US real exports of goods and services	12.2	7.7	13.4
14	Growth of US real imports of goods and services	1.0	−11.5	0.9

Memorandum items:

	Episode	Before	After
Quarters	9 (1978Q3–1980Q3)	8 (1976Q3–1978Q2)	8 (1980Q4–1982Q3)
Months	27 (7/1978–9/1980)	64 (3/1973–6/1978)	21 (10/1980–6/1982)
US intervention			
Foreign currency sales			
Amount (dollars)	23,668	6,181	417
Days	195	229	13
Foreign currency purchases			
Amount (dollars)	8,741	3,509	6,560
Days	344	329	99
Total intervention days	539	558	112
Total days	587	1,391	456

CPI = consumer price index

a. *Before* is defined as the eight quarters prior to the episode.
b. *After* is defined as the eight quarters following the episode.
c. As a percent of GDP.

Note: Indicators are calculated as averages of four-quarter changes except for items indicated by footnote c.

Sources: Bureau of Economic Analysis, Bureau of Labor Statistics, Federal Reserve Board.

to generalized floating exchange rates among their currencies in March 1973, the dollar, although weak on balance, for a couple of months did not stray substantially from its March 1973 average. It then dropped a further 5 percent (in real terms on the broad index) by July. This "third devaluation of the dollar" was used by the Europeans to persuade the US authorities to resume their defense of the dollar via sales of deutsche mark for US dollars.[26] The dollar recovered moderately and did not return to its 1973 low until July of 1977. The intervention by US and other authorities in 1975 and subsequently was reasonably successful in buying a period of relative calm in foreign exchange markets even as the US economy went through a deep recession. During the 12 months after July 1977, the dollar declined a further 6 percent and entered the first identified episode in July 1978. During the episode, the dollar did not decline substantially further on average in real terms, reaching its low in October 1978, just before the November 1, 1978, dollar rescue package.[27] However, the dollar did not recover on a sustained basis to within 10 percent of its average value until October 1980.

What was the message for US policymakers from this period of dollar weakness?

As is shown in the first line of table 9.1, the average growth rate of real GDP at 2.7 percent was 2 percentage points less than the growth rate during the previous eight quarters but substantially above the rate during the following eight quarters (only 0.5 percent), which were dominated by the recession of 1981–82.[28] On the other hand, as shown in the third line, the unemployment rate during the episode was less than during the eight quarters prior to the episode, although unemployment rose somewhat at the end of the episode as US growth slowed toward the middle of 1979 and subsequently rose substantially during the 1982 recession. Finally, global growth was essentially the same as prior to the episode but declined afterwards.

---

26. From July 11 to July 31, the US authorities sold a total of $218.8 million equivalent in deutsche mark on 12 of 16 trading days.

27. On a monthly average basis, the dollar's low in October 1978 was 3.2 percent below its value in July 1978 on the broad dollar index in both real and nominal terms. Against the major currencies, the low in October was 3.1 percent below July in real terms, but 4.3 percent lower in nominal terms, reflecting the more rapid US inflation. In nominal terms, at its low on October 30, the dollar was down 7.6 percent from its July average against the major currencies. President Carter announced the package on November 1, and the US Treasury and Federal Reserve made follow-up announcements. Those announcements featured a concern about downward pressure on the US dollar that was "hampering progress toward price stability" and causing damage to the investment and growth climate—a bit of a mixed message. The package consisted of a one percentage point boost in the Federal Reserve discount rate to a historic high of 9.5 percent; the imposition of a supplemental reserve requirement on large time deposits (intended to reduce reserve availability and to provide banks with an incentive to borrow abroad); the mobilization of $30 billion of foreign currencies via doubling of the size of swap lines with the Bundesbank, Bank of Japan, and Swiss National Bank, drawing on the IMF to obtain deutsche mark and yen, sales of SDR for deutsche mark, yen, and Swiss francs, and the issuance of up to $10 billion in foreign currency–denominated instruments (Carter bonds); and a step up in the rate of US gold sales.

28. There were two quarters of negative growth during the episode itself.

This evidence suggests that the dollar's weakness was partially a signal of relative weakness in US economic activity, but it was not necessarily signaling a need for more expansionary US economic policies—quite the reverse. As is shown in lines 5 and 6, the US consumer price inflation essentially doubled during the episode compared with the previous eight quarters, and the increase in the core CPI was almost as pronounced. The December-to-December inflation rates on the CPI and core CPI reached post–World War II record highs in 1979 and were in double digits in December 1980. Subsequently, both measures of US inflation declined substantially and after eight quarters were below the lowest rate in the eight quarters preceding the episode. During the episode the federal funds rate averaged more than twice the rate in the previous period, but it rose even higher in the following period. In real terms, during the preceding period the funds rate was slightly negative (0.4 percent). Although it averaged slightly positive during the period (0.3 percent), the real funds rate was significantly positive in the following period (5.4 percent).[29] This evidence suggests that the dollar's weakness was signaling a substantial deterioration in US inflation performance and a relative failure of the US authorities to deal with it.[30]

On the fiscal side, the federal and general government budgets (lines 9 and 10) were in modest deficit, but the deficits were smaller during the episode than prior to it. Of course, under the influence of recession and Reaganomics, the deficits widened during the subsequent period. Nevertheless, in retrospect it does not appear that exchange markets were delivering a specific vote of no confidence on US fiscal policy, in contrast with a general lack of confidence in the full range of US economic policies.[31]

Looking at the overall US trade situation, the trade deficit (line 11) narrowed during the episode compared with the previous eight quarters and narrowed further during the immediately following period. Real exports

---

29. These calculations are made in the proper manner [(1 + the interest rate)/(1 + the inflation rate) – 1]. They are not altered significantly if the core CPI is used.

30. At the time, there was a tendency to attribute US inflation to rising food and energy prices and to the decline in the dollar itself, calling for intervention to resist the dollar's decline. However, the first two factors were affecting other countries as well, even if not to an equal extent, and in retrospect too much blame was placed on the dollar.

31. However, US fiscal policy was not free from international criticism. At the Bonn summit (July 1978), the United States was criticized. In the summit declaration, President Carter pointed to his administration's scaling back of its proposed tax cut and expenditure projections. The summit declaration concluded, "Implementation of the policies described above [including the US commitment to reduce its dependence on imported oil by raising the price of domestic oil to the world level by the end of 1980] in the framework of a concerted program will help bring about a better pattern of world payments balances and lead to greater stability in international exchange markets." The Tokyo summit declaration the following year focused almost exclusively on energy issues, repeating the commitments to a concerted program by all participating countries but without any specifics on US fiscal policy.

of goods and services (line 13) during the episode increased at almost three times the rate in the prior period, though their growth rate turned negative in the subsequent period. Real imports (line 14) stagnated on average during the episode following double-digit expansion previously; they showed little growth on average after the episode. Therefore, it would not appear that the dollar was under downward pressure because the US external accounts were particularly weak compared with the immediately preceding period.

From July 1978 through September 1980, the US dollar was frequently under heavy downward pressure, and US and foreign monetary authorities often resisted those pressures through exchange market intervention to support the dollar. The US authorities operated in the foreign exchange markets on 537 days, or 92 percent of all trading days during the episode, selling $14.9 billion net of foreign currencies. The ample evidence that the root cause of the dollar's weakness was US macroeconomic, specifically monetary, policy means that we can reject the hypothesis that the market was wrong about the dollar and was generating a bubble of weakness.

The evidence from these indicators suggests that the weakness of the dollar during this episode was principally signaling that US inflation had gotten out of hand and that US monetary policy was too easy. This interpretation is consistent with the sequence of US policy actions during the period. First, the dollar's weakness was met with stepped-up US foreign exchange sales of dollars during late 1977 and the first 10 months of 1978.[32] These operations culminated in the dollar support package that was announced on November 1, 1978. It included a substantial tightening of Federal Reserve policy.[33] However, these actions proved insufficient to arrest the dollar's slide.[34]

This led to the Federal Reserve's change in operating procedure that was announced on October 6, 1979, aimed at decisively ending the inflation that afflicted the US economy. That inflation was largely a consequence of excessively easy Federal Reserve monetary policy, in the context of shocks to food and energy prices, that had been predicated on a potential growth rate that the US economy was unable to achieve because of the sharp deterioration in its productivity performance. Following the change in the Federal Open Market Committee's (FOMC) policy orientation, the federal

---

32. The net intervention amounted to foreign exchange sales of $3,134 million equivalent. As is shown in the memorandum lines of table 9.1, there were some foreign exchange purchases to recover foreign exchange sold during the period or prior to the dollar's 1971 devaluation.

33. The average federal funds rate increased 150 basis points between 1978Q3 and 1978Q4 to 10 percent. See footnote 27 for a summary of the November 1 package.

34. As shown in the memorandum lines of table 9.1, gross US foreign currency sales were $23.4 billion equivalent. Again, there also were foreign currency purchases, especially late in the period, as discussed earlier.

funds rate averaged 17.2 percent in the first quarter of 1980, substantially above the CPI inflation rate of 14.6 percent in the same quarter.[35] Although the dollar recovered somewhat on average in the wake of the Federal Reserve's policy shift, it did not move within 10 percent of its long-term average rate on a sustained basis until the fourth quarter of 1980.[36] (See Truman 2004 and 2005b for fuller descriptions of this period.)

My interpretation of the message from exchange markets during this period differs somewhat in emphasis and orientation from that offered by Bergsten and Williamson (1983). They argue (111), "renewed dollar overvaluation in 1975–76, which required a depreciation of 15 percent in 1977–78, correlated with renewal of protectionist pressure and the adoption of several new restrictive [US] measures (steel trigger price mechanism, TPM; shoes; sugar)." There is no dispute that the United States adopted during this period a series of additional protectionist measures.

However, there was not a "renewed dollar overvaluation" in 1975–76 on average; at that time the dollar (in this case on the Federal Reserve staff's major currency price-adjusted index) depreciated by 2.2 percent compared with the period from April 1973 to December 1974 and depreciated 1.3 percent between December 1974 and December 1976. In 1977–78 on average, the dollar depreciated 6.4 percent compared with 1975–76 on average, and the depreciation from December 1976 to December 1978 was 11.5 percent.[37] On the other hand, it is important to go back a bit further in history. Coming out of the US recession in 1975, US imports surged relative to exports, and the US trade balance moved back into deficit. At the same time, the surpluses of Germany and Japan were widening. When US Treasury Secretary Blumenthal in June 1977 suggested at a press conference in Paris that countries with surpluses should allow their currencies to appreciate, he was accused of talking down the dollar. His words appeared to have that effect, although he was merely echoing the agreed upon language in the statement of the OECD ministerial meeting.

These differing interpretations and emphases might be resolved as follows. There were additional US protectionist measures adopted during the

---

35. The data for the second and third quarters of 1980, when the federal funds rate fell sharply, are contaminated by the fact that the US imposition of credit controls dramatically curtailed the demand for money. Under the Federal Reserve's new operating procedure that focused on nonborrowed reserves, rather than the federal funds rate, in order to control the growth of money, the federal funds rate in the second quarter of 1980 averaged half the rate in the first quarter, and the average rate in the third quarter was affected as well.

36. The dollar was below the 10 percent upper band on average in both July 1980 and September 1980.

37. The dollar did rise by about 5 percent on average against the major currencies in real terms from a low in March 1975 through the end of 1975, but that rise was associated with intervention designed to boost the dollar, including substantial (by the standards of the time) foreign exchange sales of about $240 million equivalent in July 1975. The dollar again reached its March 1975 low by the fourth quarter of 1977.

period. They were directed primarily but not exclusively at Japan and motivated in part by the deterioration of the US trade balance, even though the dollar was adjusting—slowly.[38] However, the protectionist measures were motivated primarily not by contemporaneous dollar strength or trade weakness but in lagged reaction to the dollar's overvaluation in real terms in the late 1960s and early 1970s and the modest deterioration of the US trade position in 1976 and 1977—prior to the episode. For an extended period, US policymakers at the Federal Reserve as well as at the Treasury misinterpreted the message of dollar weakness as signaling a need for *further* dollar depreciation. In due course, the Federal Reserve, with the early support of the US Treasury and eventually other economic policy advisors in the administration, arrived at the correct interpretation of the message from the behavior of the dollar: US inflation was a serious problem that was undermining both the US economy and the role of the United States in the world economy, and US policies were pushing the economy to grow beyond its potential.

Bergsten is on the record fully signing onto the view that US inflation was a serious problem. In July 1979, he testified (Bergsten 1980) on external aspects of US inflation, noting that he would not address the internal aspects "except to reiterate the essentiality of maintaining the fight against inflation to a successful conclusion." He added, "The dollar defense program of last November [1978] was motivated largely by just such a concern and was eminently successful in strengthening and stabilizing the dollar."

The second part of this comment was a bit premature. However, reviewing the international economic policies of the Carter administration in December 1980 (Bergsten 1981, 8), he tied together the events of 1978–80:

> In November 1978, the United States also moved to more active intervention in the foreign exchange market to halt an excessive depreciation of the dollar and maintain orderly conditions necessary to global confidence. In retrospect, I believe that the program of November 1978 marked a watershed in US international monetary policy. For perhaps the first time, the US government recognized that the relationships among domestic performance, external balances, and exchange markets

---

38. This focus on Japan was not entirely consistent with the behavior of the dollar-yen exchange rate. In nominal terms the dollar rose against the yen from March 1975 to the end of the year, was essentially unchanged during 1976, and declined to well below the March 1975 level by the end of 1977 and further by October 1978. Fred Bergsten played an active role in engineering the yen's appreciation in early 1977. He informed the Japanese authorities, during a trip to Tokyo with Vice President Mondale, that they should "keep their hands off the yen-dollar exchange rate" and refrain from clandestine intervention in which the proceeds were hidden in Japanese commercial banks so they would not show up as Japanese reserves. The dollar followed a similar course against the deutsche mark. However, in 1979 in the wake of the dollar-support package of November 1, 1978, the dollar rose against the yen and stayed up, while in the summer of 1979 it declined back to its October 1978 lows against the deutsche mark.

are so strong that external factors must on occasion go far to determine our internal policies. From that date, there was unanimity within the administration (and the Federal Reserve) that fighting inflation had to be the priority objective of US economic policy—in important part because a failure to do so would continue the vicious cycle of a weaker dollar abroad and yet more inflation at home.

Bergsten in this contemporary summary put greater emphasis on the external forces of inflation than most would today, though many observers at the time agreed with him. However, his basic point is consistent with my reading of the evidence and his orientation is congruent with the motivation of this chapter to examine what exchange rates may be saying about US policies more broadly.

July 1982 to October 1986: Soaring Dollar

The dollar continued to appreciate after the inauguration of Ronald Reagan on January 20, 1981. For about a month, the US authorities accumulated additional foreign exchange, making net purchases of $1.4 billion equivalent between January 21 and February 23. On March 30, the United States authorities sold deutsche mark to settle the market when the dollar dropped sharply after the assassination attempt on President Reagan. After that date, there were no further purchases or sales of foreign exchange for a period of 326 trading days until one small operation in June 1982 in the context of a sharp rise of the dollar following an EMS realignment.

In his review of US exchange rate policy in the first Reagan administration, Bergsten (1994) characterized the dominant view at the time as one in which the exchange rate and what was happening to the external accounts was a residual of no interest and no concern to US policymakers. They thought they could learn little or nothing from the behavior of exchange rates. Bergsten also opined that the Reagan administration welcomed the strengthening dollar and widening current account deficit because the first helped to damp inflation and along with the second facilitated recovery without the need to tighten fiscal policy.

In addition, Treasury Secretary Donald Regan and Under Secretary Beryl Sprinkel believed that foreign exchange market intervention was inappropriate and ineffective. Their view was that exchange rates are and should be determined primarily by economic fundamentals, including economic policies, and they were disinclined to advocate altering US economic policies. However, as the dollar continued to strengthen through the first half of 1982, the United States was under increasing pressure to arrest the climb of its currency, which was seen to be impeding efforts in other industrial countries to combat inflation. The French and Japanese, in particular, favored intervention in this context to curb the dollar's strength.

To bridge these differences in views, it was agreed at the Versailles Economic Summit in June 1982 to conduct a joint G-7 study of the effectiveness of intervention. The conclusion of the resulting Working Group on Exchange Market Intervention (Jurgensen 1983) was that sterilized foreign exchange market intervention had a potential role to play, but it was limited to the short run. On April 29, 1983, the G-7 finance ministers and central bank governors along with representatives of the European Community, in drawing policy conclusions from the report, said that they were "willing to undertake coordinated intervention in instances where it is agreed that such intervention would be helpful."[39]

From July 1982 to December 1984, the United States did operate from time to time in the foreign exchange market, buying $571 million equivalent of foreign currencies on 12 of the 653 days and selling $423 million equivalent on seven days even as the dollar continued to appreciate. On January 17, 1985, in the context of a period of overall dollar strength and intense selling pressure against the British pound sterling, the G-5 finance ministers and central bank governors issued a statement that noted "recent developments in foreign exchange markets, expressed their commitment to work toward greater exchange market stability . . . [and] reaffirmed their commitment made at the Williamsburg Summit [in 1983 following the release of the Jurgensen report] to undertake coordinated intervention in the markets as necessary." Thus, the G-5 gave birth to a new policy instrument: coordinated oral intervention.

The United States bought deutsche mark on two days in the second half of January 1985 and an additional $643 million equivalent of foreign currency on 8 of 189 trading days after January through September 20, 1985. Meanwhile, the dollar on average in real terms peaked in March and declined by about 5 percent through August. On September 23, the G-5 finance ministers and central bank governors, following their meeting at the Plaza Hotel in New York, announced that "some further orderly appreciation of the main non-dollar currencies against the dollar is desirable." Following the Plaza Agreement, the US authorities bought $3.3 billion in foreign currency over 34 trading days through November 7. They did not intervene for the rest of the episode through the end of October 1986 as the dollar continued its decline back to where it had been on average in June 1982.

What should one take as the message from movements in the dollar's foreign exchange value during this period of almost four and a half years?

As is shown in the first line of table 9.2, the US real economy expanded rapidly during the period 1982Q2 to 1986Q4, with growth averaging 4.1 percent, substantially more than the modest rate in the preceding eight

39. I was a member of the working group. Although of course I embarked on the study with an open mind, my hope was that we would be able to demonstrate that intervention had some effectiveness and, thus, to preserve (or in the US case to revive) the instrument. In the event, our studies were less definitive than I expected, but at least we achieved my modest objective.

Table 9.2 July 1982–October 1986 episode (percent except as noted)

	Indicators	Episode	Episode less before[a]	Episode less after[b]
1	Growth of US real GDP	4.1	3.5	0.3
2	Growth of US real gross domestic purchases	4.9	4.2	1.9
3	US unemployment rate	8.1	0.0	2.3
4	Growth of world real GDP	2.8	0.6	–2.0
5	US CPI inflation	3.3	–6.6	–0.6
6	US core CPI inflation	4.5	–5.8	0.2
7	US federal funds rate	8.7	–6.4	1.4
8	10-year US Treasury bond yield	10.5	–3.0	1.8
9	US federal budget[c]	–4.4	–2.2	–1.6
10	US general government[c]	–4.1	–2.1	–1.5
11	US trade balance[c]	–2.4	–2.0	0.3
12	US current account balance[c]	–2.2	–2.4	0.7
13	Growth of US real exports of goods and services	2.6	1.4	–10.9
14	Growth of US real imports of goods and services	11.6	13.3	6.7

Memorandum items:

	Episode	Before	After
Quarters	18 (1982Q3–1986Q4)	8 (1980Q3–1982Q2)	8 (1987Q1–1988Q4)
Months	52 (7/1982–10/1986)	21 (10/1980–6/1982)	4 (11/1986–2/1987)
US intervention			
Foreign currency sales			
Amount (dollars)	423	417	50
Days	7	13	1
Foreign currency purchases			
Amount (dollars)	4,514	6,560	0
Days	42	99	0
Total intervention days	49	112	1
Total days	1,132	456	85

CPI = consumer price index

a. *Before* is defined as the eight quarters prior to the episode.
b. *After* is defined as the eight quarters following the episode.
c. As a percent of GDP.

Note: Indicators are calculated as averages of four-quarter changes except for items indicated by footnote c.

Sources: Bureau of Economic Analysis, Bureau of Labor Statistics, Federal Reserve Board.

quarters and slightly more than the rate in the following eight quarters. Excluding the first three quarters and the last quarter of the period, growth was always more than 3.0 percent, and the unemployment rate declined steadily after 1982Q4. Moreover, in every quarter gross domestic purchases (real GDP less net exports) expanded even more rapidly than output and by 0.8 percentage points more on average.[40] The rapid growth was accompanied by an expansionary fiscal policy. With the growth of demand outstripping the growth of supply (GDP), the US trade and current account deficits widened. In contrast, gross domestic purchases and output expanded at about the same rate in the previous eight quarters. During the following eight quarters gross domestic purchases expanded by 0.8 percentage points *less* than output.

Growth in the world as a whole was also somewhat stronger during the period on average than before and picked up in 1984–86, averaging 3.7 percent. Thus, the United States was an attractive place to invest, as US officials argued at the time, but its attractiveness was not all that dominant. Moreover, in the following period, US growth averaged less than growth in the rest of the world.

For the period as a whole, consumer price inflation was lower on both the headline and the core measures than in the immediately preceding period. Headline inflation declined to less than 2 percent during the last three quarters of 1986 under the influence of a collapse in global energy prices, but the core inflation rate was 4 percent, close to the average for the entire period. Subsequently, US inflation picked up, averaging 4.1 percent on the headline measure and 4.5 percent for the core during the four quarters of 1988. Thus there was the hint of a revival of inflation.

The traditional explanation for the strength of the dollar during this period lies in the combination of an easy fiscal policy and tight monetary policy. Fiscal policy certainly was easier on average than either before or after the period whether measured by the federal government or the general government budget outcomes. Deficits were around 5 percent of GDP early in the period, the real federal funds rate was more than 5.5 percent, and the 10-year bond rate was more than 10 percent through the third quarter of 1985.

Bergsten (1994) argues that the strategy of the first Reagan administration was to promote a strong dollar and tolerate a widening current account deficit in order to facilitate expansion and limit inflation. In the four quarters before the Plaza Agreement, the federal budget deficit narrowed by less than 1 percentage point compared with fiscal year 1983, and the real federal funds rate declined by about 2 percentage points but remained elevated at around 4 percent.[41] Thus the conventional macroeconomic story appears to have considerable validity except for the fact that the imbalance in the mix of fiscal and monetary policy became somewhat less pronounced during the period even as the dollar continued to appreciate

---

40. Gross domestic purchases are a measure of underlying demand in an economy while gross domestic product (GDP) is a measure of the economy's output.

41. The real federal funds rate was 3.7 percent in the third quarter of 1985 using the four-quarter change in the core CPI and 4.5 percent using the headline CPI.

through the first quarter of 1985. On average, the dollar was telling US policymakers to correct the policy mix.

Meanwhile, with respect to US external accounts, the trade and current account deficits were substantially larger during the period than before. They expanded steadily throughout the period and into 1987 in response to the earlier strength of the dollar. The growth rate of real imports was particularly rapid, but the growth of real exports was also quite strong, more than 5.5 percent on average from the fourth quarter of 1983 to the first quarter of 1985. Thereafter, export growth slowed. Thus, US external accounts were deteriorating. This deterioration, along with the unbalanced nature of the US recovery and expansion, which disfavored traditional, rust-belt industries, gave rise to intense protectionist pressures. The deterioration in the US external accounts was associated with the dollar's appreciation, which in turn was attributable in large part to the fiscal/monetary mix. The dollar was telling US policymakers that they faced potential protectionist pressures. However, they absorbed this lesson rather late in the episode, during the summer of 1985, when they cooked up the Plaza Agreement to help blunt those pressures.

In addition, the dollar also seems to have had a life of its own. From March 1984 to March 1985, it appreciated a further 14 percent in real terms on the broad index of the foreign exchange value of the dollar, bringing the dollar to 31 percent above its long-term average (1973–2008) and 54 percent above the trend. In terms of the major currencies, the appreciation during those 12 months was 18 percent, but the level was "only" 26 percent above the average and 46 percent above the trend.[42] Thus a reasonable case can be made that the dollar was experiencing a bubble.[43] That bubble in turn was contributing to protectionist pressures in the United States.

In due course, as noted earlier, US intervention policy did come to embrace purchases of foreign currencies to resist the dollar's rise and encourage its depreciation. This was done on a small scale during the first quarter of 1985 and on a larger scale immediately following the Plaza Agreement. Should the US authorities have been more proactive?

---

42. A portion of the dollar's broad appreciation during the early 1980s was associated with the global debt crises that led many emerging-market countries to untie dollar pegs, depreciating their currencies abruptly.

43. Paul Krugman (1986), in an analysis delivered at the Kansas City Federal Reserve Bank conference in Jackson Hole, Wyoming in August 1985, offered a sophisticated analysis in support of the view that the strong dollar was unsustainable and the strength involved a bubble. The analysis was grounded on the implicit market forecast derived from interest differentials that the dollar would decline only slowly over the next two decades and an explicit view that the resulting trends in the US current account and international indebtedness positions would be unsustainable. At the same conference, Bergsten (1985) was on the final overview panel. He outlined a five-step strategy to correct the dollar's overvaluation. It included joint foreign exchange market intervention by the major countries "leaning with the wind" to push the dollar down further, thus advocating a Plaza Agreement a month before it was announced.

Bergsten (1994) makes the retrospective case for more aggressive intervention earlier, but he also points out that a failure to act simultaneously on the fiscal deficit would have meant a lower dollar and a smaller net inflow of foreign saving through the current account deficit and might have caused the Federal Reserve to push up dollar interest rates by enough to slow the overall expansion of the US economy more than US policymakers wanted.

The inherent logic of this analysis was reflected in the Plaza Agreement, in which the US government pledged to "continue efforts to reduce government expenditures as a share of GNP . . . [and] implement fully the deficit reduction package for fiscal year 1986. This package passed by Congress and approved by the President will not only reduce by over 1 percent of GNP the budget deficit for fiscal 1986, but lay the basis for further significant reductions in the deficit in subsequent years." In fact, in fiscal 1986, federal outlays declined by 0.4 percent of GDP, but revenues declined as well and the improvement in the deficit was only 0.1 percent of GDP. The message may have been clear, but the implementation left something to be desired.

The messages from the dollar's movements during this episode are three: (1) a flawed fiscal/monetary mix and (2) warnings of protectionism (3) fed by a bubble in the dollar during 1984 and early 1985.

March 1987 to April 1988: Arresting the Dollar's Decline

Recall that this episode is not statistically identified as a period of protracted dollar weakness on the basis of either the broad real trade-weighted index of the foreign exchange value of the dollar relative to its 1973–2008 average or the dollar's declining long-term trend.[44] I chose to examine it because it was a period during which there was an international understanding, the Louvre Accord of February 22, 1987, to resist the dollar's decline against other G-7 currencies. The date of that agreement led me to take March 1987 as the start of this episode. The Louvre Accord was repaired several times and ultimately discarded, but cooperation on active foreign exchange market intervention continued through the dollar's low point reached in April 1988, which I have taken as the end of the episode.

By February 1987 (the month of the Louvre Accord), the dollar on the broad index had declined 17 percent in real terms from September 1985 (the month of the Plaza Agreement), and the decline in terms of the major currency index was 24 percent. In the Louvre Accord

---

44. On the basis of the average for the real foreign exchange value of the dollar in terms of the major currencies, a six-month period from December 1987 to June 1988 shows up as more than 10 percent below the 1973–2008 average, but no part of that period is as much as 10 percent below the trend of the index.

> The Ministers and Governors agreed that the substantial exchange rate changes since the Plaza Agreement will increasingly contribute to reducing external imbalances and have now brought their currencies within ranges broadly consistent with underlying economic fundamentals, given the policy commitments summarized in this statement. Further substantial exchange rate shifts among their currencies could damage growth and adjustment prospects in their countries. In current circumstances, therefore, they agreed to cooperate closely to foster stability of exchange rates around current levels.

This accord ushered in a brief period in which the parties agreed to consider positively concerted foreign exchange market intervention when bilateral exchange rates among the three major currencies (deutsche mark, dollar, and yen) rose above or below specified reference ranges—in other words, target zones.[45] The reference ranges were symmetrical and sufficiently tight (an inner band of ±2.5 percent and an outer band of ±5 percent) that they triggered initial US purchases of deutsche mark on March 11, 1987, to resist the dollar's rise, but those purchases were followed by US sales of yen by the end of March to support the dollar. Moreover, the dollar continued to decline throughout 1987, in particular against the yen, and the reference ranges were rebased and ultimately abandoned before the end of the year.[46] US and other G-7 intervention was heavy throughout this episode. The US authorities operated on 25 percent of the trading days, and the level of US foreign currency sales averaged almost $180 million equivalent each day they operated, compared with $120 million each day of foreign currency sales in 1978–79.

The US and global stock market crash on October 19, 1987 (Black Monday) and the preceding verbal fisticuffs involving Secretary Baker and German Finance Minister Stoltenberg and Bundesbank President Pöhl were the final nails in the coffin of this flirtation with target zones. Following the crash, the Federal Reserve increased liquidity, the federal funds rate declined, and the dollar depreciated further. It was only after the US Congress had passed a $76 billion two-year deficit reduction package resulting from a "budget summit" in the wake of the stock market crash that the

---

45. The Louvre Accord had been presaged by an "accord" between US treasury secretary Baker and Japanese finance minister Miyazawa on October 31, 1986, that employed the same language about exchange rates: that they were then "broadly consistent with underlying economic fundamentals." The dollar had declined substantially against the yen since the Plaza Agreement, and the Japanese felt that it had gone too far. For a period, the dollar recovered a bit, but in January 1987 it hit a new postwar low against the yen, and the US monetary authorities bought dollars for the first time since the Plaza Agreement. January also saw a realignment within the EMS, which relieved pressure in the system but increased pressure on the dollar–deutsche mark exchange rate. See Funabashi (1988) for an account of the Plaza-Louvre period.

46. Since the reference ranges were never published, the adjustment in the base rates could only be inferred from the fact that exchange rates had changed and from the fact that the G-7 continued to use the same language saying that exchange rates "broadly consistent with economic fundamentals." Unauthorized open hints from the relevant authorities also helped.

G-7 agreed to release its "Telephone Communiqué" on December 22, 1987. In an attempt to turn around market sentiment, the G-7 used new language:

> The Ministers and Governors agreed that either excessive fluctuation of exchange rates, a further decline of the dollar, or a rise in the dollar to an extent that becomes destabilizing to the adjustment process, could be counter-productive by damaging growth prospects in the world economy. They reemphasized their common interest in more stable exchange rates among their currencies and agreed to continue to cooperate closely in monitoring and implementing policies to strengthen underlying economic fundamentals to foster stability of exchange rates. In addition, they agreed to cooperate closely on exchange markets.

Despite the novelty of the Telephone Communiqué—it was the first time the G-7 issued a statement without a face-to-face meeting—market participants were disappointed that it contained no new specific measures designed to support the dollar, only the promise of more intervention. The dollar continued its decline through the end of the year, reaching lows on December 30 against the deutsche mark and yen that were 14 and 21 percent respectively below the rates just prior to the Louvre meeting. In other words, even if the Louvre bands had been set at ±10 percent, they would have been substantially breached. The G-7 experiment with reference ranges was a technical failure.[47]

However, on January 4 concerted intervention sales of foreign currencies for dollars appeared to contribute to a reversal of market sentiment toward the dollar, no doubt helped along the following day by interest rate reductions in three European countries (Cross 1988).[48] The dollar did not hit a new low against either the deutsche mark or the yen during this episode, even though on a monthly, weighted-average basis its low in real terms was recorded in April 1988, and US sales of foreign currencies did not end until that month.

What messages should US policymakers have received from the dollar's weakness during this period?

The average growth rate of US real GDP during the six quarters of this episode was essentially the same as the growth rate in the previous eight quarters and slightly higher than the growth rate in the following eight

---

47. It can always be argued that in the absence of the Louvre Accord and the substantial intervention in support of the dollar during this period, the dollar would have been even lower. It can also be argued that eventually the dollar turned around. It is possible that the dollar would have been lower, but the point is that the Louvre Accord did not prevent a substantial weakening of the dollar: It failed in this objective. As for the eventual turnaround in the dollar, that is a flawed *post hoc, ergo propter hoc* argument; the burden of proof should be on those who allege the cause and effect relationship to establish the mechanism, not on those who are skeptical.

48. For students of the effectiveness (or lack thereof) of sterilized intervention, US foreign currency sales on January 4, 1988, were $375 million equivalent; on December 28 and 29, 1987, US sales were $440 million and $464 million respectively. The timing of the operation in a new calendar year appeared to matter more than its size.

Table 9.3   March 1987–April 1988 episode (percent except as noted)

	Indicators	Episode	Episode less before[a]	Episode less after[b]
1	Growth of US real GDP	3.7	−0.1	0.3
2	Growth of US real gross domestic purchases	3.0	−1.8	0.1
3	US unemployment rate	5.9	−1.2	0.7
4	Growth of world real GDP	4.8	1.4	0.7
5	US CPI inflation	3.8	1.2	−0.9
6	US core CPI inflation	4.1	−0.1	−0.5
7	US federal funds rate	6.8	−0.6	−2.0
8	10-year US Treasury bond yield	8.6	−0.4	0.0
9	US federal budget[c]	−3.0	1.3	−0.4
10	US general government[c]	−2.7	1.0	−0.5
11	US trade balance[c]	−2.9	0.1	−1.2
12	US current account balance[c]	−3.1	0.0	−1.2
13	Growth of US real exports of goods and services	13.2	7.8	1.3
14	Growth of US real imports of goods and services	5.5	−2.1	1.2

Memorandum items:

	Episode	Before	After
Quarters	6 (1987Q1–1988Q2)	8 (1985Q1–1986Q4)	8 (1988Q3–1990Q2)
Months	14 (3/1987–4/1988)	4 (11/1986–2/1987)	8 (5/1988–12/1988)
US intervention			
Foreign currency sales			
Amount (dollars)	10,727	50	2,600
Days	60	1	13
Foreign currency purchases			
Amount (dollars)	748	0	5,147
Days	17	0	44
Total intervention days	77	1	57
Total days	305	85	175

CPI = consumer price index

a. *Before* is defined as the eight quarters prior to the episode.
b. *After* is defined as the eight quarters following the episode.
c. As a percent of GDP.

Note: Indicators are calculated as averages of four-quarter changes except for items indicated by footnote c.

Sources: Bureau of Economic Analysis, Bureau of Labor Statistics, Federal Reserve Board.

quarters (see line 1 of table 9.3). The unemployment rate continued to decline and remained at a lower level in the following period. In contrast, the average growth rate of domestic demand (gross domestic purchases) was 1.8 percentage points less than during the previous period, and the growth rate declined further in the subsequent period. Moreover, demand was growing more slowly than supply in the United States, a necessary but not sufficient condition for turning around the trade and current account deficits. Those deficits did not begin to narrow until the first half of 1988, and that trend continued through the following period (lines 11 and 12 of table 9.3). Thus, the dollar's weakness apparently was communicating that the external correction was not occurring fast enough.

If the dollar's decline was unwelcome, then the message may have been that monetary and, in particular, fiscal policy should have been tighter. At the Louvre, the US commitment on fiscal policy was to produce a federal government deficit in fiscal 1988 of 2.3 percent of GDP compared with an estimated 3.9 percent of GDP for fiscal 1987. In fact, the fiscal 1987 deficit was 3.2 percent and the fiscal 1988 deficit 3.1 percent.[49] A tighter fiscal policy and a tighter monetary policy probably would have slowed the economy and increased the US unemployment rate.[50] Of course, with a presidential election coming up in 1988, that would have been unwelcome.

The exchange rate does not appear to have been signaling much about global growth. It was somewhat higher in 1987–88 than in 1985–86. Moreover, the growth rate of US real exports was well into double digits, and twice the rate of the previous period, while the growth rate of real imports slowed. These trends continued in the subsequent period.

Thus, one possible message from the dollar's movements during this period was that internal, and therefore external, adjustment should have begun earlier. This could have been accomplished only with tighter fiscal policy and probably somewhat tighter monetary policy at the cost of less US growth and higher unemployment.

An alternative message was that the attempt to arrest the dollar's slide at the Louvre was a mistake. In February 1987, the dollar was 3 percent above its 1973–2008 average and 22 percent above its trend in terms of the real broad dollar index.[51] By April 1988, the dollar was off its December lows in nominal terms against the deutsche mark and yen but had declined a full 10 percent from its average level in February 1987 at the time of the Louvre on both the broad and the major-currency indexes for the dollar.

---

49. The fiscal 1987 deficit was less than expected because of a larger than expected revenue windfall from the 1986 tax reform, but the two-year change from fiscal 1986 to fiscal 1988 was 1.9 percentage points, not the 2.7 percentage points implied in the Louvre commitment. According to the *World Economic Outlook* database (April 2006), the improvement in the cyclically adjusted general government balance for the United States was 0.8 percentage points between calendar years 1986 and 1988. Both adjustments are reasonably impressive by the cautious standards of fiscal adjustment in vogue two decades later.

50. Given the stock market crash and the associated monetary easing as well as the influence of energy prices on the gyrations of headline CPI inflation, it is difficult to interpret US monetary policy for the episode as a whole. However, using the core CPI, the real federal funds rate in 1987Q3 before the stock market crash was about the same as in 1986Q4, close to 3 percent. Core inflation was 0.4 percentage points higher.

51. In terms of the real major currency index, the dollar was only about 4 percent below average and at the same time 15 percent above trend.

Interestingly, Williamson (1994) estimated in the first quarter of 1990, three years after the Louvre, that the dollar was overvalued by about 11 percent. Taking account of Williamson's estimated trend rate of depreciation for the dollar of 1.1 percent per year and the fact that the dollar had depreciated 4.3 percent from the first quarter of 1987 to the first quarter of 1990, the Williamson framework implies that the dollar was overvalued by about 12 percent at the time of the Louvre.[52] From this perspective, the dollar's weakness in 1987–88 does not appear to have been a bubble where the market "got it wrong."

On the other hand, the account of the period found in Volcker and Gyohten (1992), augmented by my own private conversations with Paul Volcker, suggests that he at least was concerned that the dollar might depreciate too far too fast, to the detriment of US inflation and global growth; he was less concerned about incomplete external adjustment.[53] Stephen Marris (1985 and 1987) argued eloquently in major publications by the Institute for International Economics that the US and global economies faced a hard landing (painfully low growth and other economic and financial disturbances) during this period absent preventive measures by the major industrial countries. How real that threat was and what role these warnings played in minimizing it are unanswered questions that continue to influence the debate today about the adjustment of global imbalances and the risk of a hard landing for the US and global economies.

Bergsten (1994) agrees that the Louvre left the dollar overvalued. His preferred alternative strategy would have been a controlled depreciation of the dollar using bands to guide a decline. He concludes, referring to Black Monday, "*given* the basic course of fiscal and monetary policy, exchange rate policy erred and triggered events that could have levied significant costs on the American economy." This interpretation combines the three ambiguous messages: The external adjustment should have been started earlier with supporting US macroeconomic policies, the Louvre Accord was too rigid and, if it had held, would have left the dollar overvalued, but it was desirable to try to slow if not arrest the dollar's decline.

January 1989 to April 1990: Stabilizing the Dollar?

This episode was not chosen because the foreign exchange value of the dollar deviated substantially from its average or trend. I chose it because be-

---

52. Using the dollar's broad index the resulting figure would be 15 percent, but Williamson focused primarily on the major currencies.

53. My colleagues and I in the International Finance Division of the Federal Reserve Board remonstrated with him at the time that the dollar's adjustment as of February 1987 was insufficient to address the US external imbalance and that market forces would be likely to continue to depress the dollar, undercutting the accord.

tween January 1989 and April 1990, the US monetary authorities bought $24.4 billion equivalent of deutsche mark and yen. They bought $11.3 billion deutsche mark predominantly through mid-October 1989 and $13 billion yen spread fairly evenly throughout the period on 114 trading days, or 33 percent of 346 total trading days, in an average daily amount of $214 million.

The eight months prior to the start of this episode followed the third episode in which the dollar's decline was ultimately arrested. Subsequently, the US dollar rose, on the basis of the broad measure of its real foreign exchange value, through June 1988 and declined through December, with little net change on balance.[54]

During the episode itself, the dollar rose on balance by 4 percent in terms of the broad measure and by almost 5 percent against the major currencies. However, the dollar's movements against the deutsche mark and yen were quite different. In nominal terms, the dollar rose about 13 percent through mid-September 1989 against the deutsche mark before declining by the end of April 1990 by 5 percent (compared with the end of December 1988) in the context of the unfolding process of German unification. The dollar rose in nominal terms against the yen by 19 percent by mid-September 1989 and by 26 percent by the end of April 1990 against the background of the initial bursting of the Japanese bubble in the prices of real estate and equities.[55]

Were movements in dollar exchange rates sending messages to US policymakers?

This episode involved more messages that the authorities were trying to send the foreign exchange market than messages that the foreign exchange market was trying to send the US authorities. US real GDP growth declined from the rate in the prior period, and the growth rate of domestic demand declined as well both relative to the prior period and relative to GDP (see table 9.4). The decline in foreign growth was somewhat larger. However, US real exports continued to expand at double-digit rates, and the trade and current account deficits narrowed further, though it was not until 1991 that the trade deficit shrank to less than half a percent of GDP and the current account moved into temporary surplus.

US exchange rate policy appears in retrospect to have been driven by two considerations: (1) a continued fascination with policy coordina-

---

54. Against the major currencies the dollar rose through September and subsequently declined, ending the year about 4 percent above its April 1988 average. The US authorities bought a substantial amount of deutsche mark in the first part of the period and sold deutsche mark and yen late in the period.

55. Japanese observers, with support from policy coordination skeptics (Siebert 2000), cite the post-Louvre monetary policy accommodation in Japan as a major contributing factor to the subsequent bubble in Japanese land and equity prices. In Truman (2004), along with others including Bergsten and Henning (1996, 77–78), I find little merit in these arguments. The Japanese authorities chose the wrong fiscal/monetary mix to compensate for the yen's strength.

Table 9.4 January 1989–April 1990 episode (percent except as noted)

	Indicators	Episode	Episode less before[a]	Episode less after[b]
1	Growth of US real GDP	3.2	-0.5	2.3
2	Growth of US real gross domestic purchases	2.7	-0.3	2.0
3	US unemployment rate	5.2	-0.5	-1.7
4	Growth of world real GDP	3.9	-1.0	0.9
5	US CPI inflation	4.8	0.9	0.5
6	US core CPI inflation	4.6	0.3	-0.1
7	US federal funds rate	8.9	1.7	3.3
8	10-year US Treasury bond yield	8.5	-0.2	0.6
9	US federal budget[c]	-2.6	0.3	1.1
10	US general government[c]	-2.2	0.3	1.5
11	US trade balance[c]	-1.6	1.1	-0.9
12	US current account balance[c]	-1.7	1.2	-1.3
13	Growth of US real exports of goods and services	11.1	-2.4	3.7
14	Growth of US real imports of goods and services	4.6	-0.3	2.4

Memorandum items:

	Episode	Before	After
Quarters	6 (1989Q1–1990Q2)	8 (1987Q1–1988Q4)	8 (1990Q3–1992Q2)
Months	16 (1/1989–4/1990)	8 (5/1988–12/1988)	19 (5/1990–11/1991)
US intervention			
Foreign currency sales			
Amount (dollars)	0	2,600	2,336
Days	0	13	24
Foreign currency purchases			
Amount (dollars)	24,436	5,147	550
Days	114	44	6
Total intervention days	114	57	30
Total days	346	175	414

CPI = consumer price index

a. *Before* is defined as the eight quarters prior to the episode.
b. *After* is defined as the eight quarters following the episode.
c. As a percent of GDP.

Note: Indicators are calculated as averages of four-quarter changes except for items indicated by footnote c.

Sources: Bureau of Economic Analysis, Bureau of Labor Statistics, Federal Reserve Board.

tion centered on exchange rates in the aftermath of the Plaza and Louvre experiences, which were seen within the administration as largely successful even if many outsiders were more skeptical, and (2) a desire to lock in hard-won improvements in the US external accounts.

With respect to policy coordination, the sequence of statements by G-7 finance ministers and central bank governors is instructive:

September 24, 1988   Ministers and governors emphasized their contin-
                      ued interest in stable exchange rates among their
                      currencies. Therefore, they reaffirmed their com-
                      mitments to pursue policies that will maintain ex-
                      change rate stability and to continue to cooperate
                      closely on exchange markets. They are continuing
                      their study of ways of further improving the func-
                      tioning of the international monetary system and
                      the coordination process.

April 2, 1989   The exchange rate stability over the past year has
                      made a welcome contribution to, and was sup-
                      ported by, the progress achieved in sustaining the
                      global expansion and reducing external imbal-
                      ances. The ministers and governors agreed that a
                      rise of the dollar, which undermined adjustment
                      efforts, or an excessive decline would be counter-
                      productive and reiterated their commitment to co-
                      operate closely on exchange markets.

September 23, 1989   The ministers and governors considered the rise
                      in recent months of the dollar inconsistent with
                      longer-run economic fundamentals. They agreed
                      that a rise of the dollar above current levels or an
                      excessive decline could adversely affect prospects
                      for the world economy. In this they agreed to co-
                      operate closely in exchange markets.

April 7, 1990   The ministers and governors discussed develop-
                      ments in global financial markets, especially the de-
                      cline of the yen against other currencies and its un-
                      desirable consequences for the global adjustment
                      process, and agreed to keep these developments
                      under review. They reaffirmed their commitment
                      to economic policy coordination, including cooper-
                      ation in exchange markets.

The September 1988 statement built on the experience of 1987 and early
1988 and, in hinting at additional systemic improvements, implied incor-
rectly that the reference ranges introduced at the Louvre had been rebased
and were still relevant.[56] The April 1989 statement was self-congratulatory
but warned about a rise in the dollar that undermined US external adjustment. By September 1989, the latter concerns were predominant. In April

---

56. Henning (1994, 290–97) inferred that the reference or target ranges did not unravel until
1989–90, when in fact they were history by the end of 1987.

1990, the game was over: Other members of the G-7 declined to commit themselves to resist further the decline in the yen in the absence of Japanese monetary policy action to support the yen.[57] In the event, it probably would have been a mistake for Japanese monetary policy to be tightened in the face of the bursting of their asset price bubbles. Moreover, the yen did not weaken substantially further and returned in November 1990 to the range of ¥120 per dollar, where it had been at the start of 1989.

As Henning (1994) describes in considerable, but incomplete, detail, in 1989–90 a serious rift developed between the US Treasury and the Federal Reserve concerning US intervention policy. Many Federal Reserve officials questioned the use of heavy US foreign exchange market intervention to resist the dollar's appreciation when the FOMC was struggling to contain inflation. The real federal funds rate was about 4 percent on average, and core CPI inflation averaged 4.6 percent during this episode and above 5 percent in the first half of the following period. A further appreciation of the dollar would have helped restrain US inflation, and the US foreign exchange intervention was sending the wrong message about Federal Reserve policy.

At the July 5–6 meeting (FOMC 1989a), several members raised questions about Federal Reserve foreign exchange market operations, which routinely are conducted in cooperation with the US Treasury. At the August 22 meeting (FOMC 1989b), the committee approved a proposal to conduct a thorough review of those operations by a task force on system foreign currency operation; the work of that task force was presented to the FOMC (1990) on March 27, 1990. However, pending the completion of that review and action by the committee to raise the limit on the amount of foreign currency that the Federal Reserve was prepared to "warehouse" for the Exchange Stabilization Fund (ESF) of the US Treasury Department, the Federal Reserve declined to participate in US foreign currency operations from March 5 to March 20 (Cross 1990, 69–70).[58] At the March 27 FOMC meeting, the committee approved an expansion in the warehousing arrangement with the ESF, and the Federal Reserve resumed its joint intervention with the Treasury in late March and early April. However, this episode, combined with the growing skepticism about the utility and effectiveness of the heavy US intervention, contributed to a change in US intervention policy toward more selective use of the instrument.

---

57. The US monetary authorities did buy $50 million equivalent of yen on April 9 immediately after the G-7 meeting, but that was their last yen purchase for a considerable period.

58. "Warehousing" was accomplished via simultaneous spot purchases of foreign exchange by the FOMC account from the ESF and forward sales of the same amount against dollars. This provided the ESF with additional dollars to use to purchase additional foreign currency in the market. Normally US sales and purchases in the foreign exchange markets are shared 50-50 between the FOMC's account and ESF's account. Both entities have independent legal authority to operate in foreign exchange markets, though normally the Federal Reserve does not undertake an intervention operation alone.

Bergsten and Henning (1996, 30) argue that it was a mistake to permit the yen to depreciate by as much as it did in the late 1980s because it subsequently contributed to the enlargement of the Japanese current account surplus. However, the US current account deficit continued to narrow during this period, and the yen depreciated back to only around ¥145 per dollar, where it had been in October 1987, from its high of ¥121 at the end of 1987. In other words, if ¥121 was the wrong rate at the end of 1987 because the yen was too strong, it is not clear why it was the right rate in 1989. The US Treasury, with the agreement of the rest of the G-7, had moved the goalposts. Moreover, the US and Japanese authorities used foreign exchange market intervention on an unprecedented scale to resist the yen's depreciation, which was ineffective as the yen moved to ¥158 before the coordination effort was abandoned in April 1990. Again, one can argue about the counterfactual, but the intervention was unprecedented in scale, the yen weakened anyhow, and in the end the United States and the rest of the G-7 gave up trying to arrest the yen's weakness.

Bergsten and Henning (1996, 104) also suggest that an opportunity was missed in September 1989 to coordinate monetary policy in support of exchange rate stability by easing US monetary policy and tightening policy in Germany and Japan. This was a curious argument. The deutsche mark was appreciating in any case. The Federal Reserve was easing policy, and the Bundesbank and the Bank of Japan were tightening policy. As detailed in Henning (1994, 292) and reported in FOMC (1989c), the FOMC opposed using monetary policy for this purpose because it risked undercutting the committee's longer-term efforts to achieve price stability. If the G-7 had "taken credit" for what was already occurring, the risk was that the central banks, at least the Bundesbank and the Federal Reserve, which enjoyed independence, would have altered at least the timing of their policy actions.[59]

This episode illustrates the limits of foreign exchange market intervention and the potential conflicts with other policies, in particular monetary policy (Truman 2003). The episode also suggests a conflict between using exchange rates as information to inform economic policies and using them as a straitjacket for economic policies. Moreover, to the extent that the heavy US intervention during this period was designed to limit movements of the dollar, the limits were demonstrably too tight; on the real broad index the dollar's range between its monthly high and low was only 5.4 percent, and 8.3 percent in terms of the major currencies on average. Finally, the episode underscores the fact that exchange rates are multidimensional. During the latter part of this period, the dollar was moving in different directions against the yen and the deutsche mark not because of

---

59. Although the FOMC did not ease policy at its October 1989 meeting following the G-7 meeting, the federal funds rate was 75 basis points lower by the time of the November meeting as the result of intermeeting adjustments.

what was or was not going on in the US economy but because of what was happening in the Japanese and German economies.[60] The dollar did not move very much on average during this episode. Who knows if it would have moved a great deal more without the large-scale intervention resisting dollar appreciation, but there was little scope for the dollar to send a policy message via its movements.

December 1991 to October 1992: The Dollar and the ERM Crises

The US dollar declined, on average, from the spring of 1990 to the spring of 1991 as the US economy moved into a mild recession in the context of the Gulf War. In both years the dollar recovered somewhat during the spring and summer of 1991 before tailing off again in the fall. US intervention during the period from May 1990 to November 1991 was limited to 30 of 414 trading days (7 percent), consisting of 6 days of foreign currency purchases to resist dollar appreciation and 24 days of foreign currency sales to resist dollar decline.

In December 1991 the dollar on the real broad index moved 10 percent below its average for 1973–2008 and generally remained at or below that level through October 1992 except for a brief recovery in the spring of 1992 (figure 9.1). The dollar was also more than 10 percent below the *average* against major currencies through this entire episode. In contrast, the dollar was roughly on or slightly below its *trend* on the two indexes (figure 9.2).[61] In nominal terms, the dollar declined about 4 percent against the yen and 5 percent against the deutsche mark over the 11-month period ending in October 1992, though in early September it had been down 10 percent against the deutsche mark. US foreign exchange market intervention occurred on 8 days total (only 3 percent of the 240 trading days)— 3 days of yen purchases in January and February and 5 days deutsche mark sales in July and August.

What messages were the dollar's movements sending US policymakers?

US real GDP growth was slow coming out of the 1990–91 recession even though it equaled or exceeded 3 percent for the last three quarters of 1992, unemployment continued to rise through the second quarter of 1992,

---

60. This episode also underscores another lesson about economic policy coordination: as long as both the finance minister and the central bank governors are involved in the discussions and in the policy actions, and the central banks have at least instrument independence, policy coordination begins at home. The Brady-Mulford Treasury in this period failed to achieve cooperation from the Federal Reserve, and this failure almost badly backfired by weakening the global coordination process.

61. Recall that the level of the average and the trend for the dollar in terms of the major currencies are not shown in figures 1 and 2, and the relevant lines 10 percent above and below, which are lower, are also not shown. The comments in the text refer to these lines that are not shown.

Table 9.5 December 1991–October 1992 episode
(percent except as noted)

	Indicators	Episode	Episode less before[a]	Episode less after[b]
1	Growth of US real GDP	2.9	1.8	−0.5
2	Growth of US real gross domestic purchases	2.5	1.7	−1.0
3	US unemployment rate	7.5	1.4	1.1
4	Growth of world real GDP	2.8	−0.5	−0.6
5	US CPI inflation	3.0	−2.0	0.2
6	US core CPI inflation	3.7	−1.2	0.7
7	US federal funds rate	3.7	−3.6	−0.1
8	10-year US Treasury bond yield	7.0	−1.2	0.5
9	US federal budget[c]	−4.6	−1.5	−1.0
10	US general government[c]	−4.6	−1.6	−1.1
11	US trade balance[c]	−0.6	0.5	0.6
12	US current account balance[c]	−0.7	0.1	0.8
13	Growth of US real exports of goods and services	7.4	−0.6	1.4
14	Growth of US real imports of goods and services	6.5	5.2	−3.8

Memorandum items:

	Episode	Before	After
Quarters	5 (1991Q4–1992Q4)	8 (1989Q4–1991Q3)	8 (1993Q1–1994Q4)
Months	11 (12/1991–10/1992)	19 (5/1990–11/1991)	22 (11/1992–8/1994)
US intervention			
Foreign currency sales			
Amount (dollars)	1,270	2,336	4,941
Days	5	24	8
Foreign currency purchases			
Amount (dollars)	200	550	0
Days	3	6	0
Total intervention days	8	30	8
Total days	240	414	478

CPI = consumer price index

a. *Before* is defined as the eight quarters prior to the episode.
b. *After* is defined as the eight quarters following the episode.
c. As a percent of GDP.

Note: Indicators are calculated as averages of four-quarter changes except for items indicated by footnote c.

Sources: Bureau of Economic Analysis, Bureau of Labor Statistics, Federal Reserve Board.

inflation declined, and the federal funds rate was reduced further, eventually reaching zero in real terms (see table 9.5). Global growth was also slow and somewhat less than average in the preceding period. Although the US fiscal situation deteriorated somewhat, much of that was the natural result of the recession.[62] The US trade and current account deficits were less than 1 percent of GDP.

Nothing in these data suggests that the dollar's weakness relative to its historical average should have been sending a message to US policymakers. In July and August 1992 the US authorities did sell deutsche mark. Their actions were triggered by sentiment in the market that the US authorities were indifferent to a lower dollar on the basis of remarks attributed to Treasury Secretary Brady in the wake of the Munich summit. In the context of the US presidential election, there was a desire to dissuade market participants from this view via a bit of intervention.

On the other hand, the intervention in July and August had little impact on the deutsche mark–dollar rate, and Federal Reserve officials persuaded Treasury officials that enough had been done and there was a risk of looking feckless. It soon became increasingly obvious that the dollar was caught up in the buildup to the ERM crisis that erupted in September 1992 and extended through the summer of 1993.[63]

My conclusion from this episode is that the movement in the dollar was not sending a message to the US authorities about their policies.[64] The dollar on average was not out of line with fundamentals, and the fundamentals were consistent with a somewhat weaker dollar. Was there a bubble? Not much in terms of the dollar itself. With respect to the ERM, opinions differ. The exit of sterling and the substantial adjustments in a number of other currencies appear to have been justified by European macroeconomic circumstances. The public and the politicians in the United Kingdom have not yet come to terms with their experience during this period, with the result that opinions on the United Kingdom joining the euro area range from opposition to extreme caution. The case of the French franc, which in the end was not devalued but did benefit from the wider bands implemented in the summer of 1993, might be considered a bubble in the sense that the franc was subjected to massive speculative pressures that in the end were defeated by a combination of massive intervention and a tightening of French monetary policy.

Bergsten and Henning (1996, 31–32) argue that it was a mistake by the G-7 not to engineer an appreciation of the deutsche mark in the ERM in

---

62. The IMF's *World Economic Outlook* database (April 2006) estimates that the deterioration of the US general government fiscal deficit was 2.5 percent from 1989 to 1992. Most of the deterioration was at the federal level and concentrated in 1992. On the other hand, the general government structural deficit deteriorated only half as much, though again most of the deterioration was in 1992.

63. See Truman (2002) for a fuller treatment of this episode.

64. It is true that the US jobless recovery was a political issue at the time. As noted, US fiscal policy was somewhat expansionary, and to the extent that the dollar's weakness was signaling the need for an even easier or faster easing of monetary policy, presumably that would have contributed to an even weaker dollar and the dollar's modest weakness should not have been resisted via US intervention sales of foreign currency.

the context of German unification and that the G-7 was remiss in not pay-ing more attention to the 1992–93 ERM crisis. On the first point, by late 1991 the Bergsten-Henning position can be logically defended, but it was naïve to think that a discrete deutsche mark appreciation could have been achieved prior to German monetary unification on July 1, 1990, or imme-diately thereafter, because the deutsche mark was close to its lower limit in the ERM. From the perspective of the mid-2000s, it was a bigger mis-take not to engineer a depreciation of the deutsche mark as it joined the euro in 1999.

I agree with Bergsten and Henning on the G-7 and the ERM crisis. The crisis caught the G-7 by surprise, and then they left the mop-up opera-tions to Europe. For example, the statement by G-7 finance ministers and central bank governors on September 19, 1992, in the midst of the crisis re-ferred only to "recent volatility in world financial markets" and offered nothing on the ERM itself. I argue in Truman (2002) that these ERM crises were the first financial crises of the 21st century, predating the Mexican crisis in 1995, which is conventionally described as such. I also argue that this was the beginning of the European double standard in the handling of such crises: It was perfectly all right for the public sector to bail out the private sector in the ERM crisis, but it was not OK in the Mexican and East Asian financial crises.

September 1994 to October 1995: The Birth of the Strong Dollar

The average foreign exchange value of the dollar meandered over the course of 1993 and into early 1994. However, the dollar weakened by about 20 percent against the yen between Clinton's inauguration on Janu-ary 20 and August 1993, when the rate moved close to ¥100 to the dollar. US Treasury Secretary Bentsen on February 19 responded to a question at the National Press Club that a stronger yen would boost US exports. Meanwhile, Fred Bergsten had been in Japan calling for a 20 percent ap-preciation of the yen. Bentsen immediately sought to repair the damage in foreign exchange markets, acknowledging to his colleagues that he had made a mistake to be analytical in his answer, but he contributed to some confusion in the process.[65] The new Clinton administration sold yen five times in 1993, an average amount of $286 million equivalent. Despite the dollar's weakness against the yen, it peaked on the real broad index in Jan-uary 1994 and only then began to decline. The US authorities sold yen and deutsche mark one day a month in April, May, and June; the combined av-erage was $1,170 million equivalent.

---

65. The confusion between Bentsen and Bergsten at one point was such that the US Treasury spokesperson explained to the press that it was B-E-N-T-S-E-N who was speaking as secre-tary of the treasury.

The dollar weakened further in July, reaching lows against the yen and deutsche mark on July 19. This gave rise to the "strong dollar" characterization of US exchange rate policy. In his semiannual testimony on Federal Reserve monetary policy on July 20, Chairman Alan Greenspan said, "Any evidences of weakness in [the dollar] are neither good for the international financial system nor good for the American economy." The next day, by design, Treasury Undersecretary Lawrence Summers stated in his own testimony before another committee:

> The Administration believes that a strengthening of the dollar against the yen and the mark would have important economic benefits for the United States. It would restore confidence in financial markets that is important to sustaining recovery. It would boost the attractiveness of US assets and the incentive for longer-term investment in the economy, and it would help to keep inflation low. In addition, we believe—and this view is shared by other G-7 countries—a renewed decline in the dollar would be counter productive to global recovery. (Fisher 1994, 2).

This was an example of oral intervention, as the words were not followed by action in the foreign exchange market. However, the support of the other G-7 countries was implicit. I trace the birth of the strong dollar policy to this pair of events, even though Secretary Rubin, who replaced Secretary Bentsen in January 1995, morphed the policy from a "stronger dollar" to a "strong dollar" during his confirmation hearings—an important distinction that was too sophisticated for most commentators.[66] The question of whether this policy mantra was maintained too long is addressed in connection with the next episode.

After an initial positive response to the statements by Greenspan and Summers, the dollar continued its decline. As shown in figure 9.1, the broad measure of the dollar's value crossed the line 10 percent below the 1973–2008 average in September 1994, which is the date I take for the start of this episode.[67] Following a brief rise in late 1994 and early 1995, the dollar resumed its decline, reaching a low on average in real terms in July.[68] In early 1995, the dollar was affected in mysterious ways by the Mexican financial crisis. Some market participants mistakenly believed that in providing the Mexican authorities with dollars the US Treasury was reducing

---

66. DeLong and Eichengreen (2002), while referring to the July 1994 intra-agency discussions of this issue in July 1994 and explicitly to the role of Treasury Deputy Secretary Altman, date the strong dollar policy to Secretary Rubin's January 1995 testimony. They also observe that according to press reports President-elect Clinton, on December 16, 1992, at an economic policy conference in Little Rock, Arkansas, declared his support for a strong dollar.

67. The dollar recovered to above the line after October 1995. In terms of the major currencies, the dollar fell 10 percent below the 1973–2008 average in July 1994 and stayed below that average through March 1996. On neither basis did the dollar decline 10 percent below the respective trend lines; in fact, during this period it fluctuated around them (figure 9.2).

68. In nominal terms against the yen and the deutsche mark the low was on April 19, 1995, at ¥81 and DM136 to the dollar.

its capacity to sell its deutsche mark and yen. More rationally, market participants may have anticipated an easier US monetary policy (or less restraint) or focused on the effects of the Mexican external adjustment. Because the United States is Mexico's dominant trading partner, Mexico's adjustment initially impacted disproportionately the US external position; depreciation of the dollar helped to redistribute that impact to other countries.

The US authorities sold foreign currency 10 times between November 1994 and August 1995; they sold both yen and deutsche mark eight times and twice sold just yen. The average amount of those daily operations was $915 million equivalent. The August foreign currency sales were noteworthy in that the dollar was rising at the time.

Was the dollar sending the US authorities a message about their policies?

It is difficult to substantiate a positive answer to this question. The growth of US real GDP continued at the reasonably healthy rate of the previous two years and unemployment was declining, though both indicators would perform better in the subsequent period (see table 9.6). The fiscal situation had improved, though it would later improve further. CPI inflation was low, but in 1994 the Federal Reserve was removing the substantial accommodation it had previously supplied, and the real federal funds rate by early 1995 had moved from zero into a range of more than 3 percent that most people at the time interpreted as a policy of restraint given that the long-term bond rate was significantly above the federal funds rate. Growth in the rest of the world was somewhat better than in the previous period. US external accounts were exhibiting only a minor degree of deterioration.[69] However, some members of the Clinton administration continued to express concerns about US trade relations with Japan, and some observers interpreted these comments as efforts to talk down the dollar. Nevertheless, overall export growth was strong, and global growth was faster than in the United States at that time and during the previous period.

The puzzle was and is why the dollar was weakening, in particular, given that the Federal Reserve was raising interest rates quite abruptly— a conundrum 10 years before the term came into general use. It is possible that the markets thought that the Federal Reserve was behind the curve in restraining inflation, although the data do not support that view.

Given the widening of the US trade and current account deficits, the US authorities may have been mistaken in resisting the dollar's weakness via intervention, which was significant in size even if somewhat sporadic. There certainly were pressures from major partners to restrain the dollar's decline. The G-7 finance ministers and central bank governors on April 25,

---

69. At the time the current account deficit was a bit above 2 percent of GDP, and some were beginning to be concerned. The current account data for 1994 and 1995 have subsequently been revised to show smaller deficits of 1.7 and 1.5 percent of GDP respectively.

Table 9.6   September 1994–October 1995 episode
(percent except as noted)

	Indicators	Episode	Episode less before[a]	Episode less after[b]
1	Growth of US real GDP	3.1	−0.2	−1.0
2	Growth of US real gross domestic purchases	3.1	−0.4	−0.9
3	US unemployment rate	5.6	−1.3	0.5
4	Growth of world real GDP	3.6	0.8	−0.2
5	US CPI inflation	2.7	−0.1	0.1
6	US core CPI inflation	2.9	−0.3	0.4
7	US federal funds rate	5.6	2.4	0.2
8	10-year US Treasury bond yield	6.8	0.5	0.3
9	US federal budget[c]	−2.8	1.2	−1.5
10	US general government[c]	−2.6	1.4	−1.7
11	US trade balance[c]	−1.4	−0.3	0.0
12	US current account balance[c]	−1.7	−0.4	0.0
13	Growth of US real exports of goods and services	10.5	5.9	0.3
14	Growth of US real imports of goods and services	9.7	1.0	−1.4

Memorandum items:

	Episode	Before	After
Quarters	6 (1994Q3–1995Q4)	8 (1992Q3–1994Q2)	8 (1996Q1–1997Q4)
Months	14 (9/1994–10/1995)	22 (11/1992–8/1994)	59 (11/1995–9/2000)
US intervention			
Foreign currency sales			
Amount (dollars)	9,153	4,941	0
Days	10	8	0
Foreign currency purchases			
Amount (dollars)	0	0	2,172
Days	0	0	2
Total intervention days	10	8	2
Total days	304	478	1,283

CPI = consumer price index

a. *Before* is defined as the eight quarters prior to the episode.
b. *After* is defined as the eight quarters following the episode.
c. As a percent of GDP.

Note: Indicators are calculated as averages of four-quarter changes except for items indicated by footnote c.

Sources: Bureau of Economic Analysis, Bureau of Labor Statistics, Federal Reserve Board.

1995, "agreed that recent movements [in exchange rates] have gone beyond the levels justified by underlying economic conditions in the major countries." In effect, the G-7 was saying that exchange market participants were mistaken to be driving down the dollar. If this reading is accepted, it might be said that the US authorities in cooperation with their counterparts successfully dealt with a bubble.

Bergsten and Henning (1996) express approval of the joint G-7 actions to strengthen the dollar during this period, but they argue that the yen was allowed to weaken too far beyond ¥100 to the US dollar given the size of the Japanese current account surplus at that time. If, contrary to the actual situation, there had been a notional 10 percent band for the yen-dollar rate around ¥110 per dollar, the yen would not have weakened to that level until late 1996. Moreover, target zones or reference ranges were not under serious consideration at the time, even though the new German government later raised the possibility after its election in late 1998.

In the absence of any other convincing story, my conclusion is that the dollar was caught in a negative bubble during this episode, which may have been the creation of a subset of US policymakers and others like Fred Bergsten seeking to talk the dollar down. The dollar's movements were sending no other messages to the US authorities about their policies. In due course, the strong-dollar mantra, supported by some well-timed intervention operations, became well established. The mantra has been embraced by US Treasury secretaries from Rubin to Paulson. Of course, in the opinion of some, including Fred Bergsten, that characterization of US policy is at best controversial and at worst irresponsible.

October 2000 to April 2003: Too Strong a Dollar?

As depicted in figure 9.1, the US dollar rose steadily on average from late in 1995 until early 2002, with a surge during the 1997–98 Asian financial crises that was followed by a modest correction. The dollar rose almost 25 percent from October 1995 to October 2000, in real terms on the broad index, and subsequently was unfazed by either the US recession in 2001 or the tragedy on September 11.[70] On the broad index, the real foreign exchange value of the dollar peaked in February 2002 at 17 percent above its average for the 1973–2008 period and 38 percent above the trend for that period. Interestingly, the comparable figures in March 1985, the dollar's previous peak, were 31 and 39 percent.[71]

A case can be made for using the trend rather than the average to identify periods of interest. However, as noted earlier, this approach would identify only three episodes over the past 30-plus years: the late 1970s,

---

70. The undoing by a number of countries of their currencies' formal or informal pegs to the dollar in the late 1990s had the effect of providing a series of one-time boosts to the dollar's broad foreign exchange rate index.

71. In terms of the major currencies, the dollar's performance was broadly similar, allowing for the fact that the dollar's fluctuations on the basis of this index are somewhat wider. In February 2002, the dollar's peak was 23 percent above the average and 50 percent above the trend, compared with 26 and 46 percent respectively in March 1985.

mid-1990s, and since the late 1990s. The observed behavior of US policy-makers suggests that more than these three periods should be of histori-cal interest. Therefore, I chose the period October 2000 to April 2003 for the analysis below without substantial loss in relevance.[72]

During most of the post-1995 period, there was little appetite among US policymakers to act to influence the course of the dollar. Initially, the dol-lar's strength was associated with a healthy US economy enjoying low in-flation, a budget surplus, and an investment boom, financed in consider-able part by a net inflow of saving from abroad. Moreover, during the Asian financial crises and the period immediately following, the dollar's strength facilitated the recovery of the world economy. The global stimu-lus from the US economy became even more welcome in 2002 and 2003.

During the period after August 1995, the US authorities intervened on only two occasions. On June 17, 1998, they bought $834 million equivalent of yen, in a joint operation with the Japanese authorities as the yen ap-proached ¥150 to the dollar and concerns intensified about the health of the Japanese banking system. This operation was linked in a statement by US Treasury Secretary Rubin to a commitment by Prime Minister Hashimoto to "make every effort to restore [the Japanese] banking system to health [and] achieve domestic demand-led growth. . ." and an elabora-tion by Japan's Finance Minister Matsunaga promising to dispose of the bad assets of banks more aggressively, accelerate the restructuring of fi-nancial institutions, improve the transparency of banks, and enhance standards for bank supervision. The operation was followed by an extra-ordinary meeting of the Manila Framework Group of finance ministry and central bank deputies from the Asia-Pacific region joined by Euro-pean G-7 finance deputies in which the Japanese authorities were harshly criticized for their policy inactions. Subsequently, the yen strengthened a bit, retreated briefly in August to below its June low, and finally recovered more decisively in the fall of 1998, as the dollar declined sharply against both the yen and the deutsche mark in the wake of the Russian debt de-fault and the subsequent increased turbulence and risk aversion in global financial markets.

The second US foreign exchange market operation during the post-August 1995 period occurred on September 22, 2000. After the euro had extended its decline against the dollar to almost 30 percent during the first 21 months of its existence, the US authorities bought $1,340 million equiv-alent in euros. Again, it was a coordinated operation; many days were spent in preparation and many intense hours were spent drafting the ac-companying statements. The US authorities were at pains to make it clear

---

72. The comparable period based on the dollar's index against major currencies starts in May or August 2000 but only runs through December 2002. However, recall that the choice of starting and ending dates for the identification of these episodes is intended only to be indicative.

that their participation was at the request of the European authorities. The US Treasury statement read

> At the initiative of the European Central Bank, the monetary authorities of the United States and Japan joined with the European Central Bank in concerted intervention in exchange markets, because of their shared concern about the potential implications of recent movements of the Euro for the world economy.

There were no new European economic policy commitments; the only policy hook for the intervention was the statement of shared concern for the world economy, which was code for payments imbalances. However, the US authorities were not seeking a general decline in the US dollar. US Treasury Secretary Summers that same day restated US dollar policy: "Our policy on the dollar is unchanged. As I have said many times, a strong dollar is in the national interest of the United States." The European Central Bank (ECB) intervened on three other occasions in September and November as the euro depreciated back to its level prior to September 22.[73] Subsequently the euro began its gradual recovery and by May 2003 had retraced its entire decline since its introduction on January 1, 1999.

In the six years since November 2000, neither the European nor the US authorities have operated in foreign exchange markets. The Japanese authorities operated on their own in the middle of the period, attempting either to weaken the yen or to prevent its appreciation in the context of their very weak economy and deflation. Japanese dollar purchases in 2003 and early 2004 were enormous. Until late 2003, the US authorities did not object to the fact or the scale of Japanese operations, reasoning that they facilitated the Bank of Japan's policy of quantitative ease. This rationale was technically flawed because Japanese foreign exchange market intervention is conducted for and on the account of the Ministry of Finance and thus is automatically sterilized. The Bank of Japan purchased no foreign currency assets as part of its policy of quantitative ease. Regardless of the wisdom and merits of these Japanese operations, which in my view were highly dubious, the Japanese also have been absent from exchange markets for more than two years.

Former Undersecretary John Taylor (forthcoming) describes US "exchange rate diplomacy" during his tenure at the US Treasury as being guided by five principles: (1) exchange rate policy must be supported by sound domestic economic policies; (2) exchange market intervention should be avoided, but never should be ruled out; (3) avoid verbal intervention and talking down the dollar, which has been the Bush administration's principal rationale for embracing the Clinton administration's strong-dollar mantra; (4) an exchange rate policy involves more than one country, which is where diplomacy and the IMF enter the picture; and (5)

---

73. See Henning (2006) for a detailed account of the intervention operations in 2000 and their management.

recognize that exchange rates influence, and policy may be influenced by, broader international political and security concerns, which is why exchange rate policy cannot be left to the experts.

These principles, according to Taylor, have guided US exchange rate policy since early 2001. In my view, they are not substantially different from the approach that guided US exchange rate policy during the Clinton administration. In that period, there was always a reluctance to operate in foreign exchange markets and a desire to ground any policy and operations on other economic policies. The Clinton administration undertook operations in the foreign exchange markets on 20 days over the course of eight years, but only twice after August 1995. In those days, the pragmatic view was also never to say never to the possibility of intervention. Clinton treasury secretaries may have had a somewhat higher ex ante inclination to say yes to intervention in response to requests from other countries, but no Bush treasury secretary has yet been seriously tested.

What was the strengthening of the dollar starting in October 2000, or somewhat before that date, telling US policymakers?

Economic growth in the United States had begun to slow by the end of 2000 and was slow on average from 2000Q4 to 2003Q3 compared with the previous eight quarters. There were no quarters of negative four-quarter US growth, and unemployment was at its lowest point in three decades (see table 9.7). Equity markets peaked in the first quarter of 2000. Inflation was low and considered under control, but there was a sense that there were aggregate demand pressures in the economy. Growth slowed in the global economy in 2001 and remained subdued as it did in the United States. It is difficult to make the case that the dollar's movements were conveying a message of inadequate growth in the US or the world economy.

By May 2000 the Federal Reserve stopped raising the federal funds rate, which it had been doing for a year. In early 2001 the FOMC began to reduce the funds rate; that process continued through mid-2003, when the federal funds rate reached 1 percent. Fiscal policy also was expansionary. In this context, the initial further strengthening of the dollar in foreign exchange markets in 2001 might well have been sending a message about the mix of US macroeconomic policy, but it is doubtful that it was sending a message about the overall stance of policy. Later on during the period, after the dollar was past its peak, monetary policy continued to ease and fiscal policy became even more expansionary. Thus, both monetary and fiscal policies were directed at promoting domestic expansion. I have argued elsewhere (Truman 2005a) that the Federal Reserve policy was too easy too long, especially in the context of the continuation of a profligate fiscal policy. In addition, a declining currency, which in many countries is a signal monetary policy is too easy, may have been sending the Federal Reserve a message that its policy was too easy, too long. The FOMC chose to ignore any message about impending external adjustment coming from the dollar's decline, which may initially have been appropriate. Although

Table 9.7 October 2000–April 2003 episode (percent except as noted)

	Indicators	Episode	Episode less before[a]	Episode less after[b]
1	Growth of US real GDP	1.4	–3.0	–2.5
2	Growth of US real gross domestic purchases	2.0	–3.2	–2.1
3	US unemployment rate	5.3	1.2	–0.2
4	Growth of world real GDP	2.1	–2.2	–1.5
5	US CPI inflation	2.3	–0.4	–0.3
6	US core CPI inflation	2.3	0.1	0.5
7	US federal funds rate	2.7	–2.8	1.0
8	10-year US Treasury bond yield	4.6	–1.2	0.3
9	US federal budget[c]	–1.1	–2.5	2.2
10	US general government[c]	–1.2	–3.2	2.1
11	US trade balance[c]	–4.0	–0.9	1.2
12	US current account balance[c]	–4.3	–0.8	1.2
13	Growth of US real exports of goods and services	–2.0	–8.1	–8.9
14	Growth of US real imports of goods and services	2.3	–10.0	–6.1

Memorandum items:

	Episode	Before
Quarters	11 (2000Q4–2003Q2)	8 (1998Q4–2000Q3)
Months	31 (10/2000–4/2003)	59 (11/1995–9/2000)
US intervention		
Foreign currency sales		
Amount (dollars)	0	$0
Days	0	0
Foreign currency purchases		
Amount (dollars)	0	2,172
Days	0	2
Total intervention days	0	2
Total days	707	1,283

CPI = consumer price index

a. *Before* is defined as the eight quarters prior to the episode.
b. *After* is defined as the eight quarters following the episode.
c. As a percent of GDP.

Note: Indicators are calculated as averages of four-quarter changes except for items indicated by footnote c.

Sources: Bureau of Economic Analysis, Bureau of Labor Statistics, Federal Reserve Board.

I do not believe that the Federal Reserve should target the external accounts, it should be mindful of market-driven external adjustment and does have a role to play in facilitating that process.

The US trade and current account deficits widened substantially further from late 1998 through 2000. After a brief respite during the mild recession,

US external accounts resumed their downtrends. Moreover, the growth rate of real exports of goods and services turned negative in the second quarter of 2001 and remained weak for the remainder of the episode. A reasonable message from the foreign exchange markets to US policymakers was that the dollar's continued strength coupled with the widening of US external deficits portended a rise in US protectionist pressures. Protectionist pressures did increase in the late 1990s and increased further after 2000, but observers differ about whether their increase was commensurate with the strength in the dollar or the size of US global or bilateral imbalances.

Another reasonable message from the foreign exchange markets to US policymakers was that they were observing a bubble in the market for dollar assets. The dollar's peak in 2002 was not as pronounced as it had been in 1985, but as discussed above, its movement over the course of 2001 and into 2002 was equally difficult to explain in terms of the behavior of economic fundamentals and political developments.

A basic question is why throughout the period of dollar strength, reaching a clearly unsustainable level with associated unsustainable current account deficits, there were not more frequent efforts to weaken the dollar. At least through early 2001, the answer is that there was little consensus about the need for action. Japan did not want a stronger yen; the euro was off its lows. A successful attempt to weaken the dollar would have been inconsistent with the needs of the US economy, where demand had outstripped supply and where a prescription of greater fiscal restraint and monetary ease was unheard and would have fallen on deaf ears. This was certainly the case during 1999 and 2000.

In 2001, the new Bush administration had an opportunity to jettison the strong-dollar mantra. Fred Bergsten (2001) advocated a shift in rhetoric toward favoring a "sound dollar" that would be more commensurate with smaller US external deficits at a time when the current account deficit was only in the neighborhood of 4 percent of GDP. He reiterated his call in congressional testimony in May 2002 after the dollar had peaked. Moreover, starting in 2003 he was outspoken on the need for a discrete appreciation of the Chinese yuan against the dollar. Drawing on the work of his colleagues Morris Goldstein and Nicholas Lardy (2003), Bergsten was critical of the Bush administration's calls only for additional flexibility in the Chinese exchange rate regime; he advocated in public and private the Goldstein-Lardy prescription of a two-stage process of discrete appreciation followed by a transition to a floating currency.[74]

Once the dollar and the US economy had turned down, the question was why the dollar's decline was not actively encouraged by the Bush administration following the model of the Plaza Agreement in 1985.[75] The

---

74. Goldstein and Lardy have subsequently published a large body of work on the topic of currency reform in China.

75. Cline (2005) has articulated this case.

answer appears to have been largely a reflection of a principled aversion to intervention, at least on the part of the US authorities, and perhaps concerns not to be associated (as ultimately had been the case in 1985–87) with an overly rapid decline in the dollar, in particular in the wake of the September 11 attacks.

The Europeans appear to have shared the US skepticism about the appropriateness and effectiveness of foreign exchange market intervention. It was not until the meeting of G-7 finance ministers and central bank governors in Dubai in September 2003 that one heard even a hint of oral intervention to weaken the dollar against certain currencies: "We continue to monitor exchange markets closely and cooperate as appropriate. In this context, we emphasize that more flexibility in exchange rates is desirable for major countries or economic areas to promote smooth and widespread adjustments in the international financial system, based on market mechanisms." These words were aimed at China, though that country was not mentioned by name, and some observers thought, not unreasonably, that Japan was also being identified. The statement was not reinforced by intervention operations in G-3 currencies because there was no consensus that the dollar needed to depreciate against the euro or the yen. Quite the reverse, with the dollar at ¥114 and €1.13 the Japanese and European authorities had no appetite for the appreciation of their currencies. Moreover, over the previous eight years, for better or for worse, a high bar had been erected against the use of sterilized exchange market intervention to influence the international adjustment process among the major economies.[76]

The message from the dollar's movements during 1999 and 2000 may have been to worry about protectionist pressures, which were then being actively resisted by the Clinton administration. There may have been a bubble in the foreign exchange market as well as other markets, but the US authorities were apprehensive about acting to puncture those bubbles, which at the time appeared to be linked. Moreover, the economic stimulus from a weaker dollar would have been unwelcome. In the economic environment of 2002 and 2003, the message appears to have been: Worry about a bubble especially when the dollar's strength is likely to contribute to protectionist pressures. Oral and/or actual intervention to weaken the dollar may have been the preferred policy, but it was not in the active toolkit.

Concluding Observations

The broad conclusion that I draw from reviewing these seven episodes of exchange rate adjustments for the dollar and/or heavy US exchange market intervention over the past 30-plus years is that exchange rates matter

---

76. As noted, the heavy Japanese intervention during this period was exempted from this presumption under the mistaken rationale that it was unsterilized.

and did often send useful messages to US policymakers—some of them heard, mostly with a lag, and others unheard. In the interim, the dollar's movements more often than not, at least through the mid-1990s, were met by intervention in the foreign exchange markets to resist them with limited effect.

Those messages were not exclusively or primarily about the potential for rising US protectionism, though that was the message in the mid-1980s and more recently. Sometimes, as in the 1994–95 period, the message was about protectionist pressures fomented by a subset of US policymakers themselves along with some observers outside the US government.

More broadly the messages from the dollar at times involved fundamental economic policies, for example, with respect to inflation in the late 1970s, the fiscal/monetary policy mix in the early 1980s, and arguably getting behind the curve in the adjustment process in the late 1980s—a lesson that has not been applied in 2002–06.

At other times the message was that there was a bubble—for example in 1985, 2001, and perhaps 1994–95—though what was done about those bubbles did not always follow from the content of the message. Occasionally, there was no message, as in 1991–92 in the context of the ERM crisis. In 1989–90, any message was obscured by excessive US intervention. Finally, sometimes the message was complex—for example, not to try to prevent exchange rate movements and external adjustment as in the Louvre flirtation with reference ranges.

Thus, messages from US dollar exchange rate movements are varied and sometimes ambiguous, but they are usually worth pondering by analysts and policymakers. Exchange rates can convey useful information, and careful attention to that information and its implications for policy—beyond resisting movements with intervention in the foreign exchange markets—is appropriate. From this perspective, Fred Bergsten's substantial focus throughout his career on exchange rates and their influence on trade policy, external and internal adjustment, intervention policy, and macroeconomic performance clearly has been important even if one does not embrace each element of his analysis and prescriptions. Moreover, his concern about the asymmetrical potential for the international adjustment process to lead to a chronically overvalued dollar, which dates back to his earliest writings, appears to have been well founded. Fred Bergsten's intellectual and policy contributions on exchange rates are about more than target zones!

References

Bergsten, C. Fred. 1970. The United States and Greater Flexibility of Exchange Rates. In *Approaches to Greater Flexibility of Exchange Rates: The Bürgenstock Papers*, ed. George N. Halm. Princeton, NJ: Princeton University Press.

Bergsten, C. Fred. 1975. *The Dilemmas of the Dollar: The Economics and Politics of United States International Monetary Policy*. New York: New York University Press for the Council on Foreign Relations.

Bergsten, C. Fred. 1980. *The International Economic Policy of the United States: Selected Papers of C. Fred Bergsten, 1977–79.* Lexington, MA: Lexington Books.

Bergsten, C. Fred. 1981. *The World Economy in the 1980s: Selected Papers of C. Fred Bergsten.* Lexington, MA: Lexington Books.

Bergsten, C. Fred. 1986. Overview. In *The U.S. Dollar: Recent Developments, Outlook, and Policy Options.* Kansas City: Federal Reserve Bank of Kansas City: 227–34.

Bergsten, C. Fred. 1988. The Case for Target Zones. In *The International Monetary System: The Next Twenty-Five Years.* Symposium at Basle University to Commemorate Twenty-Five Years of Per Jacobsson Lectures, June 12. Washington: Per Jacobsson Foundation.

Bergsten, C. Fred. 1994. Exchange Rate Policy. In *American Economic Policy in the 1980s,* ed. Martin Feldstein. Chicago: University of Chicago Press.

Bergsten, C. Fred. 2001. Strong Dollar, Weak Policy: A Harsh Rebuttal to Bush Advisor Lawrence Lindsey's Defense of a "Strong Dollar." *International Economy,* July/August: 8–10 and 40–41.

Bergsten, C. Fred. 2002. "The Dollar and the US Economy." Testimony before the US Senate Committee on Banking, Housing and Urban Affairs, May 1.

Bergsten, C. Fred, and C. Randall Henning. 1996. *Global Economic Leadership and the Group of Seven.* Washington: Institute for International Economics.

Bergsten, C. Fred, and John Williamson. 1983. Exchange Rates and Trade Policy. In *Trade Policy in the 1980s,* ed. William R. Cline. Washington: Institute for International Economics.

Cline, William R. 2005. *The Case for a New Plaza Agreement.* Institute for International Economics Policy Brief 05-4 (December). Washington: Institute for International Economics.

Cooper, Richard N. 2005. *Living with Global Imbalances: A Contrarian View.* Institute for International Economics Policy Brief 05-3 (November). Washington: Institute for International Economics.

Council on Foreign Relations. 1999. *Safeguarding Prosperity in a Global Financial System—The Future International Financial Architecture.* Report of an independent task force sponsored by the Council on Foreign Relations chaired by Carla Hills and Peter Peterson; Morris Goldstein, project director. New York: Council on Foreign Relations.

Cross, Sam Y. 1988. Treasury and Federal Reserve Foreign Exchange Operations: November 1987–January 1988. *FRBNY Quarterly Review* (Winter): 54–59.

Cross, Sam Y. 1990. Treasury and Federal Reserve Foreign Exchange Operations: February to April 1990. *FRBNY Quarterly Review* (Spring): 66–72.

DeLong, J. Bradford, and Barry Eichengreen. 2002. International Finance and Crises in Emerging Markets. In *American Economic Policy in the 1990s,* ed. Jeffrey A. Frankel and Peter R. Orszag. Cambridge: MIT Press.

Fisher, Peter R. 1994. Treasury and Federal Reserve Foreign Exchange Operations: July to September 1994. *FRBNY Quarterly Review* (Summer): 1–10.

FOMC (Federal Open Market Committee). 1989a. Transcript of Discussion of Foreign Exchange Operations, July 5–6: 2–8. Washington: Board of Governors of the Federal Reserve System.

FOMC (Federal Open Market Committee). 1989b. Transcript of Discussions of Foreign Exchange Operations, August 22: 1–7. Washington: Board of Governors of the Federal Reserve System.

FOMC (Federal Open Market Committee). 1989c. Transcript of Discussion of Foreign Exchange Operations and Monetary Policy, October 3: 1–18 and 38–49. Washington: Board of Governors of the Federal Reserve System.

FOMC (Federal Open Market Committee). 1990. Transcript of Discussion of Foreign Exchange Operations, March 27: 46–84. Washington: Board of Governors of the Federal Reserve System.

Funabashi, Yoichi. 1988. *Managing the Dollar: From the Plaza to the Louvre.* Washington: Institute for International Economics.

Goldstein, Morris, and Nicholas Lardy. 2003. A Modest Proposal for China's Renminbi. Op-Ed in the *Financial Times,* August 26. Available at www.iie.com.

Henning, C. Randall. 1994. *Currencies and Politics in the United States, Germany and Japan.* Washington: Institute for International Economics.

Henning, C. Randall. 2006. *The External Policy of the Euro Area: Organizing for Foreign Exchange Intervention.* Institute for International Economics Working Paper 06-4. Washington: Institute for International Economics.

Houthakker, Hendrick S., and Stephen P. Magee. 1969. Income and Price Elasticities in World Trade. *Review of Economics and Statistics* 51: 111–25.

Isard, Peter. 2006. *Uncovered Interest Parity.* IMF Working Paper SP/06/96. Washington: International Monetary Fund.

Jurgensen, Philippe. 1983. *Report of the Working Group on Exchange Market Intervention.* Washington: US Department of the Treasury.

Krugman, Paul R. 1986. Is the Strong Dollar Sustainable? In *The U.S. Dollar: Recent Developments, Outlook, and Policy Options.* Kansas City: Federal Reserve Bank of Kansas City: 103–32.

Mann, Catherine L. 2004. The US Current Account, New Economy Services, and Implications for Sustainability. *Review of International Economics* 12, no. 2.

Marris, Stephen. 1985, 1987. *Deficits and the Dollar: The World Economy At Risk.* POLICY ANALYSES IN INTERNATIONAL ECONOMICS 14. Washington: Institute for International Economics.

Miller, Marcus, Paul Weller, and John Williamson. 1989. The Stabilizing Properties of Target Zones. In *Macroeconomic Policies in an Interdependent World*, ed. Ralph C. Bryant, David A. Currie, Jacob A. Frenkel, Paul R. Masson, and Richard Portes. Washington: International Monetary Fund.

Siebert, Horst. 2000. The Japanese Bubble: Some Lessons for International Macroeconomic Policy Coordination. *Aussenwirtschaft* 55, no. 2: 233–50.

Taylor, John B. Forthcoming. *Global Financial Warriors: The Untold Story of International Finance in the Post-9/11 World.* New York: W. W. Norton.

Triffin, Robert. 1960. *Gold and the Dollar Crisis.* New Haven: Yale University Press.

Truman, Edwin M. 1977. The International Monetary System in Review. *The Journal of Economic History* 37, no. 2 (June): 461–65.

Truman, Edwin M. 2002. *Economic Policy and Exchange Rate Regimes: What Have We Learned in the Ten Years since Black Wednesday?* Remarks at the European Monetary Symposium, London School of Economics, September 16. Available at www.iie.com.

Truman, Edwin M. 2003. The Limits of Exchange Market Intervention. In *Dollar Overvaluation and the World Economy*, ed. C. Fred Bergsten and John Williamson. Washington: Institute for International Economics.

Truman, Edwin M. 2004. A Critical Review of Coordination Efforts in the Past. In *Macroeconomic Policies in the World Economy*, ed. Horst Siebert. Berlin: Springer.

Truman, Edwin M. 2005a. *Postponing Global Adjustment: An Analysis of the Pending Adjustment of Global Imbalances.* Institute for International Economics Working Paper WP 05-6. Washington: Institute for International Economics.

Truman, Edwin M. 2005b. Reflections on Monetary Policy 25 Years After October 1979. *Federal Reserve Bank of St. Louis Review* 87, no. 2 (March/April): 353–57.

Truman, Edwin M. 2006. Budget and External Deficits: Not Twins but the Same Family. In *The Macroeconomics of Fiscal Policy*, ed. Richard W. Kopcke, Geoffrey M. B. Tootell, and Robert K. Triest. Cambridge: MIT Press.

Volcker, Paul A., and Toyoo Gyohten. 1992. *Changing Fortunes: The World's Money and the Threat to American Leadership.* New York: Times Books.

Williamson, John. 1983. *The Exchange Rate System.* POLICY ANALYSES IN INTERNATIONAL ECONOMICS 5. Washington: Institute for International Economics.

Williamson, John. 1994. Estimates of FEERS. In *Estimating Equilibrium Exchange Rates*, ed. John Williamson. Washington: Institute for International Economics.

Williamson, John. 2000. *Exchange Rate Regimes for Emerging Markets: Reviving the Intermediate Option.* POLICY ANALYSES IN INTERNATIONAL ECONOMICS 60. Washington: Institute for International Economics.

10

Competitiveness and the Assessment of Trade Performance

MARTIN NEIL BAILY and ROBERT Z. LAWRENCE

No one has worked more extensively on the issue of US competitiveness than C. Fred Bergsten. He has made this issue one of the central concerns of the Institute throughout its existence, and he chaired the Competitiveness Policy Council (CPC) in the early 1990s at the request of Congress. Fred has been a tireless advocate for expanded trade and for policies worldwide that liberalize trade, but his advocacy has always been tempered by a concern that not everyone benefits from trade. In part, this concern has motivated his support for adjustment assistance programs to help those that are displaced by trade. In addition, Fred has supported policies that help US workers and companies as they compete in global markets. A strong educational system, a strong science and technology community, a high level of saving and domestic investment, and a cost-effective health care system are all goals that he has endorsed.

This chapter, intended as a tribute to Fred's accomplishments in the area of competitiveness, reviews some of the thinking on competitiveness from the 1980s and 1990s, provides a new way of framing the trade com-

Martin Neil Baily has been a senior fellow at the Institute since 2001. Robert Z. Lawrence, senior fellow at the Institute since 2001, is the Albert L. Williams Professor of Trade and Investment at the John F. Kennedy School of Government at Harvard University. Jacob Funk Kirkegaard, Katharina Plück, and Ceren Erdogan provided analysis and assistance. Michael Mussa and many other colleagues made helpful suggestions.

petitiveness issue that allows us to benchmark America's recent performance, and sets out additional work to be done.

The Competitiveness Problem Posed by the Competitiveness Policy Council

In the 1980s the persistence of slow productivity growth combined with large trade deficits created concern about the ability of the US economy to compete. To explore the problem President Reagan appointed a Commission on Industrial Competitiveness in 1983, under the chairmanship of John Young of Hewlett-Packard, which issued its report in 1985.[1] The commission defined competitiveness as "the degree to which a nation can, under free and fair market conditions, produce goods and services that meet the test of international markets while at the same time maintaining or expanding the real incomes of its citizens" (Young 1986, 502). Its key findings were:

> 1. There is compelling evidence that this nation's ability to compete has declined over the past 20 years. We see its effects both in our domestic markets and our ability to sell overseas. 2. We must be able to compete if we are going to meet our national goals of a rising standard of living and a strong national security for our people. 3. Decision makers in both the public and private sectors must make improved competitiveness a priority on their agendas. As a nation, we can no longer afford to ignore the competitive consequences of our actions—or our inaction. (Young 1986, 502)

The commission proposed a set of goals for policy and business to improve the situation: strengthening of the US technology base, increasing the supply of capital, developing a more skilled and flexible workforce, and making trade and the international trading system a priority (Young 1986, 508). The commission report was the most visible of a large number of studies reaching similar conclusions, most notably an MIT study by Michael L. Dertouzos, Richard Lester, and Robert Solow (1987) and Michael Porter's book *The Competitive Advantage of Nations*, published in 1990.[2]

In response to these concerns, the US Congress in 1988 decided to establish and fund the Competitiveness Policy Council and C. Fred Berg-

---

1. See President's Commission on Industrial Competitiveness (1985). The discussion here draws on Young (1986).

2. Porter portrayed the US economy as losing its position in the world economy. He pointed out the tremendous strength the economy had after the end of World War II and then described the subsequent decline: "American firms have diminished competitive advantage in a wide range of industries. The fundamental problem is a lack of dynamism. American industry, in too many fields, has fallen behind the rate, character, and extent of improvement and innovation. The rate of upgrading has slowed down, American industry is on the defensive, preoccupied with clinging to what it has instead of advancing" (Porter 1990, 532).

sten was appointed as its chair.[3] The CPC defined competitiveness based on four criteria:

> First, US goods and services should be of comparable quality and price to those produced abroad. Second, the sale of these goods and services should generate sufficient US economic growth to increase the incomes of all Americans. Third, investment in the labor and capital necessary to produce these goods and services should be financed through national savings so that the nation does not continue to run up large amounts of debt as in the 1980s. Fourth, to remain competitive over the long run, the nation should make adequate provisions to meet all these tests on a continuing basis. (Competitiveness Policy Council 1992, 2)

The key point, both in this definition and that of the earlier Council on Competitiveness, was that US competitiveness is not an end in itself but rather is important for its impact on US living standards. International trade, for example, is valuable to the United States to the extent that it allows Americans to achieve a higher standard of living than they would if trade were restricted or eliminated. Therefore, US participation in the global economy should be on terms that enhance living standards over a sustained period of time.[4]

In a series of three reports to Congress and the president, the CPC described in detail the areas where competitiveness in the US economy was deficient and suggested a number of policies to address the problems (Competitiveness Policy Council 1992, 1993, 1994). In its second report, the CPC (1993, 1–2) identified six indicators showing poor performance: Productivity had grown by less than 1 percent a year for the previous 20 years, real average wages were lower than in 1973, the economy had experienced four years of sluggish economic growth, high school students performed far worse than their counterparts abroad, 20 percent of adults were functionally illiterate, and the United States had run up merchandise trade deficits totaling $1 trillion and these deficits were continuing to grow.

The CPC then suggested three important national economic goals to address these problems: increasing the rate of productivity growth to 2 percent a year, increasing national investment by 4 to 6 percent of GDP, and financing new investment through increased domestic saving. In its 1992 and 1994 reports, the CPC also stressed the goals of improved education and training, increased spending on R&D, and control of health care costs.

---

3. Howard Rosen was the executive director of the council. At the time there were two other such groups, the private-sector Council on Competitiveness, chaired first by John Young of Hewlett-Packard and then by George Fisher of Motorola, and the President's Council on Competitiveness, chaired by then Vice President Dan Quayle. The private-sector group, still active today under the leadership of Deborah L. Wince-Smith, launched the National Innovation Initiative in 2004.

4. The relationship between trade and living standards continues to be a matter of study at the Institute; see the study led by Gary Hufbauer (Bradford, Grieco, and Hufbauer 2005) showing that trade accounts annually for $1 trillion of value to the United States.

It is interesting that the commission's concerns were broad. Faster productivity growth, increased saving and investment in human and physical capital, and research and development are desirable because they are associated with higher incomes rather than simply because they might improve trade performance. Indeed, one problem with the term competitiveness is that it is often used in different senses. Sometimes what people mean by "American competitiveness" is "How does America compare with other countries with respect to desirable economic goals such as productivity, employment, and equality?" At other times, they mean "How well are we performing in international trade?" In this chapter we look at each of these dimensions in turn, first asking broadly about US economic performance and then focusing more narrowly on trade. In both cases, though, the central concern is higher US living standards.

Has Recent US Economic Performance Matched the Goals of the CPC?

Growth and Productivity. Since the CPC's reports in the early 1990s, overall economic growth in the US economy has improved considerably. The most dramatic improvement has come in US productivity growth (output per hour in the nonfarm business sector), which accelerated after 1995 and has averaged 2.8 percent a year through 2005, double its earlier pace.[5] Labor force growth has slowed in recent years, but the increase in productivity fueled higher GDP growth, which averaged 3.1 percent a year from 1992 through 2005, compared to a growth rate of 2.8 percent a year from 1973 to 1992. US GDP per capita also grew more solidly and faster than for other developed-economy competitors. In the 1980s, GDP per capita in France, Germany, and other European economies as well as in Japan was converging close to the US level (OECD 2005), but by 2004 these economies had slipped back to around three-quarters or less of the US level. The CPC did not mention inflation and unemployment among its major concerns, but these have been surprisingly good also, averaging 5.1 percent for unemployment and 2.6 percent for CPI inflation (2.3 percent excluding food and energy) over the years 1995 to 2005. By these important macroeconomic measures, the US economy has performed far better than anyone would have predicted in the early 1990s.

Wages. Real wage growth remained weak in the early 1990s but has done better since then, although not stunningly well. Real average hourly earnings, which had fallen pretty steadily after 1973, rose from 1994 to

---

5. A portion of this faster growth is attributable to changes in measurement. Based on today's measurement methodology, output per hour is estimated to have grown by 1.4 percent a year over 1973–95 rather than the rate of below 1 percent a year reported by the CPC.

2003 before dipping in 2004 and 2005 in the face of rising energy costs. Real average hourly earnings in 2005 were 8.6 percent above their 1994 trough, although still well below their peak of the early 1970s. A more comprehensive measure of payments to workers is provided by real compensation per hour in the business sector. This figure, which includes benefits and covers salaried as well as hourly wage employees, rose steadily after 1973 and quite rapidly in the late 1990s, ending in 2005 at 23 percent above its 1994 level and 44 percent above its 1973 level.[6]

The gap between average earnings of hourly employees and total compensation of all employees highlights two important issues. The first is the rapid growth of benefit costs, notably health care costs (to be discussed shortly), and the second is the sharp widening of the wage and income distribution. Hourly employees have done relatively badly compared to salaried workers. Much of the gain from economic growth has gone to the most educated, skilled, and talented individuals as well as to business profits.

An important issue for the competitiveness debate is the extent to which wage trends and the widening of the wage distribution are or are not the result of international competition.[7] Popular opinion argues that competing against workers in China who earn a few dollars a day has had a depressing effect on the wages of low-skilled workers in the United States. And there is the Stolper-Samuelson trade theory to support the view that trade could put downward pressure on these earnings. Whether this theoretical finding applies to US workers to any substantial degree is open to question, however.[8] The assumptions required for this result do not hold in practice and there are many ways in which trade with low-income countries such as China has helped moderate-income US workers. As producers, US manufacturers do not specialize in the labor-intensive activities that China specializes in, so US workers generally are not competing head-to-head with low-wage workers. And in their role as consumers US workers buy the low-cost apparel and other goods made in China.

In the US economy labor demand is determined primarily by the large sectors that are not heavily exposed to international trade with low-wage countries (e.g., services, government, construction, and food processing). And a variety of factors in the broad economy have contributed to the widening wage distribution, including changing technology (skill-biased technical change) and the immigration of low-skilled workers.

---

6. Data from the Bureau of Labor Statistics, reported in the *Economic Report of the President* (Council of Economic Advisers 2004, 2006).

7. For a survey of the debate, see Lawrence (1996).

8. For a skeptical study, see Lawrence and Slaughter (1993). William Cline (1997) finds that trade is only a small contributor to the widening wage distribution.

One of the issues identified by the CPC was the US education system. In one important respect the US education system has performed well: There has been a significant increase in the fraction of the college-aged population enrolled in colleges, from 21 percent in 1960 to 40 percent in 1992, according to Cline (1997). He estimates that this increase in the supply of educated workers could have been expected to reduce wage dispersion by 40 percent from 1973 to 1993, if other things had remained equal. Other things did not remain equal, however, and the demand for skilled and educated workers has risen even faster than supply, pushing up the relative wage of skilled workers. Significant improvements in the level of skill imparted in the K–12 educational system might have alleviated the widening of the earnings gap, but such improvements do not appear to have happened.

Investment and Saving.   Fixed investment shows an increase in its share of GDP since 1990 in constant dollar terms. It is highly cyclical, of course, but nonresidential business fixed investment was 4.2 percentage points of GDP higher in 2000 and 2.7 percent higher in 2005 than in 1990. These figures are in real or price-adjusted terms and reflect the fivefold increase in investment in information processing equipment and software between 1990 and 2005. This increase is, in turn, driven both by higher business spending in dollar terms and by rapid declines in the quality-adjusted prices of computers and other equipment. The share of investment in GDP has risen because we are getting more bang for the buck (in current dollar terms nonresidential fixed investment was 10.7 percent of GDP in 1990 and 10.2 percent in 2005).

A goal of the commission was to increase saving as well as investment, and this has not happened. Household saving has declined to almost zero, and total private saving has also fallen, although by a smaller amount. Public saving is now negative again, after turning positive in 1999 and 2000. The gap between saving and investment is the current account deficit, which, of course, has grown and grown over the period.

Technology.   There was considerable concern in the 1980s and early 1990s that the United States was losing its technological strength and would be overtaken by Europe or Japan, but that did not happen. In computers and related technologies, US companies still dominate the world, and the emerging biotechnology field is centered in the United States—no other country comes close in advanced technology. However, a greater share of high-tech production manufacturing is done overseas, so that the United States now runs a small trade deficit in high-tech products.

Health Care Costs.   US health care costs have not been contained. There is an important question of who bears these costs and whether or not they are an issue for trade competitiveness. Most health care costs are paid for either by employer health insurance premiums or by tax-financed government support for Medicare and Medicaid. However, these costs are thought to be borne primarily by workers through lower wages and higher taxes. If so, any wastefulness in health care is an issue for US living standards but not something that raises employer costs. Other countries, such as many in Europe, pay a larger portion of health care costs out of taxes, but that does not directly affect their trade competitiveness. Health care costs may impact the composition of trade. Companies with strong unions and generous health care provisions for employees and retirees are facing crippling costs. General Motors reportedly pays about $1,500 per vehicle in health care costs for its US employees and retirees. Producing cars has been cheaper in Canada than in the United States in large part because health care costs are much lower in Canada (reported to be about $400 per vehicle) under its state system.

Lessons from the Past 15 Years. The CPC in the early 1990s would surely have been surprised to learn that US GDP growth and productivity growth have turned out to be as rapid as they have and that US technological performance has been so strong. But they would have been absolutely astounded to be told that the US trade and current account deficits would continue to grow, seemingly unbounded, reaching about 7 percent of GDP by 2005. Who would have believed that the rest of the world would finance a cumulative $4.5 trillion of US current account deficits between 1990 and 2005? And there have been other surprising economic outcomes:

- It had appeared to the commission that the US trade deficit was linked to, even the result of, weak productivity growth and sluggish investment. It turned out, however, that an increase in investment and an acceleration of productivity accompanied a worsening of the trade deficit. US demand expanded even more than supply.

- The other side of the coin was that competitors such as Germany and Japan experienced weak overall economic growth, slow investment, and sluggish productivity increase even though they continued to show strong export growth. Germany ran a $200 billion trade surplus and became the world's largest exporter in 2005; also that year, its GDP growth was only 1.1 percent and has averaged less than 1 percent per year since 2000. These contrasting experiences between the United States on the one hand and Germany and Japan on the other show that trade surpluses are neither necessary nor sufficient for strong economic growth.

- It had seemed that strong investment required strong domestic saving. It turned out that a higher level of domestic investment was achieved despite a decline in domestic saving. The United States consumed more, invested more, and borrowed to cover the gap.

- US dominance in technology did not translate automatically into trade surpluses. Indeed the US began to run a trade deficit even in computers and semiconductors.

- The growth rate of real wages has been slower than the growth rate of productivity for 30 years. However, faster productivity growth did translate into better average wage performance. But the distribution of wages and family incomes has widened substantially.

- In the 1980s, Europe and Japan were seen as the main competitors, while the United States was apparently mired in slow growth. Few foresaw either the strength of the US economy or the explosive growth of China and the emergence of India.

- Increased globalization and a large and rising trade deficit have not caused weak employment growth or unemployment in the United States. Except in 2001–03, private-sector employment growth has been very strong and unemployment very low. There were large job losses in US manufacturing after 2000, but overall manufacturing employment in the United States has done better since 1992 than in Germany or Japan.

In sum, in the 1980s and early 1990s a whole constellation of economic indicators suggested problems and seemed linked to overall structural weaknesses in the economy. The lessons from what happened over the next 15 years reveal that some of these problems have been solved while others remain undiminished or have worsened. Problems associated with slow productivity growth, weak investment, and technological dynamism were resolved, while weak saving, rising health care costs, increasing international indebtedness, and wage and income inequality remain. Let us turn now to consider trade performance.

Reframing the Trade Competitiveness Debate

"Competitiveness" is a highly loaded term, and many economists avoid using it because it can be so easily misunderstood. In this chapter we will focus on a particular aspect of competitiveness, namely the impact of trade on living standards. In this, we follow the Bergsten CPC and the earlier Young Commission by arguing that trade competitiveness is not sought for its own sake but rather because it allows Americans to enjoy higher living standards. While in the short term trade is a concern for issues like employment, over the long run the key metric is the implications of trade performance for living standards. In a closed economy, the only way a country can enjoy higher living standards is to increase production of goods and services. With the opportunity to trade, however, an open economy can raise its income in excess of that associated with its domestic production by exchanging domestically produced goods for imports. Everything else being equal, living standards will be higher the better the terms of this exchange—that is, the more imports a given quantity of exports can buy. Thus the terms of trade—the ratio of export prices to import prices—is a crucial link between trade performance and living standards.

By restricting our analysis to trade performance we ignore many of the issues discussed above that are part of a broader debate. For example, US living standards are primarily determined by the productivity of the US economy. Trade enters the picture because an increase in US productivity and the corresponding supply of US goods may actually lower the terms of trade: The United States would not receive the full benefit of its productivity increase because part of the benefit would be lost to the decline in its terms of trade.

Applying this perspective leads to conclusions that sometimes support but sometimes conflict with commonly held views of what changes in the global economy help and hurt the United States. It confirms that the country benefits when it can obtain higher prices for a given quantity of exports because, for example, of an increase in foreign demand due to changes in tastes, incomes, or a reduction in foreign barriers to US exports. But this perspective also implies that the United States benefits (its terms of trade improve) when it can obtain imports at lower prices, because of either improvements in foreign productivity or increases in foreign output. Most people do not think of relatively faster growth in other countries as beneficial to US competitiveness, but if it improves US terms of trade it certainly is. Likewise, people generally do not think of an improvement in the foreign ability to sell at lower prices as something that increases US competitiveness, but from the perspective of the benefits trade brings to US living standards, it certainly does.

This perspective also suggests the need to be careful in judging trade performance by the growth in exports or their share in world markets. US firms may export more because they reduced their prices or because of a weaker dollar. While these factors could mean more sales, they would not necessarily be associated with rising living standards or higher terms of trade.

We focus here on how changes in economic conditions in the United States or in the rest of the world affect US trade and on how changes in US trade in turn affect US living standards. We measure trade performance, an important component of overall competitiveness but not the whole story.

Trade Performance When Trade Is Not Balanced.   If trade were always balanced and products standardized, the terms of trade would tell us what we want to know about the implications of trade performance for living standards.[9] In fact much of the analysis of trade in the economics literature is based on the assumption of balanced trade. In practice, of course, trade is not balanced, and the general policy discussion of trade often focuses primarily on the US trade deficit rather than on the terms of trade. This is particularly the case when, as is currently true, the United States has a very large trade deficit. For many the deficit is a problem—they consider trade deficits bad and surpluses good. In fact the trade balance itself is often taken as the right measure of trade performance and countries that run large trade surpluses are considered highly competitive. Indeed, this view is so widely accepted that a shrinking of the surplus is said to reflect a "worsening" of the trade balance.

There is a disconnect, therefore, between the economists' view of trade performance and the popular view. Consider an example of the problems this disconnect creates. Suppose there were very high relative prices for US exports but the trade balance was in deficit. Would we say the United States was highly competitive because it has high terms of trade or uncompetitive because it has a trade deficit? If we look only at the terms of trade and fail to account for the deficit, we will miss the fact that by running deficits today, the United States will have more foreign debts or fewer foreign assets in the future. But by failing to take account of the high terms of trade, when we consider only the trade deficit we miss the fact that US living standards have been raised by the access to foreign goods at low prices.

This disconnect points to the need for a coherent framework for sorting out these issues. How can we take account of trade deficits and surpluses within the terms of trade framework, and how can we use this framework to appraise US trade performance?

A Model of Trade Performance with Unbalanced Trade. To motivate our subsequent empirical analysis, we will build the simplest model we can that captures the above elements. We will draw on the pure theory of international trade to show how this can be done in a simple but rigorously devised framework. We will make assumptions that will allow us to link the trade balance, the real exchange rate, and the terms of trade in a way that we believe can offer some important insights into US international trade performance.[10]

Assume there are two countries, the United States and the rest of the world (ROW). Each is fully employed and specialized in the production of a single (composite) good. Let us denote the US good as U and the ROW good as R. The quantities of U and R are U_0 and R_0 respectively. The

---

9. Trade could also affect living standards by increasing variety and changing competition, but we focus here on price.

10. Early demonstrations of the determination of the terms of trade in the pure theory of trade can be found in Marshall (1930) and Meade (1952).

price of U in dollars is (P_u) and the price of R in the foreign currency (say, euros) is P_r. If E is the dollar price of foreign exchange (i.e., \$/€), then EP_r is the dollar price of R and P_u/EP_r is the US terms of trade T. In this model changes in the real exchange rate move one for one with the terms of trade—indeed, if nominal prices were fixed they would move one for one with the nominal exchange rate.

A simple two-dimensional framework can be used to illustrate the model.[11] We will chart the terms of trade P_u/EP_r on the y-axis. On the x-axis we do something unusual: Instead of just measuring the quantity of one good, we measure the ratio of the quantity of U to the quantity of R. Since both economies are fully employed, the world relative supply of the two products, U_0/R_0, is a vertical line.

Since supplies are fixed, the terms of trade will depend on demand. To simplify, we assume that in both countries the demand curve for both products has unitary income elasticity. We can therefore draw relative demand curves for each country as downward sloping schedules that depend only on relative prices (or the terms of trade). We make an additional and crucial assumption that each country has a preference for its home good. This means that at any given world price, the relative demand for U is higher in the United States than in the rest of the world. These relationships are depicted in figure 10.1, where RD_u is the relative demand in the United States and RD_r is the relative demand for U goods in ROW. The initial world relative demand curve RD_{w0} will be a weighted average of the two curves and will lie between them. The weights reflect relative shares in spending on each product. The larger is US spending, the closer the world demand curve will be to the US relative demand curve, RD_u; the larger is ROW spending, the closer the world demand curve will be to RD_r. As the initial condition, assume there is balanced trade and an equilibrium at $(P_u/EP_r)_0$.

Transfers and a Trade Imbalance. We can now derive a relationship between trade balances and the terms of trade by thinking about the effect of transferring spending power from ROW to the United States. If ROW transfers spending power, its spending must decline relative to its income—in other words, ROW must have a trade surplus. On the other hand, if the United States now spends in excess of its income, it must have a trade deficit. So we can ask what happens to the terms of trade when the United States has a trade deficit?

We know that now more of world spending will originate in the United States. This means that the world relative demand curve will shift outward, shown in figure 10.1 as RD_{w1}, and the new equilibrium will entail a higher value for P_u/EP_r, which corresponds to an improvement in the

---

11. For a more complete explanation, see chapter 5 in Krugman and Obstfeld (2003).

Figure 10.1 Transfers and terms of trade

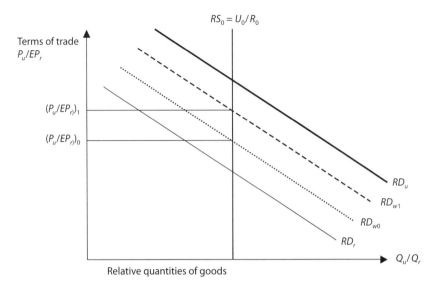

terms of trade for the United States or an appreciation in the real exchange rate to $(P_u/EP_r)_1$. We see then that a transfer to the United States induces a US trade deficit and an improvement in the terms of trade and real exchange rate appreciation. The larger the transfer from ROW, the greater the increase in the US terms of trade. Thus we can derive a schedule with a downward slope that relates the size of the US trade deficit and the US terms of trade. This is the terms-of-trade transfer (TT) schedule, shown in figure 10.2.

But can we be sure the TT schedule has a negative slope? In this model the crucial issue relates to the location of the relative demand curves. Transfers to a given country improve its terms of trade if at the margin that country has a higher marginal propensity to consume its own good than the other country's marginal propensity to consume that good. If the opposite were true in this example, then the transfer would shift world demand away from US goods and the terms of trade could actually worsen. If the countries had similar demand patterns, the terms of trade would be unaffected.[12]

---

12. There is a vast literature on the transfer problem as originally set forth in the famous debate between Keynes and Ohlin over the German transfer problem. A transfer could in principle move the terms of trade in either direction depending on the relative marginal propensities to consumers. The standard presumption, however, is that an inflow of capital (a transfer into a given country) will increase its terms of trade—the schedule slopes down to the right. Classic articles include Keynes (1929) and Ohlin (1929), Samuelson (1952, 1954), Johnson (1956), Jones (1970), and Bhagwati, Brecher, and Hatta (1983).

Figure 10.2   Shifts in the schedule as a measure of trade performance

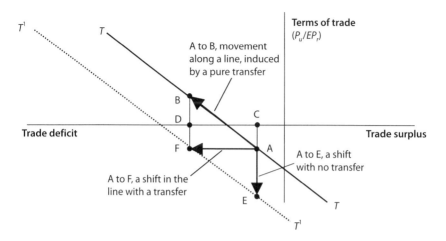

Changes in Foreign Tastes or in Technology. This model can be adapted to show how other changes could affect the terms of trade. Suppose there were a shift in foreign tastes that increased preferences for the US good. In figure 10.1, such a shift is reflected in an upward (or rightward) shift in the RD_r line and a smaller upward shift in the RD_u line. In figure 10.2, the effect is an upward (or rightward) shift in the TT schedule. Suppose now the relative global supply of the foreign good were to increase, because of an increase in either foreign growth or foreign productivity. In figure 10.1, the vertical RS line shifts to the right and the RD_u schedule shifts to the left by less than the RS line (because ROW spends some of its increased income on U). The result is that the terms of trade at balanced trade, or at any relative trade imbalance, go up. The TT schedule in figure 10.2 would shift to the right in this case also. Both of these changes affect the US terms of trade positively, but of course not all such changes will have this effect. If there were a shift in tastes toward the foreign good, this would worsen the US terms of trade at any level of the trade imbalance (indeed in figure 10.2 the case we highlight is where TT shifts to the left to T^1T^1).

Assessing Trade Performance. On the basis of this discussion we would expect at any point in time that there would be a negatively sloped line or schedule tracking the relation between the terms of trade and the trade balance. Everything else being equal, we would expect to find stronger US terms of trade associated with a larger US trade deficit. This is the schedule TT we show in figure 10.2. A pure transfer to the United States would move the economy from A to B, increasing US terms of trade but also increasing the trade deficit (from C to D). On the other hand, if there were a decline in US trade performance, due for example to a decreased foreign taste for US products, the entire schedule would move downward. With no capital transfer, this would lower the terms of trade, moving the economy to E. Alternatively, there might be a transfer that held the exchange rate constant but also increased the deficit, such as from A to F.

We propose therefore to measure trade performance (or trade competitiveness) by the position of the downward sloping TT schedule showing the relation between a transfer and the terms of trade. This allows us to separate the effects of a fundamental change in underlying trade performance associated with a shift of the TT schedule for a movement along a given TT schedule that is due to other forces affecting the trade balance (including changes in macroeconomic conditions in the United States and ROW).

The Trade Balance and the Terms of Trade in Practice

In this section we show that the relation between the trade balance and the US terms of trade identified in the simple model of the previous section has a counterpart in the actual data for the United States. We start by explaining how we formulate this relation and show how it has shifted over time. We then explore some of the ways in which other factors in the real economy, which were not taken into account in the simple model used above, could affect the findings. In particular, the US business cycle is seen by many as a major driver of the trade balance in the short run, whereas our model postulated a full employment framework.

As we move to empirical implementation, we make the assumption that there are composite US and foreign goods. This allows us to identify the real exchange rate with the terms of trade. The relative price of US goods and services in terms of foreign goods and services is expressed in a common currency.

The measure of the trade balance we use is the ratio of exports to imports. This is not perhaps as intuitive as the traditional measure of the trade balance, but it is very much in the same spirit and is consistent with the way economists have traditionally estimated import and export equations, as we show shortly. When the ratio of exports to imports is unity, trade is balanced. Deviations from balance show up as deviations from unity, so the ratio is an index of the trade balance.[13] The actual variable we plot is the percentage deviation of the ratio of exports to imports from trade balance. When our variable is zero, trade is balanced. When it is at,

---

13. One difference between our ratio trade balance and the conventional one is that the ratio improves any time exports grow faster than imports. In the dollar difference, US imports are currently so much larger than exports that the deficit can grow even if exports grow at a faster rate than imports.

say, –40 percent, then exports and imports differ by about 40 percent.[14] Appendix table 10A.1 shows the underlying data and indicates the steps leading from the dollar values of trade to the actual variable used in our relation.

The measure of the real exchange rate used is the Federal Reserve's broad real dollar index, although other exchange rate measures work pretty well also. We rebased the index to equal unity in 2000. We then use the natural log of this index as our exchange rate measure, again reflecting the trade equations, and we also multiply by 100. When the index equals zero, it is equal to its 2000 value; when it is, say, –20 percent, it is about 20 percent below its 2000 value.

We also know that there is a substantial lag in the impact of the exchange rate on trade. When the trade balance is measured in current dollars, there can actually be a worsening of the deficit for a period after a dollar decline, as the rise in the price of imports is greater than the effect of the dollar decline on real exports and imports. For our relation with real imports and exports we assume a distributed lag effect over three years. The dollar has 25 percent of its impact lagged one year, another 50 percent in the second year, and the final 25 percent in the third year.[15] Appendix table 10A.2 shows the underlying exchange rate data, again bringing out the steps along the way.

Figure 10.3 plots the resulting relationship, and it is clear that there is a powerful relation between the trade balance and the exchange rate. Other factors may indeed be at work, but it is hard to ignore this fundamental relationship. The simple model of the trade balance and the exchange rate postulated above appears to "work" in practice, showing a modest shift in the relationship after the early 1990s.

Parameters of the Estimated Relationship. We now fit a regression line to the data in figure 10.3 and find that the best fit comes from assuming a shift in the line in 1994. The regressions strongly suggest a one-time shift in the early 1990s rather than a gradual movement over the extended time period. Whether the shift took place in 1994 or a year later or earlier is not precisely estimated.

The results are illustrated in figure 10.4. It is assumed that the slope of the line remains the same in the two periods, and this assumption is supported by the data. The slope implies that a 10 percent reduction in the exchange rate will, after a lag of three years, result in a 12.5 percent reduction

---

14. We use the natural log of the ratio of exports to imports times 100. When this is equal to –40, it corresponds to exports being about 30 percent lower than imports or imports being about 50 percent higher than exports, averaging to about a 40 percent difference.

15. The exchange rate is calculated as a weighted geometric mean, and again the variable plotted is calculated as the natural log times 100.

Figure 10.3 Nominal trade balance and lagged exchange rate, 1981–2005

lagged exchange rate

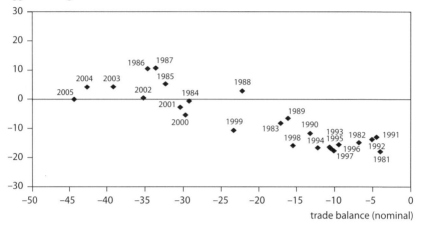

Notes: Exchange rate is lagged one, two, and three years (weighted). Exports and imports in current dollars. Federal Reserve real broad exchange rate index. Data are from the Bureau of Economic Analysis, available at www.bea.gov.

Source: Authors' calculations.

Figure 10.4 US trade performance shifted, circa 1994

lagged exchange rate

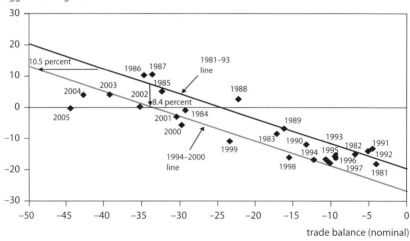

Notes: Exchange rate is lagged one, two, and three years (weighted). Exports and imports in current dollars. Federal Reserve real broad exchange rate index. Data are from the Bureau of Economic Analysis, available at www.bea.gov.

Source: Authors' calculations.

in the trade balance (the implied elasticity is 1.25). This figure is in line with mainstream estimates of the responsiveness of trade flows to exchange rate changes.[16]

We do not know what future shifts in the line may take place so we are not making predictions, but we note that the 1994–2005 line hits the vertical axis at –28 percent. Taken at face value, this says that if US and global economic conditions were to cause the dollar to settle 28 percent below its 2000 value, or 22 percent below its 2005 value, then the United States would eventually achieve trade balance.[17] This finding does not tell us, of course, what changes in global economic conditions would result in such a change in the dollar. A substantial change in the US saving-investment balance would necessarily accompany any major reduction in the trade deficit. In addition, a larger change in the exchange rate would likely be required to reach trade balance if the cost of imported oil were to remain at its current elevated level, a point further discussed below.

The Welfare Effect of the Change in Trade Performance.   Our estimated relationship allows us to evaluate changes in the US terms of trade in the presence of unbalanced trade. As estimated in figure 10.4, the real dollar exchange rate consistent with any given level of the trade balance was lower in the 1994–2005 period by 8 percent, representing a decline in the US real exchange rate and a loss of welfare to the United States. With imports equal to about 15 percent of US incomes, 0.15×0.8 equals 1.2 percent of GDP.

There is an equivalent way to look at the implications of our estimated relationship. The increase of the trade deficit has been very large over the period shown here. The ratio of exports to imports moved from close to balance in 1981 and again in 1991 to a deficit of over 40 percent by 2005. About a quarter of this (10.5 percentage points) is associated with a shift in our line, that is to say a shift in the magnitude of the deficit for any given value of the exchange rate; the remaining three-quarters is the result of a movement in the exchange rate itself. Those who look at the trade deficit that has emerged in the past 15 years and say that the United States has lost its ability to compete are partly correct but mostly wrong: The bulk of the deficit is associated with a dollar value that is higher than in prior periods of balance.

---

16. For example, Cline (2005) suggested a responsiveness of 1.5, somewhat higher than our figure, but this was based on estimates of real export and import volumes. If we repeat our regression exercise for the ratio of constant dollar trade flows, where the elasticity estimates would be expected to be higher, we find a responsiveness of 1.4, very close indeed to Cline's value.

17. This conclusion is similar to the findings based on simulations using the Macroeconomic Advisers model reported in Baily (2003).

Exploring Robustness

The estimation of import and export equations has been a central task of trade economists over the years. Typically these equations are reduced form equations that do not look at the capital transfer side of the picture. They look at how exports and imports respond to prices or the exchange rate and they yield estimated coefficients that capture the elasticities of either exports or imports with respect to the variables in question (log-linear specifications are often used). Cline (2005) provides a clear summary of the important findings of recent estimated equations, which we represent as follows:

$$X = F(Z_1)RER^{-\alpha} \tag{1}$$

$$M = G(Z_2)RER^{\beta} \tag{2}$$

$$\text{thus } tb = h(Z) - (\alpha + \beta)RER \tag{3}$$

Equation (1) shows exports depending on a set of variables Z_1, representing cyclical and shift variables, such as the growth of productive capacity in the rest of the world. Exports then also depend on the real exchange rate, RER, with an elasticity of $-\alpha$. Equation (2) shows the similar relation for imports, which depend on cyclical and shift variables Z_2 and on the exchange rate, with an elasticity of β. Equation (3) takes the natural log of the ratio of exports to imports, tb, which then depends on the log of the ratio of F(.) to G(.), expressed as $h(Z)$. The ratio of exports to imports then depends on the exchange rate (RER the log of the index) with an elasticity of $-(\alpha + \beta)$. Equation (3) gives therefore a simple linear relation between the trade balance and the exchange rate. The reduced form trade equations yield the same relationship that came out of our model and that was pictured in figures 10.3 and 10.4. (In all four figures the trade balance is on the horizontal axis and the terms of trade/exchange rate on the vertical axis. The slope is the inverse of $-(\alpha + \beta)$.)

Cyclical Effects. Estimates of import and export equations typically include other variables as well as prices or the exchange rate—the Z variables in the above specification—and cyclical effects are often included. A traditional rule of thumb on such effects is that a 1 percent rise in the level of US GDP increases imports by 3 to 4 percent after a lag. A 1 percent rise in the level of foreign GDP increases US exports by about 1.5 percent. These are not large effects compared with the massive trade balance swings that have occurred since 1981.

We tried adding cyclical variables to the relation shown in figure 10.4, using US GDP relative to potential and the US unemployment rate as proxies for the US cycle. Then we used the deviation of rest of world GDP from its trend (a five-year centered moving average) and deviations of

ROW trade from its trend as proxies for the ROW cycle. These cyclical variables were not close to being statistically significant (t-values below unity) and were rather trivial in estimated impact or even with the wrong sign. Adding them made little difference to the responsiveness of trade to the exchange rate or the shift in the line in the early 1990s. As a further check, in figure 10.4 we flagged boom years and slump years as well as years with either strong or weak economic growth. We could see no systematic pattern between years with cyclical differences.

It is generally accepted that cyclical effects on US trade are present and we do not dispute that. What we do find is that over the period 1981–2005, the net results of such effects on the US trade balance (as defined here) is very small and does not alter the estimated relation between the trade balance and the exchange rate. We note that during that period US and ROW cycles often moved together, creating offsetting impacts on US trade.

Other Specifications. In addition to cyclical variables, most trade equation estimates include variables to capture structural shifts. Our approach to this question has been a simple one: We labeled each year's data in figure 10.4 and looked at how trade performance varied over the period. A specification with a single shift in the relation, taking place in the early 1990s, then fit the data very well indeed. This approach has the advantages of transparency as well as simplicity, but it does not accord with the usual econometric approaches.

We therefore applied three alternatives to the data. The first was proposed in the famous article of Houthakker and Magee (1969). An important conclusion from this work was that the increase of US exports stimulated by a 1 percent increase in the income of the rest of the world was smaller than the increase in US imports stimulated by a 1 percent increase in US income. This "Houthakker-Magee" effect implied that if US and world GDP were growing at the same rate, then the relation between the trade balance and the exchange rate would shift over time. In fact, the value of the dollar consistent with US trade balance would decline continuously over time unless US GDP growth were far slower than world growth.

Applying the Houthakker-Magee result to the trade balance in 1981–2005 did not work at all. Over this period, US and ROW growth were similar in magnitude. Given the estimated parameters from the Houthakker-Magee study, this would imply a very large shift in the trade performance line in figure 10.4—much, much larger than actually occurred. The fact that we observed a decline in trade performance over the period is consistent with the spirit of Houthakker and Magee, but the magnitude of the effect and the fact that it did not occur continuously are very different from what they found in an earlier period.

We then turned to another trade specification described by Cline (2005) as the Krugman-Gagnon specification. We constructed an adjusted trade balance to take account of global and US trend growth and the US business cycle with the Krugman-Gagnon parameters given by Cline. This specification is symmetric, where the dollar is not forced to decline endlessly over time. It did not work well either, in terms of fitting past data or revealing the shifting relation between the exchange rate and the trade balance.

Lawrence (1990) estimated import and export equations and used a Houthakker-Magee framework that differed from the original in greatly attenuating the differences in elasticities for US and world growth. This model fit the data pretty well and is certainly a possible alternative to the one-time shift given in figure 10.4. His specification predicts that our line would move slowly down or to the left over time. The one-time shift fits the actual data better than the gradual shift, but we could not rule out the possibility that the pattern observed in this earlier work is still in effect today.

Earlier years. The real exchange rate of the dollar did not change very much from after World War II until 1971, so it is not possible to identify exchange rate effects before that year. But after 1971, the dollar moved substantially. We have added the years 1972 to 1980 to the regression analysis described earlier, looking at the entire period 1972–2005 and covering all three episodes of dollar change. With all the years included, the exchange rate continues to be a key determinant of the trade balance (t-statistic over 10), although adding the earlier years lowers the responsiveness slightly from 1.25 to 1.13.[18] The shift in the later years still occurs in 1994 and is estimated as a shift of 11.7 percentage points rather than 10.5. Overall, therefore, the results we gave earlier are not changed very much by the inclusion of the 1970s. These results may suggest that the impact of the exchange rate on trade has increased over time, perhaps because more companies are able to move their production locations to different sites around the world. More importantly, there appears to have been a dramatic shift in trade performance during the 1970s. Modeling fully what happened during this period is a topic for future research, but it appears there was an adverse shift in US trade performance in the 1970s that was 3.5 times as large as the one that occurred around 1994.

Conclusion. The US economy suffered a loss of trade performance after the 1990s, defined as a decline in the value of the dollar consistent with any given trade balance. We turn now to consider what may have caused this shift.

---

18. As there appears to be some cyclical movement of the trade balance in the 1970s, variables were included to capture the US cycle (the adult male unemployment rate) and the global cycle (the deviation of ROW GDP from a centered five-year moving average). Neither variable turns out to be significant.

Impact of Oil and Exports on Worsened Trade Performance

Note that the point for 2005 in figure 10.4 is well below the regression line. The trade deficit was worse than would have been predicted from the pattern of the post-1994 period. And based on current estimates of trade for this year, the 2006 value will be well below the regression line also. A very important reason for this is what has happened to the price of oil. The price index for imported petroleum products is set to 100 in 2000. It fell to 83 in 2001, helping the US trade position, and then rose to 185 in 2005. In addition, US demand for oil has risen over time, while domestic production has stagnated, so the quantity of oil imports has risen over time. The increased US dependence on imported oil and the rise in the world price of oil have worsened US trade performance over the past few years. If the price of oil stays as high as it is now, a larger decline in the value of the dollar will likely be necessary to bring about trade balance.[19]

How much difference has oil made? If the price of imported and exported oil had remained constant at 2000 levels, the trade balance in 2005 would have been –38.6 percent rather than the actual value shown in figure 10.4 of 43.8 percent.[20] This means that with constant oil prices the 2005 point in figure 10.4 would have been much closer to the line. In addition, apart from oil, the US trade balance (defined as the ratio of exports to imports) had started to improve in 2005. The decline in the value of the dollar since 2002 has begun to turn around the trade balance, a pattern that is masked by the rising cost of oil.

Despite its importance at times, however, oil is not the explanation for the shift in trade performance that occurred around 1994. To most people, the reason for the worsening of trade performance is obvious: The conventional wisdom is that the US has been flooded by imports, especially from China. As China and other Asian economies have developed, they have been importing advanced technology as multinationals have moved their operations and their jobs to Asia. We now seem to be buying everything overseas instead of making it here at home.

---

19. A full analysis of the consequences of a higher oil price on the sustainable exchange rate of the dollar is beyond the scope of this discussion. A higher price of oil in the long run increases the resources available to oil-exporting countries. They may save the funds or spend them; they may hold dollar assets or assets in other currencies; they may have a preference for US goods and services or of those of other countries.

20. The BEA reports total imports and nonoil imports but does not do the same for exports, except in the detailed commodity breakdown. Exports are very much smaller than imports but are not trivial. In making the above calculation we took account of the effect of price changes on both imports and exports.

As a diagnosis of the shift in US trade performance, the conventional wisdom is false. After controlling for changes in the price of oil, US imports grew more slowly from 1994 to 2005 than they did from 1984 to 1994. This is particularly the case after 2000, when US nominal imports grew more slowly than US nominal GDP (holding oil prices constant). The US was actually lowering its import intensity.[21]

Rather than imports, the reason for the deterioration in trade performance comes from weakness on the export side. Again controlling for oil prices, US exports grew at over 9 percent a year prior to 1994 and only 5.4 percent a year after that. The weakness of US exports was something we identified in an earlier paper (Baily and Lawrence 2004),[22] where we used an accounting decomposition to explore the reasons behind it. We were able to rule out a couple of possibilities. We found that the decline in US exports was not because of overall weakness in global trade but rather because of a decline in the share of US exports in total trade. Also, the US export weakness was not related either to the particular countries that the United States exports to or to the particular products exported. That left either the impact of the dollar (a prime suspect) or some other loss of competitiveness (also at work). We have updated that analysis, with very similar results. If US exports had kept their share of world trade from 2000 to 2004, exports would have increased 39 percent rather than the actual increase of 4.5 percent. Pinning down the reasons for weak US export growth is a priority for future research.

Conclusions and Directions for New Research

C. Fred Bergsten has highlighted the importance of competitiveness in his own work and that of the Institute, and the issue is increasingly in the minds of Americans today. Some of the competitiveness problems identified by Bergsten in the early 1990s have turned around, most notably sluggish productivity growth that persisted from 1973 through 1995. Since then, there has been much more rapid growth, at a level well above that of most other advanced economies. Other problems, however, have not improved or have worsened, in particular the low US national saving rate and the linked problem of the trade deficit.

With respect to the causes of the trade deficit, the message of this chapter is basically an optimistic one. Most of the increased deficit is because

---

21. It would be better to compare import growth to the growth of gross domestic purchases (the demand from US purchasers). As this measure grew faster than GDP, the above conclusion holds even more strongly.

22. See also Goldman Sachs (2006).

the value of the dollar is much higher than it was in 1981. US residents have chosen to borrow or to sell assets to foreign residents, who in turn have been willing to lend or to buy US assets on very favorable terms for the United States. The trade deficit has then effected this capital transfer. The normal case when such a transfer takes place is an increase in the terms of trade (the real exchange rate) of the country that is the recipient of the capital inflow. And this has been the case for the United States.

As well as the exchange rate effect, there is evidence of a decline in the terms of trade consistent with any given level of the trade balance—a loss of trade performance—and we explore some of the reasons this may have taken place. Oil is important and we look at the export side, exploring the reasons for weak exports since 2000. The United States has been losing its share of world markets. This is not because the US exports the wrong products or sells to the wrong countries. That leaves the continuing effect of the high dollar and a generally weakened ability of US producers to sell in world markets at a given exchange rate. Our analysis suggests it is more the former than the latter, but if the dollar keeps falling as it has recently, we will get a new test of the relative importance of these factors.

While any loss of trade performance is troubling, our analysis indicates that the impact of the change over the past 25 years has not been very large, accounting for 1.2 percent of GDP. We follow Bergsten's lead in identifying the changes in living standards as the key issue in evaluating competitiveness and apply this to the concept of trade performance. In addition, we find that the loss of trade performance since 1981 was small relative to the adjustment of the 1970s. At one time, the United States could have an exchange rate that made travel to Europe or Japan very cheap while still running trade surpluses. Those days are gone.

A host of topics could be addressed in further research. First, additional work could be done to expand our trade framework to different countries. Second, the reasons for the loss of trade performance need to be explored more fully. Third, can the distribution of the benefits be made more equitably? We believe that globalization and the expansion of trade and foreign investment have been a major source of productivity gains to the US economy, derived both from improved allocation of resources and from the competitive pressure that provides incentives for innovation and productivity increase. At the same time, workers at or below the median wage have not done well over the past 25 years. Most of the benefits of growth have gone to the top half or even the top 1 percent of the income distribution. Globalization certainly gets more of the blame for this than it deserves. But if political support for globalization is to be maintained, more of the benefits must be shared with more of the people. C. Fred Bergsten pointed out in the early 1990s that real average hourly earnings were lower then than in 1973. The same is still true today.

References

Bhagwati, Jagdish N., Richard A. Brecher, and Tatsuo Hatta. 1983. The Generalized Theory of Transfers and Welfare: Bilateral Transfers in a Multilateral World. *American Economic Review* 73, no. 4: 606–18.

Baily, Martin Neil. 2003. Persistent Dollar Swings and the US Economy. In *Dollar Overvaluation and the World Economy*, ed. C. Fred Bergsten and John Williamson. Washington: Institute for International Economics.

Baily, Martin Neil, and Robert Z. Lawrence. 2004. *What Happened to the Great US Job Machine? The Role of Trade and Electronic Offshoring.* Brookings Papers on Economic Activity 2. Washington: Brookings Institution.

Bradford, Scott C., Paul L. E. Grieco, and Gary Clyde Hufbauer. 2005. The Payoff to America from Global Integration. In *The United States and the World Economy*, C. Fred Bergsten and the Institute for International Economics. Washington: Institute for International Economics.

Cline, William R. 1997. *Trade and Income Distribution.* Washington: Institute for International Economics.

Cline, William R. 2005. *The United States as a Debtor Nation.* Washington: Institute for International Economics.

Competitiveness Policy Council. 1992. *Building A Competitive America.* First Annual Report to the President and Congress (March 1). Washington.

Competitiveness Policy Council. 1993. *A Competitiveness Strategy for America.* Second Annual Report to the President and Congress (March). Washington.

Competitiveness Policy Council. 1994. *Promoting Long-Term Prosperity.* Third Annual Report to the President and Congress (May). Washington.

Council of Economic Advisers. 2004. *Economic Report of the President.* Washington: US Government Printing Office.

Council of Economic Advisers. 2006. *Economic Report of the President.* Washington: US Government Printing Office.

Dertouzos, Michael L., Richard Lester, and Robert M. Solow. 1987. *Made in America: Regaining the Productive Edge.* Cambridge, MA: MIT Press.

Goldman Sachs, US Economic Research Group. 2006. The Case of the Missing Exports. *US Economics Analyst* 06/08 (February 24).

Houthakker, H. S., and Stephen Magee. 1969. Income and Price Elasticities in World Trade. *Review of Economics and Statistics* 51: 111–25.

Johnson, Harry G. 1956. The Transfer Problem and Exchange Stability. *Journal of Political Economy* 64, no. 3: 212–25.

Jones, Ronald. 1970. The Transfer Problem Revisited. *Economica* 184 (May): 178–84.

Keynes, John M. 1929. The German Transfer Problem. *Economic Journal* 39: 1–7.

Krugman, Paul. 1990. *The Age of Diminished Expectations.* Briefing Book. Washington: Washington Post Company.

Krugman, Paul R., and Maurice Obstfeld. 2003. *International Economics: Theory and Policy.* Boston: Addison-Wesley.

Lawrence, Robert Z. 1984. *Can America Compete?* Washington: Brookings Institution.

Lawrence, Robert Z. 1990. *US Current Account Adjustment: An Appraisal.* Brookings Papers on Economic Activity. Washington: Brookings Institution.

Lawrence, Robert Z. 1996. *Single World, Divided Nations?* Washington: Brookings Institution.

Lawrence, Robert Z., and Matthew Slaughter. 1993. *Trade and US Wages in the 1980s: Giant Sucking Sound or Small Hiccup?* Brookings Papers on Economic Activity: Microeconomics. Washington: Brookings Institution.

Marshall, Alfred. 1930. *Pure Theory (Foreign Trade—Domestic Values).* London: London School of Economics and Political Science.

Meade, James Edward. 1952. *A Geometry of International Trade.* London: George Allen and Unwin.

Ohlin, Bertil. 1929. The Reparation Problem: A Discussion. *Economic Journal* 39, no. 154: 172–82.

Organization for Economic Cooperation and Development. 2005. *Compendium of Productivity Indicators*. Paris: Organization for Economic Cooperation and Development.

Porter, Michael E. 1990. *The Competitive Advantage of Nations*. New York: The Free Press.

President's Commission on Industrial Competitiveness. 1985. *Global Competition: The New Reality*. Washington: US Government Printing Office.

Samuelson, Paul A. 1952. The Transfer Problem and Transport Costs. *Economic Journal* 62, no. 246: 278–304.

Samuelson, Paul A. 1954. The Transfer Problem and Transport Costs, II: Analysis of Effects of Trade Impediments. *Economic Journal* 64, no. 254: 264–89.

Young, John A. 1986. Global Competition—The New Reality: Results of the President's Commission on Industrial Competitiveness. In *The Positive Sum Strategy,* ed. Ralph Landau and Nathan Rosenberg. Washington: National Academy Press.

Appendix 10A

Table 10A.1   US trade data, 1981–2005 (in billions of current dollars)

Year	Exports (1)	Imports (2)	Balance (3)	Ratio of exports to imports (4)	Trade balance in figures 10.3 and 10.4ᵃ (5)
1981	305.23	317.76	−12.53	0.95	−4
1982	283.21	303.19	−19.98	0.92	−7
1983	276.99	328.64	−51.65	0.82	−17
1984	302.38	405.11	−102.73	0.73	−29
1985	302.02	417.23	−115.21	0.70	−32
1986	320.54	453.27	−132.73	0.69	−35
1987	363.91	509.10	−145.19	0.70	−34
1988	444.10	554.49	−110.39	0.79	−22
1989	503.35	591.50	−88.15	0.84	−16
1990	552.36	630.35	−77.99	0.87	−13
1991	596.83	624.31	−27.47	0.95	−5
1992	635.31	668.56	−33.24	0.94	−5
1993	655.84	720.86	−65.03	0.90	−9
1994	720.89	814.49	−93.60	0.88	−12
1995	812.22	903.58	−91.37	0.89	−11
1996	868.56	964.81	−96.24	0.89	−11
1997	955.34	1,056.90	−101.57	0.90	−10
1998	955.94	1,115.88	−159.94	0.85	−15
1999	991.24	1,251.75	−260.51	0.79	−23
2000	1,096.28	1,475.75	−379.48	0.74	−30
2001	1,032.82	1,399.85	−367.04	0.74	−30
2002	1,005.92	1,430.33	−424.41	0.70	−35
2003	1,045.65	1,546.50	−500.85	0.67	−39
2004	1,173.75	1,797.75	−624.00	0.65	−43
2005	1,301.18	2,027.68	−726.50	0.64	−44

a. Natural log of column 4 times 100.

Source: Bureau of Economic Analysis, International Transactions Accounts and National Income and Product Accounts.

Table 10A.2 Dollar exchange rate data, 1978–2005

Year	Federal Reserve real broad dollar (1)	Lagged Fed index[a] (2)	Exchange rate in figures 10.3 and 10.4[b] (3)
1978	0.82		
1979	0.84		
1980	0.85		
1981	0.92	0.84	−18
1982	1.01	0.86	−15
1983	1.05	0.92	−8
1984	1.12	0.99	−1
1985	1.16	1.06	5
1986	1.02	1.11	11
1987	0.93	1.11	11
1988	0.87	1.03	3
1989	0.89	0.94	−7
1990	0.87	0.89	−12
1991	0.86	0.88	−13
1992	0.84	0.87	−14
1993	0.85	0.86	−15
1994	0.85	0.85	−17
1995	0.83	0.85	−16
1996	0.85	0.85	−17
1997	0.89	0.84	−18
1998	0.97	0.85	−16
1999	0.96	0.90	−11
2000	1.00	0.95	−5
2001	1.06	0.97	−3
2002	1.06	1.01	0
2003	1.00	1.04	4
2004	0.95	1.04	4
2005	0.94	1.00	0

a. 25 percent lagged one year, 50 percent lagged two years, and 25 percent lagged three years. Weighted geometric mean.
b. Natural log of column 2 times 100.

Source: Federal Reserve Board.

11

International Debt: The Past Quarter Century and Future Prospects

WILLIAM R. CLINE

In the mid-1980s and again in the late 1990s, external debt crises in major developing countries posed serious risks to the stability of the international economy. Fred Bergsten and the Peterson Institute for International Economics have played an important role in providing timely research that helped shape policy responses to these crises. This chapter first provides a brief analytical review of these episodes and highlights some of the Institute studies that contributed to the ongoing policy debate. It then turns to a diagnosis of where developing-country debt stands today and considers future prospects for emerging capital markets.

Principal Phases in the Past 25 Years

The external debt of developing countries was not an issue in the first two decades of the postwar period. The widespread defaults of the 1930s had choked off the bond market, and a commodity boom and buildup in reserves in the early postwar period had limited demand for new borrowing. By the 1960s lending was rising again, but primarily in the form of of-

William R. Cline has been a senior fellow at the Institute since its inception in 1981 and now holds a joint appointment with the Center for Global Development. For comments on an earlier draft, he thanks without implicating Edwin M. Truman and John Williamson.

ficial loans. Nevertheless, by late in that decade there was rising interest in analysis of debt-carrying capacity, in part to identify critical thresholds warranting the rescheduling of export credits by the Paris Club.[1]

Two developments sharply escalated private lending to developing countries in the 1970s, setting the stage for the debt crisis that was to follow: the OPEC oil price shock and the advent of syndicated bank lending at variable interest rates. The former boosted borrowing demand in nonoil developing countries (and the borrowing capacity of those with oil) as well as the supply of foreign capital in the form of OPEC surpluses seeking an investment outlet, abetted by international public calls encouraging this "recycling" of petrodollars. The latter enabled a new form of financial intermediation to replace bonds, the dominant prewar lending vehicle discredited by the interwar defaults. Initially it was little recognized that the surge in bank lending was also potentially placing industrial-country banks in jeopardy.

The International Debt Crisis, 1982–89

Early '80s: Debt Suspension and Concerted Lending

The second oil price shock of 1980, the Volcker interest rate shock of 1979 designed to halt historically high US peacetime inflation, and the severe global recession of 1982 combined to make the rising external debt obligations of major developing countries increasingly precarious and vulnerable to a cessation of new capital inflows. Overly expansive domestic economic policies in many borrowing countries had made them vulnerable to these external shocks. Early signs of the debt crisis included Poland's debt rescheduling in 1981 and Argentina's disruption of debt servicing in early 1982, both related in part to political events (a military crackdown and the Falklands War, respectively). Then Mexico's suspension of payments on external debt in August 1982 marked the onset in force of the Latin American debt crisis. With the exception of Colombia, every country in that region soon was subsequently forced to reschedule external debt. The crisis spilled over to countries outside Latin America as well, as reschedulings of bank debt were forced in Côte d'Ivoire, the Philippines, Romania, and Yugoslavia (World Bank 2004, 66–75).

The stakes were high not only for the debtor countries but also for the industrial countries. For the 13 largest US banks, exposure to just five Latin American countries (Argentina, Brazil, Chile, Mexico, and Venezuela) amounted to an average of 153 percent of bank capital; for one large bank (Manufacturers Hanover) the ratio was 263 percent (Cline 1983, 34). A sudden loss of the bulk of these claims would have threatened bankruptcy for

---

1. For an early statistical analysis, see Frank and Cline (1971).

much of the US financial system. The vulnerability of European banks was only moderately smaller, as bank claims on the 30 or so largest developing countries stood at about 170 percent of bank capital for France, 120 percent for the United Kingdom, and 50 percent for Germany (Cline 1995, 78–83).

The international policy response was to provide financial rescue packages that involved International Monetary Fund (IMF) lending and "concerted" lending by foreign banks, combined with the rescheduling of debt coming due. In this first phase, there was largely "maintenance of value" rather than debt forgiveness, although there was some modest trimming of interest rates for the rescheduled debt. The IMF acted as the enforcer for collective action by the banks and made it clear that availability of its resources was contingent on new lending by the banks.

The strategy of new lending and principal postponement rather than forgiveness was premised on the diagnosis that most of the major debtor countries had sufficiently strong economies that they could eventually service their debt, so that the problem was one of temporary illiquidity rather than permanent insolvency. This diagnosis was based in part on the view that the "perfect storm" of high oil prices, extremely high international interest rates, and global recession in 1982 would pass and a return to more normal global economic conditions would permit developing countries to grow their way out of the debt crisis, in part through higher exports. The high-water mark of this strategy was in 1984, a year of strong global economic recovery. By 1985 debtor countries were beginning to get frustrated that private voluntary financing was not rebounding.

The Baker Plan, launched in September 1985 by US Treasury Secretary James Baker, sought to shore up the debt strategy by setting a target of $20 billion in new lending by the international banks to 15 (later 17) large debtor countries over three years, carrying further the approach of "concerted lending." Although the popular impression later was that the banks failed to meet these targets, a closer analysis shows that they broadly succeeded in doing so, after taking account of the cases in which countries did not fulfill their conditionality commitments and after recognizing that claim values kept on the banks' books often were falling more from prudential write-downs than from repayments without new lending (Cline 1995, 212).

Late '80s: From Baker Relending to Brady Relief

The collapse of oil prices in 1986 was a severe blow to the strategy of growing out of the debt problem. The damage to oil-exporting debtors such as Mexico, Nigeria, and Venezuela was proportionately much greater than the relief to oil importers such as Argentina and Brazil. There was growing debt fatigue among debtor countries more generally. One reason was that it was becoming evident there was an "internal transfer problem" that supplemented the traditionally recognized external transfer problem of scarce foreign exchange. Namely, currency depreciation needed to curb imports and boost exports also meant an increase in domestic currency fiscal costs of servicing the external debt, aggravating fiscal difficulties. Perhaps more fundamentally, political perceptions were evolving toward calls for a greater "sharing" of the burden of adjustment by the foreign bank creditors. US congressional sentiment was trending toward concern that US manufactured exports and jobs were suffering to keep up the profits of the banks. New Jersey Senator Bill Bradley called for a plan that involved moderate forgiveness of the debt.

Importantly, a secondary market for bank claims was developing. It typically carried prices in the range of 60 to 70 cents on the dollar in 1986, falling to around 50 cents on the dollar in 1987 after Brazil's suspension of payments. This in turn presented the opportunity for market-oriented debt relief in the form of discounted buybacks. In May 1987, Citibank set aside a large reserve against its developing-country debt, in part to show Brazil it could not be intimidated by default. This move somewhat undermined the notion that preservation of the value of these claims was essential to bank stability, facilitating a move toward debt reduction workout.

In this environment, in late 1988 Mexico once again became the bellwether for the debt crisis as President-elect Carlos Salinas announced that a demand for some debt reduction would be central to his debt policy, presumably for both economic and political reasons. US President-elect George H. W. Bush had met with him and was seen as sympathetic. The new US Secretary of the Treasury, Nicholas J. Brady, became convinced the Baker Plan was not working and would eventually lead to a shift of the debt risk toward the public sector. By March 1989 he announced the Brady Plan, which was designed as a form of voluntary debt relief. The two keys to the plan were the low secondary-market price on the one hand and the offer of long-term collateral for postreduction debt (US Treasury zero-coupon bonds) on the other. Banks agreeing to accept "Brady bonds" could increase their certainty of collection in exchange for a reduction either in interest rate (on "par bonds") or in principal ("discount bonds"). To apply implicit pressure on the banks to agree to debt reduction deals, the IMF changed its policy to allow "lending into arrears," financial support to countries not yet in agreement on debt in default, subject to the country's being engaged in good-faith negotiations with its creditors. Technically the Brady Plan also gave banks the alternative of keeping full face value but providing additional new money, although few availed themselves of this option (in part because "novation" in the Brady bonds in effect gutted the sharing clauses of the preexisting debt). Encompassing first Mexico in 1989, then Venezuela and other countries in 1990, and Argentina and Brazil by 1992, the Brady Plan by 1994 had carried out the conversion of nearly $200 billion in developing-country debt to banks at an effective rate of forgiveness of about 35 percent (Cline 1995, 234).

The Brady Plan had the effect of clearing the air for developing-country access to capital markets. It is arguable that several countries, especially Venezuela, sought and received greater debt forgiveness because of political imperatives than was warranted by their objective situation. Conversely, Chile, with an initially deep indebtedness, eschewed any forgiveness at all.[2] Recent statistical work suggests that the pursuit of unnecessary forgiveness for political reasons has long-term adverse effects on conditions of access to capital markets. Reinhart, Rogoff, and Savastano (2003) identify "debt intolerance" for "serial defaulters," for which safe levels of external debt relative to GDP are much lower than those for other countries. Viewed in this context, it is no accident that three major countries that received Brady relief experienced subsequent debt crises (Mexico in 1994, Brazil in 1999 and 2002, and Argentina in 2002), whereas two that did not seek Brady debt reductions have had no external debt problems in nearly two decades (Chile and Colombia).

The New Emerging Capital Markets in the 1990s

Even taking into account the healing influence of the Brady Plan, the resurgence of capital flows to Latin America in the early 1990s was remarkable. Whereas net borrowing from banks excluding change in interest arrears averaged –$2.7 billion annually for the 10 largest Latin American economies in 1987–91, this average surged to $25.3 billion annually in 1992–94 (IIF 1997). Net borrowing from other creditors, mainly in the new bond market for emerging-market economies, swung from –$900 million annually in 1987–89 to an average of $15.3 billion in 1990–91 and $32.7 billion in 1992–93 before falling to $18 billion in 1994 with the runoff in Mexican tesobonos (dollar-denominated treasury bills) in the run-up to the tequila crisis.

Wall Street popularized the term "emerging markets," which no doubt cast a better image than the previous "developing-country debt." More substantively, three factors drove the resurgence. First, there were underlying improvements for the economies, not just in debt fundamentals with Brady Plan help but also in structural and macro policy reforms. Second, the fact that bonds had been excluded in the Brady relief (mainly because they had been too small to warrant the trouble) gave a seeming preferred status to bond flows over bank claims, setting the stage for a sharp ascendancy in bond lending in the 1990s and a shift away from long-term

---

2. Perhaps the best measure of debt burden from the standpoint of the long-term external transfer problem is the ratio of net interest payments (i.e., interest paid on debt less interest received on external reserves) to exports of goods and services. This ratio reached a peak of 46 percent for Chile in 1984 and a peak of only 14 percent for Venezuela in 1986 (Cline 1995, 52), yet Venezuela received 30 percent forgiveness and Chile none.

syndicated bank loans. Third, the credit cycle in the United States created a lower-interest environment after the 1991 recession and, as was seen again at the beginning of the present decade, in such an environment investors seek yield where they can find it, whether in below-investment-grade corporate bonds or in emerging markets.[3]

Financial Crises: From Mexico to Argentina via East Asia and Russia

The boom, bust, and resurgence of the emerging capital markets over the past 15 years is shown in figure 11.1, which reports net private flows to 30 large emerging-market economies. These flows more than doubled from a total of $73 billion in 1991 to $185 billion in 1993 and nearly doubled again to a peak of $330 billion in 1996. Then, with the outbreak of the East Asian financial crises, they fell in 1997 and again in 1998 to a low of $137 billion before beginning a recovery. Their collapse would have been even greater had it not been for the resilience of direct investment flows. The sharpest downswing in the financial crises beginning in 1997 was in net lending by banks, which fell from a peak of $116 billion in 1996 to a trough of –$59 billion in 1998. Net lending through bonds and other nonbank sources peaked at $89 billion in 1997 but then fell to a low of $6 billion in 2001.

One important pattern for developing-country debt flows in the past 15 years, then, has been volatility. A second has been a steady decline in importance relative to equity flows, especially direct investment. Thus in 1991–93 banks plus bond and other nonbank sources accounted for 57 percent of total net private capital flows to the emerging-market economies; by 2003–05 this share was down to 44 percent. Direct investment alone accounted for 41 percent of total flows by the latter period.

The salient features of the emerging-market boom and bust in the late 1990s are well known. Mexico prefigured the later crises with its 1995 currency implosion. Vulnerable because of a large current account deficit, Mexico experienced a politically triggered runoff in short-term external debt, sharp interest rate increases in response, a severe recession, and a crisis in the banking sector. It also heralded the advent of the new form of financial rescue, which involved high emergency lending from the IMF (and, for Mexico, the United States) but an absence of private debt restructurings, because this time the claims in question were short-term government obligations widely held by investors in capital markets rather than long-term syndicated bank loans held mainly by a short list of large

---

3. The interest rate on the 10-year US Treasury bond fell from 8.6 percent in 1990 to 5.9 percent by 1993 before rising again to 7.1 percent in 1994 (a factor that contributed to the tequila crisis).

Figure 11.1 Net foreign private capital flows to major emerging-market economies, 1991–2005

billions of US dollars

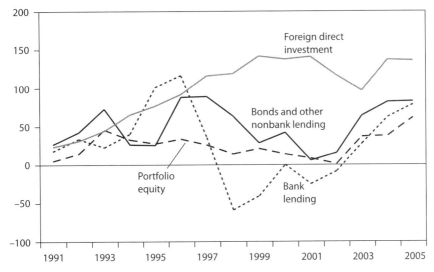

Sources: Cline (2001), IIF (2006).

banks. By 1996 the seeming success in managing the Mexican crisis coincided with a global liquidity boom marked by falling risk spreads not just for emerging markets but also for high-yield corporate bonds, fueling the surge of emerging-market lending to new highs.

In this environment, short-term bank lending to East Asia rose particularly rapidly. In the case of Korea, these flows were artificially spurred by Korea's liberalization of short-term capital flows combined with the international bank supervision practices that allowed zero risk-weighting for short-term claims on members of the Organization for Economic Cooperation and Development (OECD), which by now included Korea. In contrast, Korea in effect maintained restrictions on the safest form of capital inflow—direct investment.

Thailand initiated and typified the region's ensuing financial crisis. It maintained an overvalued fixed exchange rate in the face of a large current account deficit and reserve levels that (after adjusting for forward operations) were perilously low. The collapse of its exchange rate in mid-1997 eventually set off a round of contagion that hit Korea, which had extraordinarily high short-term debt and extraordinarily low reserves, and Indonesia, where it became clear that the much vaunted growth record was vulnerable to corruption, political upheaval, a weak banking system, and lack of an effective mechanism for collateral recovery through bankruptcy operations in the private sector. Adjustment in the region typically involved sharp exchange rate depreciation, steep increases in interest rates to keep exchange rates from falling even further, and fiscal tightening— the latter subsequently officially regretted by the IMF as overkill in the adjustment programs.

Whereas the Latin American debt crisis of the 1980s had involved long-term bank claims on governments and the tequila crisis involved short-term investor claims on the government, the East Asian crises tended to involve short-term bank claims on banks and corporations, typically linked to relending by domestic banks for speculative real estate and other investments. The crises thus became domestic banking crises that required large public-sector support to the banking systems. For Korea and Thailand, the crises were essentially liquidity crises, and indeed in the case of Korea the conversion of short-term foreign bank loans into three-year, government-guaranteed loans to Korean banks at nonpunitive spreads was a key to the solution. In contrast, in Indonesia the workout essentially took the form of self-awarded debt forgiveness to domestic corporations, which shirked collateral obligations thanks to an ineffective bankruptcy regime.

As in Mexico, in the East Asian crises there were again large IMF support programs; indeed, this time there was a formal adoption of a new IMF lending vehicle for crisis resolution, the Supplementary Reserve Facility, designed to have much higher lending limits than normal relationships to IMF quota. Debate continues to this day on whether the IMF conditions were too severe (and, in Indonesia in particular, too pervasive and intrusive); certainly the collective memory in the region seems to be that they were (in Korea the 1998 recession is called the IMF recession). Many even blame the massive accumulation of reserves in several East Asian economies today on the desire of authorities to avoid ever again being dependent on the IMF. However, reserves have by now far surpassed levels needed for this purpose and instead almost surely reflect the desire to keep exchange rates undervalued and exports highly competitive despite large current account surpluses, as well as the collective action problem that no country wants to be the only one to appreciate and thereby undermine its competitiveness.

Korea and Thailand emerged fairly promptly from their currency and financial crises, and in the region the Philippines avoided severe contagion, and Malaysia weathered it as well (whether or not due to the controversial imposition of controls on portfolio equity outflows). Whereas average real growth for these four countries fell from 6.9 percent in 1996 to 4.2 percent in 1997 and plunged to –8.1 percent in 1998, by 1999–2000 growth was back to about the 7 percent level. Large-scale liquidity support by the IMF succeeded in stemming the crises, albeit with major losses on claims against private corporations in the case of Indonesia.

Coming on the heals of the East Asian crises, Russia's default and devaluation in August 1998 turned the year into an annus horribilis for emerging-market finance. A collapse in oil prices, inadequate fiscal policy in the face of weakness in political leadership, chronic capital flight, and failure of an exchange rate–based stabilization program all contributed to the collapse. The government imposed a severe reduction in the value of short-term government bonds denominated in dollars (GKOs). Both the unilateral nature of Russia's actions and the fact that the crisis was the first to involve outright default and reduction of government debt value in the post-Brady period meant that the Russian shock to emerging markets was severe. The average spread for Latin American governments in the JPMorgan Emerging Markets Bond Index (EMBI) soared from 500 basis points in mid-1998 to 1,500 in August, and remained above 1,000 basis points until late 1999 (Cline 2003a, 481).

Contagion from Russia in turn doomed Brazil's attempt to continue the use of an exchange rate anchor for its so far successful Real Plan stabilization program dating from 1994, and by the turn of the year Brazil was forced to depreciate its currency sharply. In early 1999 there were widespread expectations of a return to high inflation in Brazil and even a new round of debt default. However, the government remained committed to fiscal adjustment and the privatization and other structural reforms of the Real Plan. Large and timely IMF support enabled the government to overcome a liquidity problem rather than slide into default. In part because of domestic recession but also thanks to fiscal restraint, Brazilian domestic prices rose far less than might have been feared based on the country's past history of response to exchange rate depreciation. After anemic but positive growth in 1999, Brazil returned to strong growth in 2000.

Ecuador did not fare as well in facing contagion from both Russia and Brazil. Its crisis in 1999–2000 took on systemic importance because as part of the resolution Ecuador became the first country to default on its already reduced Brady debt.[4] Private-market perceptions widely interpreted the move, moreover, to have been encouraged by the IMF. Even so, the impact on emerging bond markets was minimal.

In 2000 through early 2002, Turkey faced a persistent financial crisis and received successively higher IMF support that eventually reached a peak of 12 percent of GDP (Cline 2004, 2005c). The central problem was market doubt about sustainability of public sector debt, which in turn reflected extremely high real interest rates associated with the watershed transition from chronically high inflation to relative price stability, along with delays in privatization and other reforms. As the principal creditors to the government, the domestic banks particularly were in jeopardy. Forceful fiscal adjustment and a high primary surplus helped rebuild market confidence, and by 2004 inflation had fallen to single digits. Turkey had repaid

---

4. It was not the first to restructure bonds, however. Pakistan did so in 1999, when the G-7 insisted that private bondholders participate in parallel with Paris Club rescheduling. However, the restructuring was essentially on nonconcessional terms, at an interest rate of 10 percent (Cline 2003a).

about one-sixth of its peak IMF debt by the end of that year and more than half by mid-2006 (IMF 2006a).

The next major episode of emerging-market crisis in the troubled five-year period beginning in 1997 was the "3-D" crisis of Argentina, involving default, devaluation, and depression. Argentina's real output had been stagnating since its peak in 1998, reflecting in part the consequences of the fixed exchange rate under the quasi–currency board arrangement. There were external shocks from the sharp devaluation by Brazil, Argentina's largest trading partner; from the surge in emerging market spreads; and from the strong appreciation of the US dollar and hence the peso pegged to it. Recourse to high real domestic interest rates was the primary policy response, but these prolonged the recession and aggravated fiscal weakness, which was compounded by provincial deficits and a shift toward privatized social security accounts. There were increasing doubts about long-run government debt sustainability. A brief attempt to stimulate growth through fiscal incentives was followed by an about-face involving a 15 percent cut in government wages and pensions in July 2001, but by then political coherence was collapsing, in part because of the refusal of Peronist provincial governors to support the Radical Party president. After one last IMF lifeline extended in August (wrapped in ambiguous calls for debt reduction by US Treasury Secretary Paul O'Neill), by the end of 2001 there was a political collapse involving street riots supported by some Peronist groups, and after several riot-related deaths the finance minister and president resigned. The first of a flurry of successors declared a default on debt and devaluation of the currency, which promptly moved the peso from 1 to the dollar to about 3. Ensuing politically motivated measures to soften the blow for Argentine debtors owing dollars brought such anomalies as asymmetric conversion of bank assets and liabilities from dollars to pesos, causing banking system losses as well as a freeze in electricity and telephone rates despite contracts with foreign firms providing for dollar indexation. By 2003 the successor Peronist government of Nestor Kirchner imposed an essentially unilateral debt restructuring of some $100 billion in public debt. Concluded in early 2004, the restructuring was on terms far more severe for creditors than any experienced in the Brady Plan and on a par with the deep cuts usually reserved for heavily indebted poor countries (HIPCs). Crucially, the Argentine default and deep forced forgiveness appeared to have little contagion effect for emerging markets in 2002–04. The discussion below returns to the implications of the Argentine default.

The final major crisis in these difficult years for emerging markets was once again in Brazil, this time because the markets reacted severely when it became apparent that long-time radical leftist candidate "Lula" would likely win the October 2002 presidential election. The IMF called for all candidates in the election to pledge to maintain fiscal equilibrium, and Lula agreed to do so. Once again a large IMF program enabled Brazil to weather the liquidity problem, and after a surge in spreads to levels in the range of 2,000 basis points in the second half of 2002, by mid-2003 spreads were back down to about 750 basis points. Once again there was a growth recession, but by 2004 relatively strong growth had returned. Importantly, the Argentine example did not prevent Brazil from overcoming its liquidity crisis in 2002. There was no complete market cutoff stemming from Argentine spillover, nor did the G-7 put an end to large IMF rescue support on grounds that Argentina showed this strategy did not work. Instead, the IMF's requirement of presidential candidates' endorsement of fiscal equilibrium reflected the lesson from Argentina that domestic political commitment to fiscal adjustment was an important precondition for large external support.

2002–05: Easy Money and Emerging Markets Redux

Despite the experience with Argentina and the largest default on external debt in history, the first half of the present decade has turned out to be extremely favorable for emerging capital markets. The underlying reason has been the low level of global interest rates and the strong trade performance of developing countries associated with high levels of global growth. Figure 11.2 shows the strong upswing in current account balances in Asia-Pacific and Latin American emerging-market economies from the late 1990s to 2005. There was a smaller upswing in the European and Africa–Middle East emerging-market economies.

Figure 11.3 reports emerging-market borrowing spreads above US Treasury bond rates. There was a plunge of the US policy (federal funds) interest rate to historic lows in 2002–04. This decline was broadly accompanied by a systematic narrowing of emerging-market risk spreads, as measured by the JPMorgan EMBI.[5] Investors seeking higher yields boosted potential capital supply, even as a swing from current account deficit to surplus for emerging-market economies reduced potential demand, so the price premium for emerging-market borrowers fell sharply.

The concluding section of this chapter considers whether the favorable conditions for emerging capital markets will continue. At the outset, however, it should be stressed that two features of the recent configuration are troublesome. First, it involves a large aggregate current account surplus, rather than deficit, of the major emerging-market economies. This means that in recent years they have been net suppliers of real resources to the industrial countries (mainly the United States) rather than net recipients of resources. This amounts to a perverse flow of capital and resources in terms of the standard theory of capital flows and development, in which return on capital is presumed to be higher in developing countries than in industrial countries and so capital and accompanying real resources are

---

5. EMBI through July 2004; EMBI+ thereafter.

Figure 11.2 Current account balances of major emerging-market economies, 1996–2005

billions of US dollars

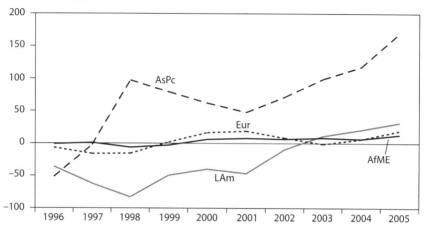

AfME = Algeria, Egypt, Morocco, South Africa, Tunisia
AsPc = China, India, Indonesia, Korea, Malaysia, Philippines, Thailand
Eur = Bulgaria, Czech Republic, Hungary, Poland, Romania, Russia, Slovakia, Turkey
LAm = Argentina, Brazil, Chile, Colombia, Ecuador, Mexico, Peru, Uruguay, Venezuela
Source: IIF (2006).

Figure 11.3 US interest rates and emerging-market spreads (EMBI), 1992–2006

percent

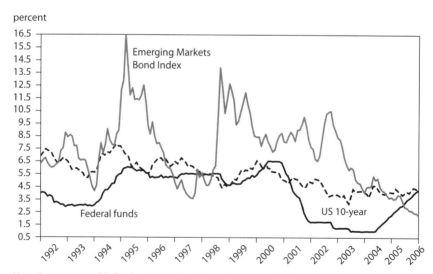

Note: Data are monthly for the years indicated and January of 2006.
Sources: IMF (2006b); JPMorgan, MorganMarkets.

presumed to flow from the industrial countries to the developing countries. Second, this unusual pattern has been the counterpart of a rise in the US current account deficit to historically high levels. The large US deficit poses a risk to both the US and global economies, and if US external adjustment does not occur smoothly, the result could be a severe shock for developing countries.

HIPC Debt Relief

A final key feature of global debt in recent years has been the arrival of debt forgiveness for HIPCs, the logical consequence of successive episodes of official debt relief for these countries, starting with bilateral debt. The Paris Club initiatives for granting forgiveness of bilateral debt owed by low-income countries constitute a string of metropolitan names each successively increasing the extent of forgiveness. Starting with the "Toronto terms" of 1988 forgiving a third of the debt for low-income countries, the bilateral donors deepened their forgiveness to 50 percent in London (1991), 67 percent in Naples (1995), 80 percent in Lyon (1996), and 90 percent in Cologne (1999). As the bilateral reductions were seen as insufficient, donors turned to including the multilateral agencies in debt forgiveness, albeit with arrangements whereby industrial countries made them whole for the losses.

Multilateral forgiveness began with the HIPC initiative of 1996, designed to cut the debt-export ratio of 41 heavily indebted poor countries to no more than 200 percent, followed by the enhanced HIPC initiative in 1999 seeking to cut the ratio to no more than 150 percent (Birdsall and Williamson 2002, 23). For 40 countries identified as having unsustainably high external debt, up to 100 percent of the debt owed to the IMF, World Bank (International Development Association, or IDA), and African Development Bank can be forgiven. Beneficiaries must develop a Poverty Reduction Strategy Paper (PRSP) and establish a favorable track record on economic policies. After a country is declared eligible at the "decision point," it receives interim relief, and if sound policies are continued and at least one year of the PRSP is implemented, the country can reach the "completion point" of the maximum multilateral relief identified as necessary. Twenty-nine countries have reached the decision point, and together with another 11 countries potentially eligible, the total present value of their debt eligible for HIPC relief in 2004 was $61 billion (IMF 2006a). As of early 2006 the HIPC initiative had reduced the debt of 18 countries by $19 billion, cutting their debt ratios in half. However, in 8 of the 13 postcompletion-point countries, the debt "ratios once again exceed HIPC thresholds" (Independent Evaluation Group 2006, vii).

The broad lesson of debt relief for poor countries would seem to be that official assistance to such countries should not have been in the form of loans in the first place but grants. So far this lesson has translated into only a modest shift in IDA and other official assistance toward grants and away from loans, in part because of some donors' fears that without future reflows the agency will not be in a position to provide new support to the countries that need it at that time.

As for the potential impact of HIPC relief, perhaps not too much should be expected, as the effect is primarily psychological rather than economic. The economic burden of HIPC debt was low even without relief because most of the debt was concessional. The average interest rate on total debt for HIPC countries in the aggregate was only 1.6 percent in 1997 and 1.1 percent in 2003, compared with 6.2 and 4.8 percent respectively for Latin America and the Caribbean (World Bank 2005a).[6] This means that even though the reported total debt was 98 percent of GDP in 1997 and 80 percent in 2003, the interest burden was only 1.6 percent of GDP in 1997 and 0.8 percent in 2003. In contrast, for Latin America and the Caribbean interest payments on external debt amounted to 2.5 percent of GDP in 1998 and 2.1 percent in 2004, considerably higher than for the HIPCs despite a much lower ratio of reported debt to GDP (39 percent in 1998 and 43 percent in 2003).[7] For its part, principal repayment tends not to pose the same type of liquidity risk for official assistance as it does for private flows because countries following sound policies tend to receive relatively reliable new inflows of assistance that offset (or more) maturities coming due (Cline 2003c).[8]

Institute Research and International Debt Policy

From the very beginning, the Institute has been deeply involved in analysis on the evolving issues in international debt policy, as shown in table 11.1. The outbreak of the Latin American debt crisis in 1982 came in the first full year of the Institute's existence. By September 1983 I had prepared a monograph providing projections that indicated prospective improvement in debt-export ratios in association with increased exports from global recovery, correction in the overvalued dollar, and reduction in abnormally high global interest rates (Cline 1983, 1984). The study supported

---

6. The estimates here for the HIPC members are obtained from aggregate data on low-income countries after subtracting the corresponding data for the four large non-HIPC countries in this grouping: Bangladesh, India, Nigeria, and Pakistan.

7. In addition, some donors may tend to provide lower volumes of new aid than they would have done if the countries had been making repayments, limiting any net flow impact of forgiving the debt.

8. There are other reasons for HIPC debt forgiveness, including the fact that tied aid is less efficient than untied debt service avoided. The point is simply that hopes for the impact of HIPC relief should not be exaggerated.

Table 11.1   Institute contributions to policy analysis on international debt

Publication	Type	Content
Cline (1983)	Policy Analyses in International Economics (PA)	Assesses debt crisis risk to global financial system and describes model of global macro conditions needed for resolution of liquidity problem
Cline (1984)	Book	Provides a more complete analysis of debt crisis, projections
Bergsten, Cline, and Williamson (1985)	PA	Reviews progress to date in managing the global debt crisis; calls for Mexico-type packages (lower spreads, new lending) and other improvements
Lessard and Williamson (1985)	PA	Calls for new instruments such as commodity-linked bonds to improve international financing after the debt crisis
Cline (1987)	PA	Provides menu approach to concerted lending, including discounted buybacks as exit tax; elaborated on Baker Plan
Williamson (1988)	PA	Calls for shift from concerted lending to voluntary debt reduction; prefigured Brady Plan
Cline (1995)	Book	Offers a retrospective on evolution of the debt crisis and international policy; includes quantitative analysis of 1983–84 model forecasts versus outcomes
Calvo, Goldstein, and Hochreiter (1996)	Conference volume	Provides early evaluation of tequila crisis of 1994 and implications for emerging markets
Goldstein (1998)	PA	Provides overview of East Asian financial crises
Noland et al. (1998)	PA	Predicts large upswing in East Asian trade balance as consequence of financial crises
Eichengreen (1999)	Book	Rejects radical architecture proposals, supports an active IMF
Hills, Peterson, and Goldstein (1999)	Book	Calls for limiting IMF lending to 100 to 300 percent of quota but adding a new contagion facility for systemic events, financed by SDR issue

(table continues on next page)

Table 11.1 Institute contributions to policy analysis on international debt *(continued)*

Publication	Type	Content
Haggard (2000)	Book	Argues that business-government ties spurred East Asian growth but also moral hazard and vulnerability to shocks; concludes that crisis advanced reform
Goldstein, Kaminsky, and Reinhart (2000)	Book	Provides empirical analysis of variables for predicting currency and banking crises
Dobson and Hufbauer (2000)	Book	Argues for extensions of Basel II reforms to further address moral hazard
Kenen (2001)	Book	Supports rule-based IMF rescue packages, mandatory standstills, collective action clauses, and floating exchange rates
Birdsall and Williamson (2002)	Book	Calls for (a) expanded HIPC debt and inclusion of Pakistan, Nigeria, (b) the use of IMF gold to finance, and (c) contingent further relief
Mussa (2002)	PA	Critiques Argentine fiscal imbalances leading to debt crisis and IMF decision to provide more support in 2001
Williamson (2002)	Policy Brief	Counters Goldstein on Brazilian debt sustainability
Krueger (2002)	Speech	Offers first statement of revised Sovereign Debt Restructuring Mechanism (SDRM) proposal
Taylor (2002)	Speech	Offers first statement of Treasury preference for collective action clauses (CACs)
Miller (2002)	Policy Brief	Argues that CACs and SDRM are compatible
Goldstein (2003)	Working Paper	Argues that Brazil's debt is unsustainable
Roubini and Setser (2004)	Book	Judges calls for an end to IMF rescue packages unrealistic, but seeks sharper IMF differentiation and insistence on debt restructuring when needed
Goldstein and Turner (2004)	Book	Calls for more attention to currency mismatches as means of crisis prevention
Williamson (2005)	PA	Calls for measures to reduce boom-bust cycles in emerging markets capital flows

HIPC = heavily indebted poor country
SDR = special drawing rights

IMF adjustment programs as the centerpiece for coordinated new lending by banks to treat the crisis as one of illiquidity rather than insolvency warranting bankruptcy-like treatment. This approach promised earlier reentry of debtor countries into capital markets, as well as less risk to the banking sectors in industrial countries, than an alternative involving default and bankruptcy-type workouts. One challenge of the approach was achieving collective action among banks, which otherwise had incentives individually to be free riders (Bergsten, Cline, and Williamson 1985). A subsequent study (Cline 1987) set forth a menu approach to this issue, including the option of "exit bond" relief granted by those banks seeking not to participate. This broad approach was adopted in the Baker Plan of 1986. Soon Williamson (1988) was shifting the emphasis further toward voluntary arrangements for debt relief, taking advantage of the by then low secondary market prices of debt. This emphasis presaged the Brady Plan adopted one year later.

By the mid-1990s it was possible to carry out an early retrospective analysis of the international debt crisis of the 1980s. In Cline (1995) I revisited my earlier projections, decomposing the gap from eventual outcomes into model error and assumption error. My early projections proved to have been broadly correct about global recovery, a correction in the dollar, and a moderation in interest rates. They had overpredicted global inflation, however, so nominal dollar export magnitudes turned out considerably smaller than projected (and hence lower relative to nominal external debt) and real interest rates turned out higher than projected. The projections had not anticipated the collapse of oil prices in 1986. Commodity prices lagged behind projected levels at first but caught up by the late 1980s. Tests rejected the theory that the debt strategy was internally inconsistent by virtue of falling terms of trade resulting from export expansion, as the heavily indebted countries did not in fact boost their shares in world commodity exports. The model had not incorporated prospective capital flight, which meant that the actual buildup in debt was much greater than projected. The retrospective analysis concluded that for nonoil countries following prudent domestic policies, the original strategy was broadly correct, as shown by the outcomes for Chile and Colombia. More broadly the study suggested that a much earlier adoption of debt forgiveness as the international strategy would likely have meant that many debtor countries would not have adopted the structural changes (trade liberalization, privatization, fiscal adjustment) that were vital to their subsequent growth prospects.

As indicated in table 11.1, by 1998 there began a five-year period in which the Institute published a large number of studies on the evolving financial crises in emerging markets and on appropriate changes in international financial architecture to avoid or deal with similar crises in the future. By 1999 there was an intense debate on whether the IMF should halt the large rescue programs typified first by Mexico in 1995 and then by

Korea, Thailand, Russia, Brazil, and later Argentina and then Brazil again. Hills, Peterson, and Goldstein (1999) essentially called for an end to such programs, whereas Kenen (2001) and Roubini and Setser (2004) recognized the need for them, albeit with caveats. Also during this period there arose a heated debate about a new quasi-bankruptcy mechanism for international debt, including at an April 2002 Institute conference where IMF First Deputy Managing Director Anne Krueger (2002) presented the case for such a mechanism on the first day and US Treasury Under Secretary John Taylor (2002) presented the opposite case and supported the alternative of collective action clauses on the second day. Among the most intriguing of the Institute contributions was the intramural disagreement between Morris Goldstein (2003), who in 2002 judged that there was a 70 percent chance Brazil would default by the end of 2003, and John Williamson (2002), who judged that it would not. Williamson proved right.

The discussion below returns to the substance of some of these issues. Suffice it to say that if the publications list of the Institute provides a barometer for tracking the salient issues of the day, financial crises in emerging markets were a predominant concern in the late 1990s and the first three years of this decade.

Prospects and Key Policy Issues

Trends in Debt Indicators

The most recent emerging-market financial crisis was the Brazil scare in 2002. As reviewed above, the rebound in private capital flows to emerging markets, rising current account balances, and falling risk spreads (figures 11.1 through 11.3) all suggest benign debt conditions during the past three years. It is useful to review further evidence on recent debt trends before considering future prospects.

One measure of the burden of external debt is the ratio of gross debt minus external reserves, or "net debt," to exports of goods and services. Although this measure does not take into account variations in the interest rate, and hence understates the reduction in debt burden associated with falling global interest rates, it does provide a gauge of potential burden when and if interest rates return to more normal levels. Figures 11.4 and 11.5 show the trend in this measure since the mid-1990s for major Latin American and Eastern European debtors respectively.

There have been dramatic declines in the ratio of net external debt to exports of goods and services for several major debtors. For Mexico the ratio fell from 185 percent in 1994 to 28 percent by 2005; for Brazil, from 379 percent in 1999 to 99 percent; for Argentina, from 428 percent in 1999 to 183 percent (and the latter overstates because of the concessional nature of postrestructuring debt). For Poland and Hungary the ratio fell from an

Figure 11.4   Net external debt as a percent of exports of goods and services: Latin America, 1993–2005

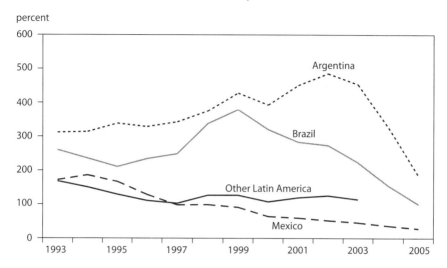

Note: Gross external debt minus reserves.

Sources: World Bank (2005a, 2005b), Deutsche Bank (2006), IMF (2006b).

Figure 11.5   Net external debt as a percent of exports of goods and services: Eastern Europe, 1993–2005

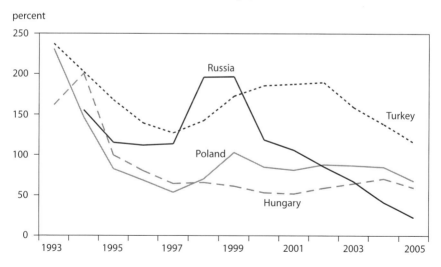

Note: Gross external debt minus reserves.

Sources: World Bank (2005a, 2005b), Deutsche Bank (2006), IMF (2006b).

Figure 11.6 Short-term external debt as a percent of external reserves: East Asia, 1994–2004

percent

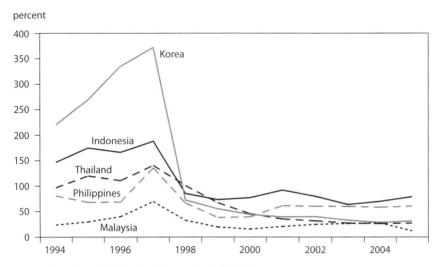

Sources: World Bank (2005a, 2003), Deutsche Bank (2006).

average of about 200 percent in 1993–94 to about 63 percent in 2005; for Russia, from a peak of 197 percent in 1999 to only 22 percent in 2005; and Turkey's ratio has also fallen substantially, from 190 percent in 2002 to 115 percent in 2005. For most of these countries, the declines in the ratio have been driven by sharply rising exports and reserves, as the nominal amount of external debt has tended to rise slowly (with the exception of a significant decline in Argentina after 2003).

For East Asia, the late-1990s financial crises were driven more by a liquidity crunch from high short-term debt than by high underlying total debt burdens (with the partial exception of Indonesia). A more relevant gauge for trends in that region is the ratio of short-term external debt to external reserves. As shown in figure 11.6, this ratio surged in the mid-1990s to a peak in 1997 but fell sharply thereafter in the region. Short-term external debt reached as high as 372 percent of reserves in Korea in 1997[9] and a range of about 150 to 200 percent in Thailand, the Philippines, and Indonesia that year. Only Malaysia maintained relatively low short-term debt (its financial stress arose from portfolio equity outflows rather than the runoff of short-term debt). By 1999, all five of the East Asian crisis economies had short-term external debt well below reserves, and as of 2005 the average ratio was about 40 percent.

---

9. The figure for Korea includes debt of overseas branches of domestic financial institutions.

In sum, the external debt indicators tend to confirm that there has been a substantial improvement in the external transfer problem for the major emerging-market economies since the late 1990s. It is less clear that the potential internal transfer problem has improved. Indeed, the IMF devoted an issue of its *World Economic Outlook* in 2003 to an analysis of what it considered troublesome levels of public debt in emerging-market economies. Among its conclusions were the following:

> High public debt is a cause for concern in many emerging market economies. At about 70 percent of GDP, the average public debt ratio in emerging market economies now exceeds that in industrial countries.... [H]istorically, many emerging market economies have not generated large enough primary budget surpluses to ensure the sustainability of their public debt.... [T]he sustainable public debt level for a typical emerging market economy may only be about 25 percent of GDP . . . emerging market economies as a group have failed in the past to respond in a manner consistent with ensuring fiscal sustainability once public debt exceeds 50 percent of GDP. (IMF 2003, 141–42)

The fundamental equation of debt sustainability is as follows:

$$1) s_p \geq (i^* - g)d$$

where s_p is the primary (i.e., noninterest) fiscal surplus as a percent of GDP, i^* is the real interest rate, g is the real growth rate, and d is the ratio of public debt to GDP. If this condition is not met, public debt rises as a percent of GDP.[10] Because real interest rates tend to be higher in emerging-market economies than in industrial economies, conventional thresholds for industrial-country public debt (such as the 60 percent ceiling set in the European Union's Maastricht Treaty) will tend to overstate the level of sustainable public debt in the absence of correspondingly more ambitious primary surplus targets.

Table 11.2 reports the path of the public debt to GDP ratios of major emerging-market economies over the past decade. These trends are far less reassuring than those for the external debt burden relative to the export base.[11] The data also reveal the vicissitudes of debt crises in recent years, for example in the large run-up in Argentina's public debt ratio in 2002 with the currency devaluation and consequential ballooning of external public debt relative to GDP, followed by a reduction with debt re-

---

10. As an approximation. More specifically, if in addition the rate of currency depreciation is r, the share of public debt denominated in foreign currency is ϕ, and the rate of inflation is p, the condition for debt to remain at an unchanged fraction of GDP becomes: $s_p = d \{[i^* - g + r\phi] / [1 + g + p]\}$. See Cline (2003b).

11. Note, however, that the data do not deduct government assets and so tend to overstate. For example, in the case of Brazil, after deducting government deposits and other public assets (most of which are relatively liquid), net public debt was about 52 percent of GDP in 2004 rather than the 72 percent gross figure shown in the table.

Table 11.2 Public debt as a percent of GDP, 1995–2005

Country	1995	1996	1997	1998	1999	2000	2001	2002	2003	2004	2005
Argentina	34.4	36.4	35.4	38.2	43.5	45.6	53.7	134.6	138.1	125.0	69.2
Brazil	38.9	41.0	41.2	55.5	79.2	74.1	70.6	72.0	78.3	71.8	74.8
Hungary	n.a.	n.a.	64.2	61.9	61.2	55.4	52.2	55.0	56.7	57.1	58.4
India	71.4	67.8	68.3	69.5	69.9	71.7	74.7	79.3	79.3	78.8	79.5
Indonesia	n.a.	15.2	24.7	44.6	86.2	92.9	82.8	75.5	68.0	69.4	63.1
Korea	7.3	7.5	13.6	30.4	32.3	30.3	36.8	33.3	32.5	31.8	29.7
Mexico	42.9	36.2	37.1	41.2	42.8	40.0	40.5	40.9	41.6	38.3	39.5
Philippines	75.7	65.0	64.3	94.7	101.5	109.8	104.8	112.5	118.2	109.8	107.7
Poland	n.a.	n.a.	44.0	39.1	40.3	36.8	36.7	39.8	43.9	41.9	42.5
Russia	40.7	32.8	55.0	79.4	88.8	56.8	42.9	36.5	26.8	21.7	14.1
Thailand	11.5	14.1	36.9	44.0	54.0	57.0	57.1	53.8	49.4	48.8	45.9

n.a. = not available

Source: Deutsche Bank (2006).

structuring by 2005. Importantly, in the East Asian economies a common pattern was a surge in public debt following the banking sector crises of the late 1990s and public-sector bailouts of the financial systems.[12]

Future public debt depends on the current fiscal deficit, and on this criterion the major emerging-market economies seem to be better positioned. Table 11.3 reports the average nominal fiscal balance as a percent of GDP in 2003–05 for 28 major developing economies. It also reports average real growth and inflation. What can be defined as the "marginal debt ratio," or the increase in public debt as a fraction of the increase in nominal GDP, can be approximated as, essentially, the nominal fiscal deficit relative to GDP as a fraction of the sum of real growth plus inflation.[13] If the fiscal deficit rate and nominal growth rate are sustained in-

---

12. More favorably, Russia's public debt ratio has fallen sharply with the combined influence of large primary surpluses associated with oil revenue and negative real interest rates on debt.

13. Debt grows by the fiscal deficit as a percent of GDP multiplied by GDP. Nominal GDP grows by the nominal growth rate multiplied by GDP. So the ratio of additional debt to additional GDP equals the ratio of the fiscal deficit as a percent of GDP to the nominal growth rate. More precisely: $z = f / [(1 + g/100)(1 + p/100) - 1]$, where f is the fiscal deficit as a percent of GDP, g is the real growth rate (percent), p is the inflation rate (percent), and z is the increase in public debt as a percent of the increase in nominal GDP, or the marginal debt ratio. This approximation implicitly assumes the GDP deflator rises at the same rate as the consumer price index.

Table 11.3 Recent fiscal performance in major emerging-market economies, 2003–05 averages

Country	Fiscal balance/GDP (percent)	Inflation (percent)	Real GDP growth (percent)	Marginal debt ratio (percent)
Argentina	2.3	9.1	8.9	−12.4
Brazil	−3.6	9.4	2.6	29.8
Bulgaria	1.2	4.5	5.2	−12.5
Chile	1.2	2.3	5.3	−16.0
China	−1.7	2.3	10.0	13.6
Colombia	1.2	2.3	5.3	−16.0
Czech Republic	−4.1	1.6	4.6	64.5
Hungary	−6.0	5.0	4.0	64.4
India	−9.1	5.7	7.9	64.5
Indonesia	−1.3	7.8	5.2	9.7
Korea	0.9	3.3	3.9	−12.7
Malaysia	−4.4	1.9	5.9	56.0
Mexico	−0.4	4.4	2.8	5.9
Philippines	−3.7	5.0	5.3	35.3
Poland	−4.3	2.2	4.1	68.2
Romania	−1.4	12.1	5.8	7.5
Russia	4.7	12.4	7.2	−22.9
Slovakia	−3.3	6.2	5.2	28.0
South Africa	−1.7	3.6	4.1	22.0
Thailand	0.0	3.1	5.9	−0.4
Turkey	−8.4	12.8	7.4	39.8
Venezuela	−3.4	22.9	6.5	11.0

Source: Country InfoBase, Deutsche Bank Research, www.dbresearch.com (accessed April 27, 2006).

definitely, the average ratio of debt to GDP should converge to the marginal ratio. On the basis of the *World Economic Outlook* study just cited, it might be suggested that somewhere in the range of 40 percent might be about as high a marginal public debt ratio as would be comfortable for an emerging-market economy.

It turns out that most of the major emerging-market economies have a lower marginal debt ratio than this range. Indeed, several of them had fiscal surpluses on average in 2003–05 (Argentina, Bulgaria, Chile, Colombia, Russia, and Korea), meaning that the marginal debt ratio was negative and the average debt ratio was being pulled down. The main exceptions to favorable fiscal performance in this period were in Eastern Europe, where the Czech Republic, Hungary, and Poland all had marginal debt ratios of about 65 percent; the ratio was also high in Malaysia (56 percent) and India (65 percent). The marginal debt ratio was below 30 percent in Brazil, China, Indonesia, Mexico, Romania, Slovakia, South Africa, and Venezuela (in addition to the list of countries with fiscal surpluses). In Turkey it was right at the notional 40 percent ceiling, and in the Philippines it was below but close to this threshold.

Overall, recent fiscal performance in major emerging-market economies appears relatively favorable, a positive factor that helps offset the sobering levels of public debt stock relative to GDP shown in table 11.2. Two major caveats are, first, that these three years have been ones of exceptionally high global growth, so a considerable portion of the favorable fiscal performance is likely to have been cyclical and, second, that several countries in the past have tended to build up "discovered" or "skeleton" debt not captured in the annual fiscal balances.

Architectural Debates and the IMF's Role

During the past decade a few central issues have dominated the debate about global financial arrangements for managing debt and financial crises in emerging-market economies. The area with the easiest agreement has been the push for transparency as a key means of crisis avoidance. The IMF's development of the Special Data Dissemination Standards (SDDS) has been a signal achievement, putting pressure on countries to report data in a timely fashion. The Web sites of central banks and finance ministries in many emerging-market economies now provide for free a wealth of data that in earlier decades was either not available, not up to date, or obtainable only through visits to the countries. Another, more controversial issue area has been the prolonged move toward Basel II standards for international banks, with its shift toward risk-based weighting for capital requirements. Some worry that this reform will provide an undue advantage for large banks capable of mounting their own sophisticated internal models; others, that the new regime will cause a disadvantage for developing countries where firms are often not rated by the standard rating agencies. At the most general level, however, it must be seen as salutary that the international community is seriously seeking to fine-tune capital requirements as part of a process of strengthening financial systems, especially considering the intensive consultation with the private sector in the process.

Perhaps the most contentious policy debate has been on whether there should be large rescue packages when financial crises arise. In Cline (2005c)

I recapitulate the case for such support and for the IMF as a lender of last resort. This role is essentially based on analogy to the Bagehot principle domestically that in a panic, the central bank should lend freely to banks with collateral but not to those that are insolvent, in order to avoid unnecessary defaults and economic disruption. The corresponding distinction between liquidity and solvency crises is also central to the policy analogy.

Major financial rescue operations have indeed been large. Outstanding IMF claims on crisis countries reached peaks of 5.5 percent of GDP in Mexico in 1995; 4.9 percent in Korea, 2.9 percent in Thailand, 8.7 percent in Indonesia, and 7.1 percent in Russia in 1998; 1.6 percent in Brazil in 1999; 5.2 percent in Argentina in 2001 (surging to 14.1 percent in 2002 with the devaluation and plunge in dollar GDP); 12.1 percent in Turkey in 2002; and 5.6 percent in Brazil in 2003 (Cline 2005c, 300–301). We can thus say that the median lender-of-last-resort financial rescue involves IMF lending amounting to about 6 percent of GDP and that in the extreme cases the amount reaches about twice this high.

There have been two criticisms of such lending. First, it is seen by many as leading to moral hazard for private-sector lenders, encouraging them to take undue risks and overlend. In Cline (2004) I briefly review the literature on this issue and suggest both that the moral hazard concern is not well borne out by the facts and that after the massive private-sector losses on Argentine debt, this concern surely must be seen as passé. Second, there is the fear that the IMF could become overcommitted to a handful of superdebtors and incapable of carrying out its normal functions. It turns out that except for Turkey, the large recipients (even including Argentina) have now repaid the IMF so fully that the institution faces the problem of too little investment income on its lending spread because of a dearth of clients, so this concern has also not been supported by experience. Instead, the broad picture of IMF lender-of-last-resort action is one of a majority of crucial successes (sequentially Mexico, Korea, Thailand, Indonesia, Brazil twice, and most likely Turkey) accompanied by a limited number of failures (Russia and Argentina). Even in the failure cases, the debtors fully repaid the Fund.

Another and related debate has been about "private-sector involvement" (see Cline 2003a, 2004). Mexico's crisis in 1994–95 was the first dominated by short-term capital market obligations rather than bank claims. Whereas the London Club and its bank advisory committees had provided a vehicle for bank rollovers and reschedulings in the 1980s, the more dispersed holdings of government securities lacked a comparable mechanism. US Treasury Secretary Robert Rubin stated that if he could have found a way to make private-sector investors pay for the Mexico bailout, he would have done so. Successive G-20 and other G-member meetings in the late 1990s called for private-sector involvement (PSI) as a necessary part of financial rescues. The high-water mark for public-sector arm-twisting in this direction was probably the Ecuador default on Brady bonds in 2000, which was widely perceived to have been counseled by the IMF as a means for forcing PSI. There was important PSI in the Korean crisis, but it was of the more familiar London Club variety as the banks converted short-term claims on Korean banks into three-year government-guaranteed paper. Similarly, there was PSI in the Brazil 1999 episode that involved a voluntary undertaking by foreign banks to roll over short-term credits so long as Brazil was meeting its policy commitments. My view has been that PSI should be achieved in the most voluntary manner possible commensurate with successfully overcoming the crisis, in order to minimize subsequent cutoff from capital market access. Once again, however, the massive Argentine default has (or certainly should have) altered the terms of the debate. It is no longer plausible to depict emerging-market crises as a one-way bet favoring private investors. Having lost some $60 billion in Argentina, private investors can reasonably take the position that they have already done their part to rebalance PSI relative to official lender-of-last-resort operations for a long time to come.

Aside from lender-of-last-resort rescues, international arrangements for debt restructuring have been the other hottest issue in the architectural debate. With the transition from developing-country debt dominated by syndicated long-term bank loans to a structure dominated by bonds and other securities, there was growing concern by the late 1990s that it would prove impossible to carry out debt restructurings for this much more dispersed investor base. There was concern that "rogue creditors" would not cooperate and would thwart the restructuring process. The image of massive public-sector bailouts for the benefit of private bondholders, not least including the ill-fated final large disbursement to Argentina in August 2001, made the political environment ripe for proposals that instead facilitated restructurings orchestrated by the public sector.

It was in this environment that Anne Krueger proposed the Sovereign Debt Restructuring Mechanism (SDRM) to deal with cases of unsustainable sovereign debt. In its initial incarnation (Krueger 2001), the SDRM gave a relatively heavy hand to the IMF. A country could come to the IMF and seek approval of a standstill. There would be an international treaty with the force of law authorizing the IMF to approve a standstill, which would involve foreign exchange controls. There would be a mechanism to "bind minority creditors" seeking to oppose a workout agreed to by the majority. Domestic debt would likely have to be included in the workout. The SDRM was to be modeled on the domestic bankruptcy process and like it would include preferred creditor status for new borrowing. The IMF would leave the terms of the restructuring to the debtor and its creditors, however, rather than dictating them; and the sanctioned standstill would expire after a given period of time.

There then ensued a debate between what was called this "statutory" approach to debt restructuring and the alternative "contractual" approach.

The latter, soon espoused by the US Treasury (Taylor 2002), sought to incorporate collective action clauses (CACs) into future bonds in order to overcome the problem that in bonds issued in New York (but not in London) unanimous consent of bondholders was required for changes in terms. The private sector soon mobilized in support of this approach, in part for fear of the SDRM alternative and its risk of politically imposed workouts tending toward the disadvantage of creditors. Without US Treasury support (despite earlier sympathetic signals from the secretary), the SDRM did not prosper, notwithstanding a reformulation attempted to make the IMF seem less the judge and jury and more a disinterested facilitator.[14] Mexico and other major borrowers were concerned that creation of an SDRM could cast doubt on their market access, and within a year Mexico led the way for the alternative approach by issuing bonds with CACs, seemingly at no risk spread penalty. CACs have become standard in new issues, although it is unclear how long it will take for the bulk of outstanding emerging-market debt to shift from previously issued obligations that require unanimous creditor consent for restructuring to new CAC-based obligations.

Viewed with some distance from that period, two observations stand out about the SDRM. First, sovereign restructurings of bonds have turned out not to be as difficult as the call for such a mechanism assumed. Pakistan, Ukraine, and Ecuador, not to mention Argentina, carried out restructurings, often using an "exchange offer" involving a proposal by the sovereign with a relatively short time period for bondholders to respond. Finding the bondholders proved not to be difficult, and responses were typically positive when reasonable terms were proposed. Second, the "rogue creditor" problem turned out not to be severe, and instead Argentina showed that it was the "rogue debtor" problem that could be more serious. Indeed, the premise that "the debtor would need protection from legal action after the suspension of payments" (Krueger 2001) has not been borne out, as shown by the experience of frustrated creditors of Argentina who still have nothing to show for years of litigation efforts.[15] In short, the problems the SDRM was designed to solve do not seem to have been compelling, in part because many of the financial crises were not associated with sovereign default on bonds.

---

14. In her initial formulation, Krueger (2001, 6) had already stated, "The international community is not going to impose the terms." In her subsequent speech to the Institute in April 2002, she further emphasized that terms of the restructuring would be based on agreement between the debtor and a supermajority of creditors and that "the Fund would not be empowered to make decisions that would undermine the enforcement of creditor rights" (Krueger 2002, 5).

15. In contrast, at the time there was much talk about a case in which Peru paid off a creditor (Elliott) to avoid legal action regarding payments on Brady bonds.

The Implications of Argentina

A clear-eyed look at debt restructuring today requires thinking carefully about the implications of the Argentine outcome. First and foremost, the Argentine default on some $100 billion and its essentially unilateral restructuring on arguably confiscatory terms has not caused a wave of international contagion against emerging-market economies. On the contrary, as shown above, emerging markets have rebounded vigorously from the financial crises of 1998–2002, albeit with the spur of low US interest rates. If creditors had taken the lesson that Argentina proved emerging-market sovereign bonds were unreliable, this would not have happened and at the very least spreads would have trended up instead of down. Instead, creditors seem to have concluded that each country makes and must live with its own reputation as creditworthy or uncreditworthy, and the spread of guilt by association to other countries is both unwarranted and unprofitable. This tends to weaken somewhat the case for large financial rescue packages, because it suggests that in contrast to what was perceived in the Mexican rescue of 1994–95 as well as the East Asian crises that followed, the stakes of sovereign default seem more likely to be confined to the country in question rather than the financial system as a whole. Both diagnoses may have been right at their respective times, given the evolution of emerging markets from a new phenomenon in the early 1990s into an increasingly standard part of international investors' portfolios more than a decade later. In any event, the potential for avoiding needless economic collapse, even if just for the country itself, still provides ample basis for lender-of-last-resort action.

Second, it should be asked whether the Argentine experience warrants reviving the call for the SDRM or something like it. The naïve argument might run as follows: If before the private sector didn't like the risk of IMF-imposed solutions, by now private firms and investors may realize that what Argentina did to them was far worse than what would have occurred under IMF auspices. However, it is extremely implausible that Argentine authorities would have played by the rules of an IMF-led SDRM workout and that the end result would have been much different. The country's wrenching political change at the end of 2001 brought to power much more populist forces. They would have been unlikely to adopt restructuring terms along more market-friendly traditional Brady Plan lines (e.g., 35 percent forgiveness instead of 70 percent) just because of the option of going to the SDRM; similarly, it is unlikely there would have been any agreement within the time limit set by the SDRM.

Another false lesson of Argentina would be that emerging-market economies can default with impunity. Argentina's high growth rates in 2003–05 might cast that illusion, but they have merely restored the economy to its level of 1998. The confidence for private-sector investment to build for the future has surely been undermined not only by the handling of the debt problem but by an associated set of populist policies ranging from unilateral revision of public utility rate agreements with multinational firms to price controls as the means of curbing inflationary consequences of undervaluation.

With respect to international policy on debt restructuring, the central lessons of Argentina are, first, that political sustainability must be at the heart of any decision for dealing with the crisis and, second, that once again it has been shown that resolving debt problems is essentially a case-by-case process rather than one that neatly fits standard treatment, especially when the international environment is benign and the roots of the problem are basically national rather than international.

The United States as the New Super-Debtor

Under today's conditions an essay on international debt would be remiss to omit the emerging issue of US external debt. In accounting terms, the United States is already the largest debtor nation in history, with net international liabilities of $2.5 trillion at the end of 2005 (BEA 2006). In terms of economic burden, the United States is just now transitioning into debtor status, as the higher rate of return on foreign direct investment than on foreign holdings of US assets kept the capital income balance positive through 2005, despite a large negative asset balance. With the US current account deficit at about 7 percent of GDP and on present trends on a path toward about 10 percent by a decade from now despite some dollar correction already, the US external imbalance poses a major risk for the international economy. Even with a smooth adjustment, the rest of the world will face the challenge of shifting the source of demand away from reliance on growing trade surpluses with the United States. This shift had better be sooner rather than later if it is to avoid being wrenching and disruptive. Otherwise there is ample scope for a global interest rate shock and recession in a hard landing for the dollar and the US and global economies (Cline 2005a).

The key to a smoother rather than harsher adjustment is for the United States to eliminate its fiscal deficit and for China and other developing countries (especially in Asia) to stop intervening in exchange markets to prevent the appreciation of their currencies, as well as a market-driven further appreciation of the euro, yen, and other major currencies against the dollar. The IMF seems to be groping toward a role in addressing this emerging potential crisis by embarking on "multilateral surveillance," but more forceful coordinated action is needed along the lines of the 1985 Plaza Agreement but with much wider participation of key economies, reflecting the change in the world economy over the past two decades (Cline 2005b).

Conclusion

Emerging-market economies have shown major improvements in recent years, as reflected by sharply falling borrowing spreads and favorable fiscal trends. However, US external adjustment will be key for a return of international capital markets to their more normal function of facilitating growth in developing countries through the provision of capital from excess saving in industrial countries. The recent phenomenon of reverse flows of resources is fundamentally perverse. The mercantilist notion that developing countries need undervalued exchange rates to keep exports and growth going, the premise of the Bretton Woods II hypothesis (Dooley, Folkerts-Landau, and Garber 2004), also seems misguided. Instead, a reorientation toward domestic demand for investment, including in infrastructure, would seem essential to a more sustainable pattern of global growth.

If this correction can be carried out, it seems highly likely that net flows of capital and resources to emerging-market economies can make an important contribution to global development over the coming decade and more. Fiscal prudence in developing countries will be a key to ensuring that such flows not get out of hand and foster renewed cycles of boom and bust, just as fiscal correction sooner or later will be essential for the United States if it is to be a positive force for, rather than an increasing threat to, sustainable global growth.

It seems unlikely that any major change in international financial architecture will be needed for a favorable functioning of international capital markets, apart from a more active process (with or without the IMF) for carrying out exchange rate realignments needed as part of the correction of US external imbalances. Increasingly each of the major debtor countries will be evaluated on its individual merits, and capital markets will maintain normal transactions with those among them that continue to demonstrate political maturity and sustain market-friendly and fiscally prudent policies. If occasions do return raising the potential need for official financial rescue, there is sufficient favorable evidence on past results that the IMF and industrial countries should step up to the plate and provide large liquidity support, if needed, to countries pursuing sound economic policies.

References

BEA (Bureau of Economic Analysis). 2006. *International Investment Position of the United States at Yearend, 2004 and 2005*. Washington: US Department of Commerce.

Bergsten, C. Fred, William R. Cline, and John Williamson. 1985. *Bank Lending to Developing Countries: The Policy Alternatives*. POLICY ANALYSES IN INTERNATIONAL ECONOMICS 10. Washington: Institute for International Economics.

Birdsall, Nancy, and John Williamson. 2002. *Delivering on Debt Relief: From IMF Gold to a New Aid Architecture*. Washington: Center for Global Development and Institute for International Economics.

Calvo, Guillermo A., Morris Goldstein, and Eduard Hochreiter, eds. 1996. *Capital Flows to Emerging Markets after the Mexican Crisis*. Washington: Institute for International Economics.

Cline, William R. 1983. *International Debt and the Stability of the World Economy*. POLICY ANALYSES IN INTERNATIONAL ECONOMICS 4. Washington: Institute for International Economics.

Cline, William R. 1984. *International Debt: Systemic Risk and Policy Response*. Washington: Institute for International Economics.

Cline, William R. 1987. *Mobilizing Bank Lending to Debtor Countries*. POLICY ANALYSES IN INTERNATIONAL ECONOMICS 18. Washington: Institute for International Economics.

Cline, William R. 1995. *International Debt Reexamined*. Washington: Institute for International Economics.

Cline, William R. 2001. Ex-Im, Exports, and Private Capital: Will Financial Markets Squeeze the Bank? In *The Ex-Im Bank in the 21st Century: A New Approach?* ed. Gary C. Hufbauer and Rita M. Rodriguez. Washington: Institute for International Economics.

Cline, William R. 2003a. The Role of the Private Sector in Resolving Financial Crises in Emerging Markets. In *Economic and Financial Crises in Emerging Market Economies*, ed. Martin Feldstein. Cambridge, MA: National Bureau of Economic Research.

Cline, William R. 2003b. *Restoring Economic Growth in Argentina*. World Bank Policy Research Working Paper 3158. Washington: World Bank.

Cline, William R. 2003c. HIPC Debt Sustainability and Post-Relief Lending Policy. Washington: Center for Global Development.

Cline, William R. 2004. Private Sector Involvement in Financial Crisis Resolution: Definition, Measurement and Implementation. In *Fixing Financial Crises in the Twenty-first Century*, ed. Andrew G. Haldane. London: Routledge.

Cline, William R. 2005a. *The United States as a Debtor Nation*. Washington: Institute for International Economics.

Cline, William R. 2005b. *The Case for a New Plaza Agreement*. International Economics Policy Brief 05-4. Washington: Institute for International Economics.

Cline, William R. 2005c. The Case for a Lender-of-Last-Resort Role for the IMF. In *Reforming the IMF for the 21st Century*, ed. Edwin M. Truman. Washington: Institute for International Economics.

Deutsche Bank. 2006. *Country Infobase*. Available at www.dbresearch.com (accessed April 25, 2006).

Dobson, Wendy, and Gary Clyde Hufbauer. 2000. *World Capital Markets: Challenge to the G-10*. Washington: Institute for International Economics.

Dooley, Michael, David Folkerts-Landau, and Peter Garber. 2004. *A Map to the Revived Bretton Woods End Game: Direct Investment, Rising Real Wages, and the Absorption of Excess Labor in the Periphery*. New York: Deutsche Bank Global Markets Research.

Eichengreen, Barry. 1999. *Toward a New International Financial Architecture: A Practical Post-Asia Agenda*. Washington: Institute for International Economics.

Frank, Charles, and William R. Cline. 1971. Measurement of Debt Servicing Capacity: An Application of Discriminant Analysis. *Journal of International Economics* 1, no. 3.

Goldstein, Morris. 1998. *The Asian Financial Crisis: Causes, Cures, and Systemic Implications*. POLICY ANALYSES IN INTERNATIONAL ECONOMICS 55. Washington: Institute for International Economics.

Goldstein, Morris. 2003. *Debt Sustainability, Brazil, and the IMF*. Working Paper 03-1. Washington: Institute for International Economics.

Goldstein, Morris, Graciela Kaminsky, and Carmen Reinhart. 2000. *Assessing Financial Vulnerability: An Early Warning System for Emerging Markets*. Washington: Institute for International Economics.

Goldstein, Morris, and Philip Turner. 2004. *Controlling Currency Mismatches in Emerging Markets*. Washington: Institute for International Economics.

Haggard, Stephan. 2000. *The Political Economy of the Asian Financial Crisis*. Washington: Institute for International Economics.

Hills, Carla, Peter G. Peterson, and Morris Goldstein. 1999. *Safeguarding Prosperity in a Global Financial System: The Future International Financial Architecture.* Washington: Institute for International Economics.

IIF (Institute of International Finance). 1997. *Comparative Statistics for Emerging Market Economies.* Washington: Institute of International Finance.

IIF (Institute of International Finance). 2006. *Capital Flows to Emerging Market Economies.* Washington: Institute of International Finance (January 19). (Also see issues for October 2, 2004, and May 15, 2003.)

IMF (International Monetary Fund). 2003. *World Economic Outlook: Public Debt in Emerging Markets.* Washington: International Monetary Fund.

IMF (International Monetary Fund). 2006a. *Debt Relief Under the Heavily Indebted Poor Countries (HIPC) Initiative.* Factsheet, April. Washington: International Monetary Fund.

IMF (International Monetary Fund). 2006b. *International Financial Statistics* (CD-Rom). Washington: International Monetary Fund.

Independent Evaluation Group. 2006. *Debt Relief for the Poorest: An Evaluation Update of the HIPC Initiative.* Washington: World Bank.

Kenen, Peter B. 2001. *The International Financial Architecture: What's New? What's Missing?* Washington: Institute for International Economics.

Krueger, Anne O. 2001. International Financial Architecture for 2002: A New Approach to Sovereign Debt Restructuring. Speech at National Economists' Club Annual Members' Dinner, American Enterprise Institute. November 26.

Krueger, Anne O. 2002. New Approaches to Sovereign Debt Restructuring: An Update on Our Thinking. Speech at Conference on Sovereign Debt Workouts: Hopes and Hazards. April 1. Washington: Institute for International Economics.

Lessard, Donald R., and John Williamson. 1985. *Financial Intermediation Beyond the Debt Crisis.* POLICY ANALYSES IN INTERNATIONAL ECONOMICS 12. Washington: Institute for International Economics.

Miller, Marcus. 2002. *Sovereign Debt Restructuring: New Articles, New Contracts—Or No Change?* International Economics Policy Brief 02-3. Washington: Institute for International Economics.

Mussa, Michael. 2002. *Argentina and the Fund: From Triumph to Tragedy.* POLICY ANALYSES IN INTERNATIONAL ECONOMICS 67. Washington: Institute for International Economics.

Noland, Marcus, Li-Gang Liu, Sherman Robinson, and Zhi Wang. 1998. *Global Economic Effects of the Asian Currency Devaluations.* POLICY ANALYSES IN INTERNATIONAL ECONOMICS 56. Washington: Institute for International Economics.

Reinhart, Carmen, Kenneth S. Rogoff, and Miguel A. Savastano. 2003. *Debt Intolerance.* NBER Working Paper 9908. Cambridge, MA: National Bureau of Economic Research.

Roubini, Nouriel, and Brad Setser. 2004. *Bailouts or Bail-ins? Responding to Financial Crises in Emerging Economies.* Washington: Institute for International Economics.

Taylor, John B. 2002. Sovereign Debt Restructuring: A US Perspective. Speech at the Conference on Sovereign Debt Workouts: Hopes and Hazards, April 2. Washington: Institute for International Economics.

Williamson, John. 1988. *Voluntary Approaches to Debt Relief.* POLICY ANALYSES IN INTERNATIONAL ECONOMICS 25. Washington: Institute for International Economics.

Williamson, John. 2002. *Is Brazil Next?* International Economics Policy Brief 02-7. Washington: Institute for International Economics.

Williamson, John, 2005. *Curbing the Boom-Bust Cycle: Stabilizing Capital Flows to Emerging Markets.* POLICY ANALYSES IN INTERNATIONAL ECONOMICS 75. Washington: Institute for International Economics.

World Bank. 2003. *Global Development Finance 2003: Striving for Stability in Development Finance.* Washington: World Bank.

World Bank. 2004. *Global Development Finance: Harnessing Cyclical Gains for Development.* Volume I: Analysis and Summary Tables. Washington.

World Bank. 2005a. *Global Development Finance 2005: Mobilizing Finance and Managing Vulnerability, Vol. II: Summary and Country Tables* (CD-Rom). Washington: World Bank.

World Bank. 2005b. *World Development Indicators* (CD-Rom). Washington: World Bank.

12

Follow the Money

MICHAEL MUSSA

In official discussions of the role of the International Monetary Fund (IMF), especially at meetings of the IMF Executive Board and of the ministerial-level International Monetary and Finance Committee, it is often observed that "surveillance" is the IMF's most important function. Indeed, this view is asserted with such frequency and solemnity that one may be quite confident that it is really not true. What has made the IMF particularly important and controversial as an international institution—often despised and sometimes admired—is the money that it chooses to lend, or not to lend, to countries facing balance of payments difficulties and the influence that it exercises because of its control over such lending.

As indicated in Morris Goldstein's overview of Institute work on the international monetary system, IMF lending has long been an issue of central concern, including in two of the Institute's earliest publications (Williamson 1982, 1983). This interest continued through the years, both in work primarily directed at IMF lending, such as Goldstein (2001) and Mussa (2002), and in a host of books and papers where the subject was of substantial importance, including contributions by Bergsten, Cline, and Williamson (1985), Cline (1983, 1984, 1987, 1995), Eichengreen (1999), Goldstein (1998, 2000, 2005), Kenen (2001), Roubini and Setser (2004), Truman (2006a, 2006b), Williamson (1988, 2005), and Williamson and Birdsall (2002).

As with virtually every other important subject on the international economic scene, Fred Bergsten has been deeply involved with issues concerning IMF lending as both author and editor in Bergsten (1991) and Bergsten,

Michael Mussa has been a senior fellow at the Institute since 2001.

Cline, and Williamson (1985). At a more practical level, as assistant secretary of the US Treasury in the administration of President Carter, Fred was responsible for US borrowing from its IMF reserve tranche, and he still holds the world record for the number of separate requests for IMF loans—all of which were granted. To balance this, Fred was also the point man for the Carter administration in the difficult task of securing congressional approval for a major increase in IMF quotas, which supply the resources for IMF lending. More recently, he dealt with key issues involving IMF lending in some of his congressional testimony[1] and as a member of both the Council on Foreign Relations Task Force on the Global Financial System (1999) and the International Financial Institutions Advisory Committee (IFIAC 2000).

This chapter continues the tradition of Institute work on IMF lending by focusing on two main issues that merit further attention in light of recent experience and likely future challenges: the significance of "moral hazard" as a serious objection to continued IMF lending and the question of whether and under what circumstances and conditions the IMF should supply large packages of financial support.

The Great Moral Hazard Bugaboo

Beginning with the exceptionally large IMF loans (and loans from the US Treasury) to assist Mexico in 1995, a new criticism has been launched against IMF lending. It comes not from those who believe that IMF conditionality is too tough but mainly from conservatives who have often been opponents of virtually any IMF lending. The argument is that large-scale IMF lending—or more precisely, the expectation of such lending—to countries facing balance of payments difficulties is itself an important cause of financial crises. The mechanism of causation for this perverse effect is "moral hazard."

Specifically, the argument is as follows: Because emerging-market countries that obtain funds in international capital markets and/or the suppliers of these funds anticipate that IMF "bailouts" will help to rescue them in the event of difficulties, the true risks of these capital flows are underestimated and the flows are thereby artificially encouraged to be undesirably large. This, in turn, increases the likelihood and severity of emerging-

1. C. Fred Bergsten, The International Monetary Fund and the National Interests of the United States, Testimony before the Joint Economic Committee, February 24, 1998 (Washington: US Congress); Reforming the International Financial Institutions: A Dissenting View, Testimony before the Committee on Banking, Housing, and Urban Affairs, March 9, 2000 (Washington: US Senate); and Reforming the International Monetary Fund, Testimony before the Subcommittee on International Trade and Finance, Committee on Banking, Housing, and Urban Affairs, April 27, 2000 (Washington: US Senate).

market financial crises when problems do arise and it eventually becomes clear that capital flows are unsustainable. This view of IMF lending as an important generator of moral hazard has been expressed by many critics and was well summarized in an op-ed column in the *Wall Street Journal* (February 3, 1998) by George Shultz, William Simon, and Walter Wriston:

> It is the IMF's promise of massive intervention that has spurred a global melt-down in financial markets. When such hysteria sweeps world markets, it becomes difficult . . . to let the private parties most involved share the pain and resolve their difficulties, perhaps with a modest program of public financial support and policy guidance. With the IMF standing in the background ready to bail them out, the parties at interest had little incentive to take these painful, though necessary steps. . . . The promise of an IMF bailout insulates financiers and politicians from the consequences of bad economic and financial practices, and encourages invest-ments that would not otherwise have been made.

These three very distinguished gentlemen are far from alone in holding these views. The report of the International Financial Institutions Advisory Committee (2000) generally endorsed the notion that IMF financing creates significant concerns about moral hazard. Both the IFIAC chairman, Allan Meltzer, and one of the committee's prominent members, Charles Calomiris (1998), were certainly advocates of this view, as were many conservative economists such as Anna Schwartz (1998). In my experience, many central bankers, particularly from Europe, were gravely concerned about the moral hazard effects of IMF lending, and these concerns continue to be an impor-tant motivation for the search for more effective means for private-sector in-volvement (PSI) in the resolution of financial crises.[2] Indeed, even some strong supporters of IMF lending, such as Stanley Fischer (1999), felt com-pelled to concede that moral hazard was a significant concern.

Economists recognize that moral hazard is a pervasive phenomenon. It is likely to arise in virtually any situation where economic agents interact in the absence of full information.[3] Thus it undoubtedly infects to some degree many aspects of IMF operations, some of which will be noted in this chapter. The issue here, however, is not whether moral hazard as a very general phenomenon is somehow relevant to the IMF but rather the bald assertion that the moral hazard effects of expectations (among either emerging-market countries or their external creditors) of "IMF bailouts" are sufficiently important to be a significant cause of the financial crises that have recently afflicted a number of emerging-market economies.

---

2. Although less extreme than some advocates of the moral hazard view (such as key offi-cials of the Bundesbank), officials from the Bank of England and the Bank of Canada have recently been prominent in pressing for more aggressive PSI; see Haldane and Kruger (2001) and Irwin and Salmon (2006).

3. The article on moral hazard in the New Palgrave (Kotowitz 1989) gives extensive refer-ences to the economic literature that makes use of this concept, including the vast literature that treats situations where economic agents have asymmetric information.

To address this key issue, it is useful to explain the concept of moral hazard, which originally arose in insurance. An insured party knows that a loss covered by insurance will result in the insurer's compensation for that loss (less any deductible or co-insurance). This arrangement creates the potential for moral hazard because the insured, knowing that losses will be covered, has less incentive to avoid risky behavior that might generate such losses. If the insurer could perfectly and costlessly observe risky behavior by the insured and charge a premium articulated in accord with such risks, the incentive for excessive risk taking could be eliminated. There would be no moral hazard because the incentives of the insured would be aligned with the efficient containment of risk.

In general, however, such perfect insurance is not possible. Sometimes, if the moral hazard problem is sufficiently large, no insurance is written. For example, life insurance policies may exclude coverage for suicide, and fire insurance policies do not pay off in the case of arson by the insured. More generally, when moral hazard cannot be eliminated but can be contained within reasonable limits, the insurer charges a premium that covers the moral hazard as well as the underlying risk. The result usually is beneficial (to the insured, the insurer, and society as a whole) but economically inefficient (relative to the full information solution). The insurer earns a fair return for the risks absorbed, whether underlying or the consequence of moral hazard. The insured is covered against both elements of risk and is charged accordingly—and prefers this arrangement to no insurance. The economic inefficiency comes because the insured could, by choosing less risky behavior, reduce risk at less cost than the insurer needs to charge to compensate for the insured's moral hazard behavior.

Returning to the case of IMF financial support for countries facing balance of payments difficulties, it is intuitively appealing to believe that moral hazard is likely to be generated. The stated purpose of IMF financial support in Article I (v) of the IMF Articles of Agreement is "To give confidence to members by making the general resources of the Fund temporarily available to them under adequate safeguards, thus providing them with the opportunity to correct maladjustments in their balance of payments without resorting to measures destructive of national or international prosperity." This "confidence" is intended to encourage countries to adopt and maintain more open policies toward international commerce that generally imply greater risks of balance of payments difficulties. But it is also commonly believed that IMF assistance to countries facing balance of payments difficulties is a bailout. As is often the case with government support to distressed people or businesses, IMF support is widely believed to be either an outright gift or a loan on exceptionally favorable terms. Thus it is not surprising that there is considerable popular appeal for the seemingly obvious conclusion that IMF lending must generate substantial moral hazard—up to the point of being itself an important cause of recent emerging-market financial crises.

IMF Bailouts?

While superficially appealing, this argument that the availability of IMF financial support generates substantial moral hazard is largely nonsense.[4] To understand why, it is essential to understand that IMF financial assistance is not a bailout.

The IMF is not a development institution and does not offer general financial assistance or low-cost loans to member countries on a continuing basis. The Fund lends to countries facing balance of payments difficulties, often in circumstances where these countries have grave difficulty in obtaining additional credit from other sources. IMF loans are usually for a term of three to five years and sometimes for up to 15 years. The amount the IMF lends to a particular country is limited, is usually disbursed in tranches, and is subject to policy conditionality. The Fund also enjoys the privilege of the preferred creditor: It is understood and accepted that loans from the IMF and their interest charges need to be paid even when a country cannot fully meet its obligations to other creditors. All of this gives the IMF exceptional security for its loans.

Policy conditionality is designed to ensure that a country undertakes policies to correct its balance of payments problem, making it possible to repay the Fund without "resorting to measures destructive of national or international prosperity" (Article I (v)). Disbursement in tranches allows the IMF to delay or withhold credits to countries with unsatisfactory policies. Limits on the amount of IMF lending—even in recent cases of very large IMF loans—to a modest fraction of a country's external debt ensure that a country will almost always have sufficient resources to meet its obligations to the IMF, even if in extreme circumstances it has to default on obligations to other creditors. The preferred creditor status enjoyed by the IMF protects the institution in precisely such extreme circumstances.[5]

The Fund charges interest on its loans at a rate (the "rate of charge") that covers the cost of funds to the IMF (which are effectively borrowed from its creditor members) plus the Fund's administrative expenses and a modest premium to build its reserves.[6] The IMF almost always collects

---

4. I have argued this point before (Mussa 1999a, 1999b, 2004, 2006), and many others share this assessment, including Cline (2004b), Roubini and Setser (2004), and Truman (2002).

5. The IMF's preferred creditor status, which is well established and known to other creditors, does not imply that the Fund can provide bailouts at the expense of other creditors. It is the responsibility of other creditors to take the Fund's status into account when they make decisions to lend. Presumably, the interest rates they charge (which are typically much higher than the IMF's rate of charge) appropriately reflect this and other risks.

6. Under a policy established in 1997, members making extensive use of the IMF's resources under the Supplemental Reserve Facility (SRF) are charged higher rates on their borrowings beyond the usual IMF limits. These interest rate surcharges have been used partly to pay for IMF operating expenses and to add to the Fund's general reserves.

its loans and charges, usually within the original maturities of the loans and sometimes sooner. Because the IMF rate of charge is essentially uniform across all of its loans and is quite low, there is virtually no opportunity for the IMF to cross-subsidize by using the excess returns garnered by loans to some countries to provide exceptionally low-cost loans to other countries.[7] In other words, the IMF cannot finance bailouts for some countries by charging high interest rates to other countries.[8]

The maturities of IMF loans are sometimes effectively extended through new IMF programs, but these loans and their associated charges are almost always paid in full.[9] There have been about a dozen cases of "prolonged" arrears where countries have not paid (or only partially paid) principal and interest due the IMF for an extended period. Most of these cases have now been resolved, with Sudan remaining the main unresolved case. Resolution has involved repayment of the IMF's general resources account for principal and accrued interest. However, it may be argued that the method of resolution involved some cost to the IMF (through concessional credit made available to the member after arrears were cleared with the aid of a bridge loan) or to the official creditor community (through debt forgiveness or direct aid). Nevertheless, adding up the costs of the resolved and still pending prolonged-arrears cases, they amount to about 1 percent of aggregate IMF lending over the past 50 years (not 1 percent per year). The general reserves that the IMF has accumulated over these years through the small premium it is rate of charge more than cover these losses.

Thus the simple notion that IMF financial assistance is a bailout for the countries receiving such assistance or their creditors is fundamentally false. The frequent description in the press of IMF assistance as a bailout, and the shameless exploitation of this fallacy by some critics of the IMF, do not make it so. This leaves the more subtle question of whether there is an important element of subsidy in IMF loans that justifies the depiction of such loans as partial bailouts.

---

7. In addition to lending from its general resources financed by drawing on IMF quotas, the Fund provides concessional financing to very poor countries through independently funded special facilities, currently the Poverty Reduction and Growth Facility (PRGF). The issue of whether the IMF should remain in the business of providing such loans or turn this activity over to the World Bank and the multilateral development banks remains controversial. However, because of its special character and limited scale, IMF concessional lending is not relevant to the issues considered here. The asserted problem of moral hazard and the issues concerning very large scale IMF loans relate to the IMF's general resource lending.

8. The IMF therefore cannot support moral hazard in the way that an insurance company can by using premiums collected from the insured who do not sustain losses to compensate those who do.

9. Cases of prolonged lending to particular IMF members constitute a relatively small fraction of total IMF lending but have received considerable attention from the IMF Executive Board.

Figure 12.1 Emerging Markets Bond Index spread, 1991–2006

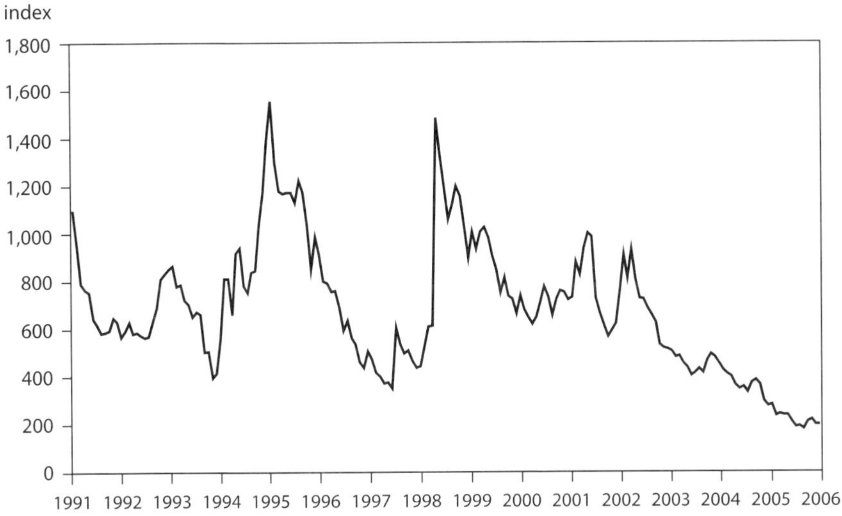

index

Source: JPMorgan Emerging Markets Bond Index.

The Low Interest Rate on IMF Loans

The argument that the IMF provides at least a "partial bailout" through its lending is often tied to the fact that the interest rate charged on IMF loans (the rate of charge) is quite low in comparison with the interest rates that emerging-market countries must pay on other credits. This argument has not only been advanced by prominent critics of the IMF such as the IFIAC (2000) and Lerrick (2003), it has even been endorsed by the responsible and usually careful Congressional Budget Office.[10] However, proper understanding of the significance of the IMF's outstanding record of collecting the principal and interest payments on its loans (even if the rate of charge is relatively low) reveals that there is not a large subsidy associated with IMF lending.

No doubt, the IMF's rate of charge is very low in comparison with the interest rates that emerging-market borrowers have typically faced in private international credit markets. During the 1990s, the average interest rate spread over US treasuries for sovereign emerging-market borrowers averaged over 600 basis points (figure 12.1). In contrast, the IMF's rate of charge

---

10. See Congressional Budget Office, Costs and Budgetary Treatment of Multilateral Financial Institutions' Activities, Testimony before the Committee on Banking, Housing, and Urban Affairs, May 19, 2004 (Washington: US Senate). The opposing view, that IMF loans involve relatively little subsidy, is presented in Jeanne and Zettelmeyer (2001) and is broadly supported by Roubini and Setser (2004).

(which is linked to short-term official interest rates in Britain, France, Germany, Japan, and the United States) usually ran 100 basis points or more below the interest rate on ten-year US treasuries. Recognizing that the emerging-market countries included in the Emerging Markets Bond Index (EMBI) were generally regarded as the best credit risks among developing countries, it would appear that IMF loans were provided at interest rates that ran 500 to 1,000 basis points below those prevailing in private international capital markets. Indeed, IMF loans to countries already in or on the brink of a financial crisis would appear to have involved even larger subsidies.

However, in judging the extent of any interest rate subsidy in IMF lending, it is essential to consider the security that the IMF enjoys for its loans. Individuals who borrow in private credit markets typically face much lower interest rates on home mortgages than on personal loans and credit card balances, because the creditor's interest is much better protected when secured by a home mortgage. Indeed, an individual who is unable to access credit on the basis of a signature alone may be able to borrow at attractive terms with the pledge of a valuable asset as collateral.

Similarly, the IMF appropriately charges a low interest rate because it enjoys exceptionally strong security for its loans, as has been demonstrated time and time again by the outstanding record of interest payments and repayment of principal on IMF loans. In contrast, private creditors have generally perceived significant risks in lending to emerging-market countries and have charged interest rates that reflect these perceived risks. Losses that private creditors have sustained when they have had to restructure and write down some of their loans, such as in the recent case of Argentina, justify this perception of risk and the higher interest rates that it implies. The virtual absence of any losses on IMF loans, in many cases where private creditors have taken substantial losses, reflects the fundamental superiority of the IMF's claims as a creditor. Thus, the argument that IMF loans generate significant moral hazard because they involve a large interest rate subsidy relative to interest rates charged by private creditors is fundamentally bogus.

Moreover, IMF loans are limited in amount and generally come with policy conditionality that requires recipient countries to adjust their policies in order to "correct maladjustments in their balance of payments." Quantitative limitations on IMF lending practically ensure that a country will be able to repay its obligations to the Fund, even if other creditors face restructurings and write-downs. Policy conditionality and the usual IMF practice of disbursing loans in tranches based on acceptable policy performance provide additional important assurance that a member will be able to meet its repayment obligations.

Policy conditionality is widely perceived as an important "cost" by countries seeking IMF loans. Indeed, despite the low interest rates on IMF loans, countries do not usually rush to seek these loans except in rather dire circumstances when other credits may not be available at virtually any price. This well-known reluctance of countries to seek IMF assistance despite its low financial cost is important evidence that countries do not regard IMF loans as a cheap way out of financial difficulties.

Moreover, the decisions of countries and their creditors that logically might be influenced by moral hazard arising from the (future) possibility of IMF lending are not made at the time when countries usually seek IMF assistance. They are the decisions to borrow and lend, perhaps excessively, before there is the likely prospect of a crisis. By the time a crisis is brewing, additional net financing from nonofficial sources is often not available. In these crisis or near crisis situations, the low cost of IMF financing relative to the very high cost of credit from nonofficial sources (reflected in yields on already outstanding private credits) is in no way an indication of moral hazard generated by IMF lending. If the prospect of IMF lending generates moral hazard, that happens much earlier, usually well before a crisis, and only to the extent that expectations of the possibility of future IMF support unduly influence emerging-market countries and their creditors to borrow and lend excessively.

The Plausible Scale of Moral Hazard

All of this, of course, does not mean that there is effectively no subsidy in the low interest rates charged by the IMF. A modest element of subsidy that encourages a modest amount of moral hazard may be associated with IMF lending. To assess whether IMF lending induces significant moral hazard, it is essential to consider the magnitude of any subsidy in IMF financing and to compare this subsidy with the costs and perceived risks of emerging-market financial crises.

The emerging-market financial crises of 1995 through 2003 involved massive economic losses both for the countries involved and for the foreign investors in these countries. One way to estimate these losses for the countries involved is to calculate the extent to which the path of GDP during the crisis and the recovery afterward deviated from the path of potential GDP (or some other reasonable estimate of the path that GDP would have followed in the absence of a crisis). Such estimates of losses are necessarily subject to a considerable margin of error and should therefore be interpreted as broad indicators of the plausible magnitude of losses.[11] No-

---

11. Williamson (2005, table 2.3) reports several estimates of cumulative output losses (based on different sources) for countries involved in the Asian crisis. These estimates range from a low of 33 percent of annual GDP in one estimate for Hong Kong to 109 percent in one estimate for Thailand. Three estimates for Korea's cumulative output loss range from 27 percent to 49 percent of annual GDP.

tably, estimates of losses are significantly larger if measured by estimated deviations of domestic demand from plausible noncrisis paths.[12]

For countries that were only marginally affected by the various crises, such as Singapore during the Asian crisis of 1997–2000, cumulative losses were probably less than 10 percent of annual GDP. For more severely affected economies, such as Hong Kong during the Asian crisis, cumulative losses were surely greater—at least 10 percent and often 20 percent or more of annual GDP. Mexico in 1995–98 had cumulative losses of about 20 percent of annual GDP, and Korea in 1998–2000 had cumulative losses of about 25 percent. For the most severely affected countries (in particular Indonesia, which has not yet fully recovered from the Asian crisis), cumulative losses have plausibly exceeded 100 percent of annual GDP. For all countries receiving substantial IMF assistance during 1995–2003, total cumulative losses were surely at least $500 billion and probably over $1 trillion.

Losses to foreign investors in countries experiencing financial crises are more difficult to estimate for both conceptual and empirical reasons. One procedure that produces a rough upper-bound estimate is to take the decline in the value of foreign investments from shortly before the onset of a crisis to its value at the height of the crisis. For sovereign bonds issued in international markets, where data on prices and quantities are reasonably reliable, this calculation generally shows more than a 50 percent decline in market value between a year before the crisis and its height. Some sovereign international bonds, however, are usually held by domestic residents (in quantities that are often difficult to determine), and losses in value for these bonds may or may not be included in estimated losses for foreign investors. In many crises, foreign residents were also holders of domestic credits issued by the sovereign, such as the Mexican tesobonos and cetes and the Russian GKOs. In many cases, data on quantities and (to a lesser extent) on market values for these foreign investments are not much better than rather crude guesses. Data on international bank loans to emerging-market sovereigns and financial institutions (collected by the Bank of International Settlements) are generally pretty good, but the values of such loans are usually not marked to market. Data on losses from defaults on bank loans are not readily available, especially for loans to nonsovereigns.

For portfolio equity investments, stock indices for emerging-market countries generally indicate that losses in market value during the series of emerging-market crises from 1995 through 2003 (measured in US dollars) were on the order of 80 percent. Data on the outstanding stocks of

---

12. This is so because a crisis generally forces a country to achieve a large improvement in its current account balance and this, in turn, requires a large fall in domestic demand relative to output. Indeed, the terms of trade loss typically associated with the large real depreciations that occur during crises usually means that the fall in domestic demand relative to output must be significantly larger than the improvement in the current account balance.

foreign portfolio investment in emerging-market equities were mainly informed guesses. There are estimates of foreign direct investment (FDI) for most of the key emerging-market countries that can be used to derive estimates of stocks. Data concerning movements in the (implicit) market value for these direct investments are not available. As a substitute it might reasonably be assumed that the (implicit) market value of foreign direct investments in a country follows the same pattern as the prices of domestic equities (measured in dollars), and these would indicate losses in value on the order of 80 percent for large FDI stocks.

Using this approach, it is relatively easy to reach estimates of losses to foreign investors in the emerging-market crises of 1995 through 2003 in excess of $1 trillion. In many cases, these estimated losses for foreign investors rival or exceed the (earlier described) estimates of the economic losses for the countries undergoing the crises. However, using the extremely depressed market values that typically prevail at the height of a crisis arguably generates unreasonably large estimates of losses. In fact in most cases the values of assets held by foreign (and domestic) investors recover considerably as a crisis is resolved. In some cases, some assets may be worth considerably more a few years after a crisis than shortly before the crisis. Russian euro bonds are a particularly dramatic example of this phenomenon.

This phenomenon is probably most relevant for foreign direct investors (who tend to be in for the long term), although it is important to recognize that foreign owners of direct investments undoubtedly feel that they are taking substantial losses in an emerging-market crisis. Such perceived losses are often registered in the value of equities of parent companies with significant foreign direct investment. For portfolio investors in either debt or equity instruments, a long-run view (beyond one year) is really not very relevant. Many portfolio investors sell out during a crisis and realize large losses, while investors who jump in at the height of a crisis and take on very large risks may ultimately be rewarded. Portfolio investors who hold on through a crisis and for years thereafter effectively make two investments: The first, on which they take very large losses, takes place before the crisis, and the second, on which they may enjoy substantial gains, comes from the new investment decision to hold on despite the crisis. Such investors would clearly have been better off avoiding the first stage.

Even for portfolio investors, however, the extremely depressed asset values at the very peak of a crisis probably do not provide an entirely reasonable basis for estimating losses. Investors who sell out do not do so at the precise bottom of the market. As a plausible compromise, it seems reasonable to take about one-half of the decline in asset values during an emerging-market crisis and the loss that foreign investors effectively perceive to result from the crisis. These figures yield an aggregate estimate of losses to foreign investors in those emerging-market countries that suffered significant crises during 1995–2003 in excess of $500 billion.

How do these losses compare with a maximum plausible estimate of the extent of IMF "bailouts" as provided by the subsidy element in IMF lending? Leaving aside the issue of default risk, the IMF does lend on a medium-term basis at a rate of charge that is linked to the interest rate on the special drawing rights (SDR), which is a weighted average of the short-term borrowing rates for the largest industrial-country governments. Arguably there may be about 100 basis points of interest subsidy involved in medium-term loans at short-term interest rates, even taking account of the fact that the IMF standard rate of charge involves a premium over the SDR interest rate.

If members could normally expect to borrow virtually unlimited amounts from the IMF to deal with balance of payments difficulties (subject only to a very firm requirement for repayment), one might argue that prospective availability of IMF loans involved an implicit subsidy on the order of 100 basis points to sovereign borrowing by member countries. But IMF lending is generally subject to quantitative limits that keep the total below a moderate fraction of a country's external indebtedness and total foreign investment. IMF financing is structured to be "catalytic," in the sense that moderate-sized IMF loans and their associated policy conditionality help to reassure and motivate a country's other creditors to supply the bulk of the required balance of payments financing. Indeed, even in recent cases of large-scale IMF financing packages (such as those for Brazil and Turkey), total IMF credits remained below one-fifth of total external debt.[13] Thus the prospective subsidy from the possibility of IMF support, spread over a country's external debt, amounts to no more than about 20 basis points and usually a good deal less.

In addition to the subsidy implicit from making medium-term IMF loans available at a rate of charge linked to short-term interest rates, one might argue that IMF lending also involves a subsidy because the IMF absorbs some default risk. As previously noted, however, the IMF has an outstanding record of collecting on its loans—implying that default risks actually absorbed by the IMF are quite small. And over the years the IMF has incorporated a small premium in its rate of charge to build up reserves that absorb losses in the event of defaults. Only to the extent that default losses might exceed these reserves is it correct to argue that there is an element of subsidy in IMF lending from the risk of such losses.

Pressing the argument to its limit, it might still be argued that, despite its fine record so far, the IMF might be forced at some point to absorb default losses significantly in excess of its reserves. There is of course no way to refute conclusively arguments about what might possibly happen in the future. Nevertheless, it is relevant to note that major creditor countries

---

13. See table 4.2 in Roubini and Setser (2004). In the 10 cases of large IMF programs reported in this table (and in table 12.1), the ratio of peak IMF lending to precrisis external debt was below 20 percent in all cases, except for Turkey in 1999, where it reached 22 percent.

that effectively control IMF lending have been extremely reluctant to see the institution take on any significant default risks. The excess of the market value of the IMF's gold holdings over their book value does provide a significant hidden reserve to cover possible default losses (in excess of measured reserves), but $10 billion is an extremely generous allowance for the maximum amount of such losses that would ever be tolerated.

Adding 10 years of a maximum annual interest subsidy of $2 billion and a one-time $10 billion maximum subsidy from IMF absorption of default risk, one arrives at a maximum conceivable subsidy from IMF lending over a decade of $30 billion. This subsidy would not, of course, be available to any single country or its creditors; rather, it might, in the most extreme and unlikely circumstances, be spread across all emerging-market countries and all of their creditors.

This maximum conceivable IMF subsidy is no more than 5 percent of a reasonable estimate of the cumulative economic losses suffered by countries that received substantial IMF assistance from 1995 through 2004. It is no more than about 10 percent of a reasonable estimate of losses suffered by foreign investors in these countries. And it is at least three times a reasonable estimate of the subsidy that was actually made available through IMF lending over that decade. Whatever the division of the IMF subsidy between countries experiencing financial crises and their foreign investors, the subsidy absorbed no more than a small fraction of these respective losses that could conceivably have been offset by this subsidy. And the maximum conceivable IMF subsidy would probably have absorbed no greater a fraction of the much larger losses that would have been sustained in situations where the maximum subsidy would have been forthcoming.

Moreover, it is clear that both emerging-market countries and their foreign (and domestic) investors understood that they were exposed to substantial risks that swamped any potential subsidy supplied by IMF lending. Foreign investors with the best security and probably most likely to benefit from IMF involvement were holders of sovereign debts issued in international markets. As previously noted, the average interest rate spread over US treasuries for holders of these emerging-market credits was over 600 basis points (on an annual-yield basis) as measured by the EMBI. This indicates a high level of perceived risk by both emerging-market borrowers and their lenders—notwithstanding any possible benefit from IMF lending. Foreign holders of domestic currency debts, portfolio equity, or direct investments were generally exposed to greater risks than holders of sovereign international bonds and were less likely to receive any protection from IMF loans; the level of risk for these investors was presumably a fair bit higher than the EMBI spread. Thus, for all foreign investment flows to emerging-market countries, the prospective subsidy from the possibility of IMF lending in the event of a crisis offset no more than a tiny fraction of the risk spread otherwise associated with these flows. The moral hazard effect of this tiny fraction of potential subsidy cannot have been very large. Certainly there is no plausible argument that through the mechanism of moral hazard, IMF lending was a meaningful cause of the recent series of devastating emerging-market financial crises.

Empirical Estimates of Moral Hazard?

It is relevant to ask whether there is any empirical evidence that IMF lending—or the expectation of such lending—had any impact on risks perceived by foreign investors in emerging markets. For example, it has been suggested that the general decline in emerging-market credit spreads following the Mexican crisis of 1995 is evidence that the unexpectedly large package of financial support to Mexico provided by the IMF and the US Treasury persuaded investors that the risks of holding emerging-market credits were lower than previously thought. This, in turn, was interpreted as evidence of a significant moral hazard effect from this large package.[14]

But this analysis (and several other attempts to measure empirically the moral hazard effect of IMF lending) is conceptually flawed. Emerging-market credit spreads generally decline as a crisis is resolved and before a new one looms, and it is very difficult to separate any effect of IMF lending (which often accompanies emerging-market financial crises) from this general phenomenon. Also, to the extent that one can reliably isolate some specific effect of IMF lending in the post-Mexico decline in emerging-market spreads, it is impossible to know whether this reflected a perceived decline in the real risk of emerging-market crises (because of the success of the Mexican government's efforts under the IMF program) or moral hazard arising from expectations of larger IMF "bailouts." The fact that the Mexican government fully and rapidly repaid its loans from the US Treasury and the IMF and, accordingly, that there was no bailout suggests that the first interpretation is more likely correct. Symmetrically, however, an empirical finding that exceptionally large IMF loans were not associated with any decline in emerging-market credit spreads does not logically imply that they have no moral hazard effect. It could be that foreign investors take on additional risks because they expect IMF bailouts, leaving credit spreads virtually unchanged.[15]

---

14. The objection that large-scale official lending to Mexico would generate substantial moral hazard was widely advanced by many of the IMF's conservative critics and by many European central bankers and finance ministry officials. In a careful empirical study, Zhang (1999) did not find persuasive evidence that official support for Mexico led to a significant decline in borrowing spreads for other emerging-market countries before the Asian crisis.

15. Careful studies that attempt to account for some of the difficulties in empirically measuring moral hazard effects have generally found little evidence that they are present or have increased as a result of IMF lending in the 1990s; see Lane and Phillips (2000) and Kamin (2002). The case of Russia, however, is different, as discussed below.

The way to deal with these (and other) conceptual difficulties in empirical estimates of the moral hazard generated by IMF lending is to apply the relevant economic theory to determine what can and should be measured empirically. The theory says that moral hazard is a rational economic phenomenon that arises because borrowers and/or lenders undertake excessive risks in the reasonable expectation that if losses are incurred, someone else will pay for some meaningful part of them. Economic theory thus insists that for moral hazard to be generated by (expectations of) IMF lending, either the countries receiving IMF loans or their foreign investors must reasonably expect that such loans will provide a bailout in which the Fund will absorb a meaningful part of their losses. Compelling empirical evidence on whether IMF lending generates moral hazard can be obtained by assessing the extent to which IMF lending normally involves significant true bailouts. This question has already been analyzed in detail: The answer is that IMF financing does not generally involve significant bailouts for emerging-market countries or their investors.

The Russian Case

In considering the issue of moral hazard generated by IMF financing, it is useful to review the special circumstances of the one case where this probably was a significant issue—IMF support for Russia before the 1998 crisis.[16]

Following the collapse of the Soviet Union at the end of 1991, there was a broad international consensus, led by the G-7, that the international community should do all it could to assist in Russia's transformation to a market-oriented economy, a democratic society, and a cooperative partner on a wide array of foreign policy issues. Significant assistance was also intended to aid the transformations of the other states of the former Soviet Union, as it had earlier for the countries of Central and Eastern Europe, but Russia was clearly the number one priority.

---

16. I have long held and frequently expressed the view that there was significant moral hazard in the case of expectations of official support for Russia. Robert Rubin, then US treasury secretary, writes in his memoir (Rubin and Weisberg 2003, 278), "I argued that providing money [to Russia] under these circumstances would create an immense moral hazard problem. I had lived in financial markets, and could feel people taking advantage of the situation." Roubini and Setser (2004), who quote this passage, clearly agree with its sentiment. They also point to IMF support for Turkey in 2000–03 as another case where markets perceived that political considerations were likely to drive IMF decisions, thereby leading to significant moral hazard concerns. I have expressed some support for this view in the case of Turkey (Mussa 2004) but, like Roubini and Setser, do not find it persuasive in other cases of large IMF lending. Chang (2000), Dell'Ariccia, Schnabel, and Zettelmeyer (2002), Sarno and Taylor (1999), and Spadafora (2001) present empirical evidence supporting the conclusion that there was some effect of moral hazard in the Russian case.

Among international institutions, the IMF was given the lead in providing financial assistance to Russia and guidance on the transformation of its economy. A substantial increase in IMF quotas was agreed to in 1992, primarily to provide the IMF with the additional financial resources needed to aid Russia and the rest of the former Soviet Union. Beginning in late 1992, the IMF negotiated a series of programs that provided financial assistance to Russia along with policy conditionality directed at both macroeconomic stabilization and economic transformation.[17] The first two programs under the IMF's Systemic Transformation Facility (STF) provided moderate assistance (50 percent of Russia's IMF quota for two years) under relatively weak policy conditionality. The one-year Stand-By Arrangement (SBA) with Russia (which covered 1995) provided financial support at the upper limit of access (100 percent of quota for one year) and had normally rigorous IMF conditionality. The subsequent three-year arrangement under the IMF's Extended Fund Facility (EFF) also featured financing at the upper limit of annual (and cumulative) access and rigorous conditionality.

Disbursements of IMF support proceeded on schedule under the 1995 SBA as the Fund assessed that Russia was meeting all of the program's key performance criteria.[18] The EFF arrangement agreed to in early 1996, however, went immediately off-track due to excessive fiscal deficits. With the reelection of President Yeltsin still pending, this transgression was waived (after a brief delay) by the IMF, and the second disbursement under the program was made—with the promise that Russia would significantly improve its fiscal performance after the election.

Beginning in 1995 until the summer of 1998, the Russian authorities maintained a crawling peg exchange rate and brought further moderation to the inflation rate (figure 12.2). However, the promised improvement in Russian fiscal performance never really materialized. Indeed, if one took proper account of the growing arrears problem (where the Russian government faced and tolerated increasing delays in tax and other receipts and delayed many of its own cash disbursements), the fiscal problem was getting worse. Faced with this situation, the fiscal performance criteria of the IMF program were repeatedly relaxed in order to allow Russia to comply with the program. There were some brief delays in disbursements of IMF support, but the Russian authorities were not pressed as hard as

17. An extensive and generally balanced description and assessment of the IMF's involvement with Russia is provided by John Odling-Smee (2006), director of the IMF's European II Department, which had responsibility for the Russian case.

18. It was later revealed that the figures were fiddled with and fiscal performance criteria (the upper limit on the fiscal deficit) were not met for end-1995, but this was not known at the time.

Figure 12.2 Russian exchange rate and price level, 1992–2006

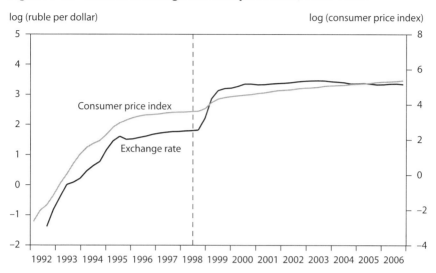

log (ruble per dollar)

log (consumer price index)

Source: IMF, *International Financial Statistics*.

other countries to live up to their fiscal policy commitments under an IMF program.[19]

All of this sent the message that Russia was a special case. The normal rules of IMF programs did not apply. Disbursements of IMF support would likely continue, with only occasional brief delays, despite clearly inadequate policy performance by the Russian authorities. When the Russian financial situation became desperate in the spring and early summer of 1998, the IMF's decision to provide a large supplemental package of financial support reinforced the notion that special efforts would be made to keep Russia financially afloat—beyond those applied for most countries.[20] This message was further reinforced by G-7 actions and statements that made it clear that continued international support for Russia

---

19. Russian fiscal performance was substantially worse than it appeared to be on the basis of the cash budget that was used as the IMF fiscal criterion. The Russian government limited the deficit in the cash budget through the buildup of large arrears on payments due from the central government to the provinces, to government suppliers, on wages and pensions, etc. In response, others delayed payments, including taxes, owed to the government. A corrosive culture of nonpayment developed as the norm in Russia. The IMF was well aware of this problem (which was particularly egregious but not unique to Russia) but did nothing serious to address it.

20. The size of the initial disbursement under the augmented IMF support package was cut back by the Fund's managing director when the Russian Duma failed to pass key legislation required as part of the strengthened program. This cutback sent a negative signal to financial markets but did not precipitate an immediate crisis—which came a few weeks later.

Figure 12.3   Russian interest rates (money market rate), 1996–2006

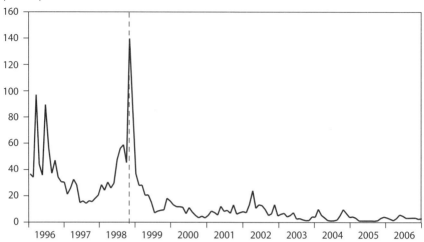

percent per annum

Source: IMF, *International Financial Statistics*.

was a critical priority. Private capital flows to Russia to purchase Russian government obligations and private equities were explicitly encouraged.

The message was clearly heard and understood in international capital markets. Indeed, private investors in Russian government obligations, including GKOs, were so persuaded of Russia's special status that they often referred to these investments as "the moral hazard play." The high yields on Russian government obligations, especially in the first half of 1998, indicate that investors understood there were significant risks. However, the perception that the IMF and/or the G-7 would step in to forestall a Russian default helped persuade many (but not all) investors that these risks were worth taking (see figure 12.3).

When the crisis hit in mid-August 1998, the IMF and the G-7 refused to offer Russia an even larger package of support. The Russian government was forced to devalue the ruble on August 18 and suspended repayment of maturing GKOs. The foreign exchange rate of the ruble crashed, prices of Russian obligations in international credit markets tumbled, and Russian banks reneged on forward contracts to deliver foreign exchange. Ultimately, foreign holders of Russian GKOs suffered losses of over 90 percent of the initial value of their claims. Foreign investors in Russia's international bonds also suffered large losses if they sold during the crisis but came out quite well if they held on to them.

IMF support for Russia was suspended after August 1998. For a time, there were discussions of resuming support under modified and strengthened economic policies. But there were also worries that Russia might not be able (or willing) to meet its obligations to repay the Fund and that IMF funds already advanced to Russia might turn into a true bailout. These issues became moot as the world oil price rose sharply in 1999–2000 and as the Russian economy and balance of payments recovered with unexpected rapidity and vigor. Russia met all of its obligations to the IMF in a timely manner and even paid off some of its IMF loans ahead of schedule.

Three important lessons follow from the Russian case for the general issue of moral hazard created by IMF financing. First, it is the expectation of a bailout, not the fact of one, that generates moral hazard. In other cases where IMF support was offered, it has been argued that the country and its foreign investors had no rational reason to expect an IMF bailout. In the Russian case, in contrast, investors were led to expect they might be offered a bailout if things went badly. Foreign investors clearly recognized that, even with the possibility of an official bailout, there were important risks from putting their money in Russia. Nevertheless, the money flowed, motivated at least in part by expectations of a possible bailout. Second, IMF financing cannot generate moral hazard by promising bailouts that it does not deliver. This indeed is the key reason why possible IMF financing cannot generate much moral hazard, provided that the Fund follows the policy of insisting that its loans be repaid with appropriate interest. Third, in the Russian case, foreign investors (especially in the GKOs) took very large losses that were not alleviated by the expected IMF bailout. This costly and unhappy surprise obviously should have dispelled any notion that true IMF bailouts are likely in virtually any circumstance.

Thus the ultimate lesson from the Russian case is that it is not reasonable to expect that IMF financing will provide bailouts either for the countries receiving such financing or for their foreign creditors. To the extent that any further demonstration of this key lesson was necessary, it was surely provided by the very large losses that foreign investors suffered in the Argentine crisis and default of 2001–05. Anyone who now engages in imprudent borrowing or lending and takes comfort in the expectation that they will be "bailed out" by the IMF is truly a fool.

Other Forms of Moral Hazard

Because the general concept of moral hazard has manifold applications, the above discussion should not be interpreted as asserting that there is *nothing* in IMF lending to which this very broad concept may be relevant (Kotowitz 1989). Indeed, aside from the mistaken assertion that IMF lending supplies bailouts that provide a significant incentive to imprudent borrowing and lending, we recognize at least three important ways in which the broad concept of moral hazard may be relevant to IMF lending activities.

First, there is a vast literature on the "principal/agent problem" that recognizes the moral hazard distortions that typically arise when a principal cannot perfectly monitor and control the actions of an agent. A version of this problem arises for IMF lending if one regards the citizens of a country as the principal and the government officials who decide on and implement economic policies as their agents. Usually, the citizens of a country do not entirely understand the implications of their government's economic policies and cannot monitor and control precisely their government's actions. But the interests of the officials who decide on and implement policies are not always perfectly aligned with the best interests of the citizens—even in a democratic country. The officials in power may favor policies that delay a potential financial crisis or offer some hope of avoiding it, even if the prospective costs of failure for the citizenry are large and not worth the gamble. Incumbent officials simply may not see that the personal and political cost to them is proportionally very much greater from a devastating crisis than from a more contained predicament. They may be willing to gamble for success on the basis of odds that (if they fully understood them) their fellow citizens would not accept. This problem may be exacerbated by a psychological tendency for officials in a desperate situation to see the prospects of success from probably futile efforts as substantially greater than would be suggested by a reasonable assessment.

The IMF necessarily deals with the incumbent government, which it assumes to represent the interests of its country. For the reasons just outlined, however, this assumption becomes somewhat suspect, particularly in those crisis situations when a government is seeking IMF financial support. The tendency is for a government to press for IMF support (or an expansion of it) for a continuation of its policies even when this offers little realistic chance of success. When failure subsequently ensues, the country is left with significant obligations to the IMF and is often worse off than would have been the case if painful adjustments had been implemented earlier. Several recent cases suggest evidence of this phenomenon, including continued IMF support for Brazil's crawling peg exchange rate at the end of 1998 and the first two weeks of 1999, continued support for Turkey's crawling peg in early 2000, and expanded IMF support for Argentina's exchange rate peg and efforts to forestall the country's default in the summer and autumn of 2001. To guard appropriately against this type of moral hazard, the IMF needs to recognize the problem and to exercise care in acceding to the requests of governments that may involve undue risks for their countries.[21] This is probably particularly important in situations where large disbursements of IMF support are at issue.

A second problem of moral hazard potentially arises because the Fund is itself an agent for the member governments that are its proximate principals. The problem here is not so much that the IMF may pursue objectives not fully in line with the interests of its principals. Rather, the worry

---

21. This form of moral hazard potentially associated with IMF lending—the principal/agent distortion for government officials—and the problem discussed in the next paragraph are also discussed in Mussa (2004).

is that the agent may be used by its proximate principals to pursue objectives in ways not entirely understood or approved of by the citizens of the IMF members who are the ultimate principals. The Fund has a substantial pool of resources that can be made temporarily available to member governments at its discretion—under the influence of its proximate principals. The ultimate principals, however, generally have only a vague understanding of IMF operations, and there is virtually no legislative oversight of IMF lending in comparison with that typically applied to other forms of government expenditure or lending. In addition, it is widely believed that some of the proximate principals, especially the government of the United States, exert disproportionate influence over the Fund and tend to guide its lending (and the conditionality associated with it) to serve their particular interests.

There is no perfect fix for this problem of potential moral hazard. The IMF is the creature of its member governments, and there is no practical and desirable alternative to this arrangement.[22] Greater openness and transparency about IMF policies and operations, however, is a useful counterbalance to this problem. More rigorous procedures for approval and review of IMF lending, including automatic requirements for evaluation of large-scale lending by the Independent Evaluation Office, are also useful safeguards. The overall quantitative limits on Fund lending implied by IMF quotas and the need to secure legislative approval (in many countries) for quota increases are important general guarantees that IMF lending practices will not get too far out of line with the interests of those who ultimately supply the Fund with its resources.

A third valid concern related to issues of moral hazard is the problem of "indirect moral hazard." Virtually all national governments engage in activities that generate significant moral hazard. For example, they regularly use resources provided by general taxpayers to help compensate for losses sustained by particular individuals and businesses; that is, they provide true "bailouts." In some cases (such as relief for those suffering from natural disasters), these bailouts enjoy wide public support. In other cases, special interests may garner bailouts that their fellow citizens neither entirely recognize nor approve. In either case, the expectation of receiving bailouts established by a fairly consistent record of providing them induces

---

22. De Gregorio et al. (1999) disagree. They propose an "independent and accountable IMF" where the members of the Executive Board would be appointed for fixed terms without the possibility of removal and would govern the IMF without taking instructions from member governments. It is highly doubtful, however, that member governments would agree to such an arrangement, particularly for an institution that potentially wields significant influence and relies on resources provided by national governments. Moreover, it is questionable whether such an "independent" executive board would really solve the moral hazard problem of better representing the interests of the Fund's ultimate principals or would be able to carry the clout that attaches to the IMF because it is the representative of its member governments.

the potential recipients to engage in moral hazard behavior. One area of particular importance as far as the IMF is concerned is the tendency of national governments to provide bailouts to private parties that suffer losses in the event of a financial crisis; these often include owners of financial institutions, their depositors and other creditors, and their borrowers.

So long as the IMF maintains the principle that its loans must be repaid with appropriate interest, it does not contribute directly to the moral hazard problems arising from the bailout policies of national governments. There is a question, however, of whether the IMF contributes indirectly to these problems by making it possible for national governments to implement their bailouts if they would not be able to do so in the absence of IMF support.[23]

There probably is some effect in this direction, but it should not be exaggerated. To the extent that IMF assistance results in lower total losses from a crisis (as we have argued was clearly the case with Mexico in 1995), there clearly is greater latitude for the national government to limit the losses to various individuals and businesses. But this is a desirable effect of reducing real hazards. Also, because national governments typically pursue policies that generate moral hazard regardless of whether they receive IMF support, the problem cannot legitimately be seen as a responsibility of the Fund. Indeed, countries are generally able to provide extensive bailouts without relying on IMF assistance.

This is so because even governments that are strapped for liquidity can and do provide extensive bailouts through debt forgiveness and promises of future compensation that are not constrained by the government' short-run liquidity or the need to supply foreign currency. For example, financial institutions that are considered insolvent based on a reasonable assessment of the market value of their assets and liabilities can be allowed to continue operations through rigged accounting rules and loans from the central bank. Only later and usually in a very nontransparent fashion does the taxpayer get the bill for such bailouts. This is what happened in Chile during the 1979–82 crisis, when the government rescued a highly insolvent domestic banking system with the aid of central bank lending (but without IMF assistance). It is also what happened in Argentina after the termination of IMF support and after the government's own default at the end of 2001: Economically insolvent banks were kept open through loans from the central bank and nonrecognition of losses on the value of assets on the commercial banks' balance sheets, with the result that deposits remained liquid (after a brief interruption to their cash convertibility). In both of these cases, and in many if not all others, use of these techniques was generally preferable to the alternative of allowing complete collapse of the banking system—even if such techniques contributed to likely future problems of moral hazard.

---

23. The general concept of "indirect moral hazard" arising from IMF lending is examined in Mussa et al. (2000).

The one area where IMF assistance may facilitate a national government's moral hazard–generating activities is by making possible immediate payments to external creditors rather than requiring them to wait for compensation. In some cases, this may increase the total amount that these creditors ultimately receive, relative to the outcome if IMF assistance were not available.[24] Indeed, if avoidance of sovereign default to external creditors was the firm policy of the IMF in virtually all cases, this would raise concerns about indirect moral hazard for external credit supplied to sovereigns. For this reason, as discussed further below, the alternative of defaulting on claims of external creditors of emerging-market sovereigns should not be ruled out in extreme cases where the sovereign is truly unable to meet its external obligations under any reasonable set of policies and circumstances.

In practice, although sovereign defaults to external creditors have not been the norm for countries receiving IMF assistance, they also have not been particularly rare.[25] Recently, sovereign defaults have occurred in the cases of Russia's GKOs and Argentina's external sovereign debt and in debt restructurings for several smaller countries. Occasional sovereign defaults in extreme situations are appropriate and serve to contain what might otherwise be a significant problem of indirect moral hazard. However, it must also be recognized that sovereign defaults typically have large real costs. Any indirect moral hazard effect of IMF assistance in facilitating payments to foreign creditors, especially for sovereign debts and debts of the financial system, must be carefully balanced against these real costs. It is not sound medicine to kill the patient as part of the standard cure for a nonfatal disease.

In addition to these three important examples, there are probably other ways in which the broad concept of moral hazard is relevant to the activities of the IMF.[26] None of this, however, supports the misguided argument that IMF lending directly creates moral hazard by encouraging imprudent international capital flows to the extent that this is a significant cause of international financial crises.

---

24. In the case of Korea in 1997–98, the rollover of commercial bank loans to Korean banks did not result in any losses. In the case of Argentina in 2001–05, the long delay in coming to terms with external creditors was associated with a substantial write-down in the value of their claims. If more IMF assistance had been provided to Argentina in 2001, foreign creditors would probably have received greater payments, but Argentines would have faced a larger bill to repay the IMF.

25. Several IMF and US officials involved in the debt crises of the 1980s insist that "defaults" were consistently avoided for those countries receiving IMF assistance. This is true in the narrow technical sense that defaults were not legally declared by creditors and courts. However, commercial banks with loans to emerging-market sovereigns were induced to roll over their loans and ultimately to write down the present value of their claims. There were many de facto defaults in the operational sense that external creditors were forced to accept significant economic losses.

26. I discuss two such mechanisms in Mussa (2004).

Problems with Large IMF Programs

Beyond the concerns about moral hazard, the advent of very large IMF lending programs since the mid-1990s has been highly controversial. Until the IMF program for Mexico in 1995, the amount of Fund lending to any country had been strictly contained by the "access limits" established by the standing policy decisions of the Executive Board. These limits were adjusted from time to time and involved some complexities, but since the early 1990s, the basic annual lending limit has been no more than 100 percent of quota and the cumulative limit has been no more than 300 percent of quota.[27] In the case of the IMF program for Mexico in early 1995, for the first time an "exceptional circumstance" was declared, and access beyond the limits (almost 600 percent of quota or about $18 billion) was granted, with most of it potentially available during the first year of the program. In conjunction with the IMF program, the US Treasury agreed to provide $20 billion in loans from its Exchange Stabilization Fund. Other pledges of official support brought the nominal total to about $50 billion—a stupendous sum in comparison with any previous package of official financial support.[28]

Following Mexico in 1995, there were nine other cases where the IMF offered exceptionally large access, often supplemented by other commitments for official lending: Thailand, Indonesia, and Korea in 1997–98, Russia in 1996–98, Brazil in 1998–99 and 2001–03, Argentina in 2000–02, Turkey in 2000–05, and Uruguay in 2002–05.[29] Table 12.1 provides some of the key facts concerning the scale and composition of the official financing packages in these cases.

---

27. Access to some IMF facilities such as the Compensatory and Contingency Financing Facility (CCFF) "floated" relative to access under the SBA and EFF. The annual and cumulative access limits for the SBA and the EFF were sometimes reduced after large increases in IMF quotas and then raised again as the effective size of quotas relative to GDP and trade declined. The annual access limit under the SBA has never been greater than 100 percent of quota and often has been less. Actual access has usually been below, often well below, the access limit.

28. Unlike the support pledged by the IMF and the US Treasury (which consisted of real, usable support), $10 billion pledged through the Bank for International Settlements (BIS) was window dressing—money that could be counted as part of Mexico's international reserves but had to be held in the form of deposits at the BIS. Despite this exaggeration, the total package of official support for Mexico was of unprecedented size, even if some allowance is made for the failure of Mexico's IMF quota to keep pace with the growth of the Mexican economy and its international trade.

29. In the programs for Argentina, Brazil (both times), Turkey, and Uruguay, the IMF's initial large amounts of pledged support were later augmented, but each of these very large programs is counted only once if it is part of what amounted to a large continuing program. Brazil is counted twice because the 1998–99 and 2001–03 programs were effectively separate arrangements.

Table 12.1   Large IMF programs, 1995–2003

Program or country	Year	IMF commitment Billions of SDR	IMF commitment Billions of US dollars	Percent of IMF quota	Percent of precrisis GDP
Argentina	2000–2002	16.9	22.4	800	7.9
Brazil	1998–99	13.0	18.4	600	2.3
Brazil	2001–03	34.2	38.0	1,125	6.9
Indonesia	1997–98	7.3	10.2	490	5.0
Korea	1997–98	15.5	21.0	1,939	3.7
Mexico	1995–96	12.1	17.8	688	4.6
Russia	1996–98	15.4	20.4	667	5.0
Thailand	1997–98	2.9	4.0	505	2.2
Turkey	1999–2005	24.5	34.0	2,534	17.0
Uruguay	2002–05	2.3	2.7	775	14.5

SDR = special drawing rights

Notes: The amounts of IMF lending commitments are set in terms of SDR. The US dollar amounts of IMF commitments are approximate, depending on the exchange rate used to convert SDR into US dollars. Because the SDR value or the US dollar value of a country's GDP often swings widely during a crisis (due to wide swings in the country's exchange rate), the figures for IMF loan commitments as a share of GDP should be regarded as gross approximations. (The amounts reported in this table differ slightly from those given in table 4.1 of Roubini and Setser 2004, but the differences are not material.)

Source: IMF press releases, available at www.imf.org.

Changes in the Character of International Capital Flows

The change in IMF policy to allow for exceptionally large access in selected cases reflected primarily a response to balance of payments crises involving large shifts in private capital flows. This problem was not entirely new. In the debt crises of the 1980s, several countries, particularly in Latin America, were confronted with sudden slowdowns and threatened reversals in large-scale capital inflows.[30] The capital flows at issue in these earlier cases, however, were primarily loans to sovereigns by syndicates of commercial banks. This made it possible to contain the crises by persuading most of the banks involved in these syndicates to roll over their existing loans as part

---

30. The debt crises of the 1980s are the subject of a large literature, including (as already indicated) many contributions from the Peterson Institute for International Economics. William Cline's chapter in this volume provides a particularly useful summary and update of this literature.

of IMF-coordinated programs that featured significant policy adjustment and moderate amounts of official financing. In these situations, the access limits on IMF financing were useful in establishing that such financing was "catalytic": large enough to provide a meaningful incentive for a deal between the debtor country and its creditors but not big enough to allow creditors to escape or permit the country to avoid necessary policy adjustments. As Managing Director de Larosiere explained at the time, it was the job of the IMF to supply and support a credible adjustment program, and it was the job of the banks to supply the bulk of the financing.

During the initial years of management of the debt crises, banks were requested to roll over only their existing loans and sometimes to provide limited amounts of "new money" at interest rates that were not exorbitant. Eventually, however, it became clear that several countries with heavy debt burdens would not be able to service them in full in the longer term. The Brady plan (proposed in 1989) provided a framework within which countries and their creditor banks could work out deals that effectively provided for partial debt write-downs, usually under the auspices of an IMF program and with limited financial support from the Fund. The banks were not entirely happy with this new policy, but they lacked a viable alternative.

Holders of sovereign bonds issued by countries caught up in the debt crises of the 1980s were generally not pressed to participate in debt rollovers or write-downs. This reflected the fact that outstanding sovereign bonds were small relative to syndicated bank loans, and bondholders were quite diverse and difficult to organize for purposes of agreeing to rollovers or write-downs. As a result, holders of sovereign bonds generally fared much better than banks with syndicated loans: Bondholder claims were paid in full as they came due, and the market value of outstanding bonds appreciated considerably as their issuers' credit problems were resolved and world interest rates fell.

Understandably, this experience made banks leery of a renewed round of large-scale syndicated lending to emerging-market sovereigns after the debt crisis was resolved. In contrast, investors became more enthusiastic about emerging-market (particularly sovereign) bonds. Thus, as capital flows to emerging markets picked up again in the 1990s, the credit component of these flows involved relatively little bank lending and a substantial expansion of borrowing through the issuance of bonds in international capital markets.

The Mexican crisis of 1995 heightened recognition that the shift in the form of international credit flows to emerging markets would create difficulties for crisis management.[31] The old strategy of convening a relatively limited number of creditor banks to agree to a debt rollover or re-

---

31. The IMF's *International Capital Markets Report* for 2005 (Folkerts-Landau and Ito 1995, 10–11) provides an early warning of this potential problem.

Figure 12.4 Mexican exchange rate and price level, 1990–2006

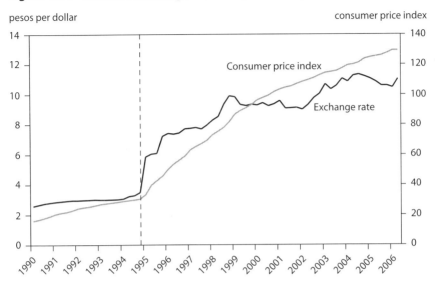

Source: IMF, *International Financial Statistics.*

structuring would not work if the bulk of creditor claims were held by a large group of individual bondholders with diverse instruments in terms of maturity, currency of denomination, and legal jurisdiction.

The Mexican Case

This is what happened in the Mexican crisis of 1995. The underlying cause of the crisis was a crawling peg nominal exchange rate that had become seriously overvalued, contributing to a Mexican current account deficit that reached almost 8 percent of GDP in 1994.[32] A botched devaluation of the Mexican peso in mid-December 1994, without a credible package of supporting policies, led rapidly to a crisis of confidence in which both Mexicans and foreign investors fled from Mexican assets. The peso crashed, and interest rates on Mexican credits (both peso- and dollar-denominated) spiked (figure 12.4). Once the crisis started, a key concern became the risk that the Mexican government might be forced to default on a large volume of debt.

---

32. The IMF was widely (and I believe rightly) criticized for its failure to foresee the Mexican crisis in 1993, especially as the situation deteriorated during 1994. An evaluation of the IMF's performance in this regard was prepared under the supervision of Sir Alan Whittome, but this evaluation has never been made public.

An important part of this debt was relatively short-term, mainly dollar-denominated loans from international banks to Mexican private banks. However, the Mexican government, like virtually any government, could not allow Mexican banks to default on these loans, and so they effectively became obligations of the government. In theory, a debt rollover and restructuring operation similar to that used in the 1980s crises might have been used to handle these interbank loans (and some officials outside Mexico suggested this approach). However, the Mexican government was extremely reluctant to go back to these practices, which would have signaled a catastrophic failure of the reforms of the past decade. The creditor banks were also unenthusiastic about such an approach, especially in view of their unhappy experience in the 1980s. In the official community (including the IMF), there was concern that the approach might set off a wider panic as other creditors of Mexico and of other emerging-market borrowers ran for the exits in advance of further possible restructurings.

Moreover, the interbank loans to Mexico were less than half of the problem. To help support the peso and keep government borrowing costs relatively low, the Mexican government had issued about $30 billion in tesobonos. These were relatively short-term, dollar-denominated obligations issued under Mexican law (mainly in 1994) and held by a diverse group of Mexican and foreign investors. There were also about $40 billion worth of longer-term, dollar-denominated international bonds of the Mexican government, primarily the Brady bonds issued to resolve the debt crises of the 1980s. With its foreign exchange reserves virtually exhausted in the vain efforts to sustain the crawling peg of the peso, the Mexican government by early 1995 was critically short of the resources needed to meet its maturing dollar obligations—even if there were a rollover of most interbank loans. Default loomed.

Facing this situation, the IMF (led by Managing Director Michel Camdessus) and key officials at the US Treasury decided that an exceptionally large package of financial support was needed and appropriate for Mexico, provided that the Mexican authorities were prepared to commit to and implement a very serious stabilization program. That program featured a moderate degree of fiscal consolidation and fairly tight limits on domestic credit creation, the use of foreign exchange reserves, and (consequently) domestic money creation. Fiscal tightening was needed to help restore confidence and to prepare for the large fiscal costs of resolving the crisis, especially the costs of resurrecting the Mexican banking system. Tight monetary policy was needed to contain the depreciation of the peso and to demonstrate the determination of the Mexican authorities to avoid a self-reinforcing cycle of catastrophic depreciation and hyperinflation.

The Mexican authorities assiduously achieved their pledged fiscal targets, but domestic credit creation and use of foreign exchange reserves at first substantially exceeded the guidelines of the IMF program. The Fund judged, however, that the excess domestic credit creation was necessary

Figure 12.5 Mexican interest rates and inflation rate, 1990–2006

percent per annum

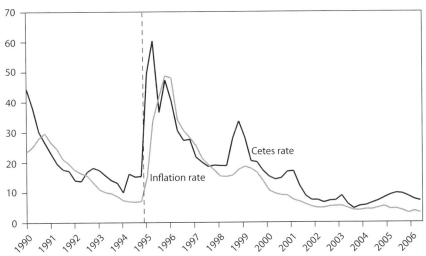

Source: IMF, *International Financial Statistics*.

to offset large losses of foreign exchange needed to meet the claims of various creditors and avoid a substantial absolute decline in the nominal domestic money supply. In real terms, the domestic money supply fell quite sharply due to a rapid escalation in the Mexican price level. Mexican domestic interest rates were pushed up substantially to over 50 percent per year (figure 12.5).

By summer 1995, the tight monetary policy succeeded in arresting the depreciation of the peso (at about 50 percent of its dollar value before the crisis). With a very sharp drop in domestic demand in Mexico, well beyond the decline in Mexican GDP, the current account moved nearly to balance by midsummer. This development, along with the strong policy efforts of the Mexican authorities and the large package of international financial support, effectively brought a restoration of confidence that allowed the Mexican economy to embark on a sustained recovery beginning in late 1995. This, in turn, led the Mexican authorities to decline much of the financial assistance pledged for 1996, to repay loans from the US Treasury well ahead of schedule, and to repay the IMF in a timely manner.

The Mexican economy had a very tough year in 1995, with real GDP falling 6.25 percent (year over year) and inflation running at 50 percent (December to December) (figure 12.6). It took more than a year for real GDP to recover its previous peak and five years for inflation to be reduced to single digits. Nevertheless, relative to Mexico's experience in the debt crisis of the 1980s, the outcome of the 1995 crisis was far more favorable. Many factors undoubtedly contributed to this result, especially the fact

Figure 12.6 Mexican current account deficit, 1992–2001

percent per annum

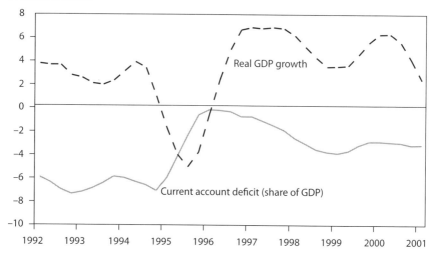

Source: IMF, *International Financial Statistics.*

that the underlying problems of the Mexican economy in early 1995 were much less severe than in mid-1982. However, most informed observers (including the Mexican and US officials, most of the staff of the IMF, the preponderance of private-market analysts, many independent scholars, and the author of this chapter and other Institute fellows) concluded that avoiding a Mexican default through the combination of determined policy action and substantial official international financial support contributed to the relative success of the response in the Mexican crisis of 1995.

The Default Option

Some have argued, explicitly or implicitly, that a Mexican default should have been allowed to happen as the preferred option.[33] This raises the intriguing question of what would have happened had Mexico followed the course of default in 1995?

A completely convincing answer to this counterfactual is, of course, not possible. But some useful insights may be gleaned by reflecting on the Mexican case in light of subsequent developments. In the other nine cases

---

33. The debate over alternatives to large-scale IMF lending, including the issue of private-sector involvement (PSI) and the possible creation of a Sovereign Debt Restructuring Mechanism (SDRM), has spawned an immense literature that is too extensive to review here. For further discussion and references, see Roubini and Setser (2004) as well as William Cline's chapter in this volume.

of exceptionally large IMF financial support, there were two (Russia in 1998 and Argentina in 2001–02) where official defaults unambiguously occurred, six where they were avoided, and one (Uruguay) where there was a debt restructuring that some might consider a de facto default.

Both Russia and Argentina—although for quite different reasons—were much better positioned to handle an official default than Mexico. In the case of Russia, persistent weakness of fiscal policy and a sharp fall of world oil prices during 1998 led to increasing fears that the Russian government would not be able to finance its fiscal deficit or roll over its burgeoning stock of GKOs. With a sharp upward spike in domestic interest rates and in interest rate spreads for Russian external debt, it became clear by late spring 1998 that the fiscal situation was unsustainable unless something was done that seriously addressed policy weaknesses and restored financial market confidence. Despite a pledge of substantial additional IMF support (and its partial disbursement), the Russian authorities (unlike the Mexican authorities in 1995) failed to implement adequate policy measures, and market sentiment continued to deteriorate. This led by mid-August to a decision by the Russian authorities that they had no alternative but to default on at least some of their debts and to allow the ruble to depreciate (see figures 12.2 and 12.3).

The government's default was limited to the ruble-denominated, domestic law–based GKOs, whose disgruntled investors had no recourse against the sovereign except through Russian courts. The Russian government assiduously maintained payments on other debt obligations, notably the euro bonds issued by the Russian government in foreign currencies and subject to foreign legal jurisdiction. Russian banks also defaulted on some of their obligations, in particular forward foreign exchange contracts held by foreign investors in ruble-denominated credits. But the Russian government (unlike the Mexican government) felt no effective pressure to make good on these losses of foreign investors.

For a relatively brief period following its default, Russia was consigned to the international financial wilderness in 1998–99 and was unable to access international capital markets. The recovery in world oil prices in 1999–2000 (and the substantial further increases after 2002) turned the Russian current account back into substantial surplus and contributed importantly to improvements in its fiscal balance. This, together with more disciplined policies, led eventually to significant fiscal surpluses and to the paying down of Russia's external and internal debt, all of which allowed Russia to regain and improve its international credit status.

For Argentina in the autumn of 2001, the situation involved the combination of a rigid nominal exchange rate that had become substantially overvalued, a rising fiscal deficit, a weakening and deflating economy since mid-1998, and exhaustion of substantial amounts of official financial assistance from the IMF and other sources. The economic and political situation did not permit a credible effort to curtail the fiscal deficit within

Figure 12.7 Argentine exchange rate and price level, 1990–2006

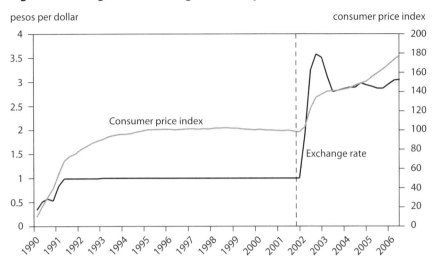

Source: IMF, *International Financial Statistics.*

anything like the available flow of financing. Comprehensive default on virtually all government obligations, abandonment of the nominal exchange rate peg, and a vast crisis in the Argentine financial system had all become unavoidable (figure 12.7).[34]

After a further sharp contraction in the early months of 2002, the Argentine economy began to turn around that summer. Not surprisingly, after a 25 percent decline from its peak in mid-1998, Argentine real GDP bounced back quite vigorously under the influence of a much depreciated real exchange rate and rising world prices for key Argentine exports (figure 12.8). Nevertheless, the default and collapse of the exchange rate peg adversely affected both domestic and foreign asset holders, including Argentine banks that were substantial (although not entirely voluntary) holders of Argentine government bonds. Through various actions of the Argentine government and courts, the losses were effectively managed in a way that domestic asset holders were partly sheltered at the expense of foreign investors (including both government bondholders and investors in Argentine banks and public utilities), who were saddled with exceptionally large losses.[35] This, of course, was quite popular with the Argen-

---

34. See Mussa (2002) for an extensive examination of the evolution of the Argentine crisis and the IMF's role therein.

35. William Cline (2004a) argues persuasively that the Argentine government could have afforded to make a more generous offer to external creditors in efforts to resolve its sovereign default. The Argentine government, however, was reluctant to impose a larger debt-repayment burden on its citizens.

Figure 12.8 Argentine current account balance, 1995–2005

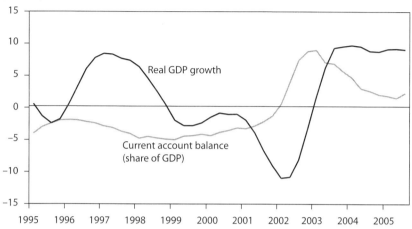

percent per annum

Source: IMF, *International Financial Statistics.*

tine public. With a substantial trade surplus and no payments to external private creditors, the Argentine economy had no need for additional foreign credit or investment and hence little to fear from becoming an international financial pariah.

In contrast to Russia and Argentina, Mexico after the 1995 crisis did not benefit from an enormous bonanza of energy export revenues, and the bounce back from the Mexican recession, although quite vigorous, was not as strong or prolonged as the recovery from the much deeper Argentine depression of mid-1998 to mid-2002. Also, Mexico is much more tightly linked to the global economy, especially to the United States, through both trade and finance than are either Russia or Argentina. The disruption of economic relations that would have followed a Mexican default in 1995 would probably have impaired the performance of the Mexican economy for a number of years. A "punish the foreign investors" approach like that aggressively adopted by Argentina (and to a lesser extent by Russia) would not have worked well for Mexico.

In six of the other seven cases of exceptionally large IMF financing, sovereign defaults were avoided, although standstills, restructurings, or defaults were employed for some, especially with regard to nonsovereign debts. In Indonesia there were widespread defaults by Indonesian companies on foreign and domestic loans and other nullifications of foreign investors' rights. In the case of Korea, the sovereign placed itself in jeopardy of default by guaranteeing a large volume of foreign bank loans to Korean banks. As the government's available foreign exchange reserves ran very low by early December 1997, the ability to make good on these guarantees became highly questionable. A rush to collect these loans by foreign banks ensued. This threat was met with a substantial augmentation of IMF support and an official effort to persuade the creditor banks to agree to roll over (but not write down) their loans. This effort was very similar to what had been done in the debt crises of the 1980s. A much softer version of this approach was also applied in the Brazilian crisis of 1998–99, where there was a somewhat vague agreement among major banks not to reduce their Brazilian exposures, and monitoring procedures were put in place to support this agreement. In other cases, international bank loans to sovereigns or to banks in the crisis countries were not sufficiently important to make this approach relevant or worthwhile.

Notably in the case of the Brazilian crisis of 2001–03, a number of analysts concluded that the prospects for surviving the intense financial pressures in the buildup to Brazil's presidential election in October 2002 and its aftermath were so poor that an early restructuring of Brazil's domestic and foreign debt was probably the best option.[36] Instead, the IMF offered the incumbent Brazilian authorities a large augmentation of the already substantial IMF financing package on the condition that the present government and the leading candidates to form the country's new government commit to maintain suitably firm fiscal and monetary policies, in particular a primary fiscal surplus of at least 4 percent of GDP. This allowed for substantial new IMF disbursements before the election and a commitment to further large disbursements after the election based on the policies of the new government.

With the aid of deft policy management by Brazil's central bank, Brazil got past the election. Thereafter the sound policies announced and implemented by the Brazilian government and central bank under new President Luiz Inácio Lula da Silva gradually restored confidence among domestic and foreign asset holders. Longer-term interest rates on Brazilian foreign currency–linked debt came down (both despite and partly because of continued tight money market conditions), and the Brazilian real recovered from its sharp preelection depreciation. A default and debt restructuring, and the highly costly financial crisis that would have accompanied them, were avoided. By 2005, Brazil was in sufficiently good financial condition to repay all of its outstanding IMF loans entirely and ahead of schedule. At this stage, no one could plausibly argue that a Brazilian default and debt restructuring in late 2002–early 2003 would have been better than the policies actually pursued by the Brazilian government with the aid of the largest package of financial support ever committed by the IMF.

Turkey (2000–2005) is another case where it appeared that a sovereign debt default/restructuring, together with a restructuring of the banking system, might have been needed. Such steps were avoided with the adoption of tough policy measures (a primary budget surplus of better than 6 percent

---

36. See Goldstein (2003) and, for opposing views, Williamson (2002) and Mussa (2002).

of GDP) and an exceptionally large financial support package from the IMF (the largest ever in relation to IMF quota). As with Brazil, few would now argue that default/restructuring would have been a superior option.

On the other hand, in the case of Uruguay (2002–05), exceptionally large IMF financial support (relative to Uruguay's GDP and IMF quota) were combined with a program that also featured agreements to restructure and write down claims on Uruguay's banking system. Also, among the many IMF programs that did not involve financial support beyond the standard access limits, there have been some cases (such as Bulgaria, the Dominican Republic, Ecuador, and the Ukraine) where debt restructurings have been used.

The Way Forward

Since the early 1990s, experience with debt restructurings and defaults for countries receiving IMF financial support has been mixed. The general conclusion that appears to be warranted in light of this experience is that in the modern world of reasonably open international capital markets providing diverse credit flows to emerging-market countries, crises may occur where there is no practicable or desirable alternative to a fairly comprehensive debt default/restructuring. There will likely be other cases, however, where potential or actual crises can be successfully resolved without costly and disruptive debt defaults/restructurings through determined policy adjustments backed by possibly very large-scale financial support from the IMF.

This leaves the important issue of how to distinguish between these two classes of crises. In the key case of Argentina, I believe the IMF went too far in providing financial assistance after it became reasonably clear that there was no realistic hope of rescuing the situation without a restructuring of Argentina's sovereign debt and an end to its rigid exchange rate peg (see Mussa 2002). In the aftermath of the Argentine case (and its evaluation even within the IMF), it was necessary and appropriate to strengthen the Fund's rules and procedures for dealing with cases of exceptionally large IMF lending where default/restructuring is a relevant issue.

The question remains as to how tightly to structure the constraints on very large scale IMF lending and especially how to determine when the situation is so grave and prospects so poor that the Fund should suspend its lending until the necessity of a sovereign debt restructuring is recognized by the country concerned.[37] At the IMF, and more broadly in the in-

---

37. A few years ago, under the impetus of proposals from the IMF's First Deputy Managing Director Anne Krueger, there was extensive discussion of the possibility of creating a Sovereign Debt Restructuring Mechanism (SDRM), which would provide an internationally agreed framework within which countries could negotiate restructuring agreements with their creditors. See Roubini and Setser (2004) and William Cline's chapter in this volume for discussion.

ternational financial community, there is no clear consensus on these issues. When the Bush administration came into office, various high officials indicated that they were firmly opposed to large-scale IMF assistance packages. Yet the Bush administration supported the three largest IMF assistance packages in history—Uruguay for the record of IMF lending relative to a country's GDP, Turkey for the record of IMF lending relative to IMF quota, and Brazil for the all-time record of total IMF lending—as well as the augmentation of the IMF loan for Argentina in the summer of 2001. Similarly, Horst Köhler, as he was assuming the duties of IMF managing director in 2000, indicated his opposition to exceptionally large-scale IMF lending. Yet he too supported the augmentation of the IMF loan to Argentina in the summer of 2001 and the huge IMF loan (relative to GDP) for Uruguay in 2002, and he was the driving force behind the Fund's very large loans to Turkey and Brazil.

This experience reconfirms the fundamental principle that in any future emerging-market financial crisis, the IMF will respond in whatever manner seems useful and appropriate at the time according to the circumstances of the particular case. The Fund's response will reflect lessons learned from the crises of the past decade as well as the somewhat modified procedures that have been agreed by the IMF Executive Board. However, no rigid set of reform proposals that is agreed now but untested in actual crises is likely to be followed precisely. Domestic and international financial markets are continually evolving, and the interactions of individual countries with the global economic and financial system are varied and changing. Just as what was done in the debt crises of the 1980s was not the relevant model for what the IMF could or should do in the emerging-market crises of the past decade, so too the actual or ideal response to these more recent crises is not likely to provide a precise guide about what to do in future crises.

References

Bergsten, C. Fred, ed. 1991. *International Adjustment and Financing: The Lessons of 1985–91.* Washington: Institute for International Economics.

Bergsten, C. Fred, William Cline, and John Williamson. 1985. *Bank Lending to Developing Countries: The Policy Alternatives.* POLICY ANALYSES IN INTERNATIONAL ECONOMICS 10. Washington: Institute for International Economics.

Calomiris, Charles. 1998. The IMF's Imprudent Role as a Lender of Last Resort. *The Cato Journal* 17: 275–95. Washington: Cato Institute.

Chang, Ha-Joon. 2000. The Hazard of Moral Hazard: Untangling the Asian Crisis. *World Development* 28, no. 4: 775–78.

Cline, William. 1983. *International Debt and Stability of the World Economy.* POLICY ANALYSES IN INTERNATIONAL ECONOMICS 4. Washington: Institute for International Economics.

Cline, William. 1984. *International Debt: Systemic Risk and Policy Response.* Washington: Institute for International Economics.

Cline, William. 1987. *Mobilizing Bank Lending to Debtor Countries.* POLICY ANALYSES IN INTERNATIONAL ECONOMICS 18. Washington: Institute for International Economics.

Cline, William. 1995. *International Debt Reexamined*. Washington: Institute for International Economics.

Cline, William. 2004a. *How Much Can Argentina Afford to Pay: Achieving a Balanced Debt Restructuring*. Washington: Economics International, Inc.

Cline, William. 2004b. Private-Sector Involvement in Financial Crisis Resolution: Definition, Measurement and Implementation. In *Fixing Financial Crises in the 21st Century*, ed. Andrew G. Haldane. London: Routledge.

Council on Foreign Relations. 1999. *Safeguarding Prosperity in a Global Financial System*. Report of an Independent Task Force. Washington: Council on Foreign Relations and Institute for International Economics.

De Gregorio, Jose, Barry Eichengreen, Takatoshi Ito, and Charles Wyplosz. 1999. An Independent and Accountable IMF. *Geneva Reports on the World Economy*, no. 1. Geneva: International Center for Monetary and Banking Studies.

Dell'Ariccia, Giovanni, Isabel Schnabel, and Jeromin Zettelmeyer. 2002. *Moral Hazard and International Crisis Lending*. IMF Working Paper 02-181 (October). Washington: International Monetary Fund.

Eichengreen, Barry. 1999. *Toward a New International Financial Architecture: A Practical Post-Asia Agenda*. Washington: Institute for International Economics.

Fischer, Stanley. 1999. On the Need for an International Lender of Last Resort. *Economic Perspectives* 13, no. 4 (Fall): 85–104.

Folkerts-Landau, David, and Takatoshi Ito. 1995. *International Capital Markets: Developments, Prospects, and Policy Issues*. Washington: International Monetary Fund.

Goldstein, Morris. 1998. *The Asian Financial Crisis: Causes, Cures, and Systemic Implications*. POLICY ANALYSES IN INTERNATIONAL ECONOMICS 55. Washington: Institute for International Economics.

Goldstein, Morris. 2000. *Strengthening the International Financial Architecture: Where Do We Stand?* Working Paper 00-8. Washington: Institute for International Economics.

Goldstein, Morris. 2001. *IMF Structural Conditionality: How Much Is Too Much?* Working Paper 01-4. Washington: Institute for International Economics.

Goldstein, Morris. 2005. The International Financial Architecture. In *The United States and the World Economy: Foreign Economic Policy for the Next Decade*, ed. C. Fred Bergsten and the Institute for International Economics. Washington: Institute for International Economics.

Haldane, Andrew, and Mark Kruger. 2001. *The Resolution of International Financial Crises: Private Finance and Public Funds*. Bank of Canada Working Paper 2001-20 (November). Ottawa: Bank of Canada.

IFIAC (International Financial Institutions Advisory Committee). 2000. *Report of the IFIAC*. Submitted to the US Congress and US Department of the Treasury, March 8. Washington.

Irwin, Gregor, and Chris Salmon. 2006. The Case Against the IMF as a Lender of Last Resort. In *Reforming the IMF for the 21st Century*, ed. Edwin Truman. Washington: Institute for International Economics.

Jeanne, Olivier, and Jeromin Zettelmeyer. 2001. International Bailouts, Moral Hazard, and Conditionality. *Economic Policy* 16, no. 33 (October).

Kamin, Steven B. 2002. *Identifying the Role of Moral Hazard in International Financial Markets*. International Finance Division Discussion Paper 736 (November). Washington: Board of Governors of the Federal Reserve System.

Kenen, Peter B. 2001. *The International Financial Architecture: What's New? What's Missing?* Washington: Institute for International Economics.

Kotowitz, Y. 1989. Moral Hazard. In *Allocation, Information, and Markets* (New Palgrave Series), ed. John Eatwell, Murray Milgate, and Peter Newman. New York: W. W. Norton.

Lane, Timothy D., and Steven T. Phillips. 2000. Moral Hazard: Does IMF Financing Encourage Imprudence by Borrowers and Lenders? *Economic Issues* 28. Washington: International Monetary Fund.

Lerrick, Adam. 2003. Funding the IMF: How Much Does It Really Cost? *Quarterly International Economics Report*. Pittsburgh: Carnegie-Mellon Gailliot Center for Public Policy.

Mussa, Michael. 1999a. Reforming the Financial Architecture: Limiting Moral Hazard and Containing Real Hazard. In *Capital Flows and the International Financial System*, ed. D. Gruen and L. Gower. Sydney: Reserve Bank of Australia (Economic Group).

Mussa, Michael. 1999b. Moral Hazard. In *The Asian Financial Crisis: Origins, Implications, and Solutions*, ed. William Hunter, George Kaufman, and Thomas Krueger. Boston: Kluwer Academic Publishers.

Mussa, Michael. 2002. *Argentina and the Fund: From Triumph to Tragedy*. POLICY ANALYSES IN INTERNATIONAL ECONOMICS 67. Washington: Institute for International Economics.

Mussa, Michael. 2004. Reflections on Moral Hazard and Private-Sector Involvement in the Resolution of Emerging-Market Financial Crises. In *Fixing Financial Crises in the Twenty-first Century*, ed. Andrew Haldane. London: Routledge.

Mussa, Michael. 2006. Reflections on the Function and Facilities for IMF Lending. In *Reforming the IMF for the 21st Century*, ed. Edwin Truman. Washington: Institute for International Economics.

Mussa, Michael, and Miguel Savastano. 1999. The IMF Approach to Macroeconomic Stabilization. In *NBER Macroeconomics Manual 1999*, ed. Ben Bernanke and Julio Rotemberg. Boston: MIT Press.

Mussa, Michael, Alexander Swoboda, Jeromin Zettelmeyer, and Olivier Jeanne. 2000. Moderating Fluctuations in Capital Flows to Emerging Market Economies. In *Reforming the International Monetary and Financial System*, ed. Alexander Swoboda and Peter Kenen. Washington: International Monetary Fund.

Odling-Smee, John. 2006. The IMF and Russia in the 1990s. *IMF Staff Papers* 53, no. 1: 151–94.

Roubini, Nouriel, and Brad Setser. 2004. *Bailouts or Bail-Ins? Responding to Financial Crises in Emerging Economies*. Washington: Institute for International Economics.

Rubin, Robert E., and Jacob Weisberg. 2003. *In an Uncertain World: Tough Choices from Wall Street to Washington*. New York: Random House.

Schwartz, Anna. 1998. Time to Terminate the ESF and the IMF. *Cato Institute Foreign Policy Briefing* 48. Washington: Cato Institute.

Sarno, Lucio, and Mark P. Taylor. 1999. Moral Hazard, Asset Price Bubbles, Capital Flows, and the East Asian Crisis: The First Tests. *Journal of International Money and Finance* 18, no. 4: 637–57.

Spadafora, Francesco. 2001. *The Pricing of Syndicated Loans to Emerging Markets: Some Further Results*. Working Paper 438 (March). Rome: Bank of Italy.

Truman, Edwin. 2002. Debt Restructuring: Evolution or Revolution? *Brookings Papers on Economic Activity* 1-2002, 341–46. Washington: Brookings Institution.

Truman, Edwin. 2006a. *A Strategy for IMF Reform*. POLICY ANALYSES IN INTERNATIONAL ECONOMICS 77. Washington: Institute for International Economics.

Truman, Edwin, ed. 2006b. *Reforming the IMF for the 21st Century*. Washington: Institute for International Economics.

Williamson, John. 1982. *The Lending Policies of the International Monetary Fund*. POLICY ANALYSES IN INTERNATIONAL ECONOMICS 1. Washington: Institute for International Economics.

Williamson, John, ed. 1983. *IMF Conditionality*. Washington: Institute for International Economics.

Williamson, John. 1988. *Voluntary Approaches to Debt Relief*. POLICY ANALYSES IN INTERNATIONAL ECONOMICS 25. Washington: Institute for International Economics.

Williamson, John. 2005. *Curbing the Boom-Bust Cycle: Stabilizing Capital Flows to Emerging Markets*. POLICY ANALYSES IN INTERNATIONAL ECONOMICS 75. Washington: Institute for International Economics.

Williamson, John, and Nancy Birdsall. 2002. *Delivering on Debt Relief: From IMF Gold to a New Aid Architecture*. Washington: Institute for International Economics and Center for Global Development.

Zhang, Xioaming. 1999. *Testing for "Moral Hazard" in Emerging Markets Lending*. Working Paper 99-1 (August). Washington: Institute of International Finance.

13

The IMF as Global Umpire for Exchange Rate Policies

MORRIS GOLDSTEIN

As a matter of logical necessity, an exchange rate involves two or more countries. The bilateral exchange rate of the Chinese renminbi against the US dollar, for example, necessarily involves both China and the United States, while the multilateral real effective exchanges rates of either China or the United States necessarily involve their exchange rates against an average of all their trading partners. For this reason, it follows that a country's exchange rate policy cannot be solely the concern of that country. China cannot unilaterally decide that eight renminbi should exchange for one US dollar while the United States simultaneously decides that one US dollar should exchange for four Chinese renminbi. Almost inevitably, controversies will arise when countries have inconsistent views and policies concerning the exchange rate that links their currencies and economies. This raises the question of how such controversies should be resolved, taking appropriate account of the interests of all countries.

This chapter presents the case for having the International Monetary Fund serve as the "global umpire" for exchange rate policies, with the key task of guarding against "currency manipulation."[1] The first section

Morris Goldstein has been the Dennis Weatherstone Senior Fellow at the Institute since 1994.

1. This chapter draws heavily on and extends the analyses presented in Goldstein (2004, 2005, 2006a) and my article "Exchange Rates, Fair Play, and the Grand Bargain," *Financial Times*, April 21, 2006. It also follows the line of argument laid out in my dinner speech on Currency Manipulation and IMF Reform, given in San Francisco on June 16, 2006, at the annual Pacific Basin conference, sponsored by the Federal Reserve Bank of San Francisco.

of this chapter explains why the issue of currency manipulation is particularly important and the second why it is attracting increasing attention. Next I outline the reasons for concluding that arguments denying the existence of currency manipulation, or maintaining that currency manipulation doesn't matter, or asserting that it should be tolerated, are misguided. Then I discuss the role of the IMF as the umpire for the exchange rate system. The final section lays out the steps that the IMF should take to discourage inappropriate exchange rate policies.

Why Currency Manipulation Is Important

When the IMF was established shortly after the end of World War II, its "founding fathers" were mindful of the unhappy experience with the competitive depreciations of the 1930s and 1940s and with the protectionist trade policy regimes of that period. They also recognized that it would be impossible to implement a desired watershed reduction in trade and payment restrictions without some assurance that there would be international safeguards against beggar-thy-neighbor exchange rate polices. Under the par value system then in force, these safeguards took the form of requiring IMF member countries to obtain the Fund's approval for proposed changes in exchange rates larger than 10 percent.[2]

When the Fund's charter was amended to accommodate the more diversified and more "flexible" exchange rate system of the early 1970s, the revised Article IV set forth obligations on exchange rate policy both for member countries and for the Fund itself. Specifically, members were directed (in Article IV, Section 1) to "avoid manipulating exchange rates or the international monetary system in order to prevent effective balance-of-payments adjustment or to gain unfair competitive advantage over other member countries." And the Fund was directed (in Article IV, Section 3) "to oversee the international monetary system in order to ensure its effective operation," "to oversee the compliance of each member with its obligations" (under Section 1), "to exercise firm surveillance over the exchange rate policies of members," and "to adopt specific principles for the guidance of all members with respect to those policies."

When the Fund in 1977 laid out principles and procedures for its surveillance over exchange rate policies, it identified a set of developments (originally thought of as "pointers") that might suggest the need for discussion with a country about its exchange rate policies. The first pointer on the list is "protracted, large-scale intervention in one direction in exchange markets." The other pointers address official or quasi-official borrowing, restrictions on trade and capital flows, monetary and domestic fi-

---

2. The Fund was to concur with a proposed change in exchange rates if it was satisfied that the change was necessary to correct a "fundamental disequilibrium."

nancial policies, and exchange rate behavior that appears unrelated to underlying economic and financial conditions. The basic idea of the pointers was to discourage policy actions that would either push the real exchange rate away from its equilibrium value or prevent the real exchange rate from moving closer to its equilibrium.[3]

The pointer on protracted, large-scale exchange market intervention was an obvious choice given the considerable difficulties in securing greater (nominal) exchange rate flexibility during the latter days of the par value system. It reflects a view that if large-scale exchange market intervention is taking place over an extended period and in the same direction, it is likely that authorities are seeking inappropriately to defend a disequilibrium exchange rate, be it an over- or undervalued rate. In other words, when the authorities' view of the right exchange rate is persistently under challenge by strong market pressure, one should give considerable weight to the market view that significant adjustment may be appropriate.

The pointers that cover official and quasi-official borrowing, trade and capital flow restrictions, and monetary and domestic financial policies are similar in spirit. That is, they were meant to discourage the use of policies (besides exchange market intervention) that might be used to substitute for a needed alteration in the exchange rate—particularly since these policy alternatives to exchange rate action could have adverse spillover costs on other economies. The inclusion of pointers in these areas was probably influenced by earlier efforts to mobilize such policies to delay needed exchange rate action during the Bretton Woods era and before. Their inclusion is also consistent with the position that the "equilibrium" real exchange rate should be defined with regard to a (theoretical) benchmark under which trade, capital, and financial policies are employed appropriately. In this connection, recall that Nurkse (1945) defined the equilibrium exchange rate as the rate that would produce equilibrium in the balance of payments but without wholesale unemployment at home or abroad, undue restrictions on trade, or special incentives to incoming or outgoing capital flows.

The final pointer on the list—exchange rate behavior that appears unrelated to underlying economic and financial conditions—was included to capture potential exchange rate misalignment under a floating exchange rate regime (a problem Fred Bergsten has stressed in some of his writings). It is different from the other pointers because it deals with market failure rather than policy failure and because it doesn't suggest an obvious policy antidote—except perhaps short-term coordinated exchange market intervention to give, if needed, the markets a nudge in the right direction.

Taken as a group, the pointers send the message that it is in neither the individual country's nor the international community's interest to seek to

---

3. In this sense, the IMF guidelines were similar in spirit to the proposals for "reference zones" recently reviewed by Williamson (2005b).

"manage" the exchange rate by heavy and prolonged reliance on exchange market intervention and sterilization operations and by manipulating restrictions on trade and capital flows.

A final historical note: The IMF's Articles of Agreement use the term "currency manipulation" to characterize inappropriate efforts both to push the real exchange rate away from the equilibrium rate and to prevent it from moving toward the equilibrium rate. Those who find the term "manipulation" misleading or too accusatory or dramatic for their taste can easily substitute "thwarting external adjustment" without loss of substance.

Why Currency Manipulation Is Important and Still Relevant

Despite the role assigned in the IMF's Articles of Agreement to IMF exchange rate surveillance in preventing currency manipulation, the issue has received little attention since two cases were considered in the 1980s. Accordingly, one may reasonably ask: Why is currency manipulation now of particular importance? There are three main answers to that question.

First, there is the problem of global payments imbalances, particularly the large US current account deficit—running at 6.5 percent of GDP in 2005 and on track to be about as large this year. The "sustainable" US current account deficit is probably no more than half as large (Mussa 2005, Cline 2005, Truman 2005, and Williamson 2005a). To get there at reasonable cost requires, among other measures, a further depreciation in the real, trade-weighted value of the dollar of between 15 and 35 percent.

But it will be difficult to achieve the needed further real depreciation of the dollar unless the Asian emerging economies and Japan—whose currencies have a combined weight in the Federal Reserve's dollar index of roughly 40 percent—participate prominently in the appreciation of nondollar currencies. If the dollar is to go "down," some other currencies have to go "up." Whereas the euro, the Canadian dollar, and the Australian dollar—among other market-determined exchange rates—exhibited strong real appreciations during the first wave of dollar depreciation (from the dollar peak in February 2002 until June/July 2006), many of the Asian currencies—including those of China, Japan, Malaysia, and Taiwan—did not;[4] indeed, some of them depreciated in real trade-weighted terms despite large current account surpluses.

If the Asian currencies do not lead the parade in the needed second wave of dollar depreciation, either the size of the overall dollar depreciation will be too small to promote substantial current account reduction in the United States or the appreciation of nondollar currencies will be

---

4. Two notable exceptions to this statement were the Korean won and the Indonesian rupiah.

skewed unreasonably toward those economies where economic circumstances would be poorly served by further large currency appreciation.[5]

Yes, the United States could and should make more of a contribution toward reducing its saving-investment imbalance by proposing a more credible medium-term plan of US fiscal consolidation, along with monetary conditions that would reduce the growth rate of domestic demand relative to that of output (Mussa 2005). But it's not an either-or choice. We need both more fiscal policy discipline in the United States and more currency appreciation in Asia. If we don't see the right amount of exchange rate adjustment, too much of the adjustment will fall on expenditure reduction in the United States, with adverse effects on growth in the United States and in its trading partners. And if we don't get appropriate fiscal and monetary policy action in the United States, there won't be enough room for the needed expansion in US net exports; instead, we will get increased inflationary pressures and higher US interest rates.

In short, an effective program of balance-of-payments adjustment requires use of both expenditure-changing and expenditure-switching policies. But if surplus countries use prolonged, large-scale, one-way sterilized intervention in exchange markets to prevent their currencies from appreciating, the expenditure-switching channel of external adjustment will be rendered impotent.[6]

A second reason for increased concern about currency manipulation is not only the recent occurrence of episodes that appear to represent departures from the IMF currency manipulation guidelines but also the fact that some of these involve systemically important economies.[7] The leading case in point is China—now the world's third largest trading nation and the second largest in terms of its GDP when calculated at purchasing power parity (PPP) exchange rates. The relevant facts about the Chinese case are as follows.

The Chinese authorities have been engaged in large-scale, one-way intervention in exchange markets for the better part of three years. The size and duration of that intervention have been dramatic—at roughly 10 percent of GDP in each of 2003, 2004, and 2005 (figure 13.1).

China's huge reserve accumulation has also coincided with a substantial increase in its global current account surplus—from approximately 2

---

5. As pointed out in Mann and Plueck (2005), a large share of the US current account deficit is in consumer goods and autos, import categories where Asian economies are large exporters to the United States.

6. In discussing the operation of the exchange rate system during the 1960s, Bergsten (1980) argued that the balance-of-payments adjustment process lacked symmetry because surplus countries were not willing to initiate the needed adjustment measures.

7. When we are dealing with exchange rate policies in systemically important economies (like China), the IMF's responsibility to "oversee the international monetary system in order to ensure its effective operation" comes into play—not just its complementary obligation to "exercise firm surveillance" over the exchange rate policies of its member countries.

Figure 13.1   Change in China's foreign exchange reserves, 1993–2005

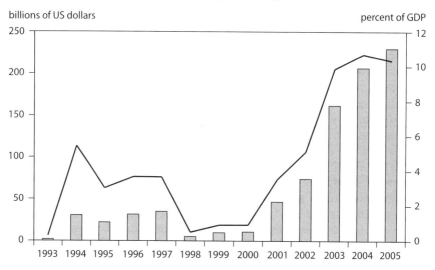

Note: The bars show billions of dollars and the line tracks percent of GDP.

Source: China State Administration for Foreign Exchange.

percent of GDP in 2003 to 3.5 percent in 2004 and to over 7 percent in 2005[8] (figure 13.2). Although final current account figures for 2006 are not yet available, China's global trade balance surplus for the first six months of 2006 ran about 55 percent ahead of last year's surplus; a global current account surplus in the neighborhood of 9 to 10 percent of China's GDP looks likely for this year.

Despite these very large global balance-of-payments surpluses, the real trade-weighted value of the renminbi has actually depreciated on a cumulative basis since the dollar peak in February 2002; according to the index compiled by Citigroup, the cumulative real depreciation of the renminbi has been about 11 percent, while JPMorgan's index shows a smaller cumulative depreciation of about 2 percent (figure 13.3). True, the real, trade-weighted value of the renminbi went up in 2005, reflecting not only the real appreciation of the US dollar but also the real depreciations of the euro and the Japanese yen. But if one believes, as is the consensus view at the Institute, that the US dollar is likely to resume its decline in the period ahead—as the US interest rate–tightening cycle is completed earlier in the United States than in either Europe or Japan, and as the large US current account deficit exerts downward pressure on the dollar—then the renminbi will again follow the dollar down. In brief, not only has the real

---

8. In 2003 and 2004 China's capital account surplus mushroomed and accounted for the largest part of the 10 percent of GDP reserve accumulation in those two years.

Figure 13.2   China's global current account position as a percent of GDP, 1994–2006E

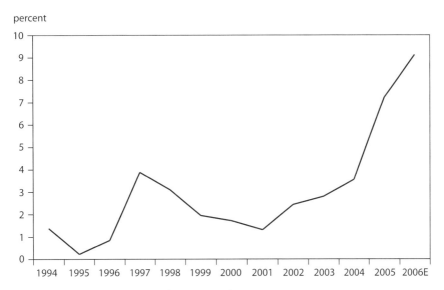

Source: China State Administration for Foreign Exchange.

Figure 13.3   Real effective exchange rate of the renminbi, January 1994–July 2006

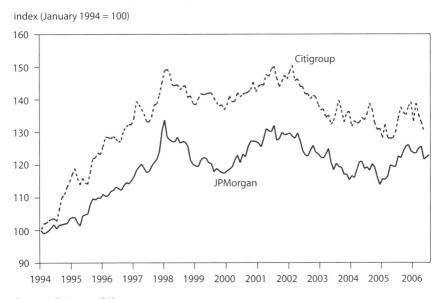

Sources: Citigroup, JPMorgan.

Figure 13.4 China's real GDP growth, 1992–2006Q3

percent

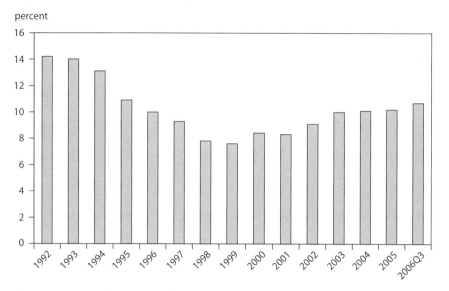

Sources: 1985–2005: *China Statistical Yearbook 2006,* p. 59, China Statistics Press; 2006Q3: National Bureau of Statistics of China, www.stats.gov.cn/index.htm.

exchange rate of the renminbi been moving in the wrong direction for most of the past three years but its misalignment could well get bigger unless more space is created soon between the renminbi and the dollar.

China's real GDP growth has been anything but weak during the 2002–05 period, averaging over 9 percent a year (figure 13.4). And during the first half of 2006, China's growth accelerated further, reaching 10.9 percent. As such, it's not persuasive to say that internal balance considerations militated against a renminbi appreciation.

China's "reform" of its currency regime in July 2005 has also so far done little to affect the renminbi's de facto behavior in exchange markets. Since the 2.1 percent appreciation of the renminbi with respect to the US dollar on July 21, 2005, the renminbi has appreciated vis-à-vis the dollar by roughly another 1.25 percent. This appreciation is small potatoes compared with the Goldstein-Lardy (2006) estimate that the renminbi is probably undervalued by 20 to 35 percent on a real trade-weighted basis and to Cline's (2005) estimate that it is undervalued by roughly 40 to 45 percent against the US dollar. At this pace, it could take a decade or more to eliminate the misalignment of the renminbi.

In July 2005, China also pledged to increase the influence of "market demand and supply" in the determination of the renminbi. But the Chinese authorities have continued to intervene by about the same massive amounts since then. Nor is there any evidence that China has been managing the renminbi with respect to a basket of currencies rather than to the

US dollar alone—thereby casting doubt on another of the key elements of the July reform (Eichengreen 2005).

While China is the most obvious and most serious case of currency manipulation, it is likely not the only episode. Malaysia, for example, has over the past several years displayed intervention, reserve, and real exchange rate behavior that appears to violate the IMF's currency manipulation guidelines. And in 2003 and the first quarter of 2004, Japan engaged in massive exchange market intervention; had that intervention continued, it certainly would have, given the accompanying circumstances, been a cause for concern. In the event, however, Japan ceased in mid-2004 intervening on a significant scale and has not resumed such operations.[9]

The worry of course is not simply with earlier episodes of apparent manipulation. It is that other economies will in the future come to the conclusion that they can benefit by using large-scale, prolonged exchange market intervention—together with sterilization of reserve inflows—to gain a competitive advantage on their trading partners.

The third reason for the increasing concern about currency manipulation is that there are preliminary signs—most evident in the United States—that it will be extremely difficult to sustain forward momentum on globalization and to resist protectionism if there isn't perceived "fairness" in exchange rate policy. As argued elsewhere,[10] the key long-term international economic challenge is to integrate further the larger emerging economies (China, India, Brazil, Russia, and some others) into the international financial and trading systems.

Both the industrial countries and the larger emerging economies should be pursuing a win-win "grand bargain." In this grand bargain, the larger emerging economies would get reliable access to the markets in industrial countries for their exports and their excess saving. They would also get increased "chairs and shares" in the international financial institutions consistent with their growing economic weight. In return, the industrial countries would get better access to fast-growing markets in the larger emerging economies as well as a commitment by the latter to play by the "international rules of the game" on trade, intellectual property, and exchange rates.

The catch is that this win-win bargain requires significant progress simultaneously on all the elements. If instead there is foot-dragging by any of the parties and if the designated umpires—the World Trade Organization (WTO) and the IMF—do not enforce the rules, then the game can descend into a lose-lose protectionist outcome.

---

9. Although it is not a member of the IMF, Taiwan's exchange rate policies over the past several years seem inconsistent with the Fund's currency manipulation guidelines.

10. Morris Goldstein, "Exchange Rates, Fair Play, and the Grand Bargain," *Financial Times*, April 21, 2006.

If, for example, certain emerging economies are perceived as having achieved large gains in market share unfairly via currency manipulation and if the IMF fails to investigate these charges, then the result may be national freelancing that would frustrate other elements of the grand bargain.[11] Likewise, emerging economies will not have the incentive to grant increased market access to industrial countries or to forgo regional alternatives to the IMF if the US Congress politicizes the approval of foreign investment plans in the United States (recall the China National Offshore Oil Corporation and Dubai Ports World cases) and if the industrial countries prevent the emerging economies from achieving a "fair" voting share in the IMF.

In short, codes of conduct on exchange rate policy may turn out over the next few years to be a necessary element in any wider proglobalization grand bargain, and IMF firm surveillance over exchange rate policies is likely to be the preferred approach to seeing that such codes of conduct are well designed and enforced. As with the WTO's role on trade policy, the most effective way to deal with high anxiety over alleged unfairness on exchange rate policy is to subject such charges to serious investigation and findings by a competent, unbiased global umpire.

Myths and Fallacies about Currency Manipulation

It is sad but true that not everyone agrees on the importance and relevance of the currency manipulation issue. This section summarizes the arguments of the skeptics as well as the reasons why their views are unpersuasive.

Fixed exchange rates can't be manipulated. Because the IMF's charter permits countries a wide choice of currency regimes (including fixed exchange rates) and because defense of a fixed exchange rate may require exchange market intervention, it is alleged that countries that maintain fixed rates cannot be guilty of manipulation.

This argument mixes up choice of currency regime with attempts to maintain a disequilibrium exchange rate. The former is allowed under IMF rules; the latter is not. IMF member countries can choose fixed rates, floating rates, or 'most anything in between; they are also free to intervene in exchange markets and indeed are expected to do so if and when they encounter disorderly markets. What is discouraged is a particular kind of intervention: large-scale, prolonged, one-way intervention in exchange

---

11. See, for example, the proposal by US Senators Charles Schumer and Lindsey Graham in early 2005 for a 27.5 percent tariff on China's exports to the United States if negotiations to end China's alleged currency manipulation did not bear fruit, or the more recent bill by Senators Charles Grassley and Max Baucus to deny an IMF quota increase and "market economy" status to any country found to be maintaining a "fundamentally misaligned currency."

markets. The latter is discouraged because it is regarded as symptomatic of a disequilibrium exchange rate that is assumed to be costly both to the home country and to its trading partners.

You can't be manipulating if you haven't changed the exchange rate. Since "manipulate" is an active verb, it is often argued that a country that has maintained the same parity over an extended period can't be guilty of manipulation because it "hasn't done anything."

This argument ignores the basic points that what matters for competitiveness is the real, trade-weighted exchange rate (that is, the trade-weighted nominal exchange rate, adjusted for cross-country differences in inflation performance) and that real exchange rate misalignment should be diagnosed against the backdrop of a country's overall balance-of-payments position. Viewed from this perspective, a misalignment of the real exchange rate could occur just as easily from nonmovement of the nominal exchange rate as from excessive movement; likewise, a given level of the nominal exchange rate might be fine when the country's balance of payments was in small surplus or small deficit but would no longer be appropriate when the balance of payments moved into persistent large surplus or persistent large deficit. Indeed, there are many cases of countries that started with reasonably valued pegged nominal exchange rates that subsequently saw their real effective exchange rates become substantially overvalued and their current accounts move into large persistent deficit. The outcome in these cases was often an eventual exchange rate crisis and a massive devaluation to correct the overvaluation. Although less frequently observed, it is obviously logically possible for a country with a pegged nominal exchange rate that is initially reasonably valued to find that its real effective exchange rate has subsequently become substantially undervalued with a large persistent current account surplus.

In 1995, China recorded a very small global current account surplus equal to 0.2 percent of GDP. By 2000, with an unchanged nominal exchange rate versus the US dollar, China's real effective exchange rate had appreciated by about 20 percent and the current account was still in modest surplus—indicating improvements in China's international competitiveness from sources other than the real effective exchange rate. By 2005, at a barely changed nominal exchange rate versus the US dollar, China's real effective exchange rate had depreciated by 7 to 15 percent from its 2000 level (depending on the exchange rate index), while the current account surplus had grown to over 7 percent of GDP. The evidence is clear that the combination of a pegged nominal rate leading to real effective depreciation together with continuing improvements in China's competitiveness from other factors led to a substantially undervalued real effective exchange rate. In short, "not doing anything" to the nominal exchange rate can thwart external adjustment and can thereby qualify as manipulation.

Undervaluation of the currency should be tolerated if it's necessary to ensure social stability. Yet a third fallacious argument is that the IMF should adopt a lenient approach to the currency manipulation guidelines for a country that purportedly needs an undervalued currency to generate enough growth and employment in its traded goods industries to keep the lid on social pressures.

But most countries have full employment objectives of one type or another, and it is difficult to see why or how some countries' concerns in this area should be elevated above those of others; should, for example, an extra worker hired in the export industry of China as a result of renminbi undervaluation be given more weight than an extra worker hired in the export industries of, say, Egypt or Bangladesh? Wholesale application of such an employment rationalization for currency manipulation would legitimize the beggar-thy-neighbor behavior that such international exchange rate guidelines were designed to prevent and that directly contradicts one of the fundamental purposes of the IMF stated in Article I, "to avoid competitive depreciation."

This is not to say that China, for example, with its large-scale migration out of agriculture and its recent history of significant employment losses in state-owned industries, does not face formidable employment challenges as part of its development strategy. But even there, the arguments that link exchange rate undervaluation with export-led growth and full employment are often exaggerated (Goldstein 2006b). In this connection, it should be recalled that between 1994 and early 2002 the real, trade-weighted exchange rate of the renminbi appreciated by almost 30 percent—yet the Chinese economy grew over this period at an average annual rate of about 9 percent and growth never dipped below 7 percent in any single year. Similarly, the appreciation in the real trade-weighted renminbi in 2005 did not prevent the value of China's exports from rising by 28 percent or its real GDP from growing by almost 10 percent. As highlighted in Anderson (2005), it is also well to note that employment in China's export industries accounts for roughly 5 percent of total employment, that China's high headline export-to-GDP ratio (35 percent) substantially overstates the value-added share of exports in GDP, and that empirical tests of export-led growth (such as correlations of net export growth with GDP growth) typically find that China's growth is much less "export-led" than growth in most other Asian emerging economies. As emphasized in Goldstein and Lardy (2004), net exports have a much lower weight (5 percent) in China's GDP than either government consumption (12 percent), private consumption (39 percent), or investment (45 percent); hence, net exports have a large effect on China's growth only in those years (e.g., 2005) when net exports change by a very large percentage. The lion's share of the time, it is investment and private consumption that lead and dominate China's economic growth.

Discussions of the impact of exchange rate changes should also not proceed as if the exchange rate were the sole instrument of macroeconomic policy. If there is concern that an exchange rate revaluation would have too negative an impact on economic growth, an option is to combine revaluation with an expansionary fiscal policy. In China's case, such an expansionary fiscal policy could be directed at its pressing social needs (pension, health, and education programs). In this way, the expenditure-switching role of the exchange rate can be retained while fiscal policy reduces the contractionary effect of revaluation on aggregate demand.

The effect of exchange rate changes on domestic financial stability should also be brought into the cost-benefit calculus. In the case of China, a much-undervalued renminbi contributes to excessive reserve accumulation, which, in turn, can spill over into excessively rapid expansion of bank credit and monetary aggregates. When bank credit expands too fast, the quality of loan decisions almost always suffers. China experienced just such a bank credit "blowout" in 2003 and the first part of 2004.[12] It was only through the use of both strong administrative controls (on bank lending, investment project approvals, and land use) and large-scale sterilization operations that runaway credit growth was contained. But the final tab for the lending excesses of 2003 and early 2004 is likely to be large (on the order of 15 percent of GDP), administrative controls and large-scale sterilization operations have their own costs, and bank credit growth has reemerged as a problem in the first half of 2006.

The de facto "fixed" nature of the renminbi currency regime has also of course limited the independence of China's monetary policy and in particular has greatly reduced the scope for using interest rate policy to rein in excesses in fixed asset investment.

In the end, one should not assume that currency manipulation is in a country's own interest—even if that country faces difficult employment challenges.

IMF guidelines on currency manipulation are not needed and will not be effective. This line of argument has a number of variants. One contention is that empirical research has demonstrated conclusively that sterilized exchange market intervention has no lasting significant effect on nominal exchange rates;[13] hence, there is no need for the prohibition on prolonged, large-scale, one-way intervention in exchange markets as such intervention will have little effect on exchange rates anyway. The rub is that while

---

12. Growth of the monetary aggregates also surged in 2003 and early 2004 and inflation rates moved up sharply for a time—contributing, inter alia, to a large fall in real interest rates. Control of the monetary aggregates again became an issue in the first half of 2006—even though inflation rates have so far remained relatively low.

13. See Jurgensen (1993); Sarno and Taylor (2001) provide more of a mixed verdict on the effectiveness of intervention.

this argument way well apply to sterilized intervention involving currencies regarded as close substitutes for one another (say, the dollar and the euro), it would not be applicable to many emerging-market currencies, which are not highly substitutable for the major reserve currencies. When it comes to emerging-market currencies (like the renminbi), there is a strong presumption that prolonged, large-scale, one-way intervention could have a significant effect on exchange rates (see Dooley 2006).

A related argument is that whatever their choice of currency regimes and whatever their interventions to affect the nominal exchange rate, countries will be able to exert little control over the real exchange rate, which after all is what matters for competitiveness. For example, a country that intervenes heavily in the exchange market in pursuit of an undervalued nominal exchange rate will eventually find that its inflation rate has risen sufficiently to restore the preintervention real exchange rate. The implication again is that IMF rules on currency manipulation are superfluous because countries will not be able via such operations to frustrate balance-of-payments adjustment or obtain an unfair competitive advantage over their trading partners. But the reality is that surplus countries can typically resist adjustment and can maintain a disequilibrium real exchange rate for longer than deficit countries. In China's case, for example, the authorities have over the past few years used large-scale sterilization operations and strong administrative controls to prevent inflation rates from rising to levels that would wipe out the real undervaluation of the renminbi; as such, the real, effective exchange rate of the renminbi has depreciated on a cumulative basis since early 2002 despite China's large balance-of-payments surpluses. If it were agreed internationally that countries engaging in large-scale exchange market intervention would refrain from sterilizing the effects on domestic monetary aggregates, then there would be a weaker link between nominal and real rate movements than has in fact been the case. But obtaining agreement on and enforcing international guidelines on sterilization policy are likely to be even more difficult than for currency manipulation. In short, experience suggests that some surplus countries can, for several years if not longer, prevent the real exchange rate from adjusting much toward its equilibrium level, with adverse consequences for their competitors as well as themselves.[14]

Another claim one hears frequently is that citing countries as "currency manipulators"—be it by the Fund or by the US Treasury—would be counterproductive. The accused would "lose face," harden their positions, and delay reform; and a finding of currency manipulation might even induce

---

14. In support of this conclusion, Cashin and McDermott (2006) find that, for a sample of 90 industrial and developing countries, the half-life of deviations from purchasing power parity (PPP) is on average three to five years. Interestingly enough, they also report that departures from PPP tend to last longer for developing than for industrial countries and that they are also longer for countries with fixed nominal exchange rates than for those with flexible rate regimes.

the US Congress to adopt protectionist trade legislation. Again, this argument is not persuasive.

It is curious that the alleged link between external criticism and lack of policy reform in the accused country seems to be peculiar to exchange rate policy. The US government, for example, does not refrain from criticizing China's human rights abuses or its military buildup for fear that doing so will slow progress. Similarly, why does it make sense for the US government to bring complaints before the WTO on Chinese trade policy and to press publicly and loudly for better protection of intellectual property rights in China but not to enforce its own guidelines on currency manipulation?

Moreover, whatever might be the effectiveness of US government efforts to persuade China to adjust its exchange rate policy to conform with international norms, would it not plausibly be more effective for the IMF to press for the same policy adjustment on behalf of, and with the support of, most of the international community? Surely there can be no valid objection from the Chinese authorities to the IMF performing tasks that are assigned to it and that its members are committed by their own agreement to support.

The IMF as Umpire for the Exchange Rate System

The discussion above establishes the need for someone in the international community to play the role of establishing and enforcing a reasonable code of practice with respect to exchange rate policies. The IMF is clearly the institution that has been assigned that role—and properly so. The problem in practice has been that neither the IMF nor its major shareholders have shown much interest in ruling on what is and is not internationally acceptable exchange rate policy, and without enforcement no code of conduct can be expected to have much impact on behavior. Several observations are revealing.

Although the Fund's surveillance guidelines allow the IMF managing director to initiate an ad hoc or special consultation with a member country whenever there is concern about its exchange rate policy, only two such special consultations have been conducted in the past 26 years (Sweden in 1982 and South Korea in 1987) and none at all in the past 19 years.

Despite overwhelming evidence of renminbi misalignment for the 2003–06 period, it took the IMF more than three years to acknowledge publicly that the renminbi needed to appreciate. Before that, the Fund was willing to conclude only that China's currency regime needed to show "greater flexibility." Even today, the Fund has still not given any indication of the order of magnitude by which the renminbi is undervalued.

In the absence of IMF action on apparent cases of currency manipulation, activities by national governments have to some extent, and not particularly effectively or desirably, filled the gap. In particular, the US

Treasury has been required, since the passage of the Omnibus Trade and Competitiveness Act of 1988, to report twice a year to the US Congress on whether any countries are manipulating their exchange rates. The implicit analytical framework involved in making such a determination appears to have been based broadly on the IMF's exchange rate surveillance guidelines. In the early 1990s, several Asian economies, including China, were designated as currency manipulators, but no country has been cited for manipulation since the mid-1990s.

During the past three years, however, the Treasury's reports have become increasingly critical of China's exchange rate policies. For example, the May 2005 report (US Treasury 2005) found that China's (economic) policies were highly distortionary and posed a risk to China's economy, its global trading partners, and global economic growth. The report went on to warn that "if current trends continue without substantial alteration, China's policies will likely meet the statute's technical requirements for designation" as a currency manipulator; as suggested earlier, trends in China's exchange rate policies over the next year did in fact "continue without substantial alteration," but Treasury opted not to cite China for manipulation. In the May 2006 report, former US Treasury Secretary Snow admitted that "we are extremely dissatisfied with the slow and disappointing pace of reform of the Chinese exchange rate regime" but argued that he didn't have sufficient evidence to conclude that China was operating its exchange rate system with the intent of either preventing effective balance-of-payments adjustment or gaining an unfair competitive advantage in international trade. In a recent paper (Goldstein 2006c), I have characterized the US Treasury's policy toward China's currency manipulation as "whine, whine, huff and puff, but then decline" to indict.

Probably partly out of frustration with the ineffectiveness of unilateral efforts, the US Treasury has turned back to the IMF, which, however, has not proved very fruitful. In interviews given during 2005, IMF Managing Director Rodrigo de Rato[15] put forth the view that the Fund should not be a "special pressure group" for changes in country policies. The question of how the Fund could exercise firm surveillance over exchange rate policies and induce corrective action—without pressure—in cases where countries have apparently violated the currency manipulation guidelines is not answered.

Over the past year or so and in the resurgent debate about IMF reform, the IMF's passivity and lack of ambition on the exchange rate policy front has finally begun to attract some unprecedented criticism. In September 2005, Tim Adams, undersecretary for international affairs at the US Treasury, lamented that "the perception that the IMF is asleep at the wheel

---

15. See Leslie Wroughton, "Under Fire, IMF's Rato Wants to Get the Job Done," Reuters, July 29, 2005; Daniel Altman, "IMF Chief Draws Fire over Style as Leader," *International Herald Tribune*, July 27, 2005.

on its most fundamental responsibility—exchange rate surveillance—is very unhealthy for the institution and the international monetary system" (Adams 2006, 135). In February 2006 Mervyn King, governor of the Bank of England, warned that the IMF could "slip into obscurity" if its mission was not examined and the institution revitalized; also, in discussing the Fund's role as an "arbiter" of the international monetary system, he expressed the hope that "the players might in time come to realize that most games improve when played according to a clear and agreed set of rules."[16] And in March 2006, Bank of Canada Governor David Dodge argued as follows:

> Let me start with the so-called umpire role. This is one area where the IMF has consistently fallen short of the mark. Too often, surveillance has shied away from the "ruthless truth-telling" that Keynes—one of the main architects of Bretton Woods—called for. Instead of making the tough calls about the rules of the game, the IMF has sat in the umpire's chair and simply asked the players whether they thought that their shot was in or out. This needs to change.[17]

At the Fund-Bank meetings in April 2006, de Rato acknowledged that the Fund should step up its exchange rate surveillance. In addition, it was agreed at those meetings that, in an effort to make greater progress on reducing global payments imbalances, the Fund would initiate a set of "multilateral consultations' with some of the larger players (the United States, the European Union, Japan, China, and Saudi Arabia). Nevertheless, de Rato remained adamant that the Fund should not seek to serve as an "umpire" for the exchange rate system—maintaining that the umpire function would conflict with the Fund's role as a "trusted adviser" to its member countries.[18] I couldn't disagree more.

The facts that emerging economies, particularly those in Asia, have over the past five years been building up international reserves hand over fist and that the Fund's largest debtors have been paying back the Fund ahead of schedule—in part because they want in the future to be less subject to IMF policy conditionality—hardly seems consistent with the claim that the Fund's policy advice is highly "trusted" in all corners. Nor is it apparent

---

16. Mervyn King, Reform of the IMF, Speech to the Indian Council for Research on International Economic Relations, New Delhi, India, February 20, 2006. Not surprisingly, this view is widely shared at the Institute; see C. Fred Bergsten, Reform of the International Monetary Fund, Testimony before the Subcommittee on International Trade and Finance, Committee on Banking, Housing, and Urban Affairs, June 7, 2005 (Washington: US Senate); and Morris Goldstein and Michael Mussa, "The Fund Appears to Be Sleeping at the Wheel," *Financial Times*, October 3, 2005.

17. David Dodge, The Evolving International Monetary Order and the Need for an Evolving IMF, Speech before the Woodrow Wilson School of Public and International Affairs, Princeton University, March 30, 2006.

18. Rodrigo de Rato, A Call for Cooperation: What the IMF and its Members Can Do to Solve Global Economic Problems, Speech at the Institute for International Economics, April 20, 2006.

why the role of "trusted adviser" should conflict with the role of exchange rate umpire unless the Fund were giving countries advice on exchange rate policy that violated its own currency manipulation guidelines.

And to the extent that the two roles do conflict, why is not the umpire role the important one? After all, the IMF's Articles of Agreement do endow the Fund with responsibility for firm surveillance over exchange rate policies but contain no corresponding requirement for the Fund to be a "trusted adviser." Most games have two teams, two coaches, and at least one umpire—not two teams, three coaches, and no umpire. de Rato seems to want the Fund to be another coach, but what is needed is an umpire— a role that only the IMF can play successfully.

As hinted earlier, if the IMF does not carry out the umpire role by exercising firm surveillance over countries' exchange rate policies, two undesirable things may happen. First, national legislatures may increasingly be tempted to make and enforce their own laws on currency manipulation, leading to more politicized analysis of exchange rate policies and possibly to more protectionist trade policies for alleged violators. Second, more and more economies may be tempted to take advantage of the de facto free-for-all on exchange rate policy by pursuing undervalued real exchange rates via large-scale, prolonged, one-way intervention in exchange markets, combined with large-scale sterilization operations. This would be a volatile mix that is unlikely to be compatible with maintaining forward progress on globalization and protecting open markets for trade and investment.

Initiatives for Discouraging Currency Manipulation

If the Fund is to reclaim its mandate to exercise firm surveillance over exchange rate policies, it will need, among other tasks, to get serious about investigating and discouraging currency manipulation. Although the Fund already has the mandate and the tools to do this, its efforts would be more effective if it undertook the following initiatives and actions.

To begin with, the Fund staff should begin issuing a semiannual report on exchange rate policies, both to discuss exchange rate developments of interest and to identify potential cases of currency manipulation. This report would cover both industrial and developing countries (including of course emerging economies), and it would hopefully contain the best objective analysis of exchange rate polices that the Fund can muster. Important input for this report could be obtained from the regular and confidential briefings on exchange rate policies presented quarterly to the Fund's Executive Board by the IMF economic counselor; these briefings (called WEMD sessions) should include, among other elements, the staff's preliminary identification of cases where real exchange rates seem to be seriously misaligned as well as a discussion of country policies that appear to be contributing to misalignment. To give the published Fund report greater authority, the US Treasury should use it as the basis for Treasury's findings on currency manipulation in the US Treasury's biannual *Report to Congress on International Economic and Exchange Rate Policies*. This would stand on its head the recent unsatisfactory practice where the evaluation of potential currency manipulation cases has been contained in the US Treasury report, with only a sentence or two reference as to whether the Fund concurs with Treasury's findings (and without any IMF report on the issue). The rest of the G-7 should also signal their support for the Fund's stepped-up surveillance over exchange rate policies by inviting the Fund to be a full and active participant in discussions of exchange rate policies during G-7 meetings. Over time, a case law would develop that would help define what is and is not internationally acceptable exchange rate policy.

The Fund should revive its special consultation tool by conducting consultations whenever another country or Fund staff has a strong concern about potential currency manipulation. Such special consultations should occur only after it becomes clear to the Fund's managing director—based on initial confidential meetings with the parties involved—that resolution of the issue requires further information and investigation. Since these special consultations are apt to take place infrequently and are likely to focus on a specific set of issues related to exchange rate policy, special consultations will probably most often be separate from both the Fund's normal Article IV consultations and the new "multilateral" consultations. Such special consultations would give the country involved a good opportunity to defend its currency policy and to explain what extenuating circumstances may have been involved in its use of, say, large-scale, prolonged, one-way intervention in exchange markets. The dialogue and information obtained in these special consultations would also serve as an essential input to the section of the Fund's semiannual report on exchange rate policies that deals with currency manipulation. If, after a special consultation, the Fund continues to believe that a member country is not complying with its obligations on exchange rate policy, the Fund can and should, subject to a 70 percent majority in the Executive Board, issue a published report criticizing the country's exchange rate policy. Although it would not likely ever come to that, prolonged noncompliance with the exchange rate policy obligations set forth in the Articles of Agreement could result in a country's expulsion from the Fund.

Finally, the Fund should review its existing guidelines for surveillance over exchange rate policies to determine if any changes are warranted. The existing guidelines are reasonable, but it is certainly possible that they can be improved. Emerging economies should participate fully in this review so that their concerns are reflected, inter alia, in the set of "pointers" used to signal potentially inappropriate exchange rate policies. It is important, however, that this review not serve as a lengthy excuse to avoid investigating current currency manipulation cases; the existing guidelines should be enforced while the review is going on.

References

Adams, Tim. 2006. The IMF: Back to Basics. In *Reforming the IMF for the 21st Century*, ed. Edwin Truman. Washington: Institute for International Economics.

Anderson, Jon. 2005. Grasping at Straws. *Asian Focus* (October 18). Hong Kong: UBS Investment Research.

Bergsten, C. Fred. 1980. Trade and Money: The Need for Parallel Progress. In *The International Economic Policy of the United States: Selected Papers of C. Fred Bergsten, 1977–1979*. Lexington, MA: D. C. Heath and Company.

Cashin, Paul, and C. John McDermott. 2006. Parity Reversion in Real Exchange Rates: Fast, Slow, or Not at All? *IMF Staff Papers* 53, no. 1. Washington: International Monetary Fund.

Cline, William. 2005. *The United States as a Debtor Nation*. Washington: Institute for International Economics.

Dooley, Michael. 2006. Impact of Intervention for Currencies of Large Emerging Economies. Paper presented at the Conference on Monetary Policy and Financial Stability, Central Bank of Argentina, June 5–6, Buenos Aires.

Eichengreen, Barry. 2005. China's Exchange Rate Regime: The Long and Short of It. Unpublished paper. Economics Department, University of California at Berkeley.

Goldstein, Morris. 2004. *Adjusting China's Exchange Rate Policies*. Working Paper 04-1. Washington: Institute for International Economics.

Goldstein, Morris. 2005. The International Financial Architecture. In *The United States and the World Economy: Foreign Economic Policy for the Next Decade*, C. Fred Bergsten and the Institute for International Economics. Washington: Institute for International Economics.

Goldstein, Morris. 2006a. Currency Manipulation and Enforcing the Rules of the International Monetary System. In *Reforming the IMF for the 21st Century*, ed. Edwin Truman. Washington: Institute for International Economics.

Goldstein, Morris. 2006b. Renminbi Controversies. *Cato Journal* 26, no. 2 (Spring/Summer).

Goldstein, Morris. 2006c. Whine, Whine, Huff and Puff, and Then Decline: The US Treasury Department's Approach to Currency Manipulation. *The International Economy* (forthcoming).

Goldstein, Morris, and Nicholas Lardy. 2004. *What Kind of Landing for the Chinese Economy?* Working Paper 04-7. Washington: Institute for International Economics.

Goldstein, Morris, and Nicholas Lardy. 2006. China's Exchange Rate Policy Dilemma. *American Economic Review* (May).

Jurgensen, Philippe. 1993. *Report of the Working Group on Exchange Market Intervention*. Washington: US Treasury Department.

Mann, Catherine, and Katharina Plueck. 2005. *The US Trade Deficit: A Disaggregated Perspective*. Working Paper 05-11. Washington: Institute for International Economics.

Mussa, Michael. 2005. Sustaining Global Growth While Reducing External Imbalances. In *The United States and the World Economy: Foreign Economic Policy for the Next Decade*, ed. C. Fred Bergsten and the Institute for International Economics. Washington: Institute for International Economics.

Nurkse, Ragnar. 1945. Conditions of International Monetary Equilibrium. *Princeton Essays in International Finance* 4. Princeton, NJ: International Finance Section, Princeton University.

Sarno, Lucio, and Mark Taylor. 2001. Official Intervention in the Foreign Exchange Market: Is It Effective and If So, How Does It Work? *Journal of Economic Literature* (September).

Truman, Edwin. 2005. *Postponing Global Adjustment: An Analysis of the Pending Adjustment of Global Imbalances*. Working Paper 05-6. Washington: Institute for International Economics.

US Treasury Department. 2005. *Report to the Congress on International Economic and Exchange Rate Policies* (May). Washington.

Williamson, John. 2005a. *A Currency Basket for East Asia—Not Just China*. International Economics Policy Brief 05-1. Washington: Institute for International Economics.

Williamson, John. 2005b. Revamping the International Monetary System. In *Reforming the IMF for the 21st Century*, ed. Edwin Truman. Washington: Institute for International Economics.

14

Institutional Strategy
for the Global Economy

C. RANDALL HENNING

The scope and function of international economic institutions evolved considerably over the second half of the last century. Formal organizations and less formal cooperative arrangements expanded in size, membership, and complexity as global economic integration progressed. This expansion gave rise to overlapping regimes and tiered governance, with steering groups to guide decision making in the organizations more effectively. Increasing size and complexity created greater distance between international organizations and domestic electorates, accentuated by tiered governance, raising in turn questions about these institutions' democratic accountability and even legitimacy. Thus international economic collaboration, both formal and informal, now faces many more domestic political and democratic-legitimacy challenges than during the half century after World War II.

C. Fred Bergsten is without doubt the most prolific proponent of innovations in formal and informal international economic institutions of his generation. As an analyst, Fred's institutional proposals have covered the substantive waterfront (trade, money, and finance) and multiple levels of governance (multilateral, regional, plurilateral, and domestic). As a practitioner, both in and out of government, he has reinforced existing institu-

C. Randall Henning, visiting fellow, has been associated with the Institute since 1986. He serves on the faculty of the School of International Service, American University. He wishes to acknowledge Fred Bergsten, I. M. Destler, Michael Mussa, Gary Hufbauer, among other Institute colleagues, and Louis Pauly for comments on a previous draft, as well as the excellent research assistance of Alina Milasiute.

tions and built new forums and organizations. A review of Fred's institutional contributions thus provides a useful backdrop for analyzing the accomplishments, shortcomings, and future challenges of institutionalized economic cooperation.

In this chapter, first, I review the highlights of Fred's contributions to institution building in international economic relations. Second, I discuss the essential institutional strategy that underpins most of these proposals, a strategy shared largely by what will be referred to here as the "second generation" of postwar economic internationalists. Third, I explore the limits of that second-generation strategy and the challenges posed by institutional complexity, domestic politics, and the backlash against globalization in the future. Fourth, in light of these limits, I examine the merits of several current proposals to reform the International Monetary Fund (IMF), warning against simply hardening rules. The final section offers suggestions for key elements of a new institutional strategy. Overall, I argue that the institutional strategy of the second generation, with which Fred's work and that of the Institute are closely associated, while outstandingly successful, has reached a point of diminishing returns, suffers from important shortcomings, and should be strengthened by, among other things, a more robust domestic political strategy and by efforts to reinforce democratic accountability.

Fred Bergsten's Contributions

Without covering Fred's contributions to institution building exhaustively—and setting aside his creation of the Institute as a nonprofit rather than a policy institution—consider the salient themes of his scholarship.

First, in his writing and as a policymaker, Fred has been consistently supportive of the multilateral institutions: the IMF, the World Bank, the General Agreement on Tariffs and Trade (GATT), and the Organization for Economic Cooperation and Development, among others. After resigning from the Nixon administration, he published his first *Foreign Affairs* article in January 1972 sharply criticizing the international component of the president's New Economic Policy. Fred lamented the marginalization of the IMF by the suspension of gold convertibility the previous August and called for strengthening the IMF's rules on exchange rates and surveillance and placing the special drawing right (SDR) at the center of the international monetary system—themes he reiterated in his 1975 book, *The Dilemmas of the Dollar*. He has revisited the subject of the IMF frequently in subsequent publications and most recently, in 2000, as a dissenting member of the International Financial Institutions Advisory Commission. Proposals that would similarly strengthen the other multilaterals surface and resurface throughout his published work.

Second, Fred has supported many, although by no means all, regional arrangements. He has been consistently supportive of European integration, including its Common Market, Single Market, and Economic and Monetary Union. He was of course similarly supportive of the North American Free Trade Agreement (NAFTA), the Free Trade Area of the Americas (FTAA), and multiple bilateral and subregional trade agreements. (By contrast, he opposes the North Atlantic Free Trade Agreement proposal.) His greatest contribution to regionalism has been in the Asia-Pacific, where he promoted the Asia Pacific Economic Cooperation (APEC) forum, created and chaired its Eminent Persons Group (EPG), and was instrumental in launching its first summit meeting (held in Bogor, Indonesia, in November 1994) and defining the goals endorsed there. Regionalism has of course been controversial among trade economists, many of whom argue that such agreements undercut the multilateral trade regime. Fred sought to reconcile regional arrangements with multilateralism by developing a particular concept of open regionalism, embodied in the EPG reports (Bergsten 1997, APEC 1993, 1994, 1995). He also encouraged "competitive liberalization" among open regional arrangements, the subject of his *Foreign Affairs* article of 1996.

Third, Fred has been an enthusiastic advocate of informal official plurilateral groups and forums. The patchwork of multilateral and regional institutions needed effective leadership, which could be provided through "steering committees" of various configurations—the "Group System." First as assistant secretary for international affairs at the Treasury, then as director of the Institute, Fred has consistently pushed the G-7 and G-8 summit process to achieve ambitious results (see, for example, Bergsten et al. 1982). He has done so most recently as cochair of the "Shadow G-8."

He promoted the G-5 and then G-7 meetings of finance ministers and central bank governors, including in a book he and I coauthored, *Global Economic Leadership and the Group of Seven* (Bergsten and Henning 1996). In his contribution to the Institute's volume on IMF reform, however, Fred gives up on the Finance G-7: "The time has come to recognize that the G-7 will remain ineffective . . . and replace it with a new steering committee that can infuse . . . new vision and leadership into the world economy. . ." (Bergsten 2005, 284). The new steering committee that he proposes would be composed of sixteen finance ministers, an "F-16."[1]

Finally, Fred has been a prolific—some colleagues would say "notorious"—proponent of "G-2s" in varying configurations. The first instance that I recall of such a proposal in Fred's work was for a US-Germany group in 1975. At least two proposals for a US-Japan group followed in

---

1. The 16 would represent Argentina, Australia, Brazil, Canada, China, the European Union (presumably the chairman of Ecofin or the Eurogroup), India, Indonesia, Japan, Korea, Mexico, Russia, Saudi Arabia, South Africa, Turkey, and the United States. He does not specifically call for inclusion of central bank governors in this group.

the 1980s and 1990s. He advocated another US-EU G-2 in his *Foreign Affairs* article of 2004 (Bergsten 2004). In his overview chapter for *The United States and the World Economy: Foreign Economic Policy for the Next Decade,* Fred outdoes himself by advocating no fewer than four G-2s, adding US-China and US–Saudi Arabia to the mix (Bergsten 2005). All configurations include the United States—although he invites others to collude benevolently against the United States when he believes that his own government is inappropriately obstinate—with each configuration designed to prod a recalcitrant third party into constructive action.

In offering multiple proposals for institution building, Fred has been undaunted by criticism that some proposals, such as those for the G-2s and regional trade agreements, contradict others, such as those to strengthen the Finance G-7 and the multilateral institutions. Fred's institutional philosophy is based on an underlying premise: that cooperation between national governments in international economic relations, a public good, is chronically undersupplied. Under these circumstances, the best institutional arrangement should not be the enemy of improvements in second-best cooperative and consultative forums. The main problem is not that an institutional "spaghetti bowl" will result from the creation of too many forums—he reasons that these complications can be sorted out by steering committees when they become binding—but the failure to use enough of them.

Before critiquing the broad strategy, I would like to highlight four additional elements of Fred's contributions with respect to institutions. First, when making institutional recommendations that would advance his economic policy objectives, Fred draws on academic work in both economics and political science with pragmatic eclecticism. Second, Fred has not shied away from advocating the use of coercive instruments when that has been necessary to defend international economic openness (elaborated below). Third, Fred takes domestic politics seriously: Rather than dismissing the US Congress as economically unsophisticated, as some analysts do, he acknowledges its responsibilities for international economic policy in the American political system. Where Congress's role complicates policymaking, Fred has sought to inform and include members rather than insulate policy from congressional purview. Fourth, Fred has long been sensitive to the importance of legitimacy in institutions and the policy process, particularly at the international level, and has sought to embed the group system in a broader political context.

Second-Generation Strategy

Fred is one of the second generation of postwar international economic policy leaders. The first postwar generation attended the Bretton Woods and Havana/ITO conferences as young aides and assisted their principals in creating the IMF and World Bank and launching the GATT. The second postwar generation inherited these institutions, brought them into their own—with the switch to convertibility in Europe and the launch of the first successful large-scale round of trade negotiations in the 1960s, the Kennedy Round—and creatively adapted them in the face of new challenges. The creation of steering groups in these organizations and outside them (the "Group System") was one of this generation's important innovations. North America, Europe, and Japan, among other regions, each contributed prominent people to this generation of economic internationalists, meeting sometimes, but by no means always, as the Trilateral Commission.

The second generation shared concepts of how institutions and international consultations among governments work to produce liberalization and cooperation. Not all of the members of this generation subscribed to a common strategy, of course, but they shared many core elements of it. This core strategy overlapped with those of academic institutionalists in political science—to which we return below—but were pragmatic and operational.

First, the second-generation internationalists were united in the belief that cross-border trade and investment were fundamentally beneficial to countries individually and the world economy as a whole, and they recognized a need for information, analysis, and rules regarding acceptable and unacceptable national policies to underpin a liberal economic order. The first-best option, in their view, was to vest those functions and rules in multilateral institutions.

Second, however, they remained acutely conscious that domestic politics, in the United States and elsewhere, often limited what could be achieved. So a tension between the desirability of robust international regimes and domestic politics was perceived to permeate international economic relations almost perpetually. Internationalists steered clear of some, though not all, domestic political obstacles for much of the second half of the twentieth century by negotiating liberalization through issue area–specific groups of national officials (often confidentially) and presenting only the final result for domestic ratification.[2]

Third, international commitments constrained backsliding, and international consultation could prepare the ground for more binding commitments when domestic politics were favorable. International collaboration works opportunistically in the spaces between domestic politics of key states to ratchet up members' obligations over time. Regimes can thus be strengthened by locking in existing commitments, facilitating further liberalization, and generally supporting openness.

The conception of how international regimes and organizations bring policy change—that is, how institutions cause member states to pursue

2. See Keohane and Nye (2001), who refer to this pattern as the "Club Model" of international cooperation.

policies that are different than they would otherwise pursue—is critical to this approach. The channels are several: information, moral suasion, threats to revoke reciprocal concessions, issue linkage, and scapegoating, among others. Meanwhile, domestic politics is conceived as divided between those favoring an internationally consistent policy and those favoring domestic determined, internationally inconsistent policies. Working through such channels, institutions can augment the coalition in favor of the internationally consistent option, tipping the balance of domestic politics on the issue (see, for example, Putnam and Henning 1989). The influence of institutions and domestic politics on international cooperation is the focus of a very large academic literature.[3]

Scapegoating became a particularly important element of the strategy: By taking the lead on enforcing a commitment to liberalization, the WTO and IMF were used by national governments in the domestic political arena as the excuse for pursuing policies that officials wished to pursue independent of international constraints. Examples of scapegoating, which are legion, include leaders of crisis-stricken emerging-market economies blaming the IMF for having to reduce government spending or raise taxes and finance ministers blaming the World Trade Organization (WTO) for having to deny domestic petitions from uncompetitive industries for protection. In Europe, they include blaming the European Commission for having to eliminate state subsidies to national champions and allowing unpopular cross-border acquisitions to proceed. In this way, governments and prime ministers often reduced their domestic political costs of compliance with international regimes. International civil servants within these organizations usually accepted their service in this scapegoating role in the belief that the damage to their institution was minor or an acceptable sacrifice for better national policies—a belief that requires reconsideration.

Second-generation economic internationalists borrowed from, and contributed to, the work on international economic cooperation by scholars in political science and economics. But the second-generation agenda was primarily applied rather than academic, leaving the overlap between the two bodies of work, while substantial, still partial. Some of the key differences between practitioners' strategy, on the one hand, and two schools of international political economy on the other—neoliberal institutionalism and neorealism—are worth highlighting.

Neoliberal institutionalists argue that states create international institutions in order to overcome dilemmas of collective action. In the classic formulation, Keohane (1984) argued that under conditions of high transaction costs and uncertainty, institutions could help states overcome market failure in efforts to reach international agreements, such as that modeled by the prisoner's dilemma game. "Chiefly by providing information to

---

3. A few of the highlights include Krasner (1983), Keohane (1984), Ruggie (1993), and Keohane and Milner (1996).

actors (not by enforcing rules in a centralized manner), institutions could enable states to achieve their own objectives more efficiently. Institutions would alter state strategies by changing the costs of alternatives; institutionalization could thus promote cooperation" (Katzenstein, Keohane, and Krasner 1998, 662). Institutions affect outcomes by (a) providing information, (b) monitoring compliance, (c) increasing iterations, (d) facilitating issue linkages, (e) defining cheating, and (f) offering salient solutions. When the coordination problem among member states has multiple equilibria, institutions can provide mechanisms for solving distributional conflict (such as side payments in the form of EU cohesion funds for accession to the Maastricht Treaty), signaling salient solutions, and reducing bargaining costs. Once a particular equilibrium solution is chosen, institutions tend to lock it in (Katzenstein, Keohane, and Krasner 1998). This logic applies similarly at the regional and multilateral levels.

A key argument advanced by this approach is that international institutions should not be understood as coercive enforcers of hard rules against the will of member states. Instead, international and regional institutions are the instruments of states in their pursuit of mutually advantageous cooperation and integration. To conceive of institutions as hard constraints on national governments rather than their tools is to begin the analysis on the wrong foot.

Second-generation internationalists in the policy realm, by contrast, have often had an ambivalent attitude toward hard rules: Most members thought such rules were desirable in principle but recognized that they were usually out of reach in practice. The exceptions, cases where rules were in fact hardened, have occurred primarily in two particular situations. The first is where cross-issue bargains were particularly dense and the costs of reneging to reputation correspondingly high, such as in Europe—although the fate of the Stability and Growth Pact demonstrates that the experience with hard rules is mixed even there. The second situation is where enforcement had the benefit of national instruments, as in the case of authorized retaliation in the WTO.

Second-generation internationalists also rested their institutional strategy on national power, the province of neorealism.[4] The coercive resources of the United States were particularly important in reinforcing the norms and rules of international institutions and economic regimes more broadly. Fred's work provides several examples of advocacy of coercion

---

4. Neorealism's analysis of international institutions emphasizes their subordination to the interests of powerful states. When hegemons create strong international institutions, in this interpretation they do so to support and defend a liberal international economic order from which they benefit. The distribution of power in the international system is thus critical to creating and sustaining both international institutions and market liberalism. A corollary, the hegemonic stability thesis, posits that liberal international economic orders cannot survive decline of the hegemon and rise of multipolarity. For a classic treatment, see Gilpin (1987).

in defense of international economic regimes, sustaining criticism from some economists in doing so. He has advocated threats of trade measures to pry open foreign markets when that has been important to sustaining domestic political support in the United States for liberal trade. Fred has also advocated depreciation of the dollar as a tool to induce foreign governments to stimulate domestic demand when that has been needed to achieve balance of payments adjustment and avoid protectionist legislation in the United States.[5] Second-generation internationalists part company with many neorealists in intending to bind the United States to the same rules and norms as the rest of the global community.

Assessment of the Strategy

By almost all relevant measures, the second generation's strategy was dramatically successful in spawning liberalization of international trade and investment. The completion of the Uruguay Round of trade negotiations (to which regional initiatives such as NAFTA and APEC contributed), establishment of the WTO and its Dispute Settlement Understanding (DSU), follow-up multilateral/plurilateral agreements such as the International Telecommunications Agreement, and expansion of the membership of the European Union represent its most recent major successes.

The strategy's record in actually *managing* the macroeconomic and financial conditions of the integrated world economy was mixed. By and large, the global macroeconomic environment has been favorable for growth and economic expansion. When growth slowed or payments imbalances became unsustainable, the G-7 countries sometimes scored successes in international coordination, such as the Bonn summit of 1978 and the Plaza-Louvre process of 1985–87. But on many occasions—managing the transition economies, the 1992–93 European currency crises, and the Asian financial crisis of 1997–98—international coordination fell short (see Bergsten and Henning 1996 and Aslund 1995).

By the mid-1990s, sectors, firms, and social movements that had suffered as a result of globalization mobilized a "backlash." Whereas the internationalists had been better organized across countries, the backlash coalition—groups knitted together across borders through internationally active nongovernmental organizations[6]—was now also able to organize with some effectiveness. The backlash movement mounted a broad, substantive challenge to the globalization agenda and the international organizations—extending beyond the problems of economic dislocation aris-

---

5. I refer to this instrument as the "exchange rate weapon" (Henning 2006).

6. The coalition that formed in the early 1990s to oppose the IMF and World Bank, "Fifty Years Is Enough," was an early prominent example.

ing from liberalization, and even beyond the labor and environmental issues linked to trade, to encompass regulation of national economies generally, democratic control, and sovereignty.

The first response of many members of the second generation of internationalists was to dismiss the backlash movement as naïve in terms of both international economics and the multilateral institutions. Some took false comfort in the diversity of political groups involved and in the decentralized character of the movement. While a number of economists have seriously analyzed backlash arguments,[7] including in publications by the Institute, it is fair to say that international economists in general have had greater difficulty than some other disciplines, such as sociology and political science, in wrapping their minds around this movement. During the previous decades, these economists had won intellectual and political fights against traditional, firm- and union-led, sector-based protectionism and had steeled themselves for more of the same. Some of them were thus blindsided by criticism from social movements in developing countries, which most economists believed would benefit greatly from globalization on the whole, and criticism on the basis of democratic accountability, sovereignty, and legitimate governance in advanced countries. By addressing these arguments largely after they had entered the public discourse, the second-generation internationalists, including Fred Bergsten, missed an opportunity to influence the terms of the debate over globalization.

As of this writing, the future of the global multilateral agenda appears quite uncertain. Notwithstanding some successes—such as reasonably broad acceptance of the WTO's dispute rulings (including in the United States)[8] and rejections by Congress of proposals to withdraw from that organization—failures are accumulating and challenges dominate the landscape. The progress of European integration was slowed dramatically by rejection of the Constitutional Treaty by referenda in France and the Netherlands in spring 2005. The Doha Round of trade negotiations collapsed in July 2006, with at best dubious prospects for revival.

The IMF faces a critical test: Its members must agree on reform of its governance, surveillance, and financial facilities to secure the organization's relevance in the coming decades (Truman 2006). Asian countries' ac-

---

7. See, for example, Baldwin and Winters (2004); Elliott, Kar, and Richardson (2004); Rodrik (1997); Stiglitz (2002); Barfield (2001); and Graham (2000). The classic treatment of the political backlash against the first wave of globalization is Polanyi (1957 [1944]). For contemporary treatments by noneconomists, see Mittelman (2000), Kahler and Lake (2003), and Broad (2002).

8. The case of the WTO inspired extensive work on "legalization" of international relations. See, among others, Goldstein et al. (2000). One current of the literature highlights the danger of overlegalizing international economic regimes, undermining institutions politically by moving from a "negotiation model," where decisions are made politically, to a "judicial model," where decisions are restricted to the legal and technical merits. See Howse and Nicolaidis (2001), Keohane and Nye (2001), and Alter (2003).

cumulation of foreign exchange reserves raises the specter of the Fund being sidelined in that region and places a premium on increasing Asian countries' quota shares and votes on the Fund's Executive Board and Board of Governors. The Board of Governors took a significant step in this direction during the 2006 annual meetings in Singapore by enlarging the quotas of four particularly underrepresented members. But the Singapore decisions only launched consideration of broader reallocation of quotas, on which obtaining consensus will be politically difficult, and these in turn represent only part of the reform agenda. Whether the membership can agree on the institutional changes needed to save the Fund from gradual erosion of standing and relevance remains very much an open question.

Softness and unpredictability of political support for trade liberalization and international institutions in the United States, among other countries, compound the difficulties facing internationalists. Congress has not offered robust support for trade promotion authority (TPA) since the Uruguay Round. President Bill Clinton did not secure such authority, and President George W. Bush secured it only in a razor-thin vote. Congressional approval of the Central American Free Trade Agreement (CAFTA) passed by a similarly narrow margin (Destler 2005). Congressional support for extension of TPA in a hypothetical effort to breathe extended life into the Doha negotiations seems unlikely.

Congressional support for the IMF has become similarly problematic. Congress agreed to the last quota increase, in 1998, only as the Asian financial crisis spread to Russia and Latin America and in the face of the collapse of the Long-Term Capital Management hedge fund and a flight to liquidity in financial markets. Softness of support on Capitol Hill will probably weigh significantly on any Treasury decision to seek a quota increase and could constrain the administration in current negotiations with other member countries over IMF reform.[9] The dubious congressional support, which stands in sharp contrast to the strong position of the United States within the institution and Fund policies that closely match US preferences, means that second-generation internationalists cannot count on being able to construct congressional coalitions in support of their agenda as they once did.

If pessimism for the globalization agenda proves to be justified, the period 2005–07 could well mark the end of the road for business as usual under the second-generation institutional strategy. Most of the generation's achievements are reasonably secure: Widespread closure of markets does not appear to be in the cards. International trade and investment will probably continue to expand relative to world output, as it has done for most of the last half century, for some time to come. Regional trade and economic arrangements will probably also continue to proliferate. How-

---

9. On congressional influence over the IMF, see Woods (2006, 27–33). For analysis of congressional voting on the Fund, see Broz and Hawes (2006) and Broz (2005).

ever, the efforts of second-generation internationalists to further develop multilateral institutions, strengthen international disciplines over national economic policies, and delegate monitoring and enforcement to these institutions could be decidedly more difficult, if not stymied.

Shortcomings of the Second-Generation Strategy

In the present environment, the standard strategy suffers from three gaps or problems that limit its effectiveness and are likely to persist. First, international organizations suffer from weak links to domestic politics. Support from domestic groups, constituencies, and bureaucracies were arguably the key to the political success of the European Union over the decades (see, for example, Kahler 1995). Most international organizations lack the kind of domestic political support from member states that the European Union commands with its members (notwithstanding the failure of the Constitutional Treaty). Moreover, the IMF and WTO, for example, have been constrained in cultivating such support by national ministries or executive agencies that insist on intermediating that relationship.

A second key weakness revolves around democratic responsiveness and accountability.[10] International organizations were constructed on the normative theory that they are responsible to their members, which are governments of member states for the most part. Their legitimacy should therefore be viewed as derived in principle from the legitimacy of their member governments; although indirect, the chain of delegation from electorates to governments to international organizations is formally unbroken. Defenders of the WTO, World Bank, and IMF argue, moreover, that markets, press and public discourse, budgeting conventions, and civil society, among other channels, can serve as alternative mechanisms of accountability for these institutions.[11]

This defense is incomplete, however, for several reasons. Not all the member governments of these institutions are democratically elected. But, even where it has a democratic source, the chain of delegation from electorate to international organization is attenuated, and slippage between the preferences of the principal and the actions of the agent is compounded at each stage. In addition, as the scope of international organizations widens and their intrusiveness into domestic policy deepens, domestic groups that prevail in national politics more often see their victory compromised or overturned by decisions at the international level. But decision making at the international level is often opaque, not sanc-

---

10. Political scientists' analysis of this problem includes Keohane and Nye (2001), Kahler and Lake (2003), and Caporaso (2003).

11. See, for example, Keohane and Nye (2003) and Grant and Keohane (2005); for similar arguments applied to the European Union, see Moravcsik (2002).

tionable for mistakes, and out of reach of these groups' political influence. In this way, political scientist Robert Dahl (1999) has argued, the degree to which the system as a whole is democratic declines.

Third, and finally, the scapegoating technique has probably reached the limits of effectiveness in smoothing the way for internationally consistent policy adjustment. When national political leaders blame international organizations for actions they must take domestically, disaffected interest groups do not simply throw up their hands and walk out of the political arena: They retarget their opposition to the organization used as the pretext for denying their demands. Thus when bills to fund the World Bank and IMF come before the US Congress, for example, members hear ample testimony from interest groups and NGOs in opposition. As this pattern is repeated over decades, scapegoating contributes to erosion of domestic political support for international organizations and a decline in their perceived democratic legitimacy. Because political support for these organizations is now tenuous in many key countries, scapegoating has become at best risky and at worst completely counterproductive.

Rule Hardening Requires Political Reinforcement

Given these shortcomings, second-generation internationalists must exercise caution when addressing the challenges facing international organizations and when building new institutions. In particular, hardening rules without also strengthening domestic political support and accountability mechanisms runs the risk of reinforcing the backlash against the international organizations that oversee international economic regimes.

Recent proposals to strengthen the IMF offer a set of examples that, in my view, run this risk. The managing director has launched "multilateral consultations" among the United States, euro area, Japan, China, and Saudi Arabia on current account adjustment.[12] John Williamson proposes world reference rates, established by the Executive Board on the basis of analysis by the Fund staff, that would guide not only intervention policy but also adjustments in other external policies (such as international borrowing) and macroeconomic policy (Williamson 2006). Bank of England Governor Mervyn King advocates a nonresident Executive Board and independence for the staff in fulfilling a mandate established by the Board.[13]

---

12. As authorized by the International Monetary and Financial Committee; see IMF (2006).

13. Mervyn King, Reform of the International Monetary Fund, Speech delivered to the Indian Council for Research on International Economic Relations (ICRIER), New Delhi, India, February 20, 2006. See also David Dodge, Lecture at the Woodrow Wilson School of Public and International Affairs, Princeton, NJ, March 30, 2006; and Tiff Macklem, Renewing the IMF: Some Lessons from Modern Central Banking, Speech delivered at the Global Interdependence Center, Philadelphia, March 9, 2006.

Morris Goldstein laments the lack of enforcement of the IMF exchange rate rules, in the case of Chinese foreign exchange intervention, and urges the Fund to act more forcefully as "umpire" by citing violators in semi-annual exchange rate reports and by convening special consultations (Goldstein 2004, 2005, 2006). Bill Cline proposes that the Fund determine whether members "manipulate" their exchange rates and that the WTO take the determination into consideration in trade cases (Cline 2005, 279–80). In testimony before Congress, Fred Bergsten has argued that the Fund has "violated" its mandate with respect to exchange rates, and he has pressed it to take a similarly assertive role.[14] Going a significant step further, he advocates that the US government adopt an escalating series of measures—including ultimately across-the-board tariffs on Chinese imports if necessary—to persuade the Chinese government to revalue.[15]

Although none of these authors propose the establishment of multilateral sanctions for violations, each of their proposals would harden existing rules substantially and constrain national policy more tightly. Consider Goldstein's proposal to stiffen the spine of the IMF with respect to exchange rate rules. I single this out not because I disagree with its economic merits; rather, because Morris's economic case is compelling and his proposal is clearly specified, his recommendation presents the most useful illustration of the incompleteness of this class of proposals. His position has the second benefit, for the purpose of this Festschrift, of being shared by Fred. Goldstein describes his proposal as "modest." During the authors' workshop for this Festschrift, Michael Mussa adds that no new amendment to the Articles of Agreement would need to be approved to implement the Goldstein proposal. Instead, the managing director must simply apply a literal interpretation of the plain language of the Second Amendment to the articles, the 1977 Executive Board decision implementing it, and the more recent reviews of that decision.

But make no mistake about it: Literal interpretation of the plain language of Article IV would be a *radical* departure from the interpretation and application of the Fund's guidelines with respect to surveillance of exchange rates since the introduction of the Second Amendment. In its interpretation of these guidelines, the General Counsel of the Fund highlighted *intent* to prevent balance of payments adjustment and gave considerable weight to members' declaration of their own intent (IMF 1977). This interpretation vitiated any effort to cite a member for manipulation,

---

14. C. Fred Bergsten, The IMF and Exchange Rates, Testimony to the Committee on Banking, Housing, and Urban Affairs, May 19, 2004 (Washington: US Senate); and Reform of the International Monetary Fund, Testimony before the Subcommittee on International Trade and Finance, Committee on Banking, Housing, and Urban Affairs, June 7, 2005 (Washington: US Senate).

15. C. Fred Bergsten, The US Trade Deficit and China, Testimony before the Finance Committee, March 29, 2006 (Washington: US Senate).

because any member could be expected to disavow intent to block adjustment even when that might be the consequence of government policy. Rejecting a member's declaration of intent as unpersuasive, thereby paving the way for formally citing the member for manipulation, would impose a new, far less deferential rule. Goldstein's review of the history of (non)enforcement of the exchange rate provisions makes it quite clear that the literal interpretation he proposes would be unprecedented.

Proposals such as this to harden soft rules reason implicitly by analogy to domestic law: They seek to create among member states something approaching the international equivalent of legal constraints on firms and individuals in the national context. Domestic legal systems, however, have the benefit of a domestic political system, court jurisdiction, enforcement capability, and mechanisms to convey legitimacy on the enforcement apparatus. Hard law and domestic politics work together as two pillars in a democratic system. Raising one without also raising the other at the international level could destabilize the structure and threaten its collapse. While solving a substantive problem, tightening the rules would compound the problem of sovereign control by member states and raise challenges to the international legitimacy of the institution.[16]

From the standpoint of institutional strategy, in my assessment this class of proposals to strengthen the IMF is incomplete, and dangerously so. They would create or strengthen rules without also giving the institution the political resources or instruments to follow through, enforce them, and protect itself against backlash from the target. If adopted alone, these recommendations run the risk of leaving the organization worse off rather than better off—more susceptible to domestic political opposition and charges of unaccountability and illegitimacy. Hardening rules without also reinforcing the institution politically would be a mistake; each such proposal should be accompanied by corresponding measures for political reinforcement.

Citing countries for violating exchange rate rules by frustrating adjustment, irrespective of the economic merits of doing so, would probably place the IMF at the center of a political maelstrom. Revaluation of the Chinese renminbi, which among other adjustments the Goldstein proposal is designed to produce, will benefit some groups and harm others, both in China and among its trading and investment partners. There is little reason to believe that national governments will be responsible and avoid using the Fund as a scapegoat. Crucially, there is little reason to believe that the Fund's supporters will outnumber the Fund's opponents. Under these circumstances, it would be completely reasonable for the managing

---

16. The Fund's political problem with respect to legitimacy was highlighted in Pauly (1997) and is also addressed by Lombardi and Woods (2005), Woods (2006), and Best (2006).

director to insist on credible commitments of enduring support from key members as a condition for applying the rules as Goldstein proposes.

Proponents of hardening the IMF's exchange rate rules point to the success in reinforcing WTO dispute settlement under the DSU and the acceptance of some key rulings by countries such as the United States. However, the WTO has several advantages over the IMF with respect to rule enforcement. First, members have negotiated periodic rounds of multilateral trade liberalization and ratified them in detail through the domestic political process, giving them multiple opportunities to review and reaffirm their consent to new and existing rules. Members' periodic approval of quota increases for the IMF does not constitute a similar domestic political review and ratification of their obligations in the Fund. Second, the economic stakes in each trade case are small on a macroeconomic scale, affecting particular sectors rather than the economy as a whole. The economic stakes of exchange rate and balance of payments rules are far larger. Third, the prospect of retaliation by national governments substantially reinforces compliance with dispute rulings. Such retaliation, "compensation" for losses arising from violations of trade agreements, is authorized by the WTO.[17] No similar national instrument reinforces IMF decisions. Unilateral action by the United States, prompted by discontent in Congress with respect to the Chinese exchange rate regime, for example, would take place outside the ambit of the Articles of Agreement and could perhaps violate other international agreements, such as the GATT/WTO. These differences render the transfer of the WTO/DSU model of rule enforcement to the IMF deeply problematic.

Conclusion

The second-generation institutional strategy, to which Fred has made leading contributions, was highly successful in sustaining and building international economic cooperation during the last three decades of the 20th century. But now the strategy is increasingly incomplete in the face of changing political conditions and, in unaltered form, faces the prospect of diminishing returns. Some of the elements of the standard strategy, such as the core functions of institutions, are worth keeping; some, such as scapegoating, should be summarily jettisoned.[18] But the general strategy must be fundamentally modified, if not replaced. Although this chapter does not offer a full replacement, it has diagnosed the directions in which

---

17. The DSU is examined in detail in Barfield (2001), Lawrence (2003), McRae (2004), and Leitner and Lester (2006).

18. A recommendation rather than a prediction.

the strategy should be developed and offers some more specific measures that I believe have promise.

When strengthening international rules and enforcement,[19] it is vital to strengthen the international organizations themselves by addressing their problems of legitimacy and accountability, by giving them links to and constituencies in domestic politics, and by developing alternative, international mechanisms of accountability. Several angles are worth pursuing and here again I use the IMF as the organizational example.

First, we must consider how key members can credibly commit their enduring support. Second, international organizations can be given deeper roots in domestic politics among groups with convergent interests. Political support for the IMF is too important to be mediated by midlevel officials in national treasuries. The managing director of the Fund should be able to testify before the US Congress, for example, or telephone the US president. The managing director should also meet with and listen to domestic interest groups and NGOs that wish to lobby the Fund on a variety of issues, including the exchange rate. Article IV missions should engage a wide variety of domestic actors at the initiative and discretion of the Fund staff.

Third, the Fund should develop deeper relationships to financial markets, which serve both as a channel for accountability and as a political constituency. Although the Fund has consulted with private financial institutions for some time on an informal basis, Fund officials should meet directly with banks, Wall Street firms, and firms based in other financial centers, for example, in the course of surveillance exercises. Finally, greater investment should be made in good old-fashioned grass-roots political activism for the Fund within member countries, of the kind that generated support for the original Bretton Woods Act in the United States. The essential point is that international institutions must be strengthened in these ways *before* they are burdened with further important responsibilities.

References

Alter, Karen J. 2003. Resolving or Exacerbating Disputes? The WTO's New Dispute Resolution System. *International Affairs* 79, no. 4: 783–800.

APEC (Asia Pacific Economic Cooperation forum). 1993. *A Vision for APEC: Towards an Asia Pacific Economic Community*. First Report of the Eminent Persons Group to APEC Ministers. Singapore: APEC Secretariat (October).

APEC (Asia Pacific Economic Cooperation forum). 1994. *Achieving the APEC Vision: Free and Open Trade in the Asia Pacific*. Second Report of the Eminent Persons Group to APEC Ministers. Singapore: APEC Secretariat (August).

---

19. An alternative is to accept that international rules and institutions, while useful, are inherently limited and instead develop domestic institutions and policymaking processes to facilitate internationally consistent policy adjustment.

APEC (Asia Pacific Economic Cooperation forum). 1995. *Implementing the APEC Vision.* Third Report of the Eminent Persons Group to APEC Ministers. Singapore: APEC Secretariat (August).

Aslund, Anders. 1995. *How Russia Became a Market Economy.* Washington: Brookings Institution.

Baldwin, Robert E., and L. Alan Winters, eds. 2004. *Challenges to Globalization: Analyzing the Economics.* Chicago, IL: University of Chicago Press.

Barfield, Claude E. 2001. *Free Trade, Sovereignty, Democracy: The Future of the World Trade Organization.* Washington: American Enterprise Institute Press.

Bergsten, C. Fred. 1996. Globalizing Free Trade. *Foreign Affairs* (May/June): 105–20.

Bergsten, C. Fred. 1997. *Open Regionalism.* Working Paper 97-3. Washington: Institute for International Economics.

Bergsten, C. Fred. 2004. Foreign Economic Policy for the Next President. *Foreign Affairs,* (March/April): 88–101.

Bergsten, C. Fred. 2005. A New Foreign Economic Policy for the United States. In *The United States and the World Economy: Foreign Economic Policy for the Next Decade,* ed. C. Fred Bergsten and the Institute for International Economics. Washington: Institute for International Economics.

Bergsten, C. Fred et al. 1982. *From Rambouillet to Versailles: A Symposium.* Essays in International Finance, no. 149: 1–7. Princeton, NJ: Princeton University.

Bergsten, C. Fred, and C. Randall Henning. 1996. *Global Economic Leadership and the Group of Seven.* Washington: Institute for International Economics.

Bergsten, C. Fred, and Marcus Noland. 1993. *Reconcilable Differences? United States–Japan Economic Conflict.* Washington: Institute for International Economics.

Best, Jacqueline. 2006. The Dilemmas of Political Economic Legitimacy: Recent IMF Reforms in Critical Perspective. Paper presented at the Centre for International Governance and Innovation workshop on The Reform of Global Financial Governance: Whither the IMF? Ottawa, Canada, June 10.

Broad, Robin, ed. 2002. *Global Backlash: Citizen Initiatives for a Just World Economy.* Lanham, MD: Rowman & Littlefield Publishers.

Broz, Lawrence J. 2005. Congressional Politics of International Financial Rescues. *American Journal of Political Science* 49, no. 3: 479–96.

Broz, Lawrence J., and Michael Hawes. 2006. Congressional Politics of Financing the International Monetary Fund. *International Organization* 60, no. 1: 367–99.

Caporaso, James A. 2003. Democracy, Accountability, and Rights in Supranational Governance. In *Governance in a Global Economy,* ed. Miles Kahler and David A. Lake. Princeton: Princeton University Press.

Cline, William R. 2005. *The United States as a Debtor Nation.* Washington: Institute for International Economics and Center for Global Development.

Dahl, Robert. 1999. Can International Organizations Be Democratic? A Skeptic's View. In *Democracy's Edges,* ed. Ian Shapiro and Casiano Hacker-Cordón. Cambridge, UK: Cambridge University Press.

Destler, I. M. 2005. *American Trade Politics,* 4th ed. Washington: Institute for International Economics.

Destler, I. M., and C. Randall Henning. 1989. *Dollar Politics: Exchange Rate Policymaking in the United States.* Washington: Institute for International Economics.

Elliott, Kimberly A., Debayani Kar, and J. David Richardson. 2004. Assessing Globalization's Critics: 'Talkers are No Good Doers?' In *Challenges to Globalization: Analyzing the Economics,* ed. Robert E. Baldwin and Alan Winters. Chicago, IL: University of Chicago Press.

Gilpin, Robert. 1987. *The Political Economy of International Relations.* Princeton: Princeton University Press.

Goldstein, Morris. 2004. *Adjusting China's Exchange Rate Policies.* Working Paper 04-1. Washington: Institute for International Economics.

Goldstein, Morris. 2005. Renminbi Controversies. Paper prepared for the Conference on Monetary Institutions and Economic Development, November 3. Washington: Cato Institute.

Goldstein, Morris. 2006. Currency Manipulation and Enforcing the Rules of the International Monetary System. In *Reforming the IMF for the 21st Century*, ed. Edwin M. Truman. Washington: Institute for International Economics.

Goldstein, Judith, Miles Kahler, Robert O. Keohane, and Anne-Marie Slaughter. 2000. Introduction: Legalization and World Politics. *International Organization* 54, no. 3: 385–99.

Graham, Edward M. 2000. *Fighting the Wrong Enemy: Antiglobal Activists and Multinational Enterprises*. Washington: Institute for International Economics.

Grant, Ruth W., and Robert O. Keohane. 2005. Accountability and Abuses of Power in World Politics. *American Political Science Review* 99 (February), no. 1: 29–44.

Held, David. 1995. *Democracy and the Global Order: From the Modern State to Cosmopolitan Governance*. Cambridge, UK: Polity Press.

Henning, C. Randall. 1994. *Currencies and Politics in the United States, Germany, and Japan.* Washington: Institute for International Economics.

Henning, C. Randall. 2006. The Exchange Rate Weapon and Macroeconomic Conflict. In *International Monetary Power*, ed. David M. Andrews. Ithaca, NY: Cornell University Press.

Howse, Robert, and Kalypso Nicolaidis. 2001. Legitimacy and Global Governance: Why Constitutionalizing the WTO Is a Step Too Far. In *Efficiency, Equity, and Legitimacy: The Multilateral Trading System at the Millennium*, ed. Roger B. Porter, Pierre Sauvé, Arvind Subramanian, and Americo Beviglia Zampetti. Washington: Brookings Institution.

IMF (International Monetary Fund). 1977. Surveillance over Exchange Rate Policies: Balance of Payments Purposes. International Monetary Fund Legal Department (SM/77/97). Washington.

IMF (International Monetary Fund). 2006. Communiqué of the International Monetary and Financial Committee of the Board of Governors of the International Monetary Fund. Washington. Available at www.imf.org (accessed April 22).

Kahler, Miles. 1995. *International Institutions and the Political Economy of Integration*. Washington: Brookings Institution.

Kahler, Miles, and David A. Lake, eds. 2003. *Governance in a Global Economy: Political Authority in Transition*. Princeton: Princeton University Press.

Katzenstein, Peter J., Robert O. Keohane, and Stephen D. Krasner. 1998. International Organization and the Study of World Politics. *International Organization* 52, no. 4: 645–85.

Keohane, Robert O. 1984. *After Hegemony: Cooperation and Discord in the World Political Economy*. Trenton, NJ: Princeton University Press.

Keohane, Robert O., and Helen Milner, eds. 1996. *Internationalization and Domestic Politics*. New York: Cambridge University Press.

Keohane, Robert O., and Joseph S. Nye Jr. 2001. The Club Model of Multilateral Cooperation and Problems of Democratic Legitimacy. In *Efficiency, Equity, and Legitimacy: The Multilateral Trading System at the Millennium,* ed. Roger B. Porter, Pierre Sauvé, Arvind Subramanian, and Americo Beviglia Zampetti. Washington: Brookings Institution.

Keohane, Robert O., and Joseph S. Nye Jr. 2003. Redefining Accountability for Global Governance. In *Governance in a Global Economy*, ed. Miles Kahler and David A. Lake. Princeton, NJ: Princeton University Press.

Krasner, Stephen D., ed. 1983. *International Regimes*. Ithaca, NY: Cornell University Press.

Lawrence, Robert Z. 2003. *Crimes and Punishments? Retaliation under the WTO*. Washington: Institute for International Economics.

Leitner, Kara, and Simon Lester. 2006. WTO Dispute Settlement from 1995 to 2005: A Statistical Analysis. *Journal of International Economic Law* 9, no. 1: 219–31.

Lombardi, Domenico, and Ngaire Woods. 2005. *Effective Representation and the Role of Coalitions Within the IMF.* Global Economic Governance Working Paper 2005/17. Oxford, UK: Oxford University.

McRae, Donald. 2004. What is the Future of WTO Dispute Settlement? *Journal of International Economic Law* 7, no. 1: 3–21.

Mittelman, James H. 2000. *The Globalization Syndrome: Transformation and Resistance.* Princeton, NJ: Princeton University Press.

Moravcsik, Andrew. 2002. In Defense of the "Democratic Deficit": Reassessing Legitimacy in the European Union. *Journal of Common Market Studies* 40, no. 4: 603–24.

Pauly, Louis W. 1997. *Who Elected the Bankers? Surveillance and Control in the World Economy.* Ithaca, NY: Cornell University Press.

Polanyi, Karl. 1957 [1944]. *The Great Transformation: Political and Economic Origins of Our Time.* Boston, MA: Beacon Press.

Putnam, Robert D., and C. Randall Henning. 1989. The Bonn Summit of 1978: A Case Study in Coordination. In *Can Nations Agree? Issues in International Economic Cooperation,* Richard N. Cooper, Robert D. Putnam, C. Randall Henning, Barry Eichengreen, and Gerald Holtham. Washington: Brookings Institution.

Rodrik, Dani. 1997. *Has Globalization Gone Too Far?* Washington: Institute for International Economics.

Ruggie, John Gerard, ed. 1993. *Multilateralism Matters: The Theory and Praxis of an Institutional Form.* New York: Columbia University Press.

Stiglitz, Joseph E. 2002. *Globalization and Its Discontents.* New York: W. W. Norton & Company.

Truman, Edwin M., ed. 2006 *Reforming the IMF for the 21st Century.* Washington: Institute for International Economics.

Williamson, John. 2006. *Reference Rates and the International Monetary System.* POLICY ANALYSES IN INTERNATIONAL ECONOMICS 82. Washington: Peterson Institute for International Economics (forthcoming).

Woods, Ngaire. 2006. *The Globalizers: The IMF, the World Bank, and Their Borrowers.* Ithaca, NY: Cornell University Press.

15

Wanted: More Effective Public Communication in Empirical International Economics

J. DAVID RICHARDSON

My thesis in this chapter is that the world needs more effective public communication in empirical international economics. *Effective* means persuasively heard or read as well as spoken or written, and with tangible results. *Public communication* involves many channels, especially the serious media for policy analysis accessible to a broad range of participants and observers beyond professional economists (but not traditional pedagogy nor popular mass communication). I will argue that the need for more effective public communication is most acute for *empirical* (including historical and institutional) *international economics*.

After all, much of economics is at first blush counterintuitive and becomes sensible (however subtly) only with patience, practice, and constant articulation, communication, and reminder. Even sophisticated commentators and policy practitioners often muddle "comparative advantage" and "competitive advantage." And both bilateral and overall trade deficits are castigated as national problems, while it is generally well understood that interpersonal trade imbalances and personal borrowing can be innocuous or even beneficial.

J. David Richardson, senior fellow at the Institute since 1991, is professor of economics in the Maxwell School of Syracuse University. This chapter is based in part on remarks given at the 12th Annual Meeting of Empirical Investigations in International Trade, Purdue University, October 22, 2005. The author is indebted to C. Fred Bergsten and Lori G. Kletzer for helpful comments.

International economics—historical, institutional, and empirical—is still more relentlessly abused and misunderstood. Even well-educated publics often seem to think that buying and spending everything as locally as possible promises stable prosperity, romantically embracing Gandhi's *swaraj* unawares. They need exposure to the massive historical evidence to the contrary.[1] And even sensible politicians mislead themselves as well as gullible followers with the notion that exports, imports, and jobs may all be controlled according to popular intuition. In contrast, even simple scatter plots show that across countries and over time, measured exports and imports covary in a tight, positive way—and that there is virtually *no* covariation in trade surpluses, deficits, and unemployment rates.[2]

So the world needs more effective public communication in empirical international economics *especially*.

A Brief Personal Retrospective

I began my career in 1970 at the University of Wisconsin, Madison, where everyone was nurtured in the "Wisconsin Idea" that "the boundaries of the University are the boundaries of the state." This meant that Madison's ivory towers ought to somehow demonstrably serve the state's citizens and government.[3] The Wisconsin Idea was vaguely appealing to me back then, but, of course, the uppermost challenges were getting my research right, getting it noticed, and getting it published. Little did I anticipate that the need to "get my research right" was soon to be supplemented by a need to "make my research relevant."

My first direct contact with Fred Bergsten and the new Institute came in the early 1980s, during an institutional competition for a distinctive experimental National Science Foundation grant. The grant was unique in mandating international economic research that was demonstrably rele-

---

1. See Maddison (1995, 2001, 2004); Williamson (2006); Aghion and Williamson (1998); O'Rourke and Williamson (1999); and Bordo, Taylor, and Williamson (2003).

2. The first correlation is the real-world counterpart of the Lerner Symmetry Theorem, which is readily demonstrated in a "general-equilibrium perspective." That same general-equilibrium perspective likewise undergirds the absence of the second correlation—in reality, market-clearing *failures* in a nation's labor markets are only rarely, loosely, and at best temporarily influenced by export-import imbalances. One need only consider how a company like GE profitably allocates its resources and workers across its many input activities, products, and multinational facilities. The answer is more provocatively simple than one might think: GE uses GE—General Electric uses general equilibrium—both within its company "boundaries" and in exporting to and importing from "other" companies, just as a country should and as smart countries do.

3. Trechter (2005) provides a recent retrospective and forward-looking assessment of the "Wisconsin Idea." Other references to the Wisconsin Idea, starting with McCarthy's (1912) seminal book, can be found at www.legis.state.wi.us (accessed May 22, 2006).

vant to the policy community. The National Bureau of Economic Research (NBER) team (for which the late William H. Branson and I were coprincipal investigators) won the micro-side competition. This led to a reorientation of my work toward policy relevance, including learning the names and reputations of Washington insiders on international economic policy and listening to them for suggestions on creative research ideas and on the most pressing research needs.

About 10 years later, Fred Bergsten offered me a special opportunity to combine my academic career with a two-year, part-time arrangement with the Institute, where I was able to hone my knowledge and skills as an international economist and as an effective public communicator.[4] Those two years mushroomed to 13 and to a personal link between academic and policy pursuits that continues to this day.

Public Payoffs and Professional Methods for Public Communication

With experience in both academic research and public policy analysis, I have a particular perspective from which to address the issue of what would enable more effective public communication of key ideas and results in international economics. What sets best-practice examples apart from otherwise commendable efforts to influence public understanding of key issues in applied international economics is precisely the policy entrepreneurship and public marketing epitomized by C. Fred Bergsten (and the theme of Michael Mussa's overview for this volume). It is these characteristics that have added the *demonstrability*, if not always the definitive persuasiveness, to the work of Institute researchers.

An example helps to clarify and amplify this point. Marvelously insightful, policy-relevant research on the virtues of outward orientation for development was carried out in the 1970s by Jagdish N. Bhagwati, Anne O. Krueger, and a stellar cast of associates.[5] But this work had limited impact because of the lack of powerful human or institutional catalysts to advance it. In contrast, cogently argued policy analyses from the Institute that focus on key international economic policy issues at or even before

---

4. I have not been alone in commuting between academics and the Institute; Mac Destler, Randall Henning, and Catherine Mann maintain such relationships. Numerous academics have had part-time arrangements with the Institute or have contributed to the Institute's work from off-site.

5. Bhagwati (1978) and Krueger (1978) distill the common and unique lessons from 10 matched book-length country case studies, authored by themselves, Robert E. Baldwin, Jere R. Behrman, Carlos Diaz-Alejandro, Albert Fishlow, Bent Hansen, J. Clark Leith, and Michael Michaely, among other luminaries.

the moment of decision making—in a manner that is easily understandable to decision makers—can and do have large impacts.

Beyond the role of such policy analysis in promoting desirable economic reforms, it is important not to underestimate the prophylactic payoff from combating pseudo-analysis that might move the United States and its trading partners in the wrong direction. Well-researched, well-documented, comprehensive, and engaging research is the natural survivor *and* the natural enforcer in the policy realm, especially when authors are able to effectively present their findings and recommendations in testimony, press briefings, and more generally in the nonprint media. The successive Institute volumes on sanctions are an excellent illustration, choking off sweeping, feel-good expressions of righteous indignation in the United States and "smartening up" the effectiveness of global sanctions.[6] John Williamson's many and meticulous contributions to the political economy of "reform," usually outward-oriented reform (in accord with the so-called Washington Consensus), were for a time just as successful.[7] Recently, however, Williamson's wisdom has been flying into strong headwinds from the increasingly well-organized skeptics of "merely" economic development and of "merely" commercial globalization. Howard Lewis and my 2001 attempt to vividly communicate the evolutionary and fitness benefits for American workers, firms, and communities of cross-border engagement in investment, exports, *or* imports was intended as a prophylactic for misunderstanding and nonsense but so far has failed to gain adequate traction.

The cautionary lesson from these examples is that communication vacuums get filled perversely by anecdotal evocation at best and "junk science" at worst. Not at all minor among the reasons for committing to more effective public communication by professionally competent applied international economists is to minimize encroachment by self-taught experts and "pop intellectuals." The world of policy discourse and practice needs far less globo-babble, either by inscrutable economists unschooled in public communication or by addled pretenders.

But how? What are the methods by which international economists might pursue more effective public communication? I have several favored techniques.

■ *Communications Artistry.* There is a real art to mastering the communications culture of public intellectuals—achieving the intersecting mix of contacts, trust, interactive attentiveness, and memorable cogency

---

6. The Institute's sanctions work includes that of Gary Clyde Hufbauer, Jeffrey J. Schott, and Kimberly Ann Elliott (Hufbauer, Schott, and Elliott 1990, forthcoming). Richardson (1993) isolated an especially large effect from national security export controls and broadened the benefit-cost apparatus of the sanctions project to calculate the antiexport bias ("cost") in a number of American regulatory areas.

7. Especially Williamson (1990, 1994) and Kuczynski and Williamson (2003).

that goes into effective communication, compounded in the case of international affairs by cultural and lingual nuance. Like many performance arts, it requires long practice and ongoing mentorship. No one masters this communications mix better than Fred Bergsten, and he has mentored his colleagues in it assiduously, from publishing in *Foreign Affairs* and on the op-ed pages of the *Financial Times* and *Nihon Keizai Shimbun* to testimony, radio and TV appearances, and in sanctioned and shadow experts groups imagining the benefits and costs of Pacific-Atlanticism, a new American "competitiveness agenda," or inclusive variations on the G-7.

- **Communications Attentiveness.** Effective public communication generally requires understanding other people's points of view and the bases for any misunderstandings they may harbor. Attentiveness thus implies good listening skills. Many of my Institute colleagues are exemplars of these skills[8] but no one more so than Fred Bergsten, who has a unique capacity to explain and refine the concerns of the policy community. He illustrates commendably the skill Paul Krugman once described in his own life as "listening to the Gentiles."

- **Turf Transfer.** Effective communication across cultures often necessitates some measure of "turf transfer." Fred and the Institute have always encouraged periodic leaves by senior staff for "public" positions, including positions abroad and in international institutions, and they have also temporarily welcomed journalists and policymakers onto the Institute research staff.[9] I would suggest greater turf transfer with academic institutions, by attracting academics on leave or sabbatical to spend time at Institute and encouraging virtually *all* Institute senior fellows to take leave for visiting academic positions at research-oriented universities.

- **"Double Writing."** A single research product is almost never suitable for *all* audiences. But it often takes little effort to rewrite suitable peer-reviewed publications for an elite, public policy community.[10] For example, in the Globalization Balance Sheet project, the 2001 books by Lori G. Kletzer and by Kenneth J. Scheve and Matthew J. Slaughter el-

---

8. My work with Monty Graham (1997a, 1997b) on multilateral competition policy for the Institute is, I believe, one example of both communications attentiveness and communications artistry.

9. John Williamson (1994) writes about the political economic value of "techno-pols"— technocrat-politicians, people with both technical expertise *and* political sensitivity. That is ideally what this sort of think-tank/public-sphere turf transfer foments. John credits Jorge Dominguez with coining the term.

10. It takes much more effort to rewrite peer-reviewed material for a broad audience. For one successful effort, see Lindert (2004a, 2004b), who says he wrote volume 1 "for human beings," and volume 2 for "social scientists" (2004a, xv).

egantly illustrate double writing, even to the point of extending their Institute research in unique directions that are not found in the work of their peer-reviewed counterparts.[11]

- *Vignettes and Stories.* Every audience has another audience. If effective writing communicates with an elite public audience, then they can usually translate it into forms suitable for their own audiences— constituents, clients, members of Congress, readers of newspapers, etc. Through this mechanism, "double writing" can become "redouble writing," spilling over from its initial target audience as far as possible toward popular reception.[12]

A Mixed Assessment

Pursuing effective public communication in empirical international economics can be extremely satisfying professionally. But, as others have also found, it is difficult to do the public policy communication while also remaining active in peer-reviewed research, mentoring successful doctoral dissertators, and helping to build academic excellence at a university. So I have some cautionary advice for the like-minded:

- *Timing and Specialization.* "For everything, there is a season." Under current custom, it is probably still advisable to spend at least 15 years after a doctoral degree fairly exclusively on peer-reviewed research, with only occasional "double writing" oriented toward economic policy. Were "custom" to change, however, including a more flexible conception of academic tenure, then I would enthusiastically welcome the idea that more empirical economists would spend an entire career specializing in public communication in international economics.

- *Seduction.* For an effective public communicator, the great temptation is the ironic mantle of "public intellectual." Unfortunately, some of the most widely acknowledged public intellectuals have abandoned their

---

11. Keith Maskus' (2000) Institute book also illustrates this handsomely. Marc Noland has the most sustained and successful record of double writing among Institute senior staff in my opinion. My impression is that several of the Institute books written under external contract by political scientists accomplish the same double-writing service, but I have not endeavored to find out.

12. In this spirit I began experimenting with interviews of real people in real stories in the real cases that were complementary to the serious empirics in my research. These vignettes appeared as sidebars in the *Why!* series (Richardson and Rindal 1995, 1996; Lewis and Richardson 2001), paying special attention to their rhetorical value. Especially in the earlier monographs, these anecdotal sidebars drew many new target readers into the serious statistical evidence that most types of global engagement could be beneficial to American workers, firms, and communities.

academic connections and accountability entirely, thereby blurring the line between scholarly discipline and public celebrity. Here is where a think tank with the root commitments of the Institute can be a close substitute for academic community and responsibility—as long as it retains membership in the professional, scholarly fold.

Closing Thoughts

Successes and exemplars notwithstanding, international economists still face a serious problem with effective public communication of their most important ideas—a problem that is probably becoming more severe. The work of the economists that is most admired for its penetrating "method" often exhibits little clear relevance to those who work in the real world of international commerce and policy. And much of the work that I most admire for its wise evaluation of real-world issues pays little attention to penetrating method. The desirable center on this continuum is too sparsely populated and perhaps even emptying.

With this problem, how can the American government and the governments of other countries sustain best-practice international economic policy? And, even if they could do so administratively, how could they politically if their ill-informed constituents and media fail to understand the requirements for and benefits of sound international economic policies?

Think tanks have burgeoned in the past few decades, but those in the Institute's and Fred Bergsten's image have not grown fast enough. May their tribe increase!

References

Aghion, Philippe, and Jeffrey G. Williamson. 1998. *Growth, Inequality and Globalization: Theory, History and Policy.* The Raffaele Mattioli Lectures. Cambridge: Cambridge University Press.

Bergsten, C. Fred. 2006. *The Peter G. Peterson Institute for International Economics at 25.* Special Anniversary Publication. Washington: Peterson Institute for International Economics. Available at www.petersoninstitute.org.

Bhagwati, Jagdish N. 1978. *Anatomy and Consequences of Exchange Control Regimes.* New York: Columbia University Press (subsequently distributed by Ballinger).

Bordo, Michael D., Alan M. Taylor, and Jeffrey G. Williamson, eds. 2003. *Globalization in Historical Perspective.* Chicago: University of Chicago Press.

Graham, Edward M., and J. David Richardson. 1997a. *Competition Policies for the Global Economy.* POLICY ANALYSES IN INTERNATIONAL ECONOMICS 51. Washington: Institute for International Economics.

Graham, Edward M., and J. David Richardson, eds. 1997b. *Global Competition Policy.* Washington: Institute for International Economics.

Hufbauer, Gary Clyde, Jeffrey J. Schott, and Kimberly Ann Elliott. 1990. *Economic Sanctions Reconsidered*, 2d ed. Washington: Institute for International Economics.

Hufbauer, Gary Clyde, Jeffrey J. Schott, and Kimberly Ann Elliott. Forthcoming. *Economic Sanctions Reconsidered*, 3d ed. Washington: Peterson Institute for International Economics.

Kletzer, Lori G. 2001. *Job Loss from Imports: Measuring the Costs.* Washington: Institute for International Economics.

Krueger, Anne O. 1978. *Liberalization Attempts and Consequences.* New York: Columbia University Press (subsequently distributed by Ballinger).

Kuczynski, Pedro-Pablo, and John Williamson, eds. 2003. *After the Washington Consensus: Restarting Growth and Reform in Latin America.* Washington: Institute for International Economics.

Lewis, Howard, and J. David Richardson. 2001. *Why Global Commitment Really Matters!* Washington: Institute for International Economics.

Lindert, Peter H. 2004a. *Growing Public: Social Spending and Economic Growth since the Eighteenth Century: The Story*, Volume 1. Cambridge: Cambridge University Press.

Lindert, Peter H. 2004b. *Growing Public: Social Spending and Economic Growth since the Eighteenth Century: Further Evidence*, Volume 2. Cambridge: Cambridge University Press.

Maddison, Angus. 1995. *Monitoring the World Economy, 1820–1992.* Paris: OECD Development Centre.

Maddison, Angus. 2001. *The World Economy: A Millennial Perspective.* Paris: OECD Development Centre.

Maddison, Angus. 2004. *Growth and Interaction in the World Economy: The Roots of Modernity.* Washington: American Enterprise Institute.

Maskus, Keith E. 2000. *Intellectual Property Rights in the Global Economy.* Washington: Institute for International Economics.

McCarthy, Charles. 1912. *The Wisconsin Idea.* Available at www. wisc.edu (accessed May 22, 2006).

O'Rourke, Kevin, and Jeffrey G. Williamson. 1999. *Globalization and History: The Evolution of a 19th Century Atlantic Economy.* Cambridge, MA: Massachusetts Institute of Technology Press.

Richardson, J. David. 1993. *Sizing Up US Export Disincentives.* Washington: Institute for International Economics.

Richardson, J. David. Forthcoming. *Global Forces, American Faces: US Economic Globalization at the Grass Roots.* Washington: Peterson Institute for International Economics.

Richardson, J. David, and Karin Rindal. 1995. *Why Exports Really Matter!* Washington: Institute for International Economics and the Manufacturing Institute (National Association of Manufacturers).

Richardson, J. David, and Karin Rindal. 1996. *Why Exports Matter: More!* Washington: Institute for International Economics and the Manufacturing Institute (National Association of Manufacturers).

Scheve, Kenneth F., and Matthew J. Slaughter. 2001. *Globalization and the Perceptions of American Workers.* Washington: Institute for International Economics.

Trechter, David. 2005. The Wisconsin Idea, Survey Research Center Report—2005/05, April. Photocopy. Available at www.uwrf.edu (accessed May 22, 2006).

Williamson, Jeffrey G. 2006. *Globalization and the Poor Periphery Before 1950: The Ohlin Lectures.* Cambridge, MA: Massachusetts Institute of Technology Press.

Williamson, John, ed. 1990. *Latin American Adjustment: How Much Has Happened?* Washington: Institute for International Economics.

Williamson, John, ed. 1994. *The Political Economy of Reform.* Washington: Institute for International Economics.

Appendix A
Publications of C. Fred Bergsten

Books

China, The Balance Sheet: What the World Needs to Know Now about The Emerging Superpower, Washington: Public Affairs, 2006 (in collaboration with Nicholas Lardy of the Institute for International Economics and Bates Gill and Derek J. Mitchell of the Center for Strategic and International Studies).

The United States and the World Economy: Foreign Economic Policy for the Next Decade, Washington: Institute for International Economics, 2005 (with senior fellows of the Institute for International Economics).

Dollar Adjustment: How Far? Against What? Washington: Institute for International Economics, 2004 (coedited with John Williamson).

From Alliance to Coalitions—The Future of Transatlantic Relations, Frankfurt: Bertelsmann Foundation, 2004 (coedited with Werner Weidenfeld, Caio Koch-Weser, Walther Stützle, and John Hamre).

Dollar Overvaluation and the World Economy, Washington: Institute for International Economics, 2003 (coedited with John Williamson).

The Korean Diaspora in the World Economy, Washington: Institute for International Economics, 2003 (coedited with Inbom Choi).

No More Bashing: Building a New Japan—United States Economic Relationship, Washington: Institute for International Economics, 2001 (with Takatoshi Ito and Marcus Noland).

Whither APEC? Washington: Institute for International Economics, 1997 (editor).

The Korea–United States Economic Relationship, Washington and Seoul: Institute for International Economics and Institute for Global Economics, May 1997, (coedited with Il Sakong).

Global Economic Leadership and the Group of Seven, Washington: Institute for International Economics, 1996 (with C. Randall Henning).

Korea–United States Cooperation in the New World Order, Washington: Institute for International Economics, 1996 (coedited with Il Sakong). Also published in Korean.

The Political Economy of Korea–United States Cooperation, Washington: Institute for International Economics, 1995 (coedited with Il Sakong). Also published in Korean.

Reconcilable Differences? United States–Japan Economic Conflict, Washington: Institute for International Economics, 1993 (with Marcus Noland). Also published in Japanese.

Pacific Dynamism and the International Economic System, Washington: Institute for International Economics, 1993 (coedited with Marcus Noland).

Japan's Growing Technological Capability: Implications for the U.S. Economy, Washington: National Academy Press, 1992 (coedited with Thomas S. Arrison, Edward M. Graham, and Martha Caldwell Harris).

International Adjustment and Financing: The Lessons of 1985–91, Washington: Institute for International Economics, 1991 (editor).

America in the World Economy: A Strategy for the 1990s, Washington: Institute for International Economics, 1988.

Auction Quotas and United States Trade Policy, Washington: Institute for International Economics, September 1987 (with Kimberly Ann Elliott, Jeffrey J. Schott, and Wendy E. Takacs).

The United States–Japan Economic Problem, Washington: Institute for International Economics, revised January 1987 (with William R. Cline). Also published in Japanese.

Bank Lending to Developing Countries: The Policy Alternatives, Washington: Institute for International Economics, April 1985 (with William R. Cline and John Williamson).

Global Economic Imbalances, Washington: Institute for International Economics, 1985 (editor).

The United States in the World Economy: Selected Papers of C. Fred Bergsten, 1981–1982, Lexington, MA: D. C. Heath and Co., 1983.

Trade Policy in the 1980s, Washington: Institute for International Economics, November 1982 (with William R. Cline).

The World Economy in the 1980s: Selected Papers of C. Fred Bergsten, 1980, Lexington, MA: D. C. Heath and Co., 1981.

The International Economic Policy of the United States: Selected Papers of C. Fred Bergsten, 1977–1979, Lexington, MA: D. C. Heath and Co., 1980.

American Multinationals and American Interests, Washington: Brookings Institution, 1978 (with Thomas Horst and Theodore H. Moran).

Managing International Economic Interdependence: Selected Papers of C. Fred Bergsten, 1975–76, Lexington, MA: D. C. Heath and Co., 1977.

The Dilemmas of the Dollar: The Economics and Politics of United States International Monetary Policy, New York: New York University Press, for the Council on Foreign Relations, 1975; reprinted by M. E. Sharpe, 1996.

World Politics and International Economics, Washington: Brookings Institution, 1975 (coedited with Lawrence B. Krause).

Toward a New World Trade Policy: The Maidenhead Papers, Lexington, MA: D. C. Heath and Co., 1975 (editor). Also published in Portuguese.

Toward a New International Economic Order: Selected Papers of C. Fred Bergsten, 1972–1974, Lexington, MA: D. C. Heath and Co., 1975.

The Future of the International Economic Order: An Agenda for Research, Lexington, MA: D. C. Heath and Co., 1973.

Leading Issues in International Economic Policy: Essays in Honor of George N. Halm, Lexington, MA: D. C. Heath and Co., 1973 (coedited with William Tyler).

Approaches to Greater Flexibility of Exchange Rates: The Burgenstock Papers, Princeton, NJ: Princeton University Press, 1970 (coarranged with George N. Halm, Fritz Machlup, and Robert Roosa).

Chapters in Edited Books

A New Steering Committee for the World Economy? In *Reforming the IMF for the 21st Century,* Special Report 19, ed. Edwin M. Truman, Washington: Institute for International Economics, 2006.

The Euro and the Dollar: Toward A Finance G-2? In *The Euro at Five: Ready for A Global Role?* Special Report 18, ed. Adam S. Posen, Washington: Institute for International Economics, April 2005.

The G-2: A New Conceptual Basis and Operating Modality for Transatlantic Economic Relations (with Caio Koch-Weser), in *From Alliance to Coalitions—The Future of Transatlantic Relations,* Frankfurt: Bertelsmann Foundation, April 2004.

Reforming the International Financial Institutions: Dueling Experts in the United States, in *Debating the Global Financial Architecture,* ed. Leslie Elliott Armijo, Albany, NY: SUNY Press, 2002.

Globalization and Sino-American Relations, in *Economic Globalisation and Sino American Economic Relations,* Hong Kong: Lingnan University, 2001.

A Framework for Fluctuations: Target Zones for the Major Currencies, in *The Currency Conundrum,* ed. Kent Hughes, Woodrow Wilson International Center for Scholars Project on America and the Global Economy, December 2001.

Fifty Years of GATT/WTO: Lessons from the Past for Strategies for the Future, in *From GATT to the WTO: The Multilateral Trading System in the New Millennium,* by the WTO Secretariat, The Hague, the Netherlands: Kluwer Law International, 2000.

The International Financial Architecture Debate—Progress to Date and Remaining Challenges, in *Emerging Market Perspectives: Reforming the International Financial Architecture,* ed. Il SaKong and Yunjong Wang, Seoul: Institute for Global Economics and Korea Institute for International Economic Policy, December 2000.

International Context for Asian Recovery, in *Regional Co-operation and Asian Recovery,* ed. Peter A. Petri, Singapore: Institute of Southeast Asian Studies, 2000.

The Dollar and the Euro, in *Research in International Business and Finance: The Quest for Exchange Rate Stability in the Next Millennium,* volume 13, ed. H. Peter Gray and Scheherazade S. Rehman, Stamford, CT: JAI Press Inc., 1999.

Exchange Rate Choices: Discussion, in *Rethinking the International Monetary System,* Federal Reserve Bank of Boston Conference Series no. 43, ed. Jane Sneddon Little and Giovanni P. Olivei, Federal Reserve Bank of Boston, June 1999.

Memo One: American Trade Leadership and the Global Economic System, in *Future Visions for U.S. Trade Policy,* Bruce Stokes, project director, Washington: Brookings Institution Press, 1998.

Open Regionalism, in *Whither APEC?* ed. C. Fred Bergsten. Washington: Institute for International Economics, October 1997.

APEC in 1997: Prospects and Possible Strategies, in *Whither APEC?* ed. C. Fred Bergsten. Washington: Institute for International Economics, October 1997.

The Impact of the Euro on Exchange Rates and International Policy Cooperation, in *EMU and the International Monetary System,* ed. Paul Masson, Thomas Krueger, and Bart Turtelboom, Washington: International Monetary Fund, 1997.

Open Regionalism, in *Global Trade Policy 1997,* ed. Sven Arndt and Chris Milner, London: Blackwell Publishers, 1998. (Also published as Working Paper 97-3, Institute for International Economics, 1997.)

The Emerging Asia Pacific Region and Trilateral Countries: APEC, in *Vancouver 96,* Trialogue: 49, ed. Charles B. Heck, New York: The Trilateral Commission, December 1996.

Moving Toward Greater Exchange Rate Stability: The Volcker Target Zone Proposal, in *Vancouver 96,* Trialogue: 49, ed. Charles B. Heck, New York: The Trilateral Commission, December 1996.

Asia-Pacific Economic Cooperation: Summary of the Second Report of the Eminent Persons Group, in *Research in Asian Economic Studies,* volume 7, part A, ed. M. Dutta, Richard Hooley, Anwar Nahution, and Mari Pangestu, Stamford, CT: JAI Press Inc., 1996.

APEC and the Multilateral Trading System, in *Stockholm Trade Policy Seminar: A Collection of Contributions by Participants,* Stockholm: The Ministry for Foreign Affairs, October 1995.

APEC: The Bogor Declaration and Its Implications for the Future, in *Emerging Growth Pole: The Asia-Pacific Economy,* ed. Dilip K. Das, Singapore: Prentice Hall, 1995.

The Bogor Declaration and the Path Ahead, in *Asia-Pacific Economic Cooperation under the WTO System*, Seoul: Institute of East and West Studies, Yonsei University, June 1995.

The IMF and the World Bank in an Evolving World, in *Fifty Years After Bretton Woods: The Future of the IMF and the World Bank* (proceedings of a conference held in Madrid, Spain, September 29–30, 1994), ed. James M. Boughton and K. Sarwar Lateef, Washington: International Monetary Fund and World Bank Group, 1995.

New Rules for International Investment, in *Multinationals in North America*, ed. Lorraine Eden, Centre for Trade Policy and Law at Carleton University and the University of Ottawa, Alberta, Canada: University of Calgary Press, 1994.

Significant Episodes in the Evolution of the International Monetary System: Discussion, in *The International Monetary System* (proceedings of a conference organized by the Banca d'Italia), ed. Peter B. Kenen, Francesco Papadia, and Fabrizio Saccomanni), Cambridge University Press, 1994.

Managing the World Economy of the Future, in *Managing the World Economy: Fifty Years after Bretton Woods*, ed. Peter B. Kenen, Washington: Institute for International Economics, September 1994.

APEC and the World Economy: A Force for Worldwide Liberalization, in *Asia Pacific Regionalism: Readings in International Economics*, ed. Ross Garnaut and Peter Drysdale, Harper Educational Publishers with The Australia-Japan Research Centre, The Australian National University, 1994.

Strategic Architecture for the Pacific, in *Asia in the 21st Century: Evolving Strategic Priorities*, ed. Michael D. Bellows, Washington: National Defense University Press, 1994.

Exchange Rate Policy: The Issue, in *American Economic Policy in the 1980s*, ed. Martin Feldstein, Chicago, IL: University of Chicago Press, 1994.

A New Vision for United States-Japan Economic Relations, in *Harnessing the Rising Sun: Managing Japan's Rise as a Global Power*, Aspen Strategy Group Report, Lanham, MD: University Press of America, 1993 (with Paula Stern).

The Collapse of Bretton Woods: Implications for International Monetary Reform, in *A Retrospective on the Bretton Woods System*, ed. Michael D. Bordo and Barry Eichengreen. Chicago: University of Chicago Press, 1993.

Commentary on Macroeconomic Policy and Long-Run Growth, in *Policies for Long-Run Economic Growth*, Symposium Sponsored by the Federal Reserve Bank of Kansas City, Jackson Hole, Wyoming, August 27–29, 1992.

Exports, Imports, and the Balance of Payments, reprinted in *The International Political Economy of Direct Foreign Investment*, ed. Ben Gomes-Casseres and David Yoffie, Cheltenham, England: Edward Elgar Publishing, December 1992.

Commentary on The Move Toward Free Trade Zones, in *Policy Implications of Trade and Currency Zones*, Symposium Sponsored by the Federal Reserve Bank of Kansas City, Jackson Hole, Wyoming, August 22–24, 1991.

The Trilateral "Steering Committee" and Its Tasks, in *Tokyo 91*, Trialogue: 43, ed. Andrew V. Frankel and Charles B. Heck, New York: The Trilateral Commission, December 1991.

The Hard Landing Scenario, in *The Risk of Economic Crisis*, ed. Martin Feldstein, Chicago: University of Chicago Press, 1991.

Domestic and International Consequences of Low U.S. Saving, in *The U.S. Savings Challenge: Policy Options for Productivity and Growth*, ed. Charls E. Walker, Mark A. Bloomfield, and Margo Thorning, Boulder: Westview Press, October 1990.

Comment: Equilibrium Exchange Rates by Paul Krugman, in *International Policy Coordination and Exchange Rate Fluctuations*, ed. William H. Branson, Jacob A. Frenkel, and Morris Goldstein, Chicago: University of Chicago Press, 1990.

America in the World Economy: A Strategy for the 1990s, in *America's Global Interests*, ed. Edward K. Hamilton, New York: W. W. Norton & Co., 1989.

The Budget and Trade Deficit: Flashpoint for Crisis? in *National Economic Commission Staff Papers*, Background Papers and Major Testimony, Washington, March 1989.

The Case for Target Zones, in *The International Monetary System: The Next Twenty-Five Years*, Symposium at Basle University to Commemorate Twenty-Five Years of Per Jacobsson Lectures, June 12, 1988.

The Dollar and the World Economic Outlook, in *United States–German Economic Yearbook*, New York: German American Chamber of Commerce, 1987.

The U.S.-Japan Economic Problem: Next Steps, in *Japan and the United States Today*, eds. Hugh T. Patrick and Ryuichiro Tachi, New York: The Center on Japanese Economy and Business, 1987.

The Trade and International Economic Outlook, in *Proceedings: Twenty-first Annual Pacific Northwest Regional Economic Conference*, Seattle: The Pacific Northwest Regional Economic Conference and The Northwest Policy Center, University of Washington, April 30–May 2, 1987.

Stabilizing the International Monetary System: The Case for Target Zones, in *Exchange Rate Targets: Desirable or Disastrous?* American Enterprise Institute Studies in Economic Policy, September 1986.

Overview, in *The U.S. Dollar—Recent Developments, Outlook and Policy Options*, Federal Reserve Bank of Kansas City, Jackson Hole, August 1985.

The Effect on Trade of Exchange Rates and Financial Policies, in *World Trade and Trade Finance*, Proceedings of the Southern Methodist University Institute on International Finance, 1985.

Can We Prevent a World Economic Crisis? in *The Challenge of Economics*, ed. Richard O. Bartel, Armonk, NY: M. E. Sharpe, 1984.

Trade Policy in the 1980s: An Overview of the Problem, in *Trade Policy in the 1980s*, ed. William R. Cline, Washington: Institute for International Economics, 1983 (coauthor).

Exchange Rates and Trade Policy, in *Trade Policy in the 1980s*, ed. William R. Cline, Washington: Institute for International Economics, 1983 (coauthor).

The International Dimension, in *Regrowing the American Economy*, ed. G. William Miller, New York: Prentice Hall, 1983.

From Rambouillet to Versailles: A Symposium, Essays in International Finance, Princeton, NJ: Princeton University, February 1983.

Mutual Interests: The "Pragmatic" Approach, in *Towards One World? International Responses to the Brandt Report*, London: Maurice Temple Smith, 1982.

The Multiple Reserve Currency System in the 1980s, in *International Framework for Money and Banking in the 1980s*, ed. Gary Hufbauer, Washington: Georgetown University International Law Institute, 1981.

Access to Supplies and the New International Economic Order, in *The Economics of the New International Economic Order*, ed. Jagdish Bhagwati, Cambridge, MA: MIT Press, 1977.

The International Economy and World Politics in the Post-Postwar Era, in *Foreign Economic Policies of Industrial States*, ed. Wilfrid L. Kohl, Lexington, MA: D. C. Heath and Co., 1977.

Stagflation—Its Origins and Implications for International Economic Relations, in *The Emerging International Monetary Order and the Banking System*, ed. Yair Aharoni, Tel Aviv: University Publishing Projects, 1976.

The United States and the Federal Republic: The Imperative of Economic Bigemony, in *United States-German Economic Survey 1975*, New York: German American Chamber of Commerce, 1975.

U.S. National Security and the Impact of Multinational Corporations, in *Defense Planning for the 1980s and the Changing International Environment*, New York: Quadrangle Books, 1975, reprinted (in Spanish) in *Estudios Internacionales*, July–September 1975.

On the Non-Equivalence of Import Quotas and Voluntary Export Restraints, in *Toward a New World Trade Policy: The Maidenhead Papers*, ed. C. Fred Bergsten, Lexington, MA: D. C. Heath and Co., 1975 (also Brookings Technical Series Reprint T-009).

International Economics and World Politics: A Framework for Analysis, in *World Politics and International Economics*, ed. C Fred Bergsten and Lawrence B. Krause, Washington: Brookings Institution, 1975 (coauthor).

The Future of World Trade, in *The International Division of Labour: Problems and Perspectives*, ed. Herbert Giersch, Tubingen: J.C.S. Mohr, 1974.

Convertibility for the Dollar and International Monetary Reform, in *Leading Issues in International Economic Policy*, ed. C. Fred Bergsten and William G. Tyler, Lexington, MA: D. C. Heath and Co., 1973.

Outlook for the Dollar, in *Business Problems of the Seventies*, The Conference Board Record, New York: New York University Press, November 1973.

International Monetary Reform: A Viewpoint from the United States, in *Europe and the Evolution of the International Monetary System*, ed. Alexander Swoboda, Leiden: A. W. Sijthoff, 1973.

International Monetary Reform and the U.S. Balance of Payments, in *U.S. Foreign Economic Policy in the 1970s*, National Planning Association, November 1971.

The United States and Greater Flexibility of Exchange Rates, in *Approaches to Greater Flexibility of Exchange Rates: The Burgenstock Papers*, ed. C. Fred Bergsten, George Halm, Fritz Machlup, and Robert Roosa, Princeton, NJ: Princeton University Press, 1970.

Reports

The Case for a Model Free Trade Agreement between the United States and New Zealand, Washington: Institute for International Economics, April 2002.

Architecture Financière Internationale, Rapport du CAE n. 18. Paris: Conseil d'Analyse Èconomique, 1999 (with Olivier Davanne and Pierre Jacquet).

Saving More and Investing Better: A Strategy for Securing Prosperity, Fourth Report to the President and Congress, Washington: Competitiveness Policy Council, September 1995.

Implementing the APEC Vision, Third Report of the Eminent Persons Group, Asia Pacific Economic Cooperation (APEC), August 1995.

Achieving the APEC Vision: Free and Open Trade in the Asia Pacific, Second Report of the Eminent Persons Group, Asia Pacific Economic Cooperation (APEC), August 1994.

Promoting Long-Term Prosperity, Third Annual Report to the President and Congress, Washington: Competitiveness Policy Council, May 1994.

A Vision for APEC: Towards an Asia Pacific Economic Community, Report of the Eminent Persons Group to APEC Ministers, Asia Pacific Economic Cooperation (APEC), October 1993.

A Competitiveness Strategy for America, Second Annual Report to the President and Congress, Washington: Competitiveness Policy Council, March 1993.

Building a Competitive America, First Annual Report to the President and Congress, Washington: Competitiveness Policy Council, March 1992.

Trade Relations Between Korea and the United States: Current Conflicts and Future Issues, Seoul, April 18, 1991.

Dangerous Dependence: The New Challenge in U.S.-Japan Relations, Washington: Rebuild America, April 1990.

Resolving the Global Economic Crisis: After Wall Street, Washington: Institute for International Economics, December 1987.

Conditions for Partnership in International Economic Management, A Report to the Trilateral Commission, The Triangle Papers: 32, 1986.

The New Protectionism and the World Economy, Seoul: Korea Institute for Economics and Technology, July 8–10, 1986.

Promoting World Recovery: A Statement on Global Economic Strategy by Twenty-Six Economists from Fourteen Countries, Washington: Institute for International Economics, December 1982.

The Reform of International Institutions, A Report of the Trilateral Task Force on International Institutions to the Trilateral Commission, The Triangle Papers: II, 1976.

The World Economy in Transition, A Tripartite Report by Fifteen Economists from North America, the European Community, and Japan, Washington: Brookings Institution, August 1975.

Completing the GATT: Toward New International Rules to Govern Export Controls, Washington and London: British-North American Committee, October 1974.

The Future of the International Economic Order: A Report to the Ford Foundation, New York: The Ford Foundation, September 1973.

Completing the GATT, Toward New International Rules to Govern Export Controls, London: British-North American Committee, 1974.

The Outlook for Raw Materials from Outside the United States, in *Chemistry in a Constrained System—An Analysis of the Options*, Report of the 8th Annual Meeting of the Corporation Associates of the American Chemical Society, December 5–6, 1974.

The Cost of Import Restrictions to American Consumers, New York: American Importers Association, March 1972.

Reshaping the International Economic Order, A Tripartite Report by Twelve Economists from North America, the European Community, and Japan, Washington: Brookings Institution, December 1971.

Working Papers and Policy Briefs

Reforming OPIC for the 21st Century, International Economics Policy Brief 03-5, Washington: Institute for International Economics, 2003.

Brunei: A Turning Point for APEC? International Economics Policy Brief 01-1, Washington: Institute for International Economics, 2001.

The Next Trade Policy Battle, International Economics Policy Brief 00-1, Washington: Institute for International Economics, 2000.

The New Asian Challenge, Working Paper 00-4, Washington: Institute for International Economics, 2000.

The Economic and Foreign Policies of the New US Administration and Congress, Occasional Paper Series, Seoul, Korea: Institute for Global Economics/Korea International Trade Association, December 12, 2000.

Globalization and Sino-American Economic Relations, Centre for Asian Pacific Studies Working Paper Series, Lingnan University, Hong Kong: Centre for Asian Pacific Studies, May 2000.

The Case for Joint Management of Exchange Rate Flexibility, Working Paper 99-9, Washington: Institute for International Economics, 1999.

The Global Trading System and the Developing Countries in 2000, Working Paper 99-6, Washington: Institute for International Economics, May 1999.

The Case for Joint Management of Exchange Rate Flexibility (coauthor with Olivier Davanne and Pierre Jacquet), Working Paper 99-9, Washington: Institute for International Economics, July 1999.

Reviving the "Asian Monetary Fund," International Economics Policy Brief 98-8, Washington: Institute for International Economics, December 1998.

A New Strategy for the Global Crisis, International Economics Policy Brief 98-7, Washington: Institute for International Economics, September 1998.

Fifty Years of the GATT/WTO: Lesson from the Past for Strategies for the Future, Working Paper 98-3, Washington: Institute for International Economics, 1998.

The New Agenda with China, International Economics Policy Brief 98-2, Washington: Institute for International Economics, May 1998.

Competitive Liberalization and Global Free Trade: A Vision for the 21st Century, Working Paper 96-15, Washington: Institute for International Economics, 1996.

APEC in 1996 and Beyond: The Subic Summit, Working Paper 96-12, Washington: Institute for International Economics, 1996.

APEC after Osaka: Toward Free Trade by 2010, Working Paper 95-6, Washington: Institute for International Economics, 1995.

Reforming the Dollar: An International Monetary Policy for the United States, Council on Foreign Relations Occasional Paper 2, September 1972.

APEC: The Bogor Declaration and the Path Ahead, Working Paper 95-1, Washington: Institute for International Economics, 1995.

World Trade Policy and a New International Role for Korea, *Distinguished Lecture Program Report Series 89-01*, Seoul: Korea Development Institute, July 1990.

Articles

Clash of the Titans, *Newsweek*, International Edition, April 24, 2006.

Rescuing the Doha Round, *Foreign Affairs*, December 2005.

The G-20 and the World Economy, *World Economics* 5, no. 3, July/September 2004.

Foreign Economic Policy for the Next President, *Foreign Affairs*, March/April 2004.

Should G-7 Policy Coordination Be Revived? *The International Economy*, November 4, 2003.

A Renaissance for U.S. Trade Policy? *Foreign Affairs*, November/December 2002.

Can the United States Afford the Tax Cuts of 2001? *Journal of Policy Modeling* 24, no. 4, 2002.

The Euro versus the Dollar: Will There Be a Struggle for Dominance? *Journal of Policy Modeling* 24, no. 4, 2002.

Ducking a Dollar Crisis, *The International Economy*, September/October 2001.

Strong Dollar, Weak Policy, *The International Economy*, July/August 2001.

America's Two-Front Economic Conflict, *Foreign Affairs*, March/April 2001.

Fifty Years of Trade Policy, *The World Economy*, January 2001.

La dollarisation: principes et enjeux, *L'economie Politique*, no. 5, 1 trimester, 2000.

America and Europe: Clash of the Titans? *Foreign Affairs*, March/April 1999.

Why The Asian Monetary Crisis? *EDI Forum* 2, no. 4, Economic Development Institute, World Bank, Spring 1998.

Open Regionalism, *The World Economy* 20, August 1997.

The Dollar and the Euro, *Foreign Affairs*, July/August 1997.

Decline of the G7, *The International Economy*, July/August 1996 (with C. Randall Henning).

Are IMF, World Bank Ready for Reform? *Foreign Service Journal*, June 1996.

Globalizing Free Trade, *Foreign Affairs*, May/June 1996.

Asia-Pacific Economic Cooperation—A Recorded Conversation with Dr. C. Fred Bergsten, Member, Eminent Persons' Group, *Journal of Asian Economics*, Winter 1995.

10th Anniversary of Plaza Accord: A Qualified Success, *The International Economy*, September/October 1995.

Freer Trade: Breaking Out All Over the Globe, *Challenge*, March/April 1995.

That Sinking Feeling—The 1994 Dollar, *The International Economy*, July/August 1994.

APEC and World Trade, *Foreign Affairs*, May/June 1994.

Toward a Competitiveness Policy for the U.S., *Science and Technology Policy Yearbook 1992*, Washington: American Association for the Advancement of Science, 1993.

A Clinton Round or a Pacific Free Trade Area? *New Perspectives Quarterly* 10, no. 2, Spring 1993.

Needed: New International Rules for Foreign Direct Investment, *The International Trade Journal* VII, no. 1, Fall 1992.

The Primacy of Economics, *Foreign Policy*, no. 87, Summer 1992.

The World Economy After the Cold War, *California Management Review* 34, no. 2, Winter 1992.

A New Economic Strategy for the U.S. and Japan, *CEO International Strategies* IV, no. VI, November/December 1991.

US External Debt & Deficits, *International Economic Insights*, September/October 1991.

Rx for America: Export-Led Growth, *International Economic Insights*, January/February 1991.

Japan and the United States in the New World Economy, *Vital Speeches*, August 15, 1990.

From Cold War to Trade War? *International Economic Insights*, July/August 1990.

The World Economy after the Cold War, *Foreign Affairs*, Summer 1990.

The Paris Summit: Lost Opportunities, *Challenge*, September/October 1989.

The Multilateral Role, *Latin Finance*, February 1989.

U.S. Economic Future, *Challenge*, November/December 1988.

Restructuring the International Monetary System, *Economic Impact*, 1988/2.

Louvre's Lesson: The World Needs a New Monetary System, *The International Economy*, January/February 1988.

Reform Trade Policy with Auction Quotas, *Challenge*, May/June 1987.

Economic Imbalances and World Politics, *Foreign Affairs*, April 1987.

Fortune Forecast: The Turn in Trade is Under Way—For Now, *Fortune*, January 1, 1987.

Third World Debt and the Global Capital Market, *Institutional Investor*, January 1987 (with Donald Lessard).

Gearing Up World Growth, *Challenge*, May/June 1986.

Trade, Debt and Investment: The Importance of Foreign Private Investment for Development, *Aussenwirtschaft*, April 1986.

The US-Japan Trade Problem, *Challenge*, July/August 1985.

The Second Debt Crisis, *Challenge*, May/June 1985 and *Vital Speeches*, April 1, 1985.

Reaganomics—The Problem? *Foreign Policy*, Summer 1985.

Wanted: A New Global Economic Strategy, *Social Education*, January 1984.

US Trade Deficit and The World Economy, *Europe*, September/October 1983.

Can We Prevent a World Economic Crisis? *Challenge*, January/February 1983.

The International Economic Policy of the United States and Europe, *United States–German Economic Survey for 1982*, January 1983.

Preventing A World Economic Crisis, *Vital Speeches*, November 1, 1982.

What to Do about the US-Japan Economic Conflict, *Foreign Affairs*, Summer 1982.

The International Implications of Reaganomics, *Kieler Vortrag*, April 1982.

The Villain Is an Overvalued Dollar, *Challenge*, March/April 1982.

The United States and the World Economy, *The Annals of the American Academy of Political and Social Science*, March 1982.

International Economic Relations, *TransAtlantic Perspectives*, no. 6, February 1982.

The Costs of Reaganomics, *Foreign Policy*, Fall 1981.

Toward Fairer International Trade: The New Subsidy-Countervailing Duty Code, *Vital Speeches*, May 1, 1979.

U.S. Commodity Policy: A Progress Report, *Vital Speeches*, November 1, 1977.

Brazil and the United States in the World Economy, *Vital Speeches*, January 15, 1977.

Reforming the GATT: The Use of Trade Measures for Balance-of-Payments Purposes, *Journal of International Economics*, February 1977.

A New OPEC in Bauxite, *Challenge*, July/August 1976 (also Brookings Reprint 316).

Let's Avoid a Trade War, *Foreign Policy*, Summer 1976.

Interdependence and the Reform of International Institutions, *International Organization*, Spring 1976.

Increasing International Economic Interdependence: The Implications for Research, *American Economic Review*, May 1976 (coauthor).

New Urgency for Monetary Reform, *Foreign Policy*, Summer 1975.

The Response to the Third World, *Foreign Policy*, Winter 1975.

New Era, New Issues, *Economic Impact*, January 1975.

Coming Investment Wars? *Foreign Affairs*, October 1974 (also Brookings Reprint 299). Reprinted as "Economic Tensions: America vs. the Third World, in *America as an Ordinary Country: US Foreign Policy and the Future*, ed. Richard Rosencrance, Ithaca: Cornell University Press, 1976, and as "A Tug of War Over the MNCS" in *Economic Impact*, 1975/3.

The New Era in World Commodity Markets, *Challenge*, September/October 1974 (also Brookings Reprint 297).

Prospects for the Atlantic World: An American Perspective, *SAIS Review*, Summer 1974 (and as "Die Zukunft der Atlantischen Welt. Ein Beitrag aus amerikanischer Sicht") *Europa Archiv*, no. 12/1974.

The Threat Is Real, *Foreign Policy*, Spring 1974, reprinted in *Growth and Its Implications for the Future*, Appendix to Hearings before the Senate Subcommittee on Fisheries and Wildlife Conservation and the Environment, May 1, 1974, and in *Controlling Multinational Enter-*

prises: Problems, Strategies, Counterstrategies, Karl P. Sauvant and Farid G. Lavipour, Denver: Westview Press, 1976.

Die Amerikanische Europe-Politik Angesichts der Stagnation des Gemeinsamen Markets, *Europa-Archiv*, no. 4/1974.

The Threat from the Third World, *Foreign Policy*, Summer 1973 (also Brookings Reprint 268). Reprinted in *A Reordered World: Emerging International Economic Problems*, ed. Richard N. Cooper, Washington: Potomac, 1973.

Future Directions for U.S. Trade, *American Journal of Agricultural Economics* 55, no. 2, May 1973 (also Brookings Reprint 275). Reprinted in *Toward a New World Trade Policy: The Maidenhead Papers*, ed. C. Fred Bergsten, Lexington, MA: D. C. Heath and Co., 1975.

Trade Policy at the Crossroads: Which Route for Negotiations? *Columbia Journal of Transnational Law*, Fall 1972.

The New Economics and U.S. Foreign Policy, *Foreign Affairs*, January 1972 (also Brookings Reprint 231).

Crisis in U.S. Trade Policy, *Foreign Affairs*, July 1971.

The United States Balance of Payments in Mid-1971 and International Flows of Short-Term Capital, *Euromoney*, June 1971.

Toward a Dollar Zone, *Interplay*, March 1969.

Taking the Monetary Initiative, *Foreign Affairs*, July 1968.

A New Monetary System? *The Reporter*, April 19, 1968. Reprinted in *Atlantic Community Quarterly*, Summer 1968.

The President's Bitter Medicine, *The Reporter*, January 25, 1968.

Social Mobility and Economic Development: The Vital Parameters of the Bolivian Revolution, *Journal of Inter-American Studies*, July 1963.

Forensics in Europe: A Lost Art, *The Forensic*, October 1960. (National Student Writing Contest Winner).

Lectures

Merrill Gaddis Memorial Lecture, Central Methodist University, October 12, 2006.

Merrill Gaddis Memorial Lecture, Central Methodist University, October 7, 2004.

David de Pury Lecture, Swiss Foundation for World Affairs, Zurich, January 19, 2004.

Eleventh Annual Bradley Lecture, University of Wisconsin, Milwaukee, November 14, 2001.

Summers International Economic Policy Lecture, The Wharton School, University of Pennsylvania, March 23, 2000.

Export Import Bank of India Annual Commencement Day Lecture, Mumbai, March 10, 1999.

Sixth Annual Bradley Lecture, University of Wisconsin, Milwaukee, October 31, 1996.

Sixth Lim Tay Boh Memorial Lecture, National University of Singapore, September 19, 1996.

Edwin O. Reischauer Center for East Asian Studies Lecture, Nitze School of Advanced International Studies, The Johns Hopkins University, October 26, 1995.

Li & Fung Public Lecture, Hong Kong, June 1, 1994.

Third Annual Bradley Lecture, University of Wisconsin, Milwaukee, November 11, 1993.

Panglaykim Memorial Lecture, Centre for Strategic and International Studies, Jakarta, Indonesia, August 24, 1993.

Weinstock Lecture, University of California, Berkeley, November 4, 1991.

Sir Winston Scott Memorial Lecture, Central Bank of Barbados, November 27, 1990.

Ernest B. Sturc Memorial Lecture, School of Advanced International Studies, The Johns Hopkins University, Washington, DC, November 13, 1986.

Merrill Gaddis Memorial Lecture, Central Methodist University, November 1, 1984.

Index

IMF role in, 266–69
over past 25 years, 243–56
rescue packages for, 245, 259–60,
266–67, 270
of 1980s, 244–47, 299–300
and dollar overvaluation, 185*n*
Institute research on, 134–35, 134*n*
debt fatigue, 245
debt relief
completion point, 255
decision point, 255
and discounted buybacks, 246
for HIPCs, 255–56
private-sector involvement in, 267–68,
270–71
voluntary, 246
debt restructuring
Argentine example, 270–71
international arrangements in, 268
during 1980s, 244–45, 245
De Gregorio, Jose, 295*n*
de Larosiere, Jacques, 300
demand
and debt burden, 271
and terms of trade, 225–26
democracy
and international cooperation, 343–44, 348
and rule hardening, 346
de Rato, Rodrigo, 329, 329*n*
Dertouzos, Michael, 216
Destler, I. M.
on costs of protectionism, 45
on forecasting of economic calamities, 6
trade experience of, 40
on trade politics, 43, 53
on trade sanctions, 71
developed countries. *See also specific*
country or region
debt fatigue among, 245
effect of debt crises on, 244–45
developing countries. *See also specific*
country or region
debt crises in (*See* debt)
foreign direct investment in, and
economic growth, 128–29
middle-income (*See* emerging-market
economies)
The Dilemmas of the Dollar (Bergsten), 164,
334
displaced workers
definition of, 101*n*
eligibility for assistance, 101
survey of, 100*n*

TAA model/proposal for, 99–100,
106–109
training for (*See* job training assistance)
Dobson, Wendy, 138
Dodge, David, 329, 329*n*
Does Foreign Exchange Intervention Work?
(Dominguez and Frankel), 152
Doha Development Round, 29, 30
assessment of, 49, 51, 52
collapse of, 31, 32, 57, 341
potential payoffs from, 46
dollar
dominance of, constraints on US due
to, 165
stabilization of, in 1989–90, 191–97
dollar appreciation
in 1981–86, 181–86
in 1984–85, 185, 185*n*
in 1995–2002, 204, 204*n*, 205
dollar depreciation
in 1973–78, 174–76
in 1987–88, 186–91
in 1991–92, 197–200
in 1993–95, 200–204
exchange rate policies and, 316
dollar-euro exchange rate, 205–206, 210
dollar exchange rate
versus common basket peg, 155–56
messages to policymakers from, 162,
167–211
July 1978–October 1980, 174–81
July 1982–October 1986, 182–86
March 1987–April 1988, 188–91
January 1989–April 1990, 192–97
December 1991–October 1992,
197–200
October 2000–April 2003, 207–210
candidate messages, 173–74
episodes of, 172
evidence, 174–210
methodology for study, 167–74
real effective average, 168*f*, 170*f*
in 1960s, 162*n*
since 1972, 162, 168*f*, 170*f*
dollar overvaluation. *See also* exchange
rate market bubbles
floating exchange rate and, 172–73
as indicator of protectionism, 16, 20–21,
23–24, 24*n*, 31
in 1970s, 179
in 1980s, 185, 185*n*, 191
in 2000s, 209
and trade deficit, 71

exchange rate regimes—*continued*
common basket pegs, 155–56
crawling band, 136, 148, 154–55
for emerging-market economies, 135–36
and fiscal and monetary policy
coordination, 151–52
floating, 146, 157–58
Institute research on, 135–36, 135n–36n,
145–58
for major industrial economies,
135n–36n
target zones, 147–51, 158, 161–62
"exit bond" relief, 259
Exon-Florio Amendment, 126–27
export(s)
decline in
due to trade sanctions, 68
US, 235–37
growth in, and trade competitiveness,
221
MNE subsidiary requirements, 118, 122
ratio to imports (*See* trade balance)
export-related industries, trade
adjustment assistance and, 100
Extended Fund Facility (EFF), 290

farmers, trade adjustment assistance for,
98–99
fast-track negotiating authority. *See* trade
promotion authority (TPA)
F-16 countries, 140–41
Federal Open Market Committee
(FOMC), 195, 196
Federal Reserve, and exchange rate
intervention policy, 1989–90, 195
financial crises, 248–53. *See also specific
country*
financial markets, IMF relationship with,
348
fiscal policy
coordination with monetary policy,
151–52
and exchange rates, 173, 315
in July 1982–October 1986, 183t, 184
July 1978–September 1980, 175t, 177
March 1987–April 1988, 189t, 190
Fischer, Stanley, 277
Fisher, George, 217n
floating exchange rates, 157–58, 166
and dollar overvaluation, 172–73
"managed," 157
move to, 146
Ford Foundation, 62

Foreign Affairs articles (Bergsten), 334, 335,
336
foreign direct investment (FDI)
and acquisition of US firms, 126–27
benefits of, 45–46, 128–29
CFIUS and, 124–27
definition of, 116
and economic growth, 128–29
and financial crises, 248, 249f
future of, 57
"greenfield," 128
liberalization of, 127, 127n
and multinational enterprises, 116
by multinational enterprises, 117–24, 130
rules governing (*See* international
investment regime)
trade policy linked to, 44
*Foreign Direct Investment in the United
States* (Graham and Krugman), 46
foreign exchange market. *See* exchange
rate(s)
foreign policy
and macroeconomic policymaking, 24
manipulation of economic flows to
influence, 61–76 (*See also* sanctions)
foreign tastes, changes in, and trade
competitiveness, 227
France
and ERM crisis, 199
and Renault's acquisition of American
Motors, 125–26
Frankel, Jeffrey, 46
Fratzscher, Marcel, 153
free trade. *See also* open economy; trade
liberalization
threats to, 16
free trade agreements (FTAs). *See also
specific agreement*
Bergsten's support for, 335
and competitive liberalization, 19, 19n
influence of Institute on, 26, 50–51
payoffs from, 46–47
shift from single to multitrack, 41–43,
49–50
splintering coalition for, 43, 53–57
Free Trade Area of the Americas (FTAA)
Bergsten's support for, 335
Clinton's initiation of, 42
WTO/NAFTA and, 51, 52
Free Trade Areas and US Trade Policy
(Schott, ed.), 50
Frenkel, Jacob, 154
"fundamental equilibrium," 146, 166

labeling, and globalization, 54
labor force
  adjustment assistance for (*See* trade
    adjustment assistance)
  GBS project on, 47–49
  and globalization, 54
  growth in, and trade competitiveness,
    218
  and protectionist backlash, 31
labor-market adjustment programs. *See*
  trade adjustment assistance
labor unions
  and free trade agreements, 43
  and protectionist backlash, 31
  and worker assistance programs, 80,
    84*n*
Lardy, Nicholas, 209
Latin America. *See also specific country*
  financial crises in, 244–45, 250
  and debt reservicing, 246–47
  and emerging capital markets,
    247*n*, 247–48, 253
  Institute research on, 256
  IMF lending, 299
  trends in, 261*f*, 261–62
  US trade policies toward, 41, 50, 51
Lawrence, Robert Z., 234
*The Lending Policies of the International
  Monetary Fund* (Williamson), 134
Lerner Symmetry Theorem, 354*n*
Lerrick, Adam, 281
Lester, Richard, 216
Levine, Ross, 129
Lewis, Howard, 356
Libya, sanctions against, 69
literacy rate, and trade competitiveness,
  217
living standards, trade competitiveness
  and, 217–18, 222–28, 237
loan defaults, 304–309
"local-content" requirements. *See* value-
  added requirements
London Club, and debt relief, 267, 268
London terms, for debt relief, 255
Louvre Accord, 149
  exchange market intervention under,
    186–87, 187*n*, 188, 188*n*, 190, 191
  fiscal policy commitment under, 190
Loy, Frank, 4, 10
Lyon terms, for debt relief, 255

macroeconomics
  and China-US trade relations, 74–75
  effect on trade, 20–21

institutional success in managing, 340
and political economy, 24–25, 29, 32
and trade competitiveness, 218
major industrial economies, currency
  regimes of, Institute research on,
  135*n*–36*n*
Malaysia
  exchange rate policies, 156
  financial crisis, 250, 262, 266
managed floating exchange rate regime,
  136, 157
Managed Floating Plus (Goldstein), 157
managed trade policy, 28, 71, 73–75
Mann, Catherine L., 29, 55, 317*n*
manufacturing, GBS project on, 47
Manufacturing Extension Program, 98
"market equilibrium," 146, 166
Marris, Stephen, 6, 22, 24, 191
Maskus, Keith, 358*n*
McDonald, David J, 80
megaregional integration, 30
Meier, Michael, 19*n*
Meltzer, Allan, 277
Meltzer Commission. *See* International
  Financial Institutions Advisory
  Committee (IFIAC)
Mexico
  benefits of NAFTA for, 130
  financial crisis in, 135, 246, 247, 248–49,
    259, 260, 267
  collective action clauses in, 269
  compared with other defaults, 307
  current account deficit and, 304*f*
  and dollar value, 201–202
  exchange rate during, 301*f*
  Institute research on, 137, 138
  IMF lending, 284, 288, 288*n*, 298,
    298*n*, 299*t*, 300–304, 301–304
  inflation and interest rates during,
    303*f*
  private-sector involvement in, 267
  rescue package for, 270
Middle East–US free trade agreement,
  50, 51
monetary policy
  coordination with fiscal policy, 151–52
  and dollar movements, 173
  in July 1978–September 1980, 178–79
  in March 1987–April 1988, 189*t*,
    190, 190*n*
  during Reagan administration,
    184–85
  during 2000s, 207–208
  and exchange rate stability, 166–67, 196

money laundering, strategies against, 70
Montreal Protocol, 56
moral hazard
    versus bailouts, 279–80
    in debt relief, 267
    empirical estimates of, 288–89
    estimating scale of, 283–88
    IMF lending and, 276–78, 293–97
    indirect form of, 295–96
    insurance and, 278
    interest rates and, 281–83
    Russian case generating, 289–93
Multilateral Agreement on Investment,
        46, 130
multilateralism, Bergsten's support for,
        334–35
multilateral trade negotiations (MTNs),
        shift from, 41–43, 49–50
multinational corporations (MNCs)
    criticism of, 43, 45–46
    GBS project on, 47
multinational enterprises (MNEs)
    definition of, 116
    foreign direct investment and, 116
    government measures promoting, 117–18
        rules limiting, 117–24, 118, 119,
            120–21, 130
    growth in 1960s and 1970s, 116–17
    investment incentives for, 117, 118,
        119–21, 122n, 124, 130
    performance requirements for, 117–18,
        119, 121–22, 122n, 123–24, 130
Mussa, Michael, 345, 355

Naples terms, for debt relief, 255
National Association of Manufacturers
        (NAM), 80–81
National Bureau of Economic Research
        (NBER), 355
National Innovation Initiative, 217n
nationalization, 125
national power, and economic
        cooperation, 339–40
national security threat, foreign direct
        investments and, 46, 126
national treatment for foreign-owned
        enterprises, principle of, 117, 125
neorealism, 339n, 339–40
newly industrialized countries (NICs),
        Institute studies on, 28, 155
Niarchos Foundation, 2
Noland, Marcus
    on forecasting of economic calamities, 6
    on Japan-US trade relations, 27, 28, 74

on NICs, 28
on North Korea, 70–71
public communication expertise, 358n
on trade deficit, 71
on trade retaliation, 72
nondiscrimination principle, 117, 125
North American Free Trade Agreement
        (NAFTA), 26
    Bergsten's support for, 335
    and competitive liberalization, 19
    environment and, 56
    Institute analysis of, 42, 51
    investment agreement in, 121n, 130
    presidential initiatives for, 41–42
    public opinion on, 43–44
    Transitional Adjustment Assistance
        program, 84–85, 86
North American Free Trade Agreement
        (NAFTA) Implementation Act (1993),
        90t
North Atlantic Free Trade Agreement,
        Bergsten's opposition to, 335
Nunn, Sam, 64
Nurkse, Ragnar, 315

offshore outsourcing, 48n, 55
    trade adjustment assistance and, 99
oil, impact on trade competitiveness, 235–37
oil-for-food program, 65
oil price shocks, 126, 244, 245, 259
Omnibus Budget Reconciliation Act of
        1981, 90t
Omnibus Trade and Competitiveness Act
        of 1988, 126–27
O'Neill, Paul, 252
open economy. *See also* free trade; trade
        liberalization
    Bergsten's evangelism for, 3–6, 15–32
open regionalism
    APEC and, 26
    Bergsten's support for, 335
ordinary least squares (OLS) estimator,
        128–29
Organization for Economic Cooperation
        and Development (OECD)
    Bergsten's support for, 334
    and financial crises, 249
outreach for awareness of programs, 98
outsourcing, 48n, 55, 99
Owens, James, 5, 12

Pakistan
    bond restructuring, 251n, 269
    free trade agreements with, 51

Special Data Dissemination Standards
(SDDS), 266
special drawing rights (SDR), 334
Sprinkel, Beryl, 181
staff recruitment, Bergsten's abilities for,
9–10
Stand-By Arrangement (SBA), 290
state governments, incentives for MNEs
from, 120
steering committees, 335
stock market crash of October 1987, 187,
191
Stolper-Samuelson trade theory, 219
stories, in public communication, 358,
358n
"strong dollar" policy, 201, 204, 206, 209
Structural Impediments Initiative, 27
Summers, Lawrence, 9–10, 11, 201, 206
Super 301, renewal of, 73n, 73–74
Supplementary Reserve Facility, 250
Switzerland, free trade agreements with,
51
Systemic Transformation Facility (STF),
290

Taiwan
exchange rate policies, 155, 156
influence of Institute on, 51
take-up rates, 88, 88n, 98
targeted sanctions, 69–70
target zones, 135n, 147–51, 161–62, 162n,
167
lack of support for, 150–51
under Louvre Accord, 187, 187n, 188
Tariff Commission, 82
tariffs, zero, impact of, 47
Task Force on International Direct
Investment, 118–22
tax incentives, for MNE subsidiaries, 117,
118
Taylor, John, 206–207, 260
technology skills. *See also* job training
assistance
assistance for upgrading, 55, 98
GBS project on, 48
"technopols," political economic value of,
357n
"Telephone Communiqué" of December
22, 1987, 188
tequila crisis, 247, 250
terms of trade
and competitiveness, 223–25, 237
in practice, 228–31
transfers and, 225–26, 226f

terms-of-trade (TT) schedule, 226, 227f
terrorist financing, disruption of, 69–70
textile industry, 31
Thailand
exchange rate policies, 156
financial crisis in, 249–50, 260, 262, 267
IMF lending to, 283n, 298, 299t
think tanks, role of, 359
Tokyo Round, 39n
Institute assessment of, 39, 40, 49
Toronto terms, for debt relief, 255
total free trade, Institute on payoffs from,
46–47
Trade Act of 1974, 21
enhancing TAA program, 82, 90t
section 301 (*See* section 301
investigations)
Trade Act of 2002, trade adjustment
assistance and, 84, 86–87, 90t
trade adjustment assistance (TAA)
alternatives to, 86–87, 97–98
Bergsten on, 16, 21–22, 79–80, 81–82,
103, 215
Chamber of Commerce task force on,
79–80, 93–94, 95–96t, 106–109
expansion and reforms of, 82–85, 85–89,
87t, 89t, 100–103
cost of, 100n, 100–103, 101t
Institute work on, 5, 21–22, 25, 55–56,
103–104
issues regarding, 94, 97–99, 105
legislative history of, 89–93, 90t, 92f,
110–11
legislature proposed for, 103, 104t
model of, 99–100
origins of, 80–82
and protectionism, 22
trade balance
cyclical effects on, 232–33
data on, 229, 240t
equations exploring, 232–34
exchange rates and, 231, 232, 234
impact of oil on, 235
measurement of, 228, 228n
in practice, 228–31
requirements for, ban on, 123
structural shifts in, 233
trade barriers. *See* protectionism
trade competitiveness, 215–37
assistance programs for, 98, 99 (*See also*
trade adjustment assistance)
debate over, reframing, 222–28
definition of, 216, 217, 218
economic goals addressing, 217–18

wage(s), and trade competitiveness, 217,
218–20, 222, 237
wage insurance
as alternative assistance, 97–98, 100
assertions regarding, 93–94
definition of, 56
provisions for, 86
"warehousing," 195, 195*n*
Washington Consensus, 356
wealth distribution. *See* income distribution
Whitman, Marina von Neumann, 11
Who's Bashing Whom? Trade Conflict in High-Technology Industries (Tyson), 41, 73
Williamson, John, 7
on debt crises, 134–35
on debt policy, 259, 260
on Eastern European transition
economies, 135
on emerging markets, 136, 138, 283*n*
on exchange rate policy, 146, 147–50,
154–55, 155–56, 157–58, 165–66,
167, 191
on fiscal and monetary policy
coordination, 151–52
on NICs, 28
on political economy of reform, 356
on rule hardening, 344
on "technopols," 357*n*

"Wisconsin Idea," 354
worker assistance. *See* job training
assistance; trade adjustment
assistance (TAA)
Working Group on Exchange Market
Intervention, 182
World Bank
Bergsten on, 140, 334
debt relief policy, 255
Executive Board, 120–21
World Investment Report, 127*n*
World Trade Organization (WTO),
115–16
dispute settlement mechanism, 74, 74*n*,
347
domestic support for, 343
exchange rate surveillance, 321–22
Institute on, 42–43, 50–51, 57
as scapegoat for trade liberalization,
338
writing, effective, for public
communication, 357–58, 358*n*
The WTO after Seattle (Schott), 42

yen depreciation, 195, 195*n*, 196. *See also*
dollar-yen exchange rate

Zoellick, Robert, 19, 19*n*

Other Publications from the Peterson Institute

POLICY BRIEFS

Narrowing the U.S. Current Account Deficit*
Alan J. Lenz/June 1992   ISBN 0-88132-103-6
The Economics of Global Warming
William R. Cline/June 1992   ISBN 0-88132-132-X
US Taxation of International Income: Blueprint
for Reform*   Gary Clyde Hufbauer,
assisted by Joanna M. van Rooij
October 1992   ISBN 0-88132-134-6
Who's Bashing Whom? Trade Conflict
in High-Technology Industries
Laura D'Andrea Tyson
November 1992   ISBN 0-88132-106-0
Korea in the World Economy*
Il SaKong
January 1993   ISBN 0-88132-183-4
Pacific Dynamism and the International
Economic System*
C. Fred Bergsten and Marcus Noland, editors
May 1993   ISBN 0-88132-196-6
Economic Consequences of Soviet Disintegration*
John Williamson, editor
May 1993   ISBN 0-88132-190-7
Reconcilable Differences? United States-Japan
Economic Conflict*
C. Fred Bergsten and Marcus Noland
June 1993   ISBN 0-88132-129-X
Does Foreign Exchange Intervention Work?
Kathryn M. Dominguez and Jeffrey A. Frankel
September 1993   ISBN 0-88132-104-4
Sizing Up U.S. Export Disincentives*
J. David Richardson
September 1993   ISBN 0-88132-107-9
NAFTA: An Assessment
Gary Clyde Hufbauer and Jeffrey J. Schott/rev. ed.
October 1993   ISBN 0-88132-199-0
Adjusting to Volatile Energy Prices
Philip K. Verleger, Jr.
November 1993   ISBN 0-88132-069-2
The Political Economy of Policy Reform
John Williamson, editor
January 1994   ISBN 0-88132-195-8
Measuring the Costs of Protection
in the United States
Gary Clyde Hufbauer and Kimberly Ann Elliott
January 1994   ISBN 0-88132-108-7
The Dynamics of Korean Economic Development*
Cho Soon/March 1994   ISBN 0-88132-162-1
Reviving the European Union*
C. Randall Henning, Eduard Hochreiter, and
Gary Clyde Hufbauer, editors
April 1994   ISBN 0-88132-208-3
China in the World Economy   Nicholas R. Lardy
April 1994   ISBN 0-88132-200-8
Greening the GATT: Trade, Environment, and
the Future   Daniel C. Esty
July 1994   ISBN 0-88132-205-9

Western Hemisphere Economic Integration*
Gary Clyde Hufbauer and Jeffrey J. Schott
July 1994   ISBN 0-88132-159-1
Currencies and Politics in the United States,
Germany, and Japan   C. Randall Henning
September 1994   ISBN 0-88132-127-3
Estimating Equilibrium Exchange Rates
John Williamson, editor
September 1994   ISBN 0-88132-076-5
Managing the World Economy: Fifty Years after
Bretton Woods   Peter B. Kenen, editor
September 1994   ISBN 0-88132-212-1
Reciprocity and Retaliation in U.S. Trade Policy
Thomas O. Bayard and Kimberly Ann Elliott
September 1994   ISBN 0-88132-084-6
The Uruguay Round: An Assessment*
Jeffrey J. Schott, assisted by Johanna W. Buurman
November 1994   ISBN 0-88132-206-7
Measuring the Costs of Protection in Japan*
Yoko Sazanami, Shujiro Urata, and Hiroki Kawai
January 1995   ISBN 0-88132-211-3
Foreign Direct Investment in the United States,
3d ed., Edward M. Graham and Paul R. Krugman
January 1995   ISBN 0-88132-204-0
The Political Economy of Korea-United States
Cooperation*
C. Fred Bergsten and Il SaKong, editors
February 1995   ISBN 0-88132-213-X
International Debt Reexamined*   William R. Cline
February 1995   ISBN 0-88132-083-8
American Trade Politics, 3d ed., I. M. Destler
April 1995   ISBN 0-88132-215-6
Managing Official Export Credits: The Quest for
a Global Regime*   John E. Ray
July 1995   ISBN 0-88132-207-5
Asia Pacific Fusion: Japan's Role in APEC*
Yoichi Funabashi
October 1995   ISBN 0-88132-224-5
Korea-United States Cooperation in the New
World Order*
C. Fred Bergsten and Il SaKong, editors
February 1996   ISBN 0-88132-226-1
Why Exports Really Matter!* ISBN 0-88132-221-0
Why Exports Matter More!* ISBN 0-88132-229-6
J. David Richardson and Karin Rindal
July 1995; February 1996
Global Corporations and National Governments
Edward M. Graham
May 1996   ISBN 0-88132-111-7
Global Economic Leadership and the Group of
Seven   C. Fred Bergsten and C. Randall Henning
May 1996   ISBN 0-88132-218-0
The Trading System after the Uruguay Round*
John Whalley and Colleen Hamilton
July 1996   ISBN 0-88132-131-1

Private Capital Flows to Emerging Markets after the Mexican Crisis*
Guillermo A. Calvo, Morris Goldstein, and Eduard Hochreiter
September 1996   ISBN 0-88132-232-6
The Crawling Band as an Exchange Rate Regime: Lessons from Chile, Colombia, and Israel
John Williamson
September 1996   ISBN 0-88132-231-8
Flying High: Liberalizing Civil Aviation in the Asia Pacific*
Gary Clyde Hufbauer and Christopher Findlay
November 1996   ISBN 0-88132-227-X
Measuring the Costs of Visible Protection in Korea*   Namdoo Kim
November 1996   ISBN 0-88132-236-9
The World Trading System: Challenges Ahead
Jeffrey J. Schott
December 1996   ISBN 0-88132-235-0
Has Globalization Gone Too Far?
Dani Rodrik
March 1997   ISBN paper 0-88132-241-5
Korea-United States Economic Relationship*
C. Fred Bergsten and Il SaKong, editors
March 1997   ISBN 0-88132-240-7
Summitry in the Americas: A Progress Report
Richard E. Feinberg
April 1997   ISBN 0-88132-242-3
Corruption and the Global Economy
Kimberly Ann Elliott
June 1997   ISBN 0-88132-233-4
Regional Trading Blocs in the World Economic System   Jeffrey A. Frankel
October 1997   ISBN 0-88132-202-4
Sustaining the Asia Pacific Miracle: Environmental Protection and Economic Integration   Andre Dua and Daniel C. Esty
October 1997   ISBN 0-88132-250-4
Trade and Income Distribution
William R. Cline
November 1997   ISBN 0-88132-216-4
Global Competition Policy
Edward M. Graham and J. David Richardson
December 1997   ISBN 0-88132-166-4
Unfinished Business: Telecommunications after the Uruguay Round
Gary Clyde Hufbauer and Erika Wada
December 1997   ISBN 0-88132-257-1
Financial Services Liberalization in the WTO
Wendy Dobson and Pierre Jacquet
June 1998   ISBN 0-88132-254-7
Restoring Japan's Economic Growth
Adam S. Posen
September 1998   ISBN 0-88132-262-8

Measuring the Costs of Protection in China
Zhang Shuguang, Zhang Yansheng, and Wan Zhongxin
November 1998   ISBN 0-88132-247-4
Foreign Direct Investment and Development: The New Policy Agenda for Developing Countries and Economies in Transition
Theodore H. Moran
December 1998   ISBN 0-88132-258-X
Behind the Open Door: Foreign Enterprises in the Chinese Marketplace
Daniel H. Rosen
January 1999   ISBN 0-88132-263-6
Toward A New International Financial Architecture: A Practical Post-Asia Agenda
Barry Eichengreen
February 1999   ISBN 0-88132-270-9
Is the U.S. Trade Deficit Sustainable?
Catherine L. Mann
September 1999   ISBN 0-88132-265-2
Safeguarding Prosperity in a Global Financial System: The Future International Financial Architecture, Independent Task Force Report Sponsored by the Council on Foreign Relations
Morris Goldstein, Project Director
October 1999   ISBN 0-88132-287-3
Avoiding the Apocalypse: The Future of the Two Koreas
Marcus Noland
June 2000   ISBN 0-88132-278-4
Assessing Financial Vulnerability: An Early Warning System for Emerging Markets
Morris Goldstein, Graciela Kaminsky, and Carmen Reinhart
June 2000   ISBN 0-88132-237-7
Global Electronic Commerce: A Policy Primer
Catherine L. Mann, Sue E. Eckert, and Sarah Cleeland Knight
July 2000   ISBN 0-88132-274-1
The WTO after Seattle
Jeffrey J. Schott, editor
July 2000   ISBN 0-88132-290-3
Intellectual Property Rights in the Global Economy   Keith E. Maskus
August 2000   ISBN 0-88132-282-2
The Political Economy of the Asian Financial Crisis   Stephan Haggard
August 2000   ISBN 0-88132-283-0
Transforming Foreign Aid: United States Assistance in the 21st Century
Carol Lancaster
August 2000   ISBN 0-88132-291-1
Fighting the Wrong Enemy: Antiglobal Activist and Multinational Enterprises   Edward M. Grah
September 2000   ISBN 0-88132-272-5

DISTRIBUTORS OUTSIDE THE UNITED STATES

Australia, New Zealand,
and Papua New Guinea
D. A. Information Services
648 Whitehorse Road
Mitcham, Victoria 3132, Australia
Tel: 61-3-9210-7777
Fax: 61-3-9210-7788
Email: service@dadirect.com.au
www.dadirect.com.au

Canada
Renouf Bookstore
5369 Canotek Road, Unit 1
Ottawa, Ontario KlJ 9J3, Canada
Tel: 613-745-2665
Fax: 613-745-7660
www.renoufbooks.com

India, Bangladesh, Nepal, and Sri Lanka
Viva Books Private Limited
Mr. Vinod Vasishtha
4737/23 Ansari Road
Daryaganj, New Delhi 110002
India
Tel: 91-11-4224-2200
Fax: 91-11-4224-2240
Email: viva@vivagroupindia.net
www.vivagroupindia.com

Japan
United Publishers Services Ltd.
1-32-5, Higashi-shinagawa
Shinagawa-ku, Tokyo 140-0002
Japan
Tel: 81-3-5479-7251
Fax: 81-3-5479-7307
Email: purchasing@ups.co.jp
For trade accounts only. Individuals will find
Institute books in leading Tokyo bookstores.

Mexico, Central America, South America,
and Puerto Rico
US PubRep, Inc.
311 Dean Drive
Rockville, MD 20851
Tel: 301-838-9276
Fax: 301-838-9278
Email: c.falk@ieee.org

Middle East
MERIC
2 Bahgat Ali Street, El Masry Towers
Tower D, Apt. 24
Zamalek, Cairo
Egypt
Tel. 20-2-7633824
Fax: 20-2-7369355
Email: mahmoud_fouda@mericonline.com
www.mericonline.com

Southeast Asia *(Brunei, Burma, Cambodia,*
Indonesia, Malaysia, the Philippines,
Singapore, Taiwan, Thailand, and Vietnam)
APAC Publishers Services PTE Ltd.
70 Bendemeer Road #05-03
Hiap Huat House
Singapore 333940
Tel: 65-6844-7333
Fax: 65-6747-8916
Email: service@apacmedia.com.sg

United Kingdom, Europe
(including Russia and Turkey), Africa,
and Israel
The Eurospan Group
c/o Turpin Distribution
Pegasus Drive
Stratton Business Park
Biggleswade, Bedfordshire
SG18 8TQ
United Kingdom
Tel: 44 (0) 1767-604972
Fax: 44 (0) 1767-601640
Email: eurospan@turpin-distribution.com
www.eurospangroup.com/bookstore

Visit our Web site at:
www.petersoninstitute.org
E-mail orders to:
petersonmail@presswarehouse.com